OVID'S *HEROIDES*

This volume offers up-to-date translations of all 21 epistles of Ovid's *Heroides*. Each letter is accompanied by a preface explaining the mythological background, an essay offering critical remarks on the poem, and discussion of the heroine and her treatment elsewhere in Classical literature. Where relevant, reception in later literature, film, music and art, and feminist aspects of the myth are also covered. The book also contains an introduction covering Ovid's life and works, the Augustan background, the originality of the *Heroides*, dating, authenticity and reception. A useful glossary of characters mentioned in the *Heroides* concludes the book. This is a vital new resource for anyone studying the poetry of Ovid, Classical mythology or women in the ancient world.

Paul Murgatroyd has lectured at the University of Natal, South Africa, and McMaster University, Canada, in a career of over 40 years. He is the author of 11 books and over 90 articles in the field of Classical literature, especially Latin poetry, and is a published Latin poet in his own right.

Bridget Reeves received a PhD from McMaster University, Canada, and currently teaches in Hamilton, Canada. Her research interests are in story-telling, both in prose and in verse, with a focus on the mythological character Europa.

Sarah Parker is a part-time instructor in the Classics department at Brock University, Canada. Her research interests are the ancient novel – those by Apuleius in particular – and Latin literature in general.

OVID'S *HEROIDES*

A New Translation
and Critical Essays

Paul Murgatroyd, Bridget Reeves
and Sarah Parker

 Routledge
Taylor & Francis Group

LONDON AND NEW YORK

First published 2017
by Routledge
2 Park Square, Milton Park, Abingdon, Oxon OX14 4RN

and by Routledge
711 Third Avenue, New York, NY 10017

Routledge is an imprint of the Taylor & Francis Group, an informa business

© 2017 Paul Murgatroyd, Bridget Reeves and Sarah Parker

British Library Cataloguing-in-Publication Data
A catalogue record for this book is available from the British Library

Library of Congress Cataloging-in-Publication Data
Names: Ovid, 43 B.C.-17 A.D. or 18 A.D., author. | Murgatroyd, Paul,
    translator, writer of supplementary textual content. | Reeves, Bridget,
    translator, writer of supplementary textual content. | Parker, Sarah
    (Classicist), translator, writer of supplementary textual content.
Title: Ovid's Heroides : a new translation and critical essays/Paul
    Murgatroyd, Bridget Reeves, and Sarah Parker.
Other titles: Heroides. English (Murgatroyd, Reeves, and Parker)
Description: Abingdon, Oxon ; New York, NY : Routledge, 2017. | Includes
    bibliographical references and index.
Identifiers: LCCN 2016053015 | ISBN 9781138722156 (hardback : alk. paper) |
    ISBN 9781138722163 (pbk. : alk. paper) | ISBN 9781315193724 (ebook)
Subjects: LCSH: Ovid, 43 B.C.-17 A.D. or 18 A.D.—Translations into English. |
    Epistolary poetry, Latin—Translations into English.
Classification: LCC PA6522.H4 M87 2017 | DDC 871/.01—dc23
LC record available at https://lccn.loc.gov/2016053015

ISBN: 978-1-138-72215-6 (hbk)
ISBN: 978-1-138-72216-3 (pbk)
ISBN: 978-1-315-19372-4 (ebk)

Typeset in Bembo
by Apex CoVantage, LLC

Visit the eResources: www.routledge.com/9781138722163

For Amy

CONTENTS

Preface   *ix*

Introduction   1

Heroides 1   Penelope to Ulysses   7

Heroides 2   Phyllis to Demophoon   22

Heroides 3   Briseis to Achilles   32

Heroides 4   Phaedra to Hippolytus   43

Heroides 5   Oenone to Paris   56

Heroides 6   Hypsipyle to Jason   66

Heroides 7   Dido to Aeneas   76

Heroides 8   Hermione to Orestes   89

Heroides 9   Deianira to Hercules   99

Heroides 10 Ariadne to Theseus   111

Heroides 11 Canace to Macareus   121

Heroides 12 Medea to Jason   132

Heroides 13 Laodamia to Protesilaus   153

Heroides 14 Hypermestra to Lynceus   164

Heroides 15 Sappho to Phaon   173

Heroides 16 Paris to Helen   186

Heroides 17 Helen to Paris   200

Heroides 18 Leander to Hero   212

Heroides 19 Hero to Leander   221

Heroides 20 Acontius to Cydippe   230

Heroides 21 Cydippe to Acontius   240

Glossary of characters in the Heroides   *250*
Select bibliography   *257*
Index   *260*

PREFACE

This work is aimed in particular at Classical Civilization students taking courses on myth, women and Ovid. Its aim is to present a translation of the *Heroides* which is both reliable and readable and basic literary criticism which will make the letters come alive and have impact, enhancing appreciation and plain enjoyment of the poetry.

The introduction covers Ovid's life and works; the Augustan background; originality of the *Heroides*; dating; authenticity; reception; and overall evaluation (e.g. feminist issues, tone, artificiality, monotony, novelty as narrative and elegy).

The translation, based on the best text available (Goold's revised Loeb), is meant to be accurate and accessible, so that the poems really reach readers. It is not literal (because that often makes for clumsiness and obscurity), but it does not leave out (or import) anything significant. This involves some explication (to avoid masses of notes) and the watering down of many erudite allusions ('Hercules' instead of 'Alcides' etc.). There is a couplet for couplet correspondence.

Each translation is preceded by a short preface, pointing out differences from the previous letter (to preclude charges of monotony), and explaining the mythological background, so students can grasp what is going on in the epistle when they read it.

Each translation is succeeded by critical remarks on the poem itself, highlighting salient features (pathos, humour, sources etc.) and bringing out different levels and layers. These are deliberately selective rather than comprehensive. As such, they are intended to appeal to readers and stimulate them; and so they will steer clear of dry scholarship (e.g. arguments about authenticity) and aim at variety (e.g. not go on about sources constantly). Feminist criticism is obviously important, but does not dominate to the exclusion of other approaches. There are questions for students, to draw them in, and references to other scholars for different points of view. These essays also go beyond the poem itself, filling out the picture with regard to the heroine and the treatment of her elsewhere in Classical literature (with stress on

Ovid and high points in other authors). Where relevant, reception in later literature and in film, music and art is also covered. There are discussion topics as well, and exercises to involve readers creatively with the heroine and her story. There is also a glossary of people mentioned in the *Heroides* to conclude the book.

As this is a wide-ranging investigation, three scholars have collaborated on it – Dr Bridget Reeves, Dr Sarah Parker and Dr Paul Murgatroyd. We would like to thank Adrienne McBride, a student of Westdale Secondary School, who carefully examined the translations and essays for clarity and appeal. In particular, we were very fortunate to be able to draw on the scholarship and expertise of Dr Ray Clark, who offered constant support, went through the whole book with great thoroughness and perception and suggested numerous improvements.

Paul Murgatroyd, Bridget Reeves and Sarah Parker

INTRODUCTION

Almost all of what we know about Ovid (full name: Publius Ovidius Naso) comes from his own poetry. He was born on the twentieth of March 43 BC and was a teenager when Augustus became Rome's first emperor. He came from a well-off middle-class family in Sulmo (an Italian town about ninety miles north of Rome). He was sent to Rome to be educated, along with his brother, who was a year older than Ovid, and who showed promise as a lawyer, but tragically died young, aged twenty. In Rome Ovid studied Latin and Greek language and literature and also rhetoric (the art of public speaking), and he finished his education by touring Greece, Sicily and Turkey. He became interested in poetry while still a boy, and during his rhetorical training showed himself a good speaker, but already his compositions seemed like free verse. His literary tastes were encouraged by the presence in Rome of the great poets of the day, whom the young Ovid worshipped. His father wanted him to follow a conventional career in the world of law and politics, and Ovid did make a start at that, but he soon rebelled and rejected it for a life as a poet, giving the first public reading of his verse when his beard had been cut once or twice.

He was one of the 'Augustan' writers (i.e. those who wrote when Augustus was emperor), and he took pleasure in being part of a golden age of poetry in Rome. In producing personal love elegy he followed in the footsteps of three other illustrious elegists – Gallus, Propertius and Tibullus. Also active during this period were Horace, who is most famous for his lyric *Odes*, and Virgil, who is best known for his epic *Aeneid*, and who is generally considered to be *the* major Roman poet. Each of these authors was distinctive and original, but they all held in common certain views on the nature of poetry. Their verse did certainly appeal to the heart, but it was also highly intellectual and very sophisticated. These were cultured men, intimately acquainted with mythology and with their (Greek and Roman) literary predecessors, and they let their erudition in these (and other) areas pervade their works. They also composed very polished poetry, paying close attention to metre, style and language. Wit, complexity and ingenuity are often in evidence too. Ovid embraced all of that, and added his own particular sparkle.

He was a prolific and versatile author and became much admired himself by younger poets. He devoted himself to the pleasures of writing and moving in intellectual circles. He had a house in Rome, and a country villa, where he could work in solitude (he enjoyed writing in his orchard in particular). He was married three times, and was especially close to his third wife, to her daughter (who was his step-daughter and a poetess herself) and also to his own daughter (by his second wife).

Ovid's enjoyable way of life in smart Roman society came to an abrupt end in AD 8, when he was banished by the emperor Augustus to Tomis, a port on the Black Sea (modern Costanza, in Romania). He tells us that this was for two reasons – a poem and a mistake. The poem was the *Ars Amatoria*, which was charged with teaching adultery (something that was now a criminal offence), even though Ovid explicitly stated in it that it was not for married women. The mistake was according to the poet a more serious matter and hurt the emperor deeply. What it was exactly remains a mystery. He says that he witnessed something unintentionally, but never explains what. He tried to win recall from Augustus and from Tiberius (his successor as emperor), but did not succeed. In his appeals to them to help him get permission to return Ovid was forced by a strange irony to send poetic letters to his wife and friends back home similar to those he invented in the *Heroides* for heroines writing to separated lovers. He spent the rest of his life at Tomis in misery and frustration, far from his beloved Rome, and finally died there in AD 17, aged fifty-nine.

The choice of Tomis as a place of exile for Ovid seems very harsh, even calculating and vindictive. It was in a barely settled province at the ends of the empire. The city had originally been founded by Greek colonists, but the majority of the population were local tribesmen, and the Greek inhabitants had largely gone native. There he was virtually cut off from Greek as well as Roman culture. This poet, who enjoyed an audience and relished their criticism as essential to the creative process, was deprived of such an audience, and complained that writing a poem you could read to nobody was like dancing in the dark. This highly urbane and civilized author was sent to live among savages, and after avoiding military service as a young man he was now exposed to raids by fierce tribesmen and had to put in time on the city walls to defend the place. Although there will be some exaggeration and omission in his depiction (due to his depression and in an attempt to win pity), Ovid paints a truly bleak picture of Tomis and the surrounding area. According to him no Latin and only a barbarous form of Greek was spoken there. He says that the food and water were bad, the air was unhealthy and the countryside was ugly, savage and treeless. He describes long winters of cold so bitter that it froze rivers and the sea and the wine in the jar (so that you had to break off chunks to drink) and made men's hair tinkle with ice, while the wind seared the skin, blew tiles off the roofs and even knocked down whole buildings. There were also marauding barbarians – wild horsemen from the steppe who rode across the frozen river

Danube, attacking the town and its outlying farms, and carrying off cattle and even the peasants themselves.

As we said, Ovid was a versatile and prolific author. He is renowned as a love poet. In addition to the *Heroides* (on which see below), he wrote the *Amores* ('Loves'), witty and amusing elegies about the ups and downs of his love life, especially with his beautiful mistress Corinna. He also composed the *Medicamina Faciei Femineae*, a treatise on women's cosmetics (of which the first 100 lines survive), and two clever and mock-solemn didactic poems (poetry of instruction). In the first, the *Ars Amatoria* ('Art of Love'), he tells men and women how to conduct a successful affair, and in the second, the *Remedia Amoris* ('Remedies for Love'), with typical inversion he explains how to terminate a liaison. The best translation of the *Amores* is that of Lee (truly in the spirit of Ovid), and there is a fine version of the *Ars Amatoria* and *Remedia Amoris* by Turner; also worth mentioning is the translation of all those poems by Green 1982. For literary criticism on the love poetry in general see Lively and Armstrong 2005.

Ovid also produced a tragedy, the *Medea* (now lost), and the *Fasti*, a poetic calendar, in which he tells a lot of mythological stories connected with the stars and rites and festivals mentioned in the poem. The first six books (on the months January to June) survive. He is perhaps most famous for the *Metamorphoses*, a great collection of myths involving change, in which he shows his narrative abilities at their best in a series of highly amusing and moving accounts. In Tomis he wrote the *Tristia* and *Epistulae ex Ponto*, pieces reflecting on his exile and trying to secure a return to Rome, and the *Ibis*, a lengthy and learned curse on an enemy. For translations see Boyle & Woodard (*Fasti*), Raeburn (*Metamorphoses*), Green 2005 (*Tristia* and *Epistulae ex Ponto*) and Mozley (the *Ibis*, and some other poems which were dubiously attributed to Ovid). For literary criticism see Murgatroyd (on the *Fasti*), Galinsky 1975 and Fratantuono (on the *Metamorphoses*), and Williams and Claassen (on the *Tristia* and *Epistulae ex Ponto*). There is an enjoyable general survey of Ovid's works by Mack. For more in-depth treatment see any of the three Companions (edited by Hardie, Boyd and Knox 2009).

The *Heroides* are twenty-one fictional letters in Latin verse (elegiac couplets). The first fifteen (called the single *Heroides*) are addressed by women to men whom they love and from whom they are in some way separated; 1–14 are by mythological heroines, while 15 is by the Greek poetess Sappho. In the double *Heroides* (16–21) there are three pairs of epistles, in each of which a man writes to a mythological female whom he loves and receives a reply from her (Paris and Helen; Leander and Hero; Acontius and Cydippe). The dating of these poems is difficult and controversial. However, most modern scholars agree that the single *Heroides* were an early work, contemporary with the *Amores* (which were composed from about 26 BC onwards), and the double *Heroides* were produced later, round about the time of Ovid's exile. The authenticity of many of these letters has been questioned, with 9, 15 and 16–21 coming in for particularly strong suspicion. The debate continues, but most critics now accept that 1–14 were by Ovid. We see no good grounds for denying Ovidian authorship of any of the *Heroides*, and feel that even if they were not all composed by Ovid, they are all interesting and well worth studying.

At *Ars Amatoria* 3.346 Ovid claimed that the *Heroides* amounted to a new poetic genre, and it does seem that there was here typical innovation by our poet, as no other collection of verse letters by mythological characters prior to him has survived. But to create this unique form he drew on various elements in the rhetorical and literary tradition. He was probably influenced to some extent by his training at school in rhetoric, especially by two exercises – the *suasoria*, in which students had to advise a mythological or historical personage to follow a certain course of action, and *ethopoeia*, in which they had to compose a speech by a mythological or historical figure at a particular point. Ovid will also have drawn on monologues by heroines in Greek and Roman tragedy, and elsewhere in literature on poems and passages in which females actually speak out or are represented as speaking out for themselves. No doubt he had an eye to actual ancient epistles (real and invented), and the idea of a poetic love letter in particular may have come from the third poem in Propertius' fourth book of elegies, which purports to be a Roman woman's letter to her man, who is absent on a military campaign (although the relative dating of the *Heroides* and the Propertian poem is uncertain).

Ovid in general has had a massive impact on subsequent literature, art and music (see Hardie 249ff., Knox 2009 395ff., Boyd 383ff. and Ziolkowski). The *Heroides* especially were picked up by Chaucer, Shakespeare, Marlowe, Donne, Pope and Tennyson, while Dryden called them Ovid's most perfect piece of poetry; they were very influential in the middle ages and reached the height of their popularity in the sixteenth, seventeenth and eighteenth centuries (see White). Tastes change. For much of the nineteenth and twentieth centuries the poems were written off by misguided and mentally lazy critics as monotonous laments, mere rhetorical exercises that were inconsistent in tone and so on. This was based on superficial skimming, and there was very little in-depth analysis or close reading. For a long time there were just two book-length studies of the epistles in English. Howard Jacobson's *Ovid's Heroides*, on the single letters (1–15) only, came out in 1974. In the first part of this work each of the fifteen poems receives its own chapter of critical appreciation, paying attention to aspects such as sources, structure, authenticity, characterization and the psychology of the heroine. The criticism is generally sober and often illuminating, but he tends to be dismissive of wit, and unfortunately the Latin is not translated, so you will experience some difficulty in following Jacobson's points. The final six chapters branch out into bigger questions, like the dating of the *Heroides*, the nature of the genre and variation within the collection. In 1985 Florence Verducci's *Ovid's Toyshop of the Heart* was published. In it there is a shrewd and spirited reaction against earlier censure of the poems for artificiality, lack of involvement and inappropriate frivolity and irreverence. She concentrates on the role of parody, irony and especially wit in *Heroides* 3, 6, 10, 11, 12 and 15 (and she provides translations of the Latin and Greek that she cites). Important articles (and a book in German by a scholar called Spoth) also started to appear at this time, studying in detail the elegiac and epistolary elements in the *Heroides*, and probing with real insight their relationship to Ovid's literary models.

At the start of the twenty-first century there was a sudden flurry of feminist criticism of the collection with three books which present interesting and challenging new ways of looking at the letters (and translate all Latin quoted). Efrossini Spentzou's *Readers and Writers in Ovid's Heroides* saw the light of day in 2003. She views the epistles as expressions of female culture, with the heroines struggling for control over their own destiny and their own stories (consciously challenging and contradicting male accounts by Homer, Euripides, Virgil etc.), as they turn themselves from girls who are written about to girls who write, and tell their tales in accordance with the female way of constructing a story. Sara H. Lindheim's *Mail and Female* came out in the same year. She maintains that on the surface Ovid empowers women to tell their own tale, but has them make the hero each time the protagonist and point of reference for their self-definition and construct themselves to ensure that they will be the hero's eternal object of desire. This leads to disjointed self-portraits, as they try on contradictory roles, and there are repetitions in the *Heroides* because Ovid gives the women a limited repertoire of roles, making them all alike, in contrast to the actual diffuseness of women. In 2005 Laurel Fulkerson's *The Ovidian Heroine as Author* was published. She sees the heroines as a community of authors who read each other's letters and base their strategy in their own epistle on that of others which they think would help them attain their end. Although they can misinterpret and be misguided about this, they can also learn from another writer's mistakes and success.

It remains to offer our own overall evaluation. The *Heroides* have suffered in particular from people approaching them with unreasonable expectations and closed and lazy minds, trying to impose on them their own view of what the poems should be like and consequently feeling disappointed and criticizing them when they do not conform to that. It is important, and only fair, to grant Ovid his prerogative as the author and allow him to make of the epistles what he wants to make of them.

Heroides 1–15, 17, 19 and 21 are letters ostensibly written by various heroines, and Ovid does give them personalities and lets them speak up and make their own points. But he is producing highly sophisticated poetry with various levels in a multifaceted performance, and he gives the women a voice and character to suit his poetic purposes (as he does with the male letter-writers in *Heroides* 16, 18 and 20). It was not his intention to catch the essence of femininity or to provide a full, detailed and nuanced recreation of the heroines. Allowing them to express their own identity or to explore women's issues was simply not a major thrust of the collection.

Given the situations of the writers and the often tragic outcomes of their stories, many readers assume that the epistles will be characterized by sadness. We do certainly find pathos in the *Heroides*, and Ovid was very skilled at creating it. However, by no means all of the poems or all parts of them are poignant (and a long succession of mournful letters would be tedious in the extreme). Some are tragicomic, with a piquant tonal mixture, while others are mainly witty and humorous. In this way there is an intellectual as well as an emotional appeal.

Some object to the artificiality of the *Heroides*. These are obviously not meant to be seen as genuine letters (often it would have been impossible for them to be written or sent to the addressees). Their epistolary form is a literary device (a means of giving an old story a new focus and so on). Ovid is not bothered about the lack of realism, and in fact sometimes jokes about it (see, for example, the opening lines of *Her.* 3). We should not be bothered by it either. After all, we don't criticize ballet or musicals for being artificial. Rather we should suspend disbelief, go along with the fiction and enjoy it.

A common complaint has been that the poems are monotonous. In fact, if one looks carefully, it is clear that on the contrary there is a tour-de-force aspect and Ovid has set himself a challenge over ringing the changes in a series of epistles. There is deliberate variation from letter to letter, as will be pointed out in the essays on the individual poems below (see also Jacobson 381ff. on the variety). At the same time, with typical dexterity, Ovid also forges links between individual *Heroides*, whether set right next to each other or widely separated (several of these are mentioned in the essays below; for more on the correspondences see Barsby 16f. and Kenney 18ff.).

Something else that makes for liveliness is the fact that this is a new form of mythical narrative. It catches a particular moment in the tale and now explores it for us by means of an epistolary setup, ensuring that our attention is taken by our ability to read over the writer's shoulder, as it were, and gain intimate insights into her or his feelings. This format also makes for an engagingly fragmentary and oblique account of events, with lots of allusion and foreshadowing (hints of what will happen subsequently). The *Heroides* also offer an elegiac retelling of stories common in epic and tragedy, with interesting and diverting spins to Ovid's sources. There is a new focus and a new perspective for myths, putting the stress on love and giving us the point of view of just one character, very often a female one for a change, and one who has frequently been peripheral or marginalized in past treatments. That makes for a very personal and often coloured version of events, with omission, distortion and so on.

This form represents a way of enlivening Latin elegy too. As in those personal poems, there is an 'I' speaking here about love, desires, experiences etc., but with a striking inversion it is a female or a hero rather than the male poet-lover who speaks (and is misused, makes appeals, behaves humbly etc.). Here too Ovid explores new erotic areas – not just the relationship of the lover and his girl, but also the love of husband and wife, stepmother and stepson, sister and brother. There are also many twists to the standard themes, language, situations and imagery of Latin elegy. See further Mack 69ff. and Liveley 59ff.

One last thing worth bearing in mind (and something that many critics have ignored) is the fact that the author of the *Heroides* is Ovid, who also wrote the brilliant *Amores, Ars Amatoria* and *Remedia Amoris*. So don't expect something dull or simple. We are moved certainly, but we are also entertained and dazzled. Here too we find cleverness and complexity; a typical admixture of ingenuity, inventiveness and versatility; and very dense poetry, with different layers beneath the appeals – in particular wit, humour (often subtle and dark), irony, stylistic polish, narrative skills and constantly a creative and combative engagement with earlier authors.

Heroides 1

PENELOPE TO ULYSSES

First of all some background information, so you will be able to understand Penelope's letter (we will do this with the subsequent *Heroides* too).

A vast Greek army sailed off to Troy (in modern Turkey) to recover Helen, the beautiful queen of Sparta (in Greece), who had eloped with the handsome Trojan prince Paris, and so the Trojan War began. The wily hero Ulysses (also known as Odysseus, the Greek form of his name) went with them. He left behind on his island kingdom of Ithaca his loving wife Penelope and also his baby son Telemachus and his mother (who died while he was away) and his father Laertes. The fighting at Troy was long and hard, and many Greeks died (see lines 15–22 below in *Heroides* 1). But there were Greek successes too: in one exploit Ulysses and a comrade put to death a Trojan spy called Dolon and also king Rhesus, who was a Trojan ally, taking his marvellous horses as spoil; and Achilles killed Troy's great defender Hector in a duel and dragged his corpse behind his chariot in revenge, because Hector had slain in battle his close friend Patroclus, when he masqueraded as Achilles, wearing his armour. It took ten years for king Priam's Troy to fall, and Ulysses had to spend another ten years getting home after that, enduring various hair-raising adventures (with monsters, cannibals etc.) and being kept prisoner on an island for seven years by a goddess who was in love with him. During his lengthy absence his devoted wife remained faithful to him, but she came under intense pressure to remarry when over a hundred young nobles turned up as suitors for her hand and abused their right to hospitality, eating and drinking away Ulysses' fortune. She bravely resisted them over a long period, keeping them at bay for three years by promising to marry one of them when she had finished making a shroud, and secretly undoing at night what she had woven during the day, until the trick was found out. But she was in a weak position, with only her young son, her aged father-in-law and a few loyal servants (see lines 103–4 below) on her side. Telemachus went to mainland Greece in the hope of getting news of his absent father from people who had fought with him at Troy (Nestor, ruler of Pylos, and Menelaus, king of Sparta), and during his absence an old beggar turned up on Ithaca, who was in fact Ulysses in disguise. When Telemachus returned, Ulysses identified himself to him and enlisted his help. Then he went to the palace and spoke to his wife, still disguised as an old stranger. The next day Penelope set up a contest, agreeing to marry any man who could string Ulysses' great bow and shoot an arrow through a line of twelve axes. The suitors who tried failed, but the 'beggar' succeeded. He then turned the bow on the suitors, and with the help of his son and two loyal servants slaughtered them. After that he finally revealed himself to his wife and was reunited with her. Ovid's letter is set after Telemachus' return and before Ulysses butchers the suitors. In it Penelope, at the end of her tether, is desperate to persuade her husband to return and rescue her.

> From Penelope to Ulysses, her dilatory husband.
>   Writing back's no good. Come in person!
> Troy, the town that Greek girls hate, has definitely fallen.
>   Priam and all Troy were hardly worth the price I've paid.
> Oh, if only the adulterer Paris had been drowned by a   5
>   raging sea when he was sailing to Sparta!
> Then I wouldn't have slept alone in a cold bed or be
>   complaining, all on my own, that the days pass slowly,
> and I wouldn't be wearing out my widowed hands weaving
>   in an attempt to beguile the long nights.   10
> I always feared dangers worse than those you actually faced.
>   Love is full of fear and anxiety.
> I imagined it was *you* that the brutal Trojans attacked;
>   I went pale whenever I heard Hector's name.
> If somebody spoke of Antilochus conquered by the enemy,   15
>   his fate made me fear for you.
> If I heard of Patroclus' death while disguised by Achilles'
>   armour, I wept, because trickery could fail.
> When told how Tlepolemus died, with his blood warming his
>   opponent's spear, I worried about you all over again.   20
> In short, whenever I got news of a Greek being killed,
>   my loving heart was colder than ice.
> But a sympathetic god looked out for my chaste love:
>   Troy is ashes and my husband survived.
> The Greek chiefs returned, altars smoked with sacrifices,   25
>   Trojan spoil was dedicated to our ancestral gods.
> Young wives made thank-offerings for the survival of their spouses,
>   who bragged of their destiny outweighing Troy's;
> righteous old men and trembling girls marvelled, and wives
>   hung on their husband's lips, as he told his tale.   30
> One man outlined brutal battles on the table-top,

tracing out the whole of Troy in a little wine:
'This is the river Simois, this is Sigeum,
    here stood old Priam's lofty palace.
There were Achilles' and Ulysses' tents; here the horses dragged   35
    off Hector's mangled corpse, frightened into a gallop.'
Old Nestor told the whole story to your son when he was sent
    to ask about you, and he passed it on to me.
He also told of Rhesus and Dolon put to the sword –
    one betrayed by sleep, the other by guile.   40
You dared – oh, all too forgetful of your family –
    to creep into Rhesus' camp at night
and kill so many enemies, with only one assistant –
    showing great caution and thinking first of me!
My heart kept fluttering with fear, until I heard that you   45
    rode Rhesus' horses back through your camp in triumph.
Troy has been torn apart by the Greeks, her walls razed
    to the ground, but what good is that to me,
if I remain as I was while Troy held out and
    must do without my absent husband forever?   50
Destroyed for others, Troy survives for me alone, even though
    the victors live there and plough with captured oxen.
Where Troy stood, there stands in the ground enriched by Trojan
    blood an abundant crop of corn ready for reaping;
curved ploughs strike the half-buried bones of   55
    warriors, and grass conceals ruined houses.
You won, but aren't here, and I'm not allowed to know why
    or where you're callously lingering and lurking.
Any foreigner who lands on our shore only goes away
    after being cross-examined by me about you   60
and being given a letter written by me to pass on
    to you, if he sees you somewhere.
I sent to Pylos, the land of aged Nestor;
    no clear news of you came back from Pylos.
I sent to Sparta; Sparta doesn't know the truth either.   65
    Where are you living or tarrying, apart from me?
Apollo's Troy still standing would be more useful to me
    (ah, my prayers for its fall annoy me now):
then I'd know where you fought, have only war to fear
    and be far from the only woman complaining.   70
I'm out of my mind, don't know what to fear, but fear
    everything; there's so much for me to worry about.
All the dangers on land and sea – I suspect every one
    of them of being behind your lengthy delay.
Those are my foolish fears. You men are so promiscuous,   75

you could be captivated by some foreign mistress.
Perhaps you tell her how unsophisticated your wife is, the sort
    whose wool isn't coarse while her manners are.
I hope I'm wrong and this accusation fades into thin air.
    Don't choose to be absent when you could return.   80
As I'm on my own, my father Icarius tries to force me
    to remarry and criticizes my endless delays.
He can criticize forever. I'm yours and must be called yours.
    I will always be Penelope, wife of Ulysses.
But my father is being softened by my devotion to you   85
    and my chaste prayers, and is easing up.
A crowd of lecherous men from Dulichium, Same and
    hilly Zacynthus descended on me as suitors
and lord it in your palace, with none to stop them,
    ravaging your wealthy possessions (our lifeblood).   90
Why tell you of dreadful Medon, Pisander and Polybus
    and the grasping hands of Eurymachus and Antinous
and the others? It's scandalous: by being absent
    you're feeding them all with your hard-won goods.
The beggar Irus and Melanthius, who brings them your goats   95
    to eat, are the crowning disgrace on top of your losses.
There are three of us, and we can't fight – your frail wife,
    your old father Laertes and our boy Telemachus.
I almost lost our son recently in a treacherous attack,
    as he prepared to go to Pylos against everyone's wishes.   100
May the gods ensure that in the natural order of things
    we die first and he is there to close our eyes.
The herdsman is on our side and so is your aged nurse
    and the faithful servant in charge of the filthy sty.
But Laertes is no use at fighting, so he can't   105
    act as king in the midst of our enemies.
If he lives, Telemachus will grow stronger, but at this
    point he needs you to help and protect him.
I don't have the strength to drive the enemies from our home.
    Come quickly, and be a great refuge for your family!   110
You have a son (may he survive!), who at his tender
    age should have been trained in his father's ways.
Think of Laertes: he is putting off his dying day
    so you can be here to close his eyes.
I was a girl when you left. Even if you come at once,   115
    believe me, you'll see that I've become an old woman.

This poem is a good introduction to the whole collection. When composing
Heroides 1, our learned poet looked back over approximately 700 years to Homer's

Odyssey in particular, a long epic poem in Greek that told of the hero's adventures on his way back to Ithaca and described how he reunited with his family there and re-established himself as king. For text and translation of the *Odyssey* (and much, much more) visit the Chicago Homer site (www.library.northwestern.edu/homer) or the Perseus Project (www.perseus.tufts.edu). Ovid here does something that he does over and over again in the *Heroides*: he takes material from a much loftier genre of poetry and converts it to elegy, putting the emphasis on love and giving the female real prominence. Here (supposedly) her story and her thoughts and feelings are related by Penelope herself, instead of the poet Homer, and there is an unwavering focus on her alone, with son, suitors and servants very much in the background. Rather than being just one character in the epic poem, she now gets a whole poem to herself, and it is her voice that we hear and her point of view that we see (so, for example, the hero's return is no longer presented as a great adventure but is something puzzling and worrying). See further Lindheim 43ff. [note that the abbreviation 'f.' means 'and the following page (or line)', so 43f. = pages 43–4, while 'ff.' denotes more than one page (or line) following].

In Homer Penelope is a figure of great beauty and pathos. She is *the* faithful and virtuous wife, devoted to her family and deeply upset by her husband's prolonged absence. She is also intelligent and crafty, but her position is not strong and she has major problems trying to assert her authority over the suitors. (For more on the Homeric Penelope see Thornton 93ff. and Felson-Rubin.) Nothing was sacred to Ovid, and typically he makes alterations to the characterization of her found in the revered Homer, and provides a very entertaining treatment of this widely admired heroine. So we are given new insights into her mind (as constructed by Ovid): for instance, there is no parallel in the *Odyssey* for her fears for Ulysses when she hears of other Greeks killed (lines 15ff.) or of his exploit with Dolon and Rhesus (45f.) or for her suspicions of Ulysses being unfaithful and mocking her (75ff.). She is also pro-active, in writing a letter of appeal to her husband (rather than just weeping and questioning strangers for news, as in Homer). This Penelope is feisty and assertive too, and Ovid enhances her cunning and devious character in the *Odyssey* by incorporating new levels of subtlety for which there is no precedent in Homer.

In *Heroides* 1 Ovid presents a Penelope who is eloquent and wily like her husband. Her letter is very focused, constantly appealing to her beloved Ulysses and trying to manipulate the arch manipulator in ways that are both touching and amusing. Directly and indirectly she often reassures him about her feelings for him and her behaviour during his time away, stressing how much she loves and misses him (enough to make her complain about his absence) and how she has remained true to him, and she frequently attempts to win pity and make him feel bad about not having returned. At 87ff. she tries scare-tactics too, dwelling on the suitors, to show Ulysses the great threat to his wife and property. As part of her strategy she also employs speculation, exaggeration and downright fabrication. So, for example, at 52ff. she speaks with assurance about the present condition of Troy, but this is mere (and incorrect) conjecture, to bring out the length of time since the city fell and the extent of Ulysses' non-appearance, to make him sorry for her. At 97f. and (after bringing out the extreme danger to his son) at 105ff. she overstates the youth of Telemachus (at twenty years old, he is no longer a 'boy') and the inability to fight of her son and father-in-law (in fact later Telemachus battles with Ulysses against the suitors, and all three of them join in combat with the suitors' relatives at the end of the *Odyssey*). At 37f. and 63ff. she maintains that she sent her son to Nestor and Menelaus to ask about his father, but in the *Odyssey* he went without her knowledge and at the instigation of the goddess Athena, so presumably Penelope is here fibbing to put herself across as desperate to get news of her sorely missed husband, and pathetically cheated of that (although in Homer Menelaus did know some of the truth about Ulysses and passed it on to Telemachus, who told her, contrary to the claim in 65). Comically in line 100 she slips up, probably because she is under stress and in such an anxious state, by suggesting that she did not want Telemachus to go to Nestor and Menelaus and he went on his own initiative. Not only is the virtuous Penelope telling lies to her husband but also it would appear that she is not quite as sly and as consistently good a liar as Ulysses.

Given the happy ending to Penelope's story, this epistle could never be really sad; but there is something that makes it particularly diverting, when we are finally allowed to piece together the timing of its composition and the identity of the recipient. From 37f. we learn that Telemachus has returned from his trip to mainland Greece, so Ulysses must be already on Ithaca. From 59–62 we learn that Penelope hands a letter from her for her husband to every stranger she meets, and at this point the 'stranger' with whom she is in contact is the hero in disguise, so she must have unwittingly given this letter to Ulysses himself. This means that, when he reads it, as somebody already there and well informed about the situation, he will see through the above-mentioned ploys by his wife (but no doubt enjoy them, as a trickster himself). It also means that there is extensive irony here, as she tries so hard to get him to come home when he is there all the time, gives him news about the state of affairs on Ithaca and about his son when he knows all that, and says that Telemachus needs his father's influence when he is already receiving it. See if you can spot for yourself similar irony throughout the poem, for example in lines 1, 18, 43, 57f., 66, 80, 93f. and 115.

Like all of the *Heroides* this is a multifaceted composition, and one final facet worth considering is allusion to specific lines in Homer. At 75–8 there is a clever use of a passage in the *Odyssey*. Penelope has heard from Telemachus the news he picked up from Menelaus that Odysseus (Ulysses) was kept as a most unwilling prisoner on the island of a goddess (Calypso), and at 75ff. she builds on that, expressing the fear that he may have fallen in love with some foreign female and be telling her mockingly about his wife's lack of sophistication. This is particularly entertaining for us because we know something that Penelope does not. At *Odyssey* 5.214ff. Odysseus did speak about his wife to a foreign female with whom he was staying (Calypso), but he did not love Calypso, and when he spoke to her, so far from criticizing Penelope, he stated his preference for his mortal wife over that beautiful deity and said how much he longed to see his spouse again, even if that meant enduring great danger at sea on his way home. Then again Penelope is not entirely wrong, as we with our superior knowledge can see, because the hero did get more involved with another female (the goddess Circe), with whom he lived of his own free will for a year. Although the *Odyssey* is the main model for *Heroides* 1, lines 39–46 refer to the story of Dolon and Rhesus as told in the other famous epic poem by Homer (*Iliad* 10.218ff.). They demote Odysseus' companion Diomedes, who is not even mentioned by name, making him a mere assistant and Odysseus the one who slaughtered king Rhesus and his men, whereas in Homer Diomedes did the killing and Odysseus just stole the horses. So, entertainingly, Penelope (a character of the *Odyssey*) blends into this letter (which is predominantly based on the *Odyssey*) an episode from the *Iliad*, and in so doing 'corrects' the account in the *Iliad*, giving greater prominence to the hero of her own *Odyssey*.

Homer depicts the sequel to this epistle – the reunion of Penelope and Odysseus – in book 23 of the *Odyssey*. It is one of the high points in the poem, touching and also amusing. Her acceptance of Odysseus is held back over many lines to create a build-up and to make us feel a similar relief and joy when she does finally recognize him as her husband. Obviously we see here the devoted wife's deep love for her man. We also see her shrewdness: she is understandably cautious after all she has been through and all the tales she has been told by strangers, and she decides to establish beyond a doubt that this is her husband. She is not intimidated by his rebukes and makes a spirited response to them at 174ff. She is quick-witted too, picking up on his demand for a bed and turning that to her advantage with a clever test for him in connection with their bed. The test succeeds, and she manages to outwit the archetypal trickster by taking him in, so that he thinks their bed has actually been moved and comes out with an unconsidered outburst that unintentionally proves his identity. This shows that she has an intelligence which matches that of her husband, and the simile (comparison) at the end of the passage also draws together subtly Penelope and the great sailor Odysseus, who had been shipwrecked himself.

At 23.1ff., after Odysseus has killed the suitors, he sends the old nurse Eurycleia to Penelope. She assures her mistress that her husband has returned. Penelope really wants to believe it, but is wary. She agrees to go and see the man who killed the suitors, and gazes at him in bewilderment, sometimes seeing a likeness to Odysseus, but at other times seeing just a beggar in rags. Telemachus criticizes her for being hard-hearted and not accepting her husband, and she tells him that she is in shock, but if it really is Odysseus, there are secret signs that will prove it. Odysseus says that she is disdainful of him because he is dirty and dressed in rags, but she will soon come round. He asks Telemachus to leave them alone, and then goes off for a bath. The goddess Athena strips away his disguise as an old beggar, gives him added beauty and makes him look like a god. He returns, sits in a chair opposite his wife and says (166ff.):

> 'You *are* a strange person. The gods who live on Olympus have
> given you a heart harder than that of any other woman.
> No other wife would steel herself like this
> to hold back from a husband who returned

home after twenty years full of suffering.   170
But come, nurse, make up a bed for me to
sleep alone, as she has a heart of iron.'
Cautious Penelope made this reply to him:
'*You* are a strange person. I'm not at all haughty or disdainful,
or overwhelmed by the change in you – I remember very well what   175
you looked like when you sailed from Ithaca on your long-oared ship.
Now, Eurycleia, take the other servants and place the sturdy bed
outside our bedroom, which he built so skilfully with his own hands;
make it up there spreading bedclothes on it –
fleeces and blankets and bright coverlets.'   180
So she spoke, testing her husband.

Odysseus now asks angrily who moved the bed from its original position in the
bedroom, and wonders how it could have been moved, because he constructed it
himself, building the bedroom around an immovable olive tree, which he trimmed
and made into one of the bedposts. Penelope's response to that comes at 205ff.:

At his words she went weak at the knees and her heart melted,   205
as she realized he had given her incontrovertible proof.
In tears, she ran straight to him, flung her arms
around his neck, kissed his head and said:
'Don't be angry with me, Odysseus: you've always been the most
understanding of men. Our misery was due to the gods,   210
who begrudged us a life together, enjoying youth
and reaching the threshold of old age with each other.
But don't be irritated with me now or indignant because
I didn't give you a loving welcome the moment I saw you.
Inside, in my heart, I was always afraid that some   215
stranger would come here and trick me with
lies (there are lots of evil, scheming people).
Helen of Argos, Zeus' daughter, fell in love with a
stranger and slept with him. She wouldn't have
done that if she'd known that Greek warriors   220
were going to fetch her back to her own country.
But a god drove her to behave so disgracefully.
Before that she hadn't contemplated that fatal madness
which immediately brought misery to her and to us.
But now, as you've given clear proof by mentioning the   225
secret of the bed, which no other human has seen
apart from you and me and a single servant-girl
(Actoris, who my father gave me when I came here,
and who was the doorkeeper for our well-built bedroom),
you really have won over my hard, hard heart.'   230

Her words made Odysseus weep, and he held his dear, loyal wife in his arms. She was in tears too, and wouldn't take her arms from his neck, as happy to see him as shipwrecked sailors are to see land after swimming to shore through a stormy sea.

This is all very affecting, but here, as generally in the *Odyssey*, Penelope is circumscribed and confined to her role as wife and mother. We learn a bit more about Penelope from literary sources other than Homer, although most of the material still concerns her role as a wife. For example, we are told that Odysseus acquired her as his bride by winning a foot-race among suitors for her hand or because her uncle Tyndareus persuaded her father to give her to Odysseus in thanks for some excellent advice he had received from him. Tyndareus was Helen's father and he was bothered that there might be a quarrel among her many suitors, until Odysseus suggested that he should get them all to swear an oath to defend the one chosen as her husband if he was ever wronged in connection with his marriage (when Paris took Helen off to Troy, this oath was called upon to assemble the great army of Greeks that went to get her back). Some relate that while Odysseus was at Troy a rumour spread that he had died there, and in great grief Penelope threw herself into the sea, but was miraculously saved by birds, which lifted her up and brought her back to shore. But others claimed that she committed adultery with the suitors and that she gave birth to the minor deity Pan, fathered either by the god Hermes/Mercury or by all of the suitors (linking Pan with the Greek word *pantes*, meaning 'all'). For more on this hostile tradition see Jacobson 246ff.

This bawdy version of Ulysses' wife is found in Latin poetry too. At *Amores* 1.8.47f. Ovid makes a foul old procuress maintain that Penelope set up the archery contest to size up her suitors as lovers, with the bow of horn used to reveal their sexual stamina. A more elaborate version occurs in Horace *Satires* 2.5, written a few years before Ovid. This poem satirizes a particularly unpleasant feature of Roman society at that time – will-hunting (i.e. courting rich people with no children as heirs, in the hope of getting included in their will). It consists of ironical advice on how to achieve that, put across in a memorable form. In the *Odyssey* during his return from Troy Odysseus visited the Land of the Dead to get advice about his journey home from the ghost of the prophet Tiresias. With a comic addition to that sombre scene in Homer, Horace makes Odysseus put one more question before their interview ends. As he faces the prospect of arriving on Ithaca with no money, he asks how he can restore his fortunes. In reply Tiresias tells him to insinuate himself into the affections of a rich old man, so that he can inherit from him. Although two Greeks are speaking, incongruously the sphere of operations is Horace's Rome, and it shows two heroic figures in a distinctly unheroic light, with the implication that even they would be infected by the rampant immorality there. So the wise and revered prophet offers immoral advice, and the great warrior is perfectly ready to put it into practice and demean himself. Penelope is dragged into all this at 75ff. First Tiresias actually advises Odysseus to prostitute his own wife to a rich old man. In his response Odysseus is not shocked or outraged, and doesn't defend the virtue of his paragon of a spouse, but just doubts if he could persuade her to do that.

Tiresias then easily removes his doubts with a few cynical remarks (which also leave Odysseus unmoved).

> 'If he's a lecher, don't wait to be asked, be obliging and   75
> readily hand over Penelope to your better.' 'Do you think
> she can be persuaded, a lady so pure and proper, who the
> suitors weren't able to tempt away from the straight and narrow?'
> 'Yes! The lads who turned up are mean with their presents,
> more interested in the palace cooking than in sex.   80
> *That* is why your Penelope is chaste. Just you make her
> your partner and let her taste some cash from one old man –
> she'll be like a dog that can't be scared away from a juicy bone.'

The image in that final line conjures up a picture of the heroine aggressively protecting her interests, absolutely unwilling to give up her prize, snarling, slavering and so on. But all this is not so much anti-Penelope as anti-Rome. The idea is that even as noble and virtuous a woman as Penelope would be corrupted by degenerate Roman society.

Penelope's popularity in literature (and cinema) extends well beyond the ancient world down to our own day (see Grafton & Most & Settis 699f.). Probably the most bizarre use of the heroine was made by Jacopo Ugone in 1655. He claimed that the *Odyssey* was an allegory that prophesied events in connection with the Catholic church. Thus Ulysses represents St Peter, and Penelope stands for the church threatened by wicked reformers (the suitors), while the pope (Telemachus) protects the church until St Peter returns and defeats the reformers. I have to admit that this does leave me wondering what St Peter was doing with Calypso for seven years. Even more amusing than that is the Coen brothers' film *O Brother, Where Art Thou?* (released in 2000), which is a very creative and ingenious updating of the *Odyssey*. In it Penelope is even more feisty than she is in *Heroides* 1; in fact she is the dominant partner in the relationship, and although she has only one suitor (who beats up Ulysses) she is perfectly prepared to marry him.

James Joyce's long and challenging novel *Ulysses* concerns the thoughts and actions of two men in the Irish city of Dublin one day in 1904. The men are Stephen Dedalus, a young schoolmaster who decides to give up his job and wander the town, and Leopold Bloom, an advertising agent who roams the streets while his wife (the infamous Molly Bloom) entertains her lover at home. Leopold Bloom (= Ulysses) and Stephen Dedalus (= Telemachus) reenact those two heroes' experiences in the *Odyssey* among modern equivalents of characters and places in the epic poem and finally come together. This is a naturalistic novel of early twentieth-century city life, exposing much of its shabbiness and shoddiness. There are ironic contrasts between the worlds of Homer and Dublin, bringing out the mundane, sordid and provincial nature of the Irish town. A particularly strong contrast is that between the wives of the ancient Ulysses and the modern Bloom. The Irish Penelope is a fading singer who has had many lovers and is currently having an affair with her manager, Blazes Boylan. Her husband, who is unfaithful himself, knows about it and feels jealousy, but does nothing about the situation. In the *Odyssey* the hero and his wife are joyfully reunited and retire to bed, where they make love, talk about all that has happened during their years apart and then fall asleep. *Ulysses* ends with Leopold Bloom returning home, joining his wife in bed and giving her a short (edited) account of what had happened that day and then falling asleep, while she lies awake, thinking about her erotic encounter with Boylan earlier that day and about her other lovers, at length and in lecherous detail.

Recently Margaret Atwood has produced an entertaining and thought-provoking new take on Penelope's story in her novel *The Penelopiad*. In it the dead heroine tells her own story, and proves to be sharp-witted and sharp-tongued, given to amusing asides about our modern world. There is a down to earth and deflating realism: what the suitors really wanted was Odysseus' kingdom and his posses-sions, as his wife was by then ageing and had put weight on around the middle; and she herself sometimes daydreamed about going to bed with one or more of them. This Penelope is also smart and more in control of events when her husband returns: she sees through his beggar disguise at once, but pretends to be taken in so as not to hurt his feelings, and she deliberately sets up the contest with the bow so that he can win it and claim her as his wife. The book also explores with sympathy and indignation the story of the twelve unfaithful maids in the palace, who were involved with the suitors and who were subsequently hanged on Odysseus' orders, and they provide interludes as a sort of chorus. For more on later versions of Penelope see Stanford (index under Penelope), Graziosi & Greenwood 62ff., 243f. and Hall 115ff.

Penelope also figures in art. In both the Greek and the Roman worlds artists focused almost exclusively on her role as the dutiful yet grieving wife. The heroine is often seen pining away for her beloved husband, either seated mournfully on her own or in the company of others, who seem to try unsuccessfully to engage the inconsolable woman in conversation. The Chiusi Vase (about 440 BC) by the Penelope Painter illustrates such a pathetic scene (type in Chiusi Vase in the Google Images search engine and view the first image), and encapsulates very well the pres-entation of Penelope as the archetypal Greek wife. This red figure skyphos shows in the foreground a weary Penelope seated on a stool, her head leaning on her right hand, as her arm rests on her leg. To the left is a standing Telemachus, holding two lances in his left hand, as he looks down at his broken-hearted mother. Single ornate palmettos frame the scene. In the background stands an upright, warp-weighted loom with a partially woven cloth depicting silhouetted gryphons in profile (see further Roller & Roller 14). With her downcast eyes and slouched body, Penelope looks forlorn and tired. While Roller & Roller 18 argue that her sadness stems from knowing that she is about to unravel a section of the shroud which she has just completed, a psychologically dismaying task for a weaver, perhaps a more likely cause for her grief is the fact that her husband is absent. Here sits a woman weary of the charade of the shroud and tired of wondering where her husband is. And having her son in attendance is a poignant reminder for Penelope, and for us, the viewers, that she has raised Telemachus alone in the absence of his father. No wonder she looks wiped out!

Deviations from the mourning Penelope are extremely rare in antiquity – actually, even when reunited with Odysseus, the heroine is frequently depicted as seated sadly as her husband approaches her. But an intriguing mosaic from Apamea dating to the third quarter of the fourth century AD illustrates how the Homeric couple were possibly employed for allegorical purposes (type in Ulysses Penelope mosaic Apamea Brussels in the Google Images search engine and view the first image). The multi-coloured mosaic, which was found in a building beneath a cathedral, is a piece extending over two metres in length, most of which is decorated with geometric patterns, though there are other panels too (see further Dunbabin 169f.). In one panel, labelled *Therapenides* (Maidservants), are a number of dancing maidservants, welcoming home the wandering Odysseus who, recognizable from his traveller's cap, stands beneath an arch in the embrace of a veiled Penelope. Both appear to the left of the panel. Dunbabin notes that there are several other panels and figures (like Socrates and Poseidon, as well as personifications such as *Bythos* = Judgment) on this mosaic and acknowledges that Apamea was a centre for Neoplatonic philosophy. Others, however, go further, suggesting that Odysseus stands for the Sage who is welcomed home from his travels by Philosophy, represented by Penelope (see, for example, Montiglio 183 n. 69), due to the philosophic interest at Apamea. Philosophy, therefore, wraps her arms around the wise Sage who has wandered but finally returned.

Away from ancient art the iconography of Penelope expands somewhat, so that by the sixteenth century the heroine is not just languishing on her derrière, although those types of scenes do still persist. For instance, there is an exquisite painting by the renowned Bernardino di Betto (1454–1513), nicknamed il Pintoricchio 'the little painter' (see further Hartt & Wilkins 327f.). This shows Penelope weaving as her suitors enter the room (type in Pintoricchio Penelope in the Google Images search engine and view the first image). One of three frescoes by Pintoricchio for Petrucci's palace in Siena, this painting of Penelope with her suitors (about 1509) demonstrates the interest artists of the early 1500s had in showing perspective on multiple planes.

In the foreground Penelope, elegantly dressed in a contemporary blue gown, sits to the left of the composition at her loom, with her lady's maid seated on the ground and holding a tray of yarn. To the right four suitors enter from a doorway at the back of the room. As the men approach, each grows in size, indicating some perspective. Far in the back the last man to enter is Odysseus, wearing the disguise of a beggar. The foreground is also marked by the frame of the loom, which takes up much of the area of the room. Painters of this time were particularly keen on incorporating open windows to extend the canvas view (see Hagen & Hagen 121). Thus out through the window, in the background, scenes of Odysseus' adventures are depicted. To the right is Odysseus' ship, with the hero tied to the mast, as the Sirens sing to him. His crew-members, unable to endure the Sirens' song further, plunge themselves into the water. Off to the left is a scene depicting Odysseus' meeting with Circe. The two are surrounded by Odysseus' men who were turned into swine by the witch. The painting is a complex composition, seemingly focused on Odysseus (his trials and soon now his revenge – note the bow and arrows on the wall against which Penelope sits); however, Penelope does figure largely. She still appears as the dutiful wife who awaits her husband's return, but, as Hagen & Hagen 112 shrewdly point out, the focus is on the loom and Penelope's trickery. Just as Odysseus used his cunning against the Sirens and Circe, and now uses it in his disguise in order to enter his home and seek his revenge, so too Penelope employs great deceit against the suitors.

When commissioned by King Francis I of France in 1532 to decorate the royal chateau Fontainebleau, the Italian-born painter Francesco Primaticcio began an extensive and elaborate gallery of scenes from the *Odyssey* (see further Fiorenza 795ff.). Most of the murals have been destroyed, but a splendid scene entitled *Ulysses and Penelope* (painted about 1560) survives and resides now in the Toledo Museum of Art (type in Primaticcio Penelope in the Google Images search engine and view the first image). The painting is an exceptional work which, while drawing attention to the couple, really highlights Penelope. In this scene Primaticcio recalls *Odyssey* 23.30ff., where after making love the married pair recount to each other their trials and tribulations before being reunited. Both figures are nude, though covered by bed-sheets from the waist down. Ulysses, who is to the left of the composition, raises himself up with his right elbow as he turns his head towards Penelope, who faces forward and is seated to her husband's left. The hero turns his wife's head with his upraised left hand so that she faces him and a profile of her face is shown. Penelope appears to be engrossed in her narrative, as her hands are raised and she seems to count with her fingers the number of her past troubles, but with that subtle turning of the head the two lovers are caught in a spellbinding gaze.

Primaticcio makes Penelope the central figure of this composition – she is located in the middle of the painting, but attention is drawn to her in other ways as well. There is a definite chiaroscuro effect, with the light falling on her, while Ulysses is shadowed and the background even more so. In addition, by making Ulysses grasp the heroine's chin the painter draws the eye towards her. Penelope's animation also seems to give her prominence in the piece. Lastly, Primaticcio deviates from Homer by drawing attention to the heroine – in the *Odyssey* it is the hero who recounts his story at length, not Penelope, so what is depicted here is a reversal of roles in which the heroine and her account are the real focus, as Fiorenza 807 astutely recognizes.

In the eighteenth century the Swiss-born history painter Angelica Kauffman embraced Penelope and made the heroine the focus of her oeuvre. Kauffman came to London in 1766 and established herself as a leading artist in Neoclassical England and was one of the founding members of the Royal Academy in 1768 (see further Roworth 11ff.). During her time in England Kauffman produced numerous paintings of Penelope, some of which had never appeared before in the iconography of the heroine. *Penelope Invoking Minerva's Aid for the Safe Return of Telemachus* (1774) is just such a novel work of art (type in Kauffman Penelope Minerva in the Google Images search engine and view the first image). Penelope is centrally located in this composition at an altar upon which stands a miniaturized full-length bronze statue of the Roman goddess Minerva (= Greek Athena). The heroine is framed by her attending maidservants, three on the left and one on the right behind her, all of whom are carrying gifts for the goddess. Penelope wears a brilliant embroidered white gown, which further stresses her prominence in this painting, especially as it stands in marked contrast to the darker jewelled gowns of her servants. Neoclassical elements are present, such as the classicizing decoration of the altar, the women's attire and pale aquiline profiles (see further Rosenthal 20ff.). While Penelope's maidservants are occupied in tasks and conversation, the heroine gives her attention solely to the goddess, raising her right hand along with her gaze, as she implores the deity for the safe return of Telemachus from Greece. A real sense of Penelope's helplessness comes across in her supplication of the goddess, which is in striking contrast to the portrayal of her as a cunning woman in her iconography. Although she is often shown as the one in control as she deceives her suitors, Kauffman's painting depicts a mother caught up in the world of men (compare Rosenthal 25).

Where is Penelope? You might be asking yourself why there was a lack of interest in Penelope in art. A Google search on artistic representations of her in comparison to, say, Medea or Helen of Troy or any number of ancient heroines would lead you to the conclusion that Penelope appears only rarely in art. Why is that, and, when she does figure, what is the motivation behind her appearance? Does a painter need an ulterior motive beyond painting something that hasn't been painted before? These are just some of the questions that you may be asking yourself, so consider the following, and see if you agree.

Penelope could be viewed as a bit of a bore. As Roworth 37 rightly claims, Penelope was not suicidal, a passive victim or suitable for erotic representation. One could infer that because she was not a virgin she would not pique the interest of a god looking down for an easy conquest. Rather she was a faithful wife and devoted mother of a grown man. In short she may not have appealed to many artists intent on arousing voyeuristic patrons. But the fact that she does appear in art suggests that she holds great appeal for some painters. For Pintoricchio it has been suggested that in a corrupt period, in which trickery was key to survival, artwork demonstrating skill at deception was valued, at least by Petrucci, the artist's patron, who considered himself rather crafty (see further Hagen & Hagen 122). Primaticcio seems to have turned to the female protagonist after exhausting himself with Ulysses in the *Galerie d'Ulysse* at Fontainebleau; but Fiorenza 812 also points out that Penelope captivated aristocratic females looking for models for themselves. And what about Kauffman, whose repertoire, for the most part, centred on the Odyssean heroine? This painter appears to have dedicated her life to Penelope. Rosenthal 18 perceptively argues that for Kauffman Penelope was the 'metaphorical embodiment of the female historical narrator' and that Kauffman had a close affinity to this female protagonist. Just as Penelope wove her shroud and controlled the narrative of her future, so too Kauffman, as one of a handful of female history painters, wove her own narrative in her paintings.

For some, and maybe even for you, there is only one question: why *wouldn't* Penelope be painted? Here is a great example of the idea that numbers don't matter. The representations of Penelope that are out there simply give us something more from antiquity to enjoy.

Heroides 2

PHYLLIS TO DEMOPHOON

The *Heroides* have been accused of being repetitious, and to a lazy reader taking a superficial view they may seem to be just a series of complaints by abandoned females. But in fact Ovid is careful to ensure a lively variety, and there is even a tour-de-force aspect, as he constantly rings the changes (as well as forging links between some letters) in a typically clever and complex display. So there are marked differences between this poem and the last one, with regard to the writer's character (Phyllis is a naive young woman of Thrace, a land to the north of Greece) and her situation (she has been deceived, used and deserted by her man, who will not come back to her), and the epistle's tone, which is consistently sad, and its purpose (on which see below).

Demophoon, an Athenian prince, sailed into a harbour in Thrace with his ships seriously damaged and was given shelter there by queen Phyllis. She fell in love with him, and he pretended to love her, married her and took her virginity, before sailing on to Athens when his fleet was repaired. He promised to return a month later, but did not. She writes this letter four months after his departure, still very much in love, but deeply hurt by his continued absence and accusing him of breaking his word. At 69ff. she contrasts him with his father, the great hero Theseus, who killed brigands, conquered monsters, murdered the king of the Greek city of Thebes, and even went down to the Underworld, trying to abduct its queen from her palace there. She also accuses Demophoon of admiring his father's treachery in abandoning the princess Ariadne, who had helped him beat the monstrous Minotaur, and who was later rescued and claimed by the god Bacchus as his wife (79f.). After maintaining at 117ff. that her marriage to him was an ill-omened affair, attended by the Furies (sinister goddesses of the Underworld), she ends by telling how she still paces the shore looking for his ship and is now set on committing suicide.

> Demophoon, this is your Phyllis (who gave you shelter in Thrace),
>   complaining that you didn't return when you promised to.
> It was agreed you would sail back and anchor here

a month later, when the moon was full again.
The moon has waned and waxed four times since then,   5
    but your ship hasn't appeared in our waters.
If you count the days (and we lovers count them carefully),
    this complaint of mine isn't premature.
My hope lingered, like you. We're slow to believe what it hurts us to believe.
    Now you are guilty, but your lover hardly credits it.   10
I've often lied to myself for you, often imagined the gusty
    south wind was bringing back your white sails.
I cursed Theseus for not letting you go, but perhaps he
    wasn't the one who stopped you setting out.
Sometimes I feared your ship had sunk on its way to our   15
    river Hebrus, wrecked by foam-white waves.
I often begged and prayed to the gods for you to be well,
    you criminal, and burnt incense in supplication.
Often, when I saw in the sky and on the sea that the wind was
    favourable, I said to myself: 'If he's well, he's on his way.'   20
In short your faithful lover came up with all the things that slow
    someone down, and I was good at finding excuses.
But you're lingering somewhere else. Your oaths by the gods don't
    bring you back and you're not moved to return by love for me.
The winds took your sails and your words. It hurts that   25
    your sails don't return and your words aren't true.
Tell me, what did I do wrong except love unwisely? That's
    a mistake that might have won your heart.
You criminal, my only crime was taking you in, but that
    crime is equal and equivalent to a kindness.   30
What happened to your obligations, the pledge of your hand-clasp
    and Cupid, who was always on your lying lips?
What happened to the marriage-god, the guarantor vouching
    for our promised years together as man and wife?
You swore to me by the sea (all churning with winds and waves),   35
    on which you had surely sailed and would sail again,
and by Neptune, your grandfather (unless that's a lie too),
    who calms the ocean when it's whipped up by winds,
and by Venus too, Demophoon, and her son's bow and
    torches, those weapons that work on me all too well,   40
and by kindly Juno, who presides over the marriage-bed,
    and by torch-bearing Ceres' secret rites.
If all those wronged gods punished your perjury, just one
    of you won't be enough for their vengeance.
Ah, I was actually mad enough to refit your battered fleet,   45
    so you could safely sail off and abandon me,
and I supplied you with oars when you intended deserting me.
    Oh, it was my own weapons that wounded me.

I trusted your seductive words (there were lots of them),
    I trusted your illustrious ancestry, 50
I trusted your tears – or are they also taught to pretend,
    are they crafty too, flowing as ordered?
I trusted the gods as well. Why swear all those oaths by them?
    You could have taken me in well enough with just a few.
I'm not upset over helping you with a port and a place to stay, 55
    but my kind hospitality should have stopped there.
I regret the disgrace of going further by sharing my bed with you
    as your wife and pressing my body to yours.
I wish the night before that had been my last,
    when I could have died with my good name intact. 60
I hoped for better treatment, because I thought I deserved it;
    any hope based on what one deserves is reasonable.
There's no glory in easily tricking a trusting girl! You should
    have been considerate to someone so naive.
I was in love and a woman, so I was deceived by your words. 65
    God grant that's your only claim to fame!
Let your statue join your family's in the middle of Athens,
    with pride of place for your father's, inscribed with his feats.
When men have read there how he slew Sciron, grim
    Procrustes, Sinis and the Minotaur, 70
and conquered the Thebans and routed the Centaurs
    and knocked at the doors of dark Pluto's gloomy palace,
let this be inscribed on your statue's base behind his:
    HE DECEIVED THE GIRL WHO SHELTERED AND LOVED HIM.
Out of all your father's exploits his desertion of Ariadne 75
    is the one that made a lasting impression on you.
The only deed he makes excuses for is the only one you admire;
    you act as the heir of his deceitfulness, you traitor.
Ariadne – I don't begrudge it – now enjoys a better husband,
    sitting on high in Bacchus' tiger-drawn chariot. 80
But the Thracians I turned down won't marry me, because of
    the rumour I preferred a stranger to my own people.
One of them says: 'Let her go off to learned Athens right now;
    we'll find somebody else to rule warlike Thrace.
Judge what she did by its outcome.' God damn the man who 85
    thinks actions should be condemned because of how they turn out!
But if your ship came back, they'd claim then that I
    acted in the best interest of my subjects and myself.
But I didn't. You'll never live here, caring about my palace,
    and bathing in a local river after tiring yourself out. 90
I can still picture you as you were leaving, when your fleet
    filled my harbour on the point of departing.

You had the nerve to embrace me, draped over your lover's
    neck, pressing on me long, lingering kisses,
and to mingle your tears with my tears and to   95
    complain that you had the right breeze for sailing
and to say as your final, parting words to me:
    'Phyllis, expect your Demophoon back!'
Expect you back, when you went intent on never seeing me again?
    Expect back sails forbidden to my seas?   100
Yet I do expect you back – just return to your lover, even though
    late, untrue to your word only in terms of time.
A stupid request! Perhaps you've another wife now and are
    in love (something that turned out badly for poor Phyllis).
Now, I suppose, you've forgotten me and know no Phyllis.   105
    Ah, if you ask who Phyllis is and where she lives,
I'm the one who gave you access to a port in Thrace and hospitality,
    after you'd wandered and been driven far and wide,
the rich queen so generous to you in your time of need, who gave
    you many gifts, was going to give you many more,   110
who put you in control of her father's vast kingdom
    (which can hardly be governed by a female ruler) –
where icy Rhodope extends to shady Haemus
    and the sacred river Hebrus rushes along –
the one who offered you her virginity amid sinister omens   115
    and let your treacherous hands undress her.
Tisiphone as my bridal attendant shrieked in that bedroom,
    while a screech-owl gave ill-omened hoots.
Allecto was there, with little snakes around her neck, and the
    wedding-torches lit for me came from a funeral.   120
Broken-hearted, I pace the shore with its rocks and bushes,
    the shore that extends far and wide before my gaze.
Whether the stars shine cold or the ground thaws in the sun,
    I look to see which way the winds blow out at sea.
Whenever I see sails approaching from afar, at once I   125
    suppose they're yours, bringing my god to me.
I run out into the water, scarcely impeded by the waves,
    into the shallows at the edge of the surging sea.
The closer the sails come, the less able I am to stand;
    I faint and collapse into the arms of my maids.   130
There's a bay that curves gently like a drawn bow;
    at its outermost tips are hard, steep crags.
I have decided to leap from there down into the sea; and since you
    continue to be false to me, I'll keep to that decision.
When I've jumped, I hope the waves take me to your   135
    shores and you set eyes on my unburied body.

Even if you were harder than iron and adamant and yourself,
  you'll say: 'You shouldn't have followed me like this.'
I often thirst for poison; often dying a bloody
  death run through by a sword appeals to me;   140
putting a noose around my neck also appeals,
  because it let you embrace it, you traitor.
I *will* atone for the loss of my virginity by dying soon;
  choosing the form of death won't take long.
This epitaph (or one like it) inscribed on my tomb will make   145
  you notorious and hated as the cause of my death:
DEMOPHOON SLEW PHYLLIS, WHO SHELTERED AND LOVED HIM;
  HER HAND KILLED, HE CAUSED HER TO KILL.

Several critics think that the purpose of Phyllis' letter is to get her man to
return, and initially that might well seem to be what is going on here, and we
are subtly inclined to make that assumption right after reading Penelope's epistle,
which did have such an aim. But typically Ovid goes for something different here.
Suddenly at 133ff. Phyllis announces her firm intention to kill herself, soon, and
has even gone so far with that plan as to compose an epitaph for herself. It appears
that in fact she has just about completely given up on the idea of Demophoon
ever coming back – hence her decision to end it all. Lines 89f. and 133f. make
clear her despair, and in the course of the whole letter she overtly appeals to
him to reappear only once, late on and very briefly (at 101f.), and immediately
retracts that as a stupid and pointless request. So *Heroides* 2 takes the form of a
suicide note, explaining why Phyllis is about to terminate her life. She may be
going over things in her own mind, getting straight for herself what led to her
resolution (which we know from the myth that she will carry out), but the missive is addressed specifically to Demophoon, so it would be intended to come to
his notice. As such, it points out to him at length and in detail how badly he has
treated her (stressing his exploitation of her, his lies, ingratitude, perjury and per-
fidy), how much misery he has caused her and how responsible he is for her death
(emphasized in the final line, for him to take away with him). She wants him to be
clearly aware of all this, presumably so that he will feel shame, remorse and guilt,
as he should. But even now she is not as hard on him as she could be, and does
not attack him furiously (because she still feels deeply for him), and part of what
she is doing here is assuring him of how much she loved him and continues to
love him right up to the point of imminent death despite all he has done to her.
That is tragic, and there is much else that is poignant in this poem.

The *Heroides* give readers the impression that they are listening to the authentic
words of various heroines, but this is, of course, just an illusion. The Phyllis encoun-
tered in *Her.* 2 will not be the real Phyllis (if there ever was such a person). Ovid's
Phyllis is a constructed character (read Wyke for an interesting treatment of the
construction of the female). The fact that here and elsewhere in the collection the
women are created by a man raises some interesting questions. Is there patriarchal

arrogation of femininity? Is the poet trying to deny the heroines their diversity and otherness (compare Lindheim on this)? Or is he giving them a voice (which is generally denied them elsewhere in Classical literature), and is he often sympathetic to them? In their representation of females male writers are frequently guilty of over-simplifying and producing stereotypes, like woman as whore, woman as destroyer and woman as gullible victim (see Ginsburg 106ff.; Gorsky and Blinderman in Cornillon 28ff. and 55ff.). So you should always consider how individual and complex the writers in the *Heroides* are. You should also always bear in mind that with mythical characters, and even with genuine historical figures (compare Ginsburg 9ff.), the portrait serves a literary purpose, and in line with that end the author colours his account and manipulates material, emphasizing traits, repeating themes, omitting details and so on.

Ovid is a famously flippant and witty author, but he was also a master at creating pathos (a mood of sadness in a piece of literature) and arousing sympathy for his characters. These are important elements in many of the poems in this collection and so merit quite detailed analysis here. The story of what happened to Phyllis is in itself moving, but our poet's presentation of it makes it still more moving, as he builds on the basic outline in various ways. With regard to plot, Ovid drops the rather off-putting detail found in some versions of Phyllis causing Demophoon's death (see below); and he alone makes the hero arrive with his ships badly damaged and has the queen herself (rather than her father) hand over her kingdom to him, so as to heighten his ingratitude and our outrage at it and pity for her. The poet chooses to take up the tale at a very sad point. He also goes in for an emotive opening to his poem, making us really feel for the queen from the very start, where she is kind and loving but also deceived, miserable and despairing. And we feel for her throughout *Heroides* 2. This is partly thanks to her isolation: her father is apparently dead; there is no mention of any other relatives or friends or servants who are close to her; and she has alienated some of her subjects too (81ff.), because of her affection for Demophoon. And the characterization of her is consistently affecting (and realistic): in particular, she is gentle, hospitable and very loving (even now, despite everything); she is also a young girl, inexperienced and naive; she was very trusting too, and is now incredulous at his maltreatment of her and ashamed of her own behaviour. We are also sorry for her throughout because Ovid's Demophoon is shown again and again as such a villain, an exploitative and immoral predator, who makes her look even more noble and vulnerable beside him. The conclusion of the poem has a bleak impact as well, with its sudden and saddening revelation of imminent suicide. Placement also plays its part, increasing the poignancy by means of the contrast with *Heroides* 1, as we progress from a crafty and amusing letter to an ingenuous and pathetic one, and from the mature Penelope who has years with her husband ahead of her to the young woman here who will never see her lover again and who will shortly die.

In myth there are many more females who help men like this and several of them appear later on in the *Heroides*. This kind of Helper is an important type of figure in the collection, and so we will fill out the picture by presenting a well-known example from Homer's *Odyssey* – Nausicaa, the captivating young princess who lived in the land of the fairy-tale people called the Phaeacians, and who assisted Odysseus on his way home from Troy. In addition, comparing Phyllis with Nausicaa highlights some more Ovidian techniques for producing a mournful mood. In the *Odyssey*, in contrast to *Heroides* 2, we see that a female can offer aid without pain and misery, and the whole episode is light and charming: there is just a glancing contact between the hero and heroine, with delicate hints of a marriage that might take place rather than an actual wedding, and Nausicaa does not get involved emotionally or sexually with Odysseus, and so is not devastated over his departure. As you read the account below, see if you can find more differences in the way in which Homer and Ovid present their stories and so sharpen further your perception of the pathos in Phyllis' epistle.

At the end of *Odyssey* 5 the shipwrecked hero, after a long struggle, manages to get ashore on the Phaeacians' island and falls asleep, exhausted, near a river mouth. At the start of book 6 the goddess Athena goes to the room of the lovely princess Nausicaa and appears to her in a dream, telling her to go and wash her clothes, which she has been neglecting, as she will soon need beautiful clothing when she gets married. Next morning Nausicaa asks her beloved father for the use of a waggon, so she can go and do the family washing (too shy to mention her thoughts of her own marriage). Her fond father agrees, knowing that she is really thinking of clothes for her own wedding. Her mother gives her a picnic lunch, and she rides off to the river with her maids. They do the washing, eat and play ball, with Nausicaa singing and keeping time for their game, and looking like the goddess Artemis. When the ball falls into the river, they all shriek, waking up Odysseus. As a result of the shipwreck he is naked, so he puts a branch in front of himself to conceal his private parts and, all grimy with salt, advances on the girls, like a mountain lion. The maids run off in a panic, but the princess bravely stands her ground. In an eloquent speech Odysseus artfully compliments her, saying that she looks like a goddess, and remarking on how happy her family must be with her, and how the happiest of all will be the man who marries her. He begs her to give him some clothes and tell him the way to town, so he can get help there. Sympathetic and self-possessed, Nausicaa replies:

> 'Stranger, for you don't seem to be a bad man or a fool,
> and Olympian Zeus himself assigns prosperity to men
> (to the good and the bad, to each as is His will)
> and perhaps he inflicted this on you, which you must just endure.   190
> Now, since you have come to this city and land,
> you won't want for clothes or anything else that
> an unfortunate suppliant can expect from those he meets.
> I'll show you the town and tell you who we are.
> The men who live in this city and land are called Phaeacians,   195
> and I am the daughter of great-hearted king Alcinous,
> who is the source of the people's might and strength.'

She then calls the maids back, tells them to give Odysseus food and drink, as it is important to offer hospitality to those in need, and orders them to bathe him. He is embarrassed at the latter idea and goes off to bathe on his own. Athena makes him more handsome and tall and sturdy. When he returns, Nausicaa gazes at him in admiration, wishing that she could have such a godlike man as her husband. As he eats, she tells him to follow her in her waggon to the city; when they reach it, he must turn aside and wait for a while in a grove, because she is afraid that if the people in the town see him in her company, they will gossip and ruin her reputation, imagining that the tall and handsome stranger with her must be her future husband; then he must make his way to the palace and go through the great hall to her mother, as she is the one to ask for help to get home. Odysseus duly follows her waggon and waits in the grove, as Nausicaa proceeds to the palace and retires to her quarters. At this point she drops out of the narrative, as Odysseus goes on to ask the queen for aid. He is hospitably received, and the next day attends some splendid games and then a banquet. There we glimpse Nausicaa for the last time, as her encounter with Odysseus ends with a touching brevity and dignity (8.457ff.):

> Nausicaa in her heaven-sent beauty
> was standing by the doorpost of the well-built hall.
> She looked at Odysseus, full of admiration,
> and spoke, sending her words winging to him: 460
> 'Good luck, my friend. When you get back to your own country,
> remember me, because it's chiefly to me that you owe your life.'
> Resourceful Odysseus said to her in reply:
> 'Nausicaa, daughter of great-hearted Alcinous,
> may Hera's husband, Zeus The Thunderer, grant 465
> that I do see the day of my return and reach my home.
> Then I would pray to you there all my days as though
> to a god: for you gave me life, young lady.'

At the banquet he is urged to tell the story of his adventures so far, and does so at length (in books 9–12), before finally being taken on to his native island of Ithaca by a Phaeacian ship and crew.

In the *Odyssey* there are lots of distracting mundane details and even some gentle humour, but *Heroides* 2 concentrates solely on the tragedy. Ovid also achieves emotional impact by keeping the focus entirely on the suffering heroine (whereas in Homer lots of other people figure, and Nausicaa is not prominent from the start and all the way through the episode) and by giving her a whole free-standing poem to herself (while Homer makes Nausicaa's help just a short interlude in a long series of adventures recounted in a lengthy epic). In the *Odyssey* there is third person narrative as an account is given by the uninvolved and fairly detached poet, but in *Heroides* 2 Ovid comes up with a version coloured by the thoughts and feelings of someone who was deeply involved in events, to draw us in and touch us more.

We don't hear very much about Phyllis elsewhere in Classical literature (for what we do have see Jacobson 59 and Fulkerson 24), but there are a few extra items of information that fill out her story. In a tradition deliberately ignored by Ovid, as Demophoon left, Phyllis gave him a casket and told him not to open it until he had abandoned all hope of returning to her. He went off and settled on the Greek island of Cyprus. When the time appointed for his return went by without him appearing, she called down curses on him and killed herself. He opened the casket, was struck by fear and galloped off wildly on a horse, which stumbled, throwing him on to his sword and killing him. Another author says that when he did not return Phyllis ran down to the shore looking for him nine times, as a result of which the place was named Nine Roads. After her death her parents erected a tomb for her, and trees grew there, which at a fixed time shed their leaves in mourning for Phyllis (hence the Greek word *phylla,* meaning 'leaves'). According to a third writer Phyllis hanged herself in despair and was turned into a leafless almond tree; but Demophoon did come back, although too late, and he embraced the tree, which grew leaves as if aware of the return of the hero. The possibility that Demophoon might actually return (as in this account) makes Phyllis' impending suicide in *Her.* 2 even more terrible.

Of references to Phyllis elsewhere in Ovid the most substantial is at *Remedia Amoris* 591ff., where he takes us on to her death:

> What else harmed Phyllis but the secluded forest?
>   The cause of her death is certain – lack of company.
> She rushed along, as barbarians do with dishevelled hair
>   when they celebrate a festival of Thracian Bacchus;
> and now she gazed at the vast ocean, where she could do that,   595
>   and now she lay down on the shore, exhausted.
> 'Demophoon, you traitor!' she shouted to the deaf waves,
>   her words broken by sobs as she spoke.
> There was a narrow path darkened by long shadows,
>   along which she often made her way to the sea.   600
> As she walked on it for the ninth time, the poor girl said:
>   'On his head be it!' She turns pale, looking at her girdle
> and the branches. She hesitates, shrinking from the reckless
>   act, and moves her trembling fingers to her neck.
> Phyllis, I really wish you hadn't been alone at that point: 605
>   then the trees wouldn't have shed their leaves in mourning for you.
> Going by Phyllis' example, beware of too much seclusion,
>   lovers hurt by their girl, and girls hurt by their man.

Typically our versatile poet makes some changes when he revisits Phyllis. The depiction of her end is in itself moving, and Ovid shows a delicate restraint in not describing the actual hanging. But there is also a light-hearted aspect and a typical tonal blend. Phyllis is here used as an example of the dangers of solitude for a flippant piece of advice in a frivolous poem on the trivial subject of how to terminate a love affair successfully. The advice is that when you have broken up with a girl, you should not go off on your own (because you will be miserable and think of her) and you should avoid lonely places; you need company, and should always have a friend with you. The heroine is cited to prove all this, but in an unserious way, because the Phyllis that we know was in such deep despair that the presence of a companion would certainly not have stopped her from killing herself sooner or later.

Heroides 3

BRISEIS TO ACHILLES

This is a letter by Briseis, the captive awarded to Achilles as his prize by the Greek army after he took her city and killed her husband and three brothers. At the start of Homer's long epic poem called the *Iliad* king Agamemnon, the commander-in-chief of the Greek forces at Troy, is forced to return his captive girl Chryseis, to save the army from a plague visited on them by a god because of his earlier refusal to give her back to her father. The king demands immediate compensation, quarrels with Achilles and claims his slave Briseis as recompense for the loss of his own prize. In his rage Achilles nearly kills Agamemnon, but is checked by the goddess Athena (Minerva). He retires to his hut, refuses to fight any more and asks his mother (the sea-nymph Thetis) to get Zeus (Jupiter) to make the Greeks start losing, so the king will realize how mad he is not to respect the Greeks' best fighter. When the Trojans later get the upper hand, in book nine of the *Iliad*, a desperate Agamemnon sends an embassy to lure Achilles back, offering to return Briseis and give him very generous gifts by way of compensation. Still proud and angry, Achilles rejects the offer and threatens to sail home at dawn on the next day. It is at this point that Briseis (who has fallen in love with Achilles, has apparently persuaded herself that he loves her and longs to be reunited with him) writes her epistle, adding her appeals to those of the ambassadors. Her letter does not succeed. On the next day the Greeks suffer further serious reverses, and Achilles allows his great friend Patroclus to masquerade as him by wearing his armour and drive the Trojans off. But when he does this, Patroclus is killed. Achilles is distraught and set on taking revenge on Hector, the Trojan prince who dealt the fatal blow to Patroclus, even though he knows that his own death will follow soon after Hector's. He and Agamemnon end their quarrel, and Briseis and the gifts are produced, but Achilles has only thoughts for vengeance now and goes off and kills Hector. The *Iliad* ends with Achilles restoring Hector's body to his father (king Priam) and with the funeral of Hector, Troy's finest warrior.

In contrast to the previous poem, *Her.* 3 is not a despairing announcement of imminent suicide but an attempt to persuade the addressee to bring about reunion with the writer. In addition, unlike Phyllis, Briseis will be reunited with her man, who did not deliberately go off and abandon her, but was pressurized into handing her over to another unwillingly, and who only threatens to sail away. Further differences in the two heroines' situations are discussed below.

What you're reading comes from stolen Briseis,
    written in a foreigner's clumsy Greek.
Whatever smears you see were made by tears,
    but tears are also as weighty as words.
If I may complain briefly about you, my master and my man,   5
    I will complain briefly about my master and my man.
Since the king claimed me, it's not your fault that I was
    swiftly surrendered; but it also *is* your fault.
For the moment that his two heralds asked for me,
    I was immediately handed over to go with them,   10
which made them look at each other, silently
    wondering what had become of our love.
You could have stalled, pleased me by postponing the pain.
    Ah, I went away without giving you a kiss.
But I kept on and on crying and tearing my hair. I was   15
    miserable, I felt I'd been taken captive all over again.
I've often wanted to slip by the guards and return to you,
    but the enemy was there, to seize your timid Briseis.
I was afraid that if I left at night I'd be caught and be
    given to one of Priam's daughters-in-law as a slave.   20
You had to give me up, but I've been away all these nights,
    not demanded back. All you do is rage on and on.
When I was handed over, Patroclus himself whispered to me:
    'Why are you crying? You'll be back here soon.'
You don't demand me back. Worse than that, you actually oppose   25
    my return. Call yourself an ardent lover after that?
Achilles, your cousin Ajax and your comrade Phoenix
    and Ulysses (son of Laertes) came to you, offering
great gifts to reinforce their coaxing pleas,
    trying to secure my return to you, accompanied by   30
twenty ornate cauldrons of yellow bronze and
    seven tripods of equal weight and craftsmanship;
added to those were ten talents of gold and twelve
    stallions that always win all their races
and something superfluous – Lesbian girls of outstanding   35
    beauty, taken captive when their island was sacked,
and with all of that one of Agamemnon's three daughters

as your wife – not that you're short of a wife.
You would have had to pay this to buy me back from
   Agamemnon, but refuse to accept it as recompense! 40
What have I done to deserve your contempt?
   Where has your fickle love for me fled so soon?
Or does bad luck dog its miserable victims permanently,
   with no respite once trouble has started?
I saw the walls of my city (where I had been a 45
   person of rank) levelled by your soldiers;
Achilles, I saw my three brothers fall,
   comrades in birth and in death as well;
I saw my husband stretched out at full length on the
   gory ground, his bloody chest heaving. 50
You were my compensation for the loss of so many:
   you were my master and husband, you were my brother.
You personally assured me, swearing by your sea-nymph mother,
   that being taken captive was a good thing for me –
only to reject me now, though I come to you with a dowry, 55
   only to shun me along with the riches on offer.
What's more, there's even a rumour that tomorrow morning
   you'll spread your sails before the cloudy winds.
When I heard of that criminal plan, in my misery
   and fear I went pale and fainted. 60
Ah, you'll go, heartless Achilles, but who are you leaving me to,
   who will gently comfort me when I'm abandoned?
May I be swallowed up by some sudden earthquake or
   incinerated by a flying thunderbolt's bright-red fire
before your oars churn up the sea without me on board 65
   and I see your fleet sail off and leave me!
If you're now set on returning to your ancestral home,
   I'm not a heavy load for your ship to carry.
I'll follow my conqueror as captive, not as a wife;
   my hands are skilled at spinning soft yarn. 70
The most beautiful woman in Greece by far will enter
   your bedroom as your bride (and let her!),
worthy of your father (the grandson of Jupiter and Aegina),
   and worthy of Nereus (your mother's aged father).
I, as your humble slave, will spin the wool I'm told 75
   to spin, drawing the thread from the full distaff.
Only please don't let your wife persecute me
   (I know she'll be hard on me somehow),
don't let her tear my hair in front of you, while you
   disown me as just another girl who used to be yours. 80
Or *do* let her, provided you don't spurn me and leave me.

Ah, fear of that makes me shudder in misery.
But why are you waiting? Agamemnon repents his anger,
    and Greece lies at your feet, in tears.
Conquer your pride and rage, as you conquer everything else.   85
    Why is Hector still busily ravaging Greek troops?
To arms, Achilles! But take me back first. With Mars
    on your side, rout the enemy and press them hard!
As your rage began, so let it finish, because of me;
    let me cause and end your sullenness.   90
Don't think it degrading to yield to my pleas:
    his wife's pleas persuaded Meleager to fight.
I've only heard the story, you know it. When he killed her brothers,
    his mother cursed him – her own son, her hope for the future.
There was a war. He defiantly laid down his arms,   95
    withdrew and stubbornly refused to help his country.
Only his wife changed his mind. She's luckier than me:
    my words have no weight and are wasted.
But I'm not resentful, and I've not acted like a wife because
    I've often been called to my master's bed as a slave.   100
I remember, a captive girl called me 'mistress';
    I said: 'That word makes my slavery harder to bear.'
But by my husband's bones, which were only half-buried
    in haste, but will always be revered by me,
by the brave souls of my three brothers (gods to me),   105
    who died nobly for their country as it died,
by your head and mine, which shared a pillow,
    by your sword, a weapon my relatives knew well,
I swear that Agamemnon has never been in my bed.
    If I'm lying, leave me, with my blessing!   110
You're red-blooded. If I asked you now to swear that
    you too have not had sex, you'd refuse.
The Greeks think you're moping – you're strumming a
    lyre, in the warm embrace of a willing girlfriend.
If anyone asks why you won't fight – fighting hurts,   115
    but the lyre and song and love are enjoyable.
It's safer to lie on your couch with a girl in your arms
    and play a tune on the Thracian lyre
than to hold a shield and a sharp-pointed spear
    and support a heavy helmet on your head.   120
You used to prefer illustrious exploits to safety
    and get pleasure from the glory won in warfare.
Did you only favour fierce war so you could capture me?
    Was the end of my country the end of your prowess?
God forbid! I want you to hurl your spear with that   125

mighty arm of yours right into Hector's side.
Greeks, send me as your envoy! I'll plead with my master
   and give him lots of kisses along with your message.
I'll achieve more than Phoenix, more than eloquent Ulysses
   and more than Ajax, believe me.   130
To put the arms he knows so well around his neck and let him
   see me in person and remember me – that's no small thing.
You may be pitiless, more savage than your mother's waves, but
   even if I don't speak, you'll be broken by my tears.
I pray that your father lives out his full span of years   135
   and your son enjoys your good fortune as a warrior,
so have some thought for your poor, worried Briseis now, brave Achilles,
   don't keep on cruelly tormenting me by doing nothing.
If you've wearied of me and don't love me any more, instead of
   making me live without you, make me die.   140
What you're doing now will kill me. I'm thin and pale;
   only my hope of you sustains what life is left in me.
If that goes, I'll rejoin my brothers and husband;
   but leaving a woman to die is no great achievement.
But why just leave me to die? Draw your sword, stab   145
   me in the chest: there's still blood in my body to be shed.
Stab me with the sword that you would have plunged in
   Agamemnon's chest, if Minerva hadn't stopped you.
Ah, rather save my life, which you spared when victorious:
   I'm asking as a friend for what you gave me as your enemy.   150
Neptune's Troy has better people for you to kill:
   look for victims for your sword among the enemy.
Whether you're preparing to sail off or are remaining here,
   as my master just order me to come to you.

As part of an intricate network of links in the collection Ovid here makes connections with the two earlier *Heroides*, although typically he does also go in for enlivening variation. For a start, this is a sad letter, like *Her.* 2, and again we feel great sympathy for the heroine. In the *Iliad* (on which Ovid draws heavily: see Mack 73ff.) Briseis is a pawn in a male struggle over status. Although Achilles claims to love her at 9.335ff., he is exaggerating to heighten the insult in Agamemnon's seizure of her. He does not really love her, but is more concerned with his honour and with Patroclus (the one for whom he does have strong feelings). So in her absence he sleeps with another captive girl (9.664f.). When he is reconciled with the king (at 19.56ff.), he says that he wishes that Briseis had died rather than causing the deaths of so many Greeks because of his withdrawal from the fighting, and he is not bothered about getting her back, but is intent on revenge instead. When she is returned to him he pays no attention to her, and there is no emotional reunion (there is only a brief reference to him sleeping with her at the end of the poem). In line with all that, there is no reason to think that Ovid's Achilles has much genuine affection for Briseis either (so this letter fails to persuade him to get her back). But Ovid gets added poignancy by bringing out how much she loves him. Ovid seizes on and makes much of the brief and lone *aekous'* (= 'unwilling') in *Iliad* 1.348, when Briseis is taken away to Agamemnon unwillingly. That word may imply affection for Achilles, but Ovid makes her definitely and very much in love with him, plausibly enough, as he is handsome, brave and manly, and showed her some kindness (see lines 53f.), and is now the protector on whom she is reliant (for the psychological insight in this early instance of the 'Stockholm Syndrome' see Kelly). Tragically her talk of his love for her is self-delusion, as she virtually admits herself (at lines 5f., 26, 42 and 111ff.), hurt by his inactivity. Her world crumbled, all she has now is Achilles and she is in the terrible situation of being in love with the man who killed her husband and brothers. At this point she is totally isolated, uncertain and afraid for her future, as he is doing nothing to get her back. She longs to be reunited, but is too timid and vulnerable to speak up strongly and comes out with only mild reproach, carefully combined with a show of devotion and servile humility. She will rejoin Achilles very soon, but not because of this epistle, and she will return only to find that her friend Patroclus is dead (see below for her great grief over that).

Look for the wide variety of appeals throughout the poem, indicating how desperate Briseis is, and look at the opening and closing to see how the poet builds up pathos at those significant points. Consider also how Ovid (who loved to set himself challenges) actually manages to top himself, making *Heroides* 3 even sadder than 2. Do this before going on to the next paragraph, where we mention some of the major differences in circumstances which make Briseis an even more affecting figure than Phyllis.

Phyllis was married to her man, whereas Briseis is a concubine, a sex-slave forced (initially at any rate) to have intercourse with Achilles. Phyllis kept her status and freedom, unlike Briseis. In contrast to Phyllis, Briseis has witnessed the deaths of her husband and brothers, and will soon have to deal with two more deaths. When she wrote her letter, Phyllis was on the point of escaping from her misery, but for Briseis the suffering will go on, and get worse.

There is a link with *Heroides* 1 as well, via another Homeric heroine and more Homeric subject-matter. Again Ovid takes epic material and puts an amatory spin on it, giving the woman real prominence and presenting an elegiac retelling (for more on this elegiac aspect and on the extra layer in the clever play with the themes and language of elegy see Bolton). Again Ovid provides us with the point of view of a female involved in the action, who is made to speak out for herself (in place of the third person male narrator Homer). Rather as he developed the Penelope of the *Odyssey*, our poet really builds on the Briseis of the *Iliad* (a distinctly minor character in that epic), giving her considerably more of a voice, letting us learn what she (as opposed to Achilles) feels about her seizure, and turning a pawn and a plot-device into a person. He also offers us an interesting and touching new take on the quarrel, with the stress on love rather than anger and pride.

But this is a much more provocative poem than *Heroides* 1. Ovid had rather irreverent fun with Penelope there, but here the treatment of Achilles is tart and there is pointed criticism of him. *Heroides* 3 is not just sympathetic to Briseis but also diminishes Achilles. It amounts to a love poet's indictment of *the* epic hero, the greatest of the Greeks at Troy. This letter comes right after the embassy to Achilles. By the Homeric code he was unreasonable in refusing the offer of recompense made by the official envoys, but on top of that he turns a blind eye to this personal plea. This epistle clarifies for him Briseis' sorry state, showing him the massive impact their separation has had on this loving woman who is totally dependent on him, and it contains a whole series of desperate appeals to tug at the heart-strings. When he ignores all of that, he has to appear very cold, callous and selfish. He is undermined in other ways too. Amid constant complaints and sniping, we see not Achilles the splendid warrior but Achilles the defective lover. The stress is on him as an inactive non-fighter rather than a vigorous fighter (the only feat of his mentioned appears at 47ff., and that is turned into a reproach). At 113ff. there is undercutting mockery of his momentous withdrawal from the war. And Ovid cheekily uses reminiscences of Homer to debunk the Homeric hero. For example, at 23f. he picks up the detail of Patroclus comforting Briseis (*Iliad* 19.295f.) to make Achilles look bad by way of contrast. At 57ff. he makes much of Achilles' brief threat to sail home, showing the awful prospects for her resulting from that, which were apparently not even contemplated by the self-centred hero. And at 111ff. he seizes on and develops censoriously Homer's mention of him sleeping with another captive while deprived of Briseis.

Compare and contrast the handling of Achilles by Ovid at *Metamorphoses* 12.64ff., where he encounters an invulnerable enemy and is comically slow on the uptake and frustrated in his attempts to engage him in proper epic combat.

Not much has come down to us from antiquity about Briseis (see Jacobson 12ff. for what there is), and in surviving Classical literature Ovid alone fleshes her out, giving us here much more than the shadowy outline of the affectionate and mourning beauty that we find elsewhere. He also adds new twists at *Remedia Amoris* 475ff. and 777ff., where he makes Agamemnon fall in love with her and copulate with her, airily correcting Homer, whose king denies having sex with her, and also contradicting the claim of chastity by his own Briseis here. The two fullest pictures of her outside of Ovid occur in Greek epic. At *Iliad* 19.282ff. Homer describes her sorrow when she returns from Agamemnon to find Patroclus dead (Ovid would have expected his Roman readers to be familiar with this passage and so be aware of the grief awaiting her shortly after this letter):

> But then Briseis, who looked like golden Aphrodite,
> saw Patroclus mangled by the sharp bronze spears.
> She flung herself on top of him with a piercing scream and tore
> with her hands at her breasts, her soft throat and her lovely face,   285
> as beautiful as a goddess. In tears she said:
> 'Dear, darling Patroclus, my heart is broken.

When I went from this hut, I left you alive,
but now I return to find you dead, my prince.
For me one grief always follows on another like this.   290
I saw in front of our city mangled by sharp bronze spears
the husband to whom my father and queenly mother gave me
and my three brothers (the same mother bore us all),
my beloved brothers, who all met their day of doom.
But when swift-footed Achilles killed my husband   295
and sacked the city of godlike Mynes, you would
not let me weep but said that you'd make me
godlike Achilles' wedded wife and take me by ship
to Greece and give me a marriage-feast among his people.
You were always kind, so I'll mourn your death forever.'   300

In about the third century AD Quintus of Smyrna wrote an epic called the
Posthomerica which told of the fall of Troy and filled in the gap in events between
Homer's *Iliad* and *Odyssey*. At 3.551ff. he depicts Briseis a little later on, after Achilles has been killed in the fighting. He often echoes scenes from the *Iliad*, and here
clearly has in mind the above passage, but makes her love and lamentation more
intense for her man than for her friend.

Most of all, in an agony of grief, Briseis, who had
shared the bed of the great warrior Achilles, kept
circling the corpse, tearing her beautiful flesh
with both hands and screaming. She raised
bloody bruises on her breasts as she struck   555
them – it looked like crimson gore had been poured
on milk. But even as she mourned bitterly, her beauty
retained its radiant allure, and grace was all around her.
Groaning in misery, Briseis said:
'Ai! I've never felt agony like this before.   560
I wasn't as crushed by the killing of my brothers
or the sacking of our spacious city as I am by
your death. For me you were the blessed day,
the light of the sun and my life's sweetness,
my hope of good, my great protector against adversity,   565
more important to me than all my beauty and my parents.
Although I was your captive, you alone were everything to me.
You freed me from my servile duties and made me your wife.
But now some other Greek will take me on his ship
to fertile Sparta or to thirsty Argos. As his   570
slave I'll be absolutely miserable and suffer
terribly, separated from you. I wish I'd died
and been buried before setting eyes on your death.'

Such were her words of lament for the dead Achilles,
as she mourned her lord and her man, along with the   575
miserable slave-girls and grieving Greeks. The painful
tears dripped from her eyes to the floor, and
never stopped.

Whereas Ovid deliberately moved away from Homer, gave his heroine more of a personality and used her for more than just pathos, Quintus' Briseis may seem to you so close to the beautiful mourner in the *Iliad* as to be repetitious. You may also feel that the misery and love in the *Posthomerica* are overdone, and the relative restraint in Homer is more effective. Or do you think that Quintus gets more impact?

Quintus (7.723ff.) relates that when Achilles' son (Pyrrhus) turned up at Troy, he found Briseis among the slaves of his father whom he took over, but we do not learn of any later event than that. Come up with your own version of how Briseis' story ended, and compose a reminiscence by her near death looking back over her life.

Women often figure in myth as prizes and rewards (e.g. Andromeda, Hippo-damia and Philonoe, who was given to Bellerophon as a wife). In this category should be included captives of war, the spoil taken by the victor. Briseis is just one of many enslaved in the course of the fighting at Troy. We are best informed about the Trojan royal family and their chilling fall from eminence into servitude. The fifth-century Greek tragedian Euripides wrote three powerful plays on their plight (*Hecuba, Andromache* and *The Trojan Women*), and a little before him Aeschylus in his famous tragedy *Agamemnon* handled the end of Priam's daughter Cassandra. She was raped at the fall of Troy, and then was taken back to Greece by Agamemnon as his concubine, where she was murdered along with the king by his wife (Clytaemnestra) and her lover. Priam's aged wife Hecuba, after losing so many of her sons and daughters, was also allocated as a slave, but was turned into a snarling bitch (see especially the grim narrative in Ovid *Metamorphoses* 13.439ff.).

Hector's wife Andromache was taken as booty too, after her young boy Astyanax had been flung from the battlements of Troy to his death, and was given as a captive to Pyrrhus. The Roman poet Virgil has a poignant account of her experiences in the third book of his epic *Aeneid*. There the Trojan hero Aeneas, who survived and escaped with other Trojans, is telling of his adventures after he sailed off in search of a new home. In the course of his voyage he lands in Greece and hears an extraordinary story – that Helenus (one of Priam's sons) was a king there and had Andromache as his wife. When Aeneas goes to investigate, he meets Andromache. For our first glimpse of her Virgil shows a sorrowful figure still devoted to Hector (despite being married to the Trojan prince Helenus) and performing a sad rite all on her own in a gloomy grove, in an attempt to get some sort of contact with her beloved husband. While summoning the dead, she is thrown into shock when she suddenly sees Aeneas and his men. She is incredulous, reasonably imagines that they might be ghosts, and, if they are, immediately wants to know where Hector's spirit is.

> I set out from the harbour, leaving behind the ships and the shore. 300
> Just then by chance in a grove before the city, by a counterfeit
> river Simois, Andromache was offering a ritual feast,
> a gift of grief, to Hector's ashes and was summoning his ghost
> to the empty tomb (a mound of green turf, which she had
> consecrated along with two altars as a place for tears). 305
> When she saw me approaching and the Trojan warriors
> with me, she was astounded and frightened out of her mind.
> She stiffened in mid-gaze, went cold all over and
> fainted. After a long time she barely managed to speak:
> 'Son of Venus, is it really you, with news for me, not some 310
> phantom? Are you alive? Or if the kindly light of life has left you,
> where's Hector?' With that she burst into tears, and filled the
> whole grove with her cries, distraught.

Aeneas assures her that he is real, and asks what has happened to her since she lost her noble husband. Her reply makes it clear that she has loathed her life since his death. She actually envies Priam's daughter Polyxena, who was beheaded as an offering at the tomb of Achilles, but at least remained at Troy and unviolated, in contrast to all of Andromache's suffering. This included impregnation by a hated enemy (and she gets no comfort for the loss of Astynanax from the product of a rape). She is so broken that she does not give any sign of pleasure over escaping from Pyrrhus by being passed on to Helenus or exulting over Pyrrhus' death. All she has is a pathetic and unsatisfying reproduction of Troy. The only point at which she becomes animated is when she asks Aeneas about his young son Ascanius, showing that she still has a maternal instinct and is worried that he might have died like her own Astynanax.

> She looked down and said in a low voice: 320
> 'Ah, Priam's virgin daughter was the luckiest of us all:
> she was sentenced to die at her enemy's tomb beneath
> Troy's lofty walls, and didn't endure being drawn by lot
> and didn't enter her conquering master's bed as a captive.
> But I, when Troy burned down, was taken over distant seas, 325
> endured young Pyrrhus' haughty arrogance and bore him
> a child in slavery. He then pursued marriage to a Spartan,
> to Leda's grand-daughter Hermione, and passed me on
> as a possession to Helenus, one slave to another slave.
> But Pyrrhus was stealing the intended bride of Orestes. 330
> Fired with love, and driven by the madness brought on by his crime,
> he caught Pyrrhus off guard and killed him at his father's altars.

At his death part of the kingdom passed by bequest
to Helenus, who called the plains Chaonian and
the whole area Chaonia after Chaon of Troy,   335
and built on the ridge here a Pergamum, our own Trojan citadel.
But what winds, what destiny brought you sailing here?
Or did some god drive you, all unknowing, to our shores?
What about Ascanius? Is he still alive and breathing,
the boy who now Troy for you . . .   340
But does the boy ever think of the mother he lost?
Do his father Aeneas and the thought of his uncle Hector
awake in him the old-time courage and manliness at all?'
As these words poured out, she was crying, weeping
useless tears, on and on.

At this point Helenus turns up and takes Aeneas and his comrades back to his city. He is delighted to see them and entertains them for several days, until Aeneas feels that it is time to move on. He asks Helenus, who is a prophet, for advice about the journey ahead of him. Helenus prophesies at length, and then is also very generous with gifts for the Trojans as they prepare to depart. Andromache now reappears in the narrative. She has presents too, for Aeneas' son Ascanius. This is a thoughtful touch (so the boy does not feel left out) and a poignant one (because he is a substitute for her Astyanax), and she has selected special gifts, to make him think of her and home (Troy). Again Hector is still in her thoughts (and despite her other husbands she still sees herself as his wife), but Astyanax dominates the end of her speech, and we are left with a final picture of her missing her son terribly and about to lose the only living image of him that she has.

Andromache too, sad at the final parting, and not to be
outdone in showing honour, brought robes embroidered with
gold thread and a Trojan cloak for Ascanius.
She loaded him down with these woven gifts and said: 485
'Have these too, my boy, as reminders of my handiwork
and tokens of the enduring love for you of Andromache,
Hector's wife. Take them, the final gifts from your people.
Ah, you're the only image left to me now of my Astyanax.
He had the same eyes, the same hands, the same expression.   490
He would have been your age now, growing up to manhood like you.'

Heroides 4

PHAEDRA TO HIPPOLYTUS

After the last two mournful epistles Ovid produced by way of relief the amusing and outrageous *Heroides* 4 (in which he indulges in levity in connection with the grave crime of incest). This time we have a letter of seduction, as an older woman (who flatteringly refers to herself as a 'girl' in line 1 below) propositions a young man (her own stepson), trying to start rather than resume a relationship, and this time the writer is not physically separated from the addressee, but there is a gulf between them due to character and outlook.

Phaedra was the daughter of Minos (king of the Mediterranean island of Crete) and Pasiphae, who notoriously fell in love with a bull, had intercourse with it while concealed within a fake cow and gave birth to the Minotaur, a monster that was half-man and half-bull. Phaedra's sister was Ariadne, who helped the Athenian hero Theseus kill the Minotaur and eloped with him, only to be abandoned by him on a Greek island. Subsequently Phaedra was given in marriage to Theseus and had two sons by him. But she became infatuated with his earlier son by an Amazon queen. This was Hippolytus, who devoted himself to Diana, the virginal goddess of hunting and the wilds, and scorned Venus and women and love. In a famous play called *Hippolytus*, the fifth-century Greek tragedian Euripides made the goddess of love punish Hippolytus by causing Phaedra to fall disastrously in love with him, and Ovid's Phaedra also talks darkly of his neglect of Venus and suggests that a curse has been put on her family by Her (53ff., 88). *Heroides* 4 represents a missive sent to Hippolytus trying to entice him into an affair, while Theseus is away, staying with his great friend Pirithous in northern Greece.

What happens after this is well known. The chaste and prudish Hippolytus is horrified at the proposal and angrily turns Phaedra down. Afraid that he might reveal her advances to Theseus, she tells her husband on his return that Hippolytus had raped her (in many versions she does this in a letter). Theseus believes her, banishes his son and calls on the sea-god Neptune to punish him. As Hippolytus goes

off along the coast into exile in a chariot, a huge bull comes from the sea, terrifies
the horses and makes them bolt; the chariot crashes and, entangled in the reins, he
is dragged along and fatally injured. Phaedra also dies, committing suicide in one
tradition after she sends her accusing letter to Theseus, in another after she learns
that she has brought about the death of Hippolytus.

> From the Cretan girl to Hippolytus: I hope that all is well
>   with you; all being well with me depends on you.
> Read this through – what harm will there be in reading a letter?
>   You may even find something here to please you.
> Writing transmits secrets over land and sea;   5
>   even enemies accept and look at letters from their enemies.
> Three times I tried to speak to you; three times my tongue froze
>   and failed me, and the words died on my lips.
> Love should be combined with decency, where they can and do go
>   together;
>   love made me write what it wasn't decent to say.   10
> It's not safe to disregard anything that Love orders:
>   He is supreme and controls even the almighty gods.
> At first I hesitated, but He told me to write:
>   'Write! His hard heart will soften and yield.'
> May He come and grant my wishes by shooting you,   15
>   just as His avid fire burns me to my very marrow.
> I won't break my marriage vows just out of promiscuity:
>   my reputation (just ask!) is above reproach.
> The later it comes, the harsher love is. I'm on fire inside,
>   on fire, and my heart has a hidden wound.   20
> As the steer's tender neck is chafed by its first yoke
>   and a captive colt fresh from the herd resists the reins,
> so my inexperienced heart can hardly, scarcely bear love,
>   and that burden does not sit well on me.
> A person who learns to misbehave from early on becomes adept   25
>   at love; one who comes to it late suffers.
> You'll reap the first-fruits of my unsullied reputation;
>   we'll both be equally guilty.
> It's something to pluck fruit from an orchard's heavily-laden branches
>   and to pick the first rose with one's delicate nails.   30
> If the purity of my blameless life so far had
>   to be sullied by some novel stain,
> it's good that I'm smitten with someone of my own rank:
>   a discreditable lover is worse than an adulterous affair.
> If Juno offered me Jupiter (her husband and   35
>   brother), I think I'd prefer Hippolytus.
> Now (you'll hardly believe it) I'm turning to pastimes new to me.

I feel the urge to go off hunting wild animals.
The chief goddess for me now is Diana, famed for her curved
    bow. I share your preference for Her.   40
I like going to the woods, driving deer into the nets,
    urging on swift hunting-hounds over the highest ridges
or vigorously hurling a quivering spear
    or lying down to rest on the grassy ground.
I often enjoy driving a team of galloping horses, pulling   45
    on the reins to turn them and churning up dust.
Now I rush along like Bacchantes driven by their frenzied god
    or Cybele's Trojan devotees shaking their tambourines
or women touched by the Dryad nymphs or horned
    Fauns and crazed by their divine power.   50
When my frenzy has passed, they tell me all this;
    I say nothing, knowing it's love that burns me.
Perhaps my love is due to a curse imposed on my family
    by Venus, and she wants the whole line to pay.
Our family originated with Europa, and she was loved   55
    by duplicitous Jupiter, in the form of a bull.
My mother inside a fake cow was mounted by a bull
    and gave birth to a shameful child – the Minotaur.
Theseus escaped the Labyrinth by following the guiding thread
    that my sister gave him, but later broke his word to her.   60
Now, see, I'm the latest to encounter the fate laid down for all
    my line, to make it clear that I'm one of that family.
It was also fated for one house to entice two women:
    I fell for your beauty, Ariadne fell for your father.
Theseus and Theseus' son have two sisters as conquests: 65
    set up a double trophy over our house.
That time your father and I went to Eleusis (Ceres' city) –
    I wish now I'd never left my own land of Crete:
I'd found you attractive earlier, but it was then in particular
    that a violent love took root deep inside me.   70
You were dressed in white and wore a garland of flowers;
    a modest blush had tinged your bronzed cheeks;
the face that other women call hard and harsh
    to my eye was not hard but strong.
I want nothing to do with girlishly glamorous youths: 75
    a handsome man shouldn't do much to enhance his looks.
That hardness of yours, your artless hairstyle and the
    light coating of dust on your splendid face suit you.
If you ride a stubborn and spirited horse in the ring,
    I marvel at how you steer it in a small circle.   80
My gaze is drawn to your fierce and powerful arm,

whether you hurl a tough javelin with it
or grasp broad-headed hunting-spears of cornel wood.
    In short I enjoy watching whatever you do.
Just leave your ruthlessness behind on the wooded ridges.   85
    I'm not prey to be tracked down and killed by you.
What's the use of devoting yourself to the huntress
    Diana and depriving Venus of her dues?
Relaxing now and then renews strength and refreshes
    tired limbs. Without that nothing lasts.   90
Model yourself on Diana's weapons: a bow will grow
    slack if you never stop stretching it.
Cephalus was a famous hunter in the woods who
    brought down many animals with his arrows,
but he did well to make himself available as Dawn's lover,   95
    and it was sensible of her to go to him from her old husband.
Venus and Adonis often lay down together
    on some grassy spot underneath oak trees.
Meleager burned with love for Atalanta and showed it
    by awarding her the hide of the Calydonian boar.   100
Let's join all these people as soon as possible!
    Without love your forest has no refinement.
I'll hunt with you as your attendant, undaunted by rocky lairs
    or boars with dread sideways-slashing tusks.
Two seas hurl their waves at an isthmus, and that narrow   105
    strip of land hears the roars of both of them.
I'll live there with you in Troezen, the city ruled by Pittheus;
    it's already more precious to me than my homeland.
Opportunely Theseus is away and will be away for a long time,
    staying in the kingdom of his dear Pirithous.   110
Unless we deny the obvious, Theseus has preferred
    Pirithous to Phaedra and Pirithous to you.
And this isn't the only wrong that he has done to us.
    We've both suffered major harm at his hands.
With a knotted club he smashed my brother's bones in a spray   115
    of splinters, and left my sister as prey for wild animals.
The bravest of the axe-wielding Amazons bore you,
    a suitable mother for such a vigorous son.
If you ask where she is – Theseus drove his sword into her side;
    producing such a great son didn't save her life.   120
And she wasn't even married to him, no formal wedding for her,
    clearly so you couldn't inherit his kingdom, as a bastard.
He also fathered your brothers on me, and he was the one who
    acknowledged them all as his legitimate sons (not me).
Oh, you lovely, lovely boy, I wish my womb had split open   125

in childbirth before it could harm you like this.
Such a deserving father! Now show respect for the marriage
    which he abandons and renounces by his own actions!
You see me as a stepmother who would bed her stepson,
    but you shouldn't let empty names frighten you.   130
Such old-fashioned respect for family was unsophisticated way
    back in the Golden Age and died out soon after that.
Jupiter equated devotion to family with pleasure; his marriage to
    his sister means that no action is immoral.
Ties of kinship are only firm when Venus herself   135
    strengthens them with her own bonds.
We'd be doing wrong, but it's not hard to hide our love:
    the label 'relative' can conceal our misconduct.
If anyone sees us embracing, we'll both be praised;
    they'll say I'm a stepmother dedicated to her stepson.   140
You won't need to slip in at night through some hard
    husband's front door or elude a watchman.
We were and will continue to be under the same roof;
    you kissed and will continue to kiss me openly.
You'll be safe with me, and you'll win praise for your misconduct,   145
    even if you're seen in my bed.
Just hurry, start our affair soon! If you do, then may
    Cupid (who's so harsh to me now) go easy on you!
I'm not above humbly begging and pleading. Ah,
    where's my pride now and my haughty words? Fallen.   150
It was definite (if anything is definite in love): I'd put up
    a long fight against doing wrong and not give in.
But I'm beaten and begging, imploring you, even though
    I'm a queen: lovers are blind to propriety.
I've lost all shame, my shame has deserted and fled;   155
    forgive my confession, and soften your hard heart.
Even though my father is Minos, who rules the seas, and I'm
    descended from Jupiter who hurls the thunderbolt,
and my grandfather is the Sun with his crown of pointed rays
    and the glittering chariot that brings the warm daylight,   160
love tramples on noble birth. Pity my ancestors, and if
    you won't have mercy on me, have mercy on them.
My dowry is Crete, the island where Jupiter was raised;
    let my whole court serve my Hippolytus!
Give in, you savage! My mother managed to seduce a   165
    bull – will you be crueller than a fierce bull?
Spare me please, in Venus' name (she's here with me in all her power).
    If you do, may you never love a girl who could spurn you,
may swift Diana help you when you hunt in remote glades,

may the deep forest supply you with game to kill,   170
may the Satyrs and Pans (those mountain gods) show you favour,
   may you bring down boars head-on with your spear,
and may the nymphs (even though they say you hate girls)
   give you water to quench your parching thirst.
I'm adding tears to my request. You're reading the   175
   request; picture the tears in your mind's eye.

We have already touched on the elegiac spin given to material taken over from epic in connection with *Heroides* 1 and 3, but here the flavour of elegy is much more developed and significant. Phaedra's world is in important respects like that of the Latin elegists, a world of love letters, deceived husbands and furtive love affairs (see especially 141f.). Phaedra herself is in many ways a creature of elegy. She resembles the standard elegiac mistress: in the very first couplet she calls herself *puella* 'girl', a word commonly applied to such females, even though she is an older woman and mother of two; and her advanced views on morality, her sexual availability and her propensity for infidelity also recall them. In addition, with lively switches, at several points she also recalls the elegiac poet-lover, coming out with learned mythological parallels (93ff.) and professing humility towards the beloved (149ff.) as he frequently does, and often writing like Ovid in particular. So she shows an Ovidian contempt for rusticity and old-fashioned morals (102, 131f.), and her idea that men should not take pains over their appearance parallels Ovid's advice in the *Art of Love* (1.509, 523f.). So too she often demonstrates his type of elegant expression: see, for instance, the balanced arrangement, pointed repetition of words and melodious sound at 112 (in the Latin *Pirithoum Phaedrae Pirithoumque tibi*) and 144 (in the Latin *oscula aperta dabas, oscula aperta dabis*). For more on this elegiac aspect see Armstrong 2006 261ff.

This aura of contemporary elegy is incongruous in connection with a mythological character and subverts the figure of the queen familiar from tragedy. All of this has its playful side. There is also much else that is clearly intended to amuse in what is in fact an often ludicrous letter, which Phaedra presumably wrote blinded by passion. To appreciate this fully, you need to have a proper idea of the kind of character that she is propositioning here. In Euripides' *Hippolytus* the young prince is intolerant and rather fanatical, a virginal misogynist who will have nothing to do with love or sex. In that play it is Phaedra's nurse who reveals to him that Phaedra loves him, presumably expressing herself much more moderately and discreetly than the queen does here, but that still evokes revulsion and a furious denunciation of the whole female sex by this extremely moralistic young man, who at 616ff. says to her:

'Zeus, why did you inflict this plague on mankind, why
place women on earth with their fake glitter?
If you wanted to produce human beings,
you shouldn't have done it by means of women;

instead men should deposit in your temples   620
bronze or iron or a mass of gold
to buy children (each one paying as
much as he can afford) and live in
their homes free from the female sex . . .
Obviously women are a plague: the man   627
who fathers and raises one gives away a dowry and
sends her to a new home to get rid of trouble for himself;
and the poor husband who takes this poisonous creature   630
into his home gets pleasure from putting fine jewellery
on this foul idol and gives her lovely clothes as the
finishing touch, gradually exhausting the family fortune . . .
It's easiest for the man whose wife is a nonentity (although   638
no good comes of a stupid woman enshrined in your house).
But I hate a clever female. I wouldn't give house room to   640
a woman who's more intelligent than a woman should be.
Aphrodite makes the clever ones more promiscuous,
whereas a simpleton because of her lack
of brains is saved from immorality.
Slaves should not have access to a woman.   645
Instead women should be housed with wild animals
that bite but lack speech, so they can't talk to
other people or get a reply back from them.
But as things are evil females sit at home devising evil
schemes, and their servants go out to further them.   650
That's how you've come to fix up an unholy
affair with my father's wife, you evil creature.
I'll pour water into my ears and wash away
your words. How could I be evil like that,
when just hearing the proposal makes me feel dirty? . . .   655
I curse all women. I'll never have my fill of hating   664
them (even if I'm accused of always talking about   665
them), because they never stop being evil.
So someone should teach them to control themselves
or let me trample them underfoot for all time.'

There is nothing that Phaedra could have said that would seduce such a character. But comically she makes a real mess of her attempt. She does not just come out
with remarks that are hardly likely to impress him or win him over (like claims of
illustrious ancestry). She writes things that would actually put him off: for example,
in 15 she pictures Cupid shooting him; at 55ff. and later she talks of her amorous
family, which includes a mother guilty of bestiality and a monstrous brother; at 73ff.
she puts herself across as some sort of stalker, obsessively observing the young man;
and at 125f. she conjures up the grotesque image of her womb bursting. Worse than

that, she includes material that would have him writhing in embarrassment, shame and disgust. So there is obvious phallic symbolism at 91f. in the reference to the taut bow (his revered Diana's own weapon). In 107 she pictures herself shacked up with him. At 109ff. she suggests outrageously that Theseus is off having an affair with his friend Pirithous. At 129ff. she is shamelessly cynical about incest. And at 139ff. she dilates on how easily she and Hippolytus could get away with an incestuous liaison and depicts them embracing, kissing and in bed together. Imagine the reactions of the chaste and prudish youngster as he reads all this! And the length of the letter means he would go on and on squirming.

There is more to the facetiousness than that. The queen indulges in absurd exaggeration, lies and fantasy, posing as a virgin (30), maintaining that she goes hunting (37ff.) and envisioning her stepson as wanting her along with him when he hunts (103f.). There is irony too: for instance, in 4 she thinks that there may be something to please Hippolytus in this letter; in 39 she claims allegiance to the virginal Diana, while trying to seduce the young man; and at 113ff. she complains that Theseus has done her wrong while she is in the process of trying to wrong him. There is also dark wit in the extensive foreshadowing. Hippolytus will turn down Phaedra, and she will then write a very different kind of letter, accusing him of attempted rape (so her question in 3 about what harm there is in reading a letter is grimly amusing). What happens after that is hinted at by numerous references to chariots, horses, bulls, the sea, Neptune and death. There is lots more humour, which you can now find for yourself (look in particular at lines 17, 18, 33f., 85f., 97f., 148, 161f., 167 and 168).

The above seems to me a valid assessment of *Heroides* 4, but another approach is also feasible. In *The Resisting Reader* Judith Fetterley advocates a feminist reading that resists the male point of view and has one enter the text from a new critical direction, not thinking as a man but identifying its patriarchal assumptions and ideas and the role that it assigns to women, perceiving how the female in the text is excluded, undermined, denigrated etc., rejecting its tacit inducement to make her think and behave in a particular way, and pointing out how a woman feels when she tries to make something of the piece of writing. Essentially this kind of analysis (always very relevant to the *Heroides*) looks at what is said about women, how they are represented and what is assumed about them and recommended for them implicitly or explicitly. In the case of *Her.* 4 a resisting reader would see Ovid (who could have made changes to the story) as taking over and being complicit with a myth that reflects male fear of female sexuality, wants the heroine to conform to a patriarchal society's standards and reinforces ancient stereotypes (women lack rationality, find it hard to restrain themselves sexually and are bad when they do not act in the family's interest). Such a reader might well object to Ovid's depiction of the queen (as scheming, shameless, undignified, subservient to a man etc.) and take exception to his levity in general and mockery of Phaedra in particular.

As an exercise compare and contrast Ovid's treatment of the theme of incest at *Metamorphoses* 9.454ff. (Byblis).

Heroides 4 is paired with *Heroides* 2. What are the major links between the two poems, and in what ways does Ovid also achieve enlivening variation?

There were many other versions of Phaedra both before and after Ovid, and it is fascinating to see how this character changes from creator to creator and is employed in very diverse ways. We only have the space to pick out for comment here some of the more famous and interesting representations of the queen and her story. For much more on Phaedra in literature, music and film see Mills 109ff., Mayer 75ff., James & Jondorf 89ff. and Grafton & Most & Settis 707f.

Three fifth-century tragedies were concerned with her story – the *Phaedra* of Sophocles (of which we know very little, as most of it is lost) and two plays called *Hippolytus* by Euripides (of which only the second has survived intact). Going by the fragments of the first *Hippolytus* and ancient references to it, we gather that in it Phaedra was an immoral and shameless woman who approached the prince in person and tried to seduce him; and, when he turned her down, acted out of anger and in self-defence (in case he told Theseus) and accused him of rape or attempted rape. Ovid obviously had an eye to that depiction of the heroine; but he also looked to the second *Hippolytus* (on the relation of *Her.* 4 to these tragedies see Jacobson 142ff. and Armstrong 2006 271ff.). In that second play we see a very different Phaedra, a highly sympathetic character. Now she is an honourable and virtuous woman, who has been tormented by her love for her stepson and bravely tried to resist, but has been unable to master it. She has kept silent about her passion, and only reveals it under intense pressure from her old nurse. At 392ff. she tells her and the chorus of her intention to starve herself to death rather than yield to dishonour in a moving speech that shows clearly her anguish, integrity and nobility:

> When love wounded me, I looked for the best way
> to endure it. I began by saying nothing
> about my sickness and keeping it secret.
> For there's no trusting the tongue: it knows how to   395
> criticize other people's ideas, but when you talk about
> your own failings, you do yourself a lot of damage.
> My next plan was to master this madness by using
> self-control and endure it successfully that way.
> Then, when I didn't manage to overcome my   400
> passion by that means, I decided to die –
> the best course, as all will agree.
> I don't want lots of people to see me behaving shamefully,
> just as I do want them to notice when I act honourably.
> I knew my sickness and its consummation were disgraceful,   405
> and I was also well aware that I was a woman,
> something everyone hates. I wish the most agonizing
> of deaths on the wife who first defiled her
> marriage-bed with other men. This evil that infects
> the female sex originated with the aristocracy: 410
> when noble ladies approve of shameful conduct,
> the lower classes will certainly think it's respectable.

I also hate women who profess purity but in
secret have the effrontery to behave scandalously.
Sea-born queen Aphrodite, how do they look   415
their husband in the face and not shudder for fear
that the darkness (their accomplice) and the house's
timbers might some day reveal what they have done?
That's why I'm going to commit suicide, my friends,
so I'm not found guilty of bringing disgrace on my husband   420
and children, and so they can live and flourish in
glorious Athens as free men, speaking out freely,
their good name not tarnished by their mother.
When a man learns of crimes committed by his mother or father,
even if he's bold-hearted, he feels demeaned, like a slave. 425
They say you only hold your own in life's struggles
if you have a just and honest character.
Sooner or later Time holds up a mirror (like a
young girl's) to show what bad people are really
like. I don't want to be seen as one of them, ever.   430

After this the well-meaning but misguided nurse, in an attempt to save her mistress' life, acts against Phaedra's instructions and tells Hippolytus of the queen's feelings for him. He thinks this is a proposition that comes from Phaedra and launches into the furious tirade against women at 616ff., which was translated above. The queen fears that he will speak out about what has happened, and so she hangs herself, leaving a letter for Theseus accusing Hippolytus of rape, to discredit what he will say and to protect her children's reputation. After Theseus banishes and curses his son, the dying Hippolytus is brought on stage, and the goddess Artemis (Diana) appears to explain his innocence, leaving Theseus in agony. Phaedra is a particularly tragic figure as she is just a pawn and the helpless victim of a vastly superior power. Because Hippolytus neglected her, the goddess Aphrodite (Venus) avenged that slight by making Phaedra fall violently in love with him, which resulted ultimately in him being wrongfully discredited, banished by his father and suffering an appalling end (and incidentally in Phaedra dying too). This is a gloomy, disturbing and thought-provoking play. We witness human blindness, frailty and total inferiority (to the gods). We see a chillingly callous and vindictive Aphrodite. And we are left to deduce things like the need to achieve balance (not be one-sided and intolerant) and to recognize and not suppress the sexual side of our nature. Those who wish to go into this play in more detail should consult Mills.

In the first century AD the Roman writer Seneca produced another bleak tragedy based on this story. His *Phaedra* combines elements of the versions of the heroine in *Her.* 4 and Euripides' *Hippolytus*: she propositions her stepson in person, but she is essentially a good woman, who is initially repelled by her own desire and wants to resist it. The gods are hardly in evidence in this play, and the humans are the victims of their own feelings, which are what really do the damage. As a Stoic philosopher

Seneca believed that if the passions (intense emotions) are allowed to outweigh reason, that leads to irrational acts and madness, and here he shows us the terrible things that happen in that situation. We witness the moral degeneration of Phaedra, as her self-control is overwhelmed by a mad desire which makes her do bad things. And Theseus also succumbs to passion (anger and a lust for revenge), and that makes him bring about his own son's death and leaves him at the end a broken man.

After Phaedra tells the nurse of her longing for the prince and proves unable to master it, the nurse makes an indirect approach to him unsuccessfully, and then Phaedra openly confesses her love to him. He is outraged and flees in horror, dropping his sword. To protect her mistress' reputation, the nurse pretends that he tried to rape the queen and points to the dropped sword as proof of his violence. When Theseus returns, Phaedra weeps and tears her hair to gain credibility, and with seeming reluctance claims that she was raped. Enraged, he curses his son, and Neptune sends the bull from the sea. When the fragments of his severely mangled body are returned to Theseus and brought on stage, he grieves, and then Phaedra enters. The sight of the corpse brings to her the reality of what she has done. She comes to her senses again and reverts to being a basically good person. At 1159ff. she confesses to her deception, asserts Hippolytus' innocence and tries to atone and recover some of her honour by killing herself. Her speech, in the grand style of tragedy, arouses both pity and admiration:

> It's *me* you should attack, *me*, savage lord Neptune,
> send against *me* the monsters of the blue deep – 1160
> all that the remotest sea has in its inmost
> recesses, all that the ocean hides in its furthest
> waters, enveloped in its wandering waves.
> Theseus, you're always cruel, you've never returned without
> harming your relatives. Your son and father paid for your 1165
> homecomings with their deaths. You always wreck your family,
> destroying them through love or hatred of your wives.
> Hippolytus, is this your face, did I make it look
> like this? Has some savage Sinis or Procrustes torn
> you limb from limb? Were you ripped apart by some 1170
> Cretan bull-monster, some ferocious horned beast
> filling the Labyrinth with its massive roars?
> What happened to your beauty, and your eyes (my
> stars)? I can't believe you're lying there dead.
> Be with me for a little while, listen to my words 1175
> (none of them shameful). I'll make amends, plunging the
> sword into my black heart with my own hands,
> freeing myself from life and guilt together,
> and I'll follow you frantically across the waters and lakes
> of the Underworld, across the Styx and the river of fire. 1180
> Let me placate your ghost: accept this hair stripped

from my head, cut from the brow I've scratched in grief.
We couldn't be united in love, but at least we can be in
death. [*To herself*] Die — if faithful, for your husband; if not,
for your lover. Should I return to the marriage-bed which my   1185
criminal conduct defiled? *One* crime I avoided — pretending innocence
and sleeping there as if my honour had been vindicated.
Death is the only remedy for my evil love and it will bring
me the greatest glory now that my honour is ruined.
Death, give me refuge, opening wide your merciful arms.   1190
Hear me, Athens, and you, Theseus, a father deadlier than a
deadly stepmother: I didn't tell the truth, I made it up,
I lied about the sinful coupling that I had obsessed over
in my madness. You punished your son for a fiction,
and this pure youth lies here the victim of an impure accusation,   1195
chaste and innocent. [*To Hippolytus*] Have your real character back.
It's right to bare my evil breast to this sword.
My blood is a funeral-offering to a good man.

                                   [*She stabs herself*]

After that Theseus gives his son due mourning and a proper cremation at length, but ends the play with just two lines for Phaedra, telling his slaves to bury the woman and praying that the earth weigh heavily on her wicked body. For more on Seneca's play see Mayer.

The famous seventeenth-century French playwright Jean Racine looked to both Euripides and Seneca in creating his *Phèdre*, which many regard as his masterpiece. He followed the main outline of the myth, while adapting it to suit the current vogue for politics and love in drama and also the sensibility of his audience. He adds a political dimension by having Theseus believed to be dead at one point, so that there is a dynastic struggle over who will succeed to the throne. He develops the love interest by introducing a new character — Aricia, who is a princess in a rival Athenian royal family that Theseus has suppressed, and who loves Hippolytus and is loved by him (which means that he is no longer misogynistic or prudish but a young lover). Phaedra's character is also softened, in line with the contemporary French sense of decorum. She feels great horror over her love for the prince, and had earlier fought it by getting Theseus to send him away from Athens, so that temptation was removed. She only reveals her attraction to Hippolytus when she thinks that Theseus is dead and there would be nothing wrong any more in a relationship. And as well as not accusing him of rape herself (the nurse alone does that) she begs Theseus to relent when he curses his son. There is extra suffering for her too, when she learns of the love of Aricia and Hippolytus and feels deep pain and also jealousy. For more information on this tragedy (best read in the free verse translation by Ted Hughes) consult James & Jondorf.

June Rachuy Brindel's *Phaedra: A Novel of Ancient Athens* (published in 1985) gives the myth a decidedly feminine focus (via the female narrator, who concentrates on Phaedra) and a feminist slant. The story is told by Aissa, a servant who looked after Phaedra, and who recounts a version of events different from the standard tale that has come down to us (a tale which consists of lies put out by Theseus' palace). Phaedra was still a child when the brutal and duplicitous Theseus took her from Crete, after he had conquered and plundered the island. He wanted her to become his queen so that he could ensure power for himself in Crete through this member of the Cretan royal family. She was also a representative of the old worship of the mother-goddess and had the mystic power to speak for that deity as her incarnation. The violent hero scorned that peaceful matriarchal religion and wanted to control Phaedra as part of his campaign to wipe it out. But the goddess still had many worshippers, and they fought back, and Phaedra and Aissa (and Hippolytus) were drawn into that dangerous struggle.

Sarah Kane's play *Phaedra's Love* (first performed in London in 1996) is an 'in-yer-face' modern adaptation of the myth, based very loosely on Seneca's *Phaedra*. Kane has been grouped with other contemporary writers under the label of the New Brutalists, and her play is fairly brutal, with its violence, sexuality, coarse language and nihilism. It opens with Hippolytus watching TV and eating a hamburger, and then blowing his nose on one sock and masturbating into another (note that the socks are discarded and he is not wearing them at the time). Hippolytus is the drama's focus, and he is a spoiled, jaded and cynical prince, overweight and smelly, and cruelly truthful. This Hippolytus is not a virgin or a prude (in fact he indulges in lots of sex, but gets no pleasure from it), and he is not a simple misogynist (although he takes out his frustrations on women, he hates all people, men included). In this play Phaedra is rather different too. She comes with presents for the prince from the people (it is his birthday), and he tries to make her hate him, asking her when she last had a fuck and why she married into all this shit in the palace (was Theseus a great shag?). She explains that she loves him despite the fact that he is moody, bitter, fat, decadent and selfish, and adds: 'You're in pain. I adore you.' She wants to change him, to make him happy by means of her love. For his birthday present she performs oral sex on him, but during it he watches television and eats sweets, and he has nothing to say to her after it is over, reducing her to tears. When she says that she wants to have full intercourse with him, he tells her to fuck someone else and imagine it is him. Then he informs her that he had sex with her daughter and made her come, and that he has gonorrhoea, and asks her if she hates him now. She says no, but subsequently hangs herself, leaving a note which claims that he raped her. The people riot in anger over the queen's death, but Hippolytus refuses to deny the charge of rape (life is a void for him and he is waiting for death to take him away from it). In jail he refuses the help of a visiting priest, denies the existence of God and lures the priest into fellating him. Subsequently on his way to the law court he is torn apart by an angry mob. A woman cuts off his genitals and throws them on to a barbecue. A child takes them off and hurls them at another child, amid much laughter. Finally they are thrown to a dog. Hippolytus dies, and a vulture descends and begins to eat his body. This is a provocative and disturbing play, which probes violence, the nature of love and belief in god. Kane also described it as 'my comedy', and there is a savage humour in Hippolytus' cynicism and brutal honesty.

Heroides 5
OENONE TO PARIS

Paris was the son of king Priam of Troy and his queen Hecuba. When she was pregnant with Paris, she dreamed that she gave birth to a flame which burned down Troy. This was interpreted to mean that the child when born would cause the destruction of the city. So when she gave birth to Paris, he was left on Mount Ida nearby to die. But a shepherd found him and brought him up as his own son. Acting as a humble herdsman, Paris grew up to be so handsome that a local nymph and daughter of a river-god called Oenone fell in love with him and married him. Subsequently his true identity was revealed and he was welcomed back into the royal family. When the three goddesses Juno, Minerva and Venus asked him to judge which of them was the most beautiful, Venus bribed him by offering him the most beautiful woman in the world and he accepted the bribe. The woman in question was Helen, wife of Menelaus, who was the king of Sparta (in Greece), and Paris sailed there, seduced Helen and took her back to Troy as his new wife. The Greeks demanded her return, and it is at this point that Oenone writes this letter to Paris, urging him to renew their relationship and give Helen back. He did not return her, so a huge Greek expedition led by Agamemnon (Menelaus' brother) besieged Troy for ten years to get her back, and finally captured it and burnt it down. Shortly before that Paris was severely wounded and appealed to Oenone to heal him with her great medical skills. After the way he had treated her, she refused. But then she relented and wanted to heal him, but found that he had already died, and so she committed suicide.

By way of a change the writer of this letter is a minor goddess rather than a human (and she is very much on her dignity instead of humiliating herself). There is no question of incest here, and she is already in a relationship with the addressee, which she is trying to revive (rather than undermining the institution of marriage).

And in this letter the man is the adulterous one, and he is in so many respects opposite to the prudish, virginal and misogynistic Hippolytus.

> Are you reading this? Or won't your new wife let you?
>   Read on! This isn't a letter from Agamemnon.
> It's from Oenone, your girl (with your leave), a water-nymph of
>   real renown in the local forests, complaining of your betrayal.
> Is some powerful god opposing my desires? Am I   5
>   being punished for some crime by losing you?
> Suffering that is deserved should be endured calmly;
>   punishment that is unmerited rankles.
> You weren't so grand when I (a nymph and daughter of a
>   mighty river) was content to have you for my husband.   10
> Priam's son now, you were a slave then (I won't suppress the truth
>   out of deference). Though a nymph, I deigned to marry a slave.
> We often rested under a shady tree among the flocks,
>   with the grass and leaves providing a bed for us.
> We often lay on straw or in deep hay,   15
>   protected from the hoar-frost by a humble hut.
> Who used to show you the glades good for hunting and the
>   rocky lairs where wild animals hid their young?
> I often went with you and spread out the meshed nets,
>   I often drove on your swift dogs over the long ridges.   20
> My name is still there on the beeches inscribed by you,
>   and people read OENONE carved by your blade;
> as the trunks grow bigger, so does my name;   25
>   trees, grow tall and straight, and make me famous!
> Please live on, you poplar planted on the bank of Xanthus
>   with this couplet on your wrinkled bark:
> WHEN PARIS CAN LEAVE OENONE AND SURVIVE WITHOUT HER,
>   THIS RIVER WILL TURN AND FLOW BACK TO ITS SOURCE.   30
> Xanthus, turn, flow back, and quickly reverse your course:
>   Paris has abandoned Oenone and *can* bear it.
> That day spoke doom for poor Oenone, the awful storm
>   of blighted love began for me on that day
> when Venus, Juno and Minerva (who's more attractive with   35
>   her armour on) came to be judged naked by you.
> When you told me of this, my heart lurched in shock
>   and a cold shudder ran through my hard bones.
> I was really terrified and consulted male and female elders.
>   They all agreed that it was very bad.   40
> Firs were felled, planks were cut, ships were built
>   and caulked and launched on the blue sea.

You wept as you left – don't deny that at any rate;
    we were both miserable and mingled our tears.   46
The elm isn't clasped by the clinging vine as tightly
    as my neck was embraced by your arms.
Ah, how often your crew laughed when you complained
    about the wind (which was favourable) detaining you!   50
How often you sent me away, then called me back for more
    kisses! How hard you found it to say 'goodbye'!
A gentle breeze stirred the sails that hung from the rigid
    mast, and your oars churned the water into foam.
My sad eyes followed your sails as long as they   55
    could, and soaked the sand with tears.
I prayed to the green sea-nymphs for a swift return,
    oh yes, for a swift and ruinous return.
So, you came back for the benefit of another, not me?
    Ah, my persuasive prayers helped a sinister rival.   60
A massive crag that has tumbled down faces the
    boundless sea, forming a natural breakwater.
From there I first recognized your ship's sails, and I
    felt an urge to rush through the waves to you.
I held back, then glimpsed a gleam of purple up on the prow;   65
    I became very scared: you didn't wear purple.
In the swift breeze your ship approached and reached land;
    with a trembling heart I saw a woman's face.
Worse than that (why was I mad enough to stay there?),
    the slut was clinging to you, your mistress.   70
Then I ripped my dress, beat my breasts and tore
    my tear-drenched cheeks with my hard nails,
filling holy Ida (my mountain) with howls of
    outrage and going back there in tears.
I hope Helen weeps like that, abandoned by her man,   75
    feeling the pain and suffering that she caused me.
Now you've a taste for women who leave their lawfully wedded
    husbands and sail away with you over the open sea.
But when you were a poor herdsman, Oenone (and nobody
    else) was your wife, poor though you were.   80
I'm not impressed by your wealth, I don't care about your palace
    or being called a wife of one of Priam's many sons –
not that he'd refuse to have a nymph for a daughter-in-law,
    not that Hecuba would have concealed our relationship:
I am worthy of becoming a powerful lord's spouse;   85
    my hands could add lustre to a sceptre.
Don't look down on me because I lay with you on beech
    leaves: I'm better suited to a bed of royal purple.

Lastly, my love is not dangerous: it doesn't lead to war
    or an avenging fleet coming across the waves.   90
Armed enemies demand the return of runaway Helen –
    this is the dowry that arrogant bride brings with her.
Ask your brother Hector or Deiphobus and Polydamas
    if she should be given back to the Greeks;
find out the advice of stern Antenor and Priam himself,   95
    who have learned things in their long lives.
Don't begin as prince by valuing your spoil above Troy.
    You should be ashamed; her husband is right to fight.
If you've any sense, don't count on fidelity in one who
    so quickly turned to you and fell into your arms.   100
Menelaus roared out in rage at the violation of his marriage,
    wronged and pained by her love for a stranger,
and you will too. Purity, once spoiled, can't possibly be
    restored; it's lost and gone for good.
She burns with love for you? She loved gullible   105
    Menelaus like that too, and he now sleeps alone.
Lucky Andromache, happily married to faithful Hector!
    You should have been a husband like him to me.
You're more lightweight than dried out, sapless
    leaves wispily drifting on a shifting breeze;   110
there's less substance to you than there is to the tip of a corn-ear
    burnt light and crisp by the sun day after day.
I remember, your prophetic sister once predicted all this
    to me, with her hair streaming about her:
'What are you doing, Oenone? Why sow seeds in sand,   115
    uselessly ploughing a beach with oxen?
A Greek heifer is coming, to destroy you, your home and your
    land. Ho, keep her away! A Greek heifer is coming.
Trojans, sink that ill-omened ship while you can!
    Ah, it carries a heavy cargo of Trojan blood.'   120
She was still speaking in an inspired frenzy when her slaves
    hurried her off; my blonde hair stood on end.
I'm so miserable. Her prophecy was all too true:
    see, that heifer has taken over my pastures.
However beautiful she is, she's an adulteress (that's clear):   125
    she fell for her guest and betrayed the gods of marriage.
Someone called Theseus (unless I'm mistaken over the name)
    stole her from her homeland before you.
Who'd imagine that passionate young man returned her still a virgin?
    How am I so sure about this? I'm in love.   130
You can call it rape, using that word to conceal her guilt;
    a woman so often abducted invited abduction.

But I am still true to my cheating husband, even though
    by your rules I could have cheated on you.
Swift and shameless, the Satyrs ran round looking   135
    for me (but I lay low, hidden in the woods),
and so did Faunus, with a wreath of sharp pine on his horned
    head, on the vast slopes of swelling mount Ida.
Apollo, the illustrious lyre-player and builder of Troy's walls,   145
    loved me. He gave me access to his gifts:
I have all the potent remedial herbs and roots used by
    physicians, wherever they grow in the whole world.
Poor Oenone – love can't be cured by herbs.
    I'm a skilled expert, but my skill fails me.   150
The earth that produces so many medicinal plants can't help me,   153
    nor can Apollo the Healer, but *you* can.
You can, and I'm entitled. Have pity on a deserving girl.   155
    I don't come with Greeks, bringing bloody war.
No, I'm yours; we were together when we were young,
    and I want to be yours for the rest of time.

Ovid here gives prominence to another minor female character connected with the Trojan War (like the contrastingly humble and timid Briseis in *Her.* 3), as he seizes on and develops what is essentially something of a sideshow to the main action. Oenone is in a rather awkward situation but handles it with style. Mortifyingly, she is a goddess in love with a human who has been jilted by that human, for another mortal; and despite that she still loves him and wants him back. Here she is trying to get him back, but she is careful to maintain her dignity while doing that in a delicate balancing-act. Obviously she is hurt and angered by what Paris has done, but she stays self-possessed and in control, and she will not lower herself by begging. On the contrary she is proud and superior, feisty and combative, disdainful and sharp-tongued. Ovid's Oenone is very much a goddess (albeit a minor one) and very intelligent (especially in contrast to the short-sighted Paris, who is about to pass up this last chance to rejoin the nymph and escape war, a prolonged siege and death).

All of this is evident from the very start of *Heroides* 5. At 1f. Oenone begins the digs at Helen (undermining her rival as a domineering shrew) and Paris (with an ominous allusion to the great trouble that the fool has brought on himself from the Greeks). In 3f. she tartly reminds him of the established relationship which he has betrayed (to make him feel bad) and highlights her superiority (to him and his foreign mistress). In the next couplet disarmingly she intimates her love for him and also tries to win his sympathy; but then at 7f. she works in a subtle barb (she is innocent and suffering unfairly, whereas he is the one who has done wrong and deserves to be punished). At 9–12 for emphasis she again brings out his inferiority, cuttingly exaggerating the lowliness of his status in the past, and sniping at his newly acquired grandeur now, while also toning down the condescension a bit by means of further indirect indication of her love for him. The wistful dwelling on their former happiness together at 13–20 is eloquent of her feelings for him, and it also craftily shows him what he will be missing – an idyllic, peaceful and safe existence, a free, harmonious and relaxed way of life (in contrast to being a target himself and enduring all the anxiety and misery of siege and warfare).

The rest of the letter is also consistently dense and pointed like this, and these main lines of attack are picked up and developed further there, as you can see for yourself. Look in particular for more of the overt digs at Helen and Paris (e.g. in 60, 70, 77f. and 91f.) and more of the cunning barbs (e.g. in 97, 105f. and the various unflattering implications about Paris in the comparisons at 109–112). Later on in this spunky performance Oenone adds extra thrusts, bringing in supporters for her point of view at 93ff. and (Cassandra) 113ff., attempting to arouse jealousy at 135ff., and being more open in her appeals at the very end. There is an engaging tonal blend in all of this, a bittersweet mixture of the amusing (in the snootiness, jibes and innuendo) and the sad (in Oenone's overall unhappiness, in the letter's futility and in the clear hint of the denouement at 147ff. with the references to absence of a cure, Oenone's skill achieving nothing and the appeal for help, which is about to be turned down).

To sharpen your appreciation of how developed and lively the character of Ovid's Oenone is, compare and contrast her with the softer nymph in the poem *Oenone* by the nineteenth-century English poet Tennyson.

In *Heroides* 5 the upcoming death of Oenone forms part of the gloomy undercurrent. The late Greek epic poet Quintus Smyrnaeus brings out the sadness of that fully in his account of her end in book ten of his *Posthomerica* (quoted below). After he is shot, Paris is most unwilling to approach Oenone, but has to, because he can only escape death if she is willing to help him. He goes to her, claiming feebly that he did not willingly desert her but was led to Helen by inescapable fate, and asking her to save his life. She angrily refuses, telling him to go and ask Helen to cure him. He departs and dies. When she hears the news, she bitterly regrets her refusal to tend him and determines on suicide. At this point lots of pathos is built up. So, for example, we are shown her continuing great love for Paris, whose death she has helped bring about. Her unstoppable rush to his pyre through the atmospheric moonlight makes for an awful sense of inevitability, although her actual arrival there is held off for many lines, so there is a build-up to it. At his pyre there are nymphs and shepherds mourning for Paris, which increases the overall poignancy. And then there is Oenone's brisk and resolute leap on to the blazing pyre, and the affecting tribute to her made by one of the nymphs.

> Groaning terribly, she said to herself:
> 'Oh, I did wrong. Oh, I hate being alive.
> I loved my luckless husband and had hoped for a   425
> fine death with him in frail old age after a life
> of harmony together. But the gods willed otherwise.
> I wish black death had carried me off

before I was separated from Paris.
Even if he left me in his lifetime, I'll join him   430
in death, undaunted. There's no pleasure for me in living.'
As she said this, she wept piteous tears,
remembering her husband who had met his doom.
She melted with grief, like wax in a fire, but in secret
(wary of her father and the maids with their lovely robes),   435
until night rose from broad Ocean and flowed
across the glorious earth, bringing men release from toil.
Then while her father and the slave-girls slept
in the halls, she tore open the palace gates
and rushed off, like a storm-wind, sprinting.   440
Think of a heifer on heat, whose passion
drives her to rush along mountains on swift feet;
in her longing to couple with a bull she doesn't fear
her herdsmen at all; an uncontrollable impulse carries her
along in the hope of seeing a mate in the thickets: 445
just like that Oenone sped over long paths,
keen to quickly mount the dreadful funeral pyre.
Her legs were tireless, and her speeding feet flew
along ever faster, spurred on by deadly Doom and
Aphrodite. And she had no fear of the shaggy beasts   450
she met in the dark, though terrified of them earlier.
She trod every rock and crag of those overgrown
mountains and crossed every ravine.
The moon-goddess on high saw Oenone then and,
remembering her own lover (the noble Endymion),   455
pitied her speeding along so swiftly. She shone down
for her brightly and illuminated the long paths.
Oenone quickly made her way along a mountain to the
place where other nymphs were wailing round Paris' pyre.
A huge blaze enveloped him still.   460
Shepherds had come from the various hills
and heaped up a great mass of wood, performing this
last sad service for their comrade and prince, streaming
with tears as they stood around him. When she saw him there
clearly, she didn't groan at all, although broken-hearted,   465
but covered her beautiful face with her cloak and swiftly
leapt on to the pyre. And they gave a great groan.
She burned beside her husband. All the nymphs were
astounded when they saw her collapsed at his
side, and one of them said this to herself: 470
'Paris was really wrong deserting a wife who was absolutely
devoted to him and coming back with a whore as his new wife,

bringing pain and death to himself and the Trojans and Troy,
the fool! He didn't show any respect for his prudent wife's
broken heart, while she revered him more than life, 475
even though he detested her and didn't love her.'

Quintus adds that when the bodies had been consumed by the flames, their joint
ashes were collected in a golden urn and buried in a funeral-mound which had two
gravestones aptly facing away from each other.

Oenone is one of the nymphs (on whom see especially Larson). They were minor
female divinities, usually very long-lived, or even immortal. There were nymphs of
the sea and of islands at sea, and there were also nymphs of the countryside, who
inhabited streams, rivers, trees, woods, mountains and whole regions. They were
mainly benevolent, often consorting with and helping herdsmen (like Paris) by
protecting and increasing their flocks (see Larson 78ff.), and also aiding hunters.
But they did sometimes assume a sterner aspect, punishing, for instance, those who
violated their habitat and also unresponsive lovers. Sometimes they had the power
of prophecy (as Oenone did according to other authors). In general they led a life
of great freedom (dancing, singing, hunting, weaving and reveling, as they wished),
and frequently they acted as the attendants of a major goddess (such as Diana) or
god (such as Bacchus). In myth and literature they are closely connected with love,
and they are the willing or unwilling partners of various divinities (see Larson 91ff.)
and humans (like Paris), being pursued and raped, and also having consensual sex, and
also abducting and detaining handsome youths and men whom they fancy (like
Hylas and Ulysses). In Ovid's poetry they have a predominantly erotic function,
and rapes (successful and unsuccessful) of nymphs are particularly common, with
the mood varying from frivolous (e.g. Daphne and Io at *Metamorphoses* 1.452ff. and
588ff.) to sad (for example, Callisto at *Met.* 2.406ff.) and a combination of both
(for instance, Juturna and Lara at *Fasti* 2.585ff.). Examine *Met.* 4.285ff., where the
nymph Salmacis is the would-be rapist, and look for humour there and clever twists
to the normal situation. On the topic in general see Murgatroyd 63ff.

Paris reappears in *Heroides* 16 and 17, and he refers to Oenone at 16.96ff. He
is trying to seduce Helen with what he writes to her there, but his smugness and
unloving dismissiveness show him in a bad light again:

It's not just the daughters of kings and chieftains who have courted me: 95
nymphs too have cared for me and loved me.
Who was there to surpass Oenone's marvellous beauty? After you
nobody in the world is more worthy of being Priam's daughter-in-law.
But I despised all of those females once I was
given the hope of marrying you, Helen. 100

The negative portrayal of Paris begins with Homer. In the *Iliad* he appears
overall as a rather unheroic figure, more of a lover than a fighter, one who excels
in beauty and the gifts of Aphrodite. He can be brave and fight well, especially

when rebuked and shamed by his brother Hector; and he does accept those rebukes gracefully. But he tends to be dilatory in battle and emerges badly from the contrast with his more serious and heroic sibling. Paris' weapon was the bow, which was regarded as somewhat unmanly (the spear was the standard weapon of the warrior), and in book 3 of the *Iliad* he performs poorly in a duel with Menelaus. At 3.15ff. Paris challenges the best of the Greeks to combat (a typically showy and thoughtless gesture), but when Menelaus immediately steps out to meet him, Paris slinks back into the Trojan ranks. When taunted by Hector as a pretty boy who disgraces the Trojans with his cowardice, he agrees to fight. A formal truce is established so the duel can take place. Both heroes hurl their spears ineffectually. Then Menelaus draws his sword and brings it down on Paris' helmet, only for the weapon to shatter. He seizes Paris by the helmet and drags him towards the Greeks, choking him with the strap, which is pulled tight. But Aphrodite snaps it, snatches Paris away from death with the greatest of ease and sets him down in Helen's perfumed bedroom. Helen rounds on him, telling him she wishes he had been killed by Menelaus, a much better man. The insouciant Paris says in reply that Menelaus has beaten him for the time being with divine help, but will himself be beaten by Paris at another time. He then takes Helen to bed and makes love to her, while back on the battlefield Menelaus is prowling through the ranks trying to find Paris and continue the duel (an eloquent contrast between the two men). None of the Trojans can point out Paris to him, but would if they could, because after all the years of warfare thanks to him they hate him like black death.

After that the truce is broken and battle is joined again. The Greeks begin to do very well in the combat, and so in book 6 (237ff.) Hector slips back to Troy to get the women to make an offering to Athena in the (vain) hope of persuading her to help the Trojans. While there, he encounters Helen and Paris, and accuses him of shirking combat. Paris says he will rejoin the fighting and, if Hector goes ahead, he'll arm and then catch up with him. Hector sets off, but meets his loving wife Andromache with his baby son at the city walls. She anxiously begs him to stay inside the walls. He explains that his code of honour would make him ashamed to do such a thing, and also that he knows that Troy will fall some day and is most tormented by the thought of her being dragged off to slavery. When he reaches for his son, the baby shrinks back, terrified by his helmet with its nodding plume, and the husband and wife burst out laughing. Hector takes off his helmet, kisses his son and prays (futilely) for him to grow up a great warrior and king, a much better man than his father. He hands the boy to Andromache, who is laughing and crying simultaneously. Pitying her, he tells her that nobody will kill him before his time is up and sends her back to their house. She goes off, weeping and looking back at him. When she reaches home, she and the maids mourn for Hector as if he is already dead (which he soon will be).

The light-hearted Paris breaks in on this serious scene, looking particularly lightweight in contrast. As Hector stands there, his brother (by now armed) comes rushing up to him, and is compared to a horse (at 6.506ff.):

Just as a stallion in his stable breaks his halter after feeding
at the manger and gallops over the plain with thudding hooves
to a lovely river (where he likes to plunge in the water),
exulting and confident in his beauty, his head
held high and his mane rippling over his shoulders,   510
as he speeds along to the horses' familiar pastures,
so Paris, son of Priam, strode down from the lofty citadel,
glittering in his armour like the sun, and laughing,
as he sped along. He quickly came up on his brother, glorious
Hector, who was still lingering before turning away   515
from the spot where he had been talking intimately
with his wife. Godlike Paris was the first to speak:
'Dear Hector, you're in a hurry, and I must have kept
you waiting by not coming quickly as you told me.'
Hector of the flashing helmet said in reply: 520
'You strange man. No reasonable person would underrate
what you actually do in battle, as you *are* a good fighter.
But you're too ready to hang back and refuse to fight,
and it pains me to hear the contemptuous remarks made about
you by the Trojans, who have so much trouble because of you.   525
But let's be off. We'll settle our differences later,
if Zeus ever allows us to honour the immortal gods
with a feast in the palace to celebrate our freedom
after we've driven the Greek warriors away from Troy.'

As well as cutting a brilliant figure as he speeds along up to his static and sober
brother, flippant Paris (who actually jokes) seems particularly trifling beside the
diplomatic Hector with his moving attempt at optimism. The simile (comparison)
of the horse at 506ff. is economically suggestive: like the stallion Paris is sated, has
left home and is moving quickly; he is also similarly handsome (and knows it),
strong, proud, confident and self-centred; and he goes to war as the animal goes
to the river and the pastures – carefree, thoughtless and lacking in seriousness. The
simile at 513 is also effective, implying that like the sun Paris is dazzling, but can also
be tiring, dangerous and destructive.

Heroides 6

HYPSIPYLE TO JASON

Jason was the son of Aeson (who was a king in Thessaly, in northern Greece), but Aeson's kingdom (Iolcus) was taken from him by his half-brother Pelias. When he grew to manhood, Jason came to ask for the kingdom back, and Pelias agreed to restore it, if Jason would get for him the Golden Fleece. This was the fleece of a mythical golden ram, which belonged to a fierce oriental king (Aeetes, who lived in remote Colchis, at the east end of the Black Sea), and which was guarded by a huge, unsleeping serpent. Jason sailed off on that very dangerous quest on the ship Argo with fifty heroes as companions (called the Argonauts). On the way they stopped off at the island of Lemnos. There the women had killed their husbands, who had rejected them (in one version because they neglected Aphrodite, who made their bodies smell by way of punishment) and had taken up with some female captives taken from nearby Thrace instead. The Lemnian women killed the captives and all the males on the island, except for the unmarried Hypsipyle, who secretly saved her father's life and smuggled him away to safety. He was king Thoas, and as his daughter she had been made queen. The women of Lemnos had been without men for a while now and needed to ensure their survival by means of children, so they gave the Argonauts a warm welcome. According to Ovid, Hypsipyle married Jason and became pregnant by him. After a lengthy stay he had to sail off on his quest, before she gave birth to twin boys. Once the Argonauts reached Colchis, Aeetes agreed to let Jason have the Fleece if he performed some tasks – yoking the bronze-footed, fire-breathing bulls of Mars, ploughing a field with them and sowing some dragon's teeth (from which ferocious armed men would grow). This too was meant to be the end of Jason, but Aeetes' daughter (the beautiful and powerful witch Medea) fell in love with him and was persuaded by him to help him, thereby betraying her father. Her help was vital. She gave him a magic drug (so the bulls' fiery breath could not harm him) and told him how to deal with the armed men (he threw a rock among them and they killed each other fighting over it). Even though Jason had performed the tasks, Aeetes wouldn't give him the Fleece. So Medea used her magic to put the guardian snake to sleep and Jason grabbed the Fleece. He sailed back to Thessaly with it, taking Medea with him and marrying her on the way. She did him another important service on the journey back. She had her brother Apsyrtus with her, and when Aeetes pursued them, she killed the boy, hacked him to pieces and scattered them around, so Aeetes would stop to pick them up and they could escape. Jason and Medea got back to Thessaly safely (avoiding Lemnos), and it is when Hypsipyle hears news of all this that she writes this letter to Jason.

From the goddess Oenone we are now taken back to a human letter-writer. Although there are some similarities between this epistle and the last one, there are also distinct differences. With regard to situation, Hypsipyle has two children by her husband. Rather than returning with another wife before her eyes, her man has sailed off to another woman and gone out of her life totally, never to be seen by her again, and this time the rival is portrayed as much more sinister. There are differences in personality too. Hypsipyle is less intelligent and subtle than Oenone, and although she tries to stay in control and maintain her dignity at the start, that breaks down, and she humiliates herself, becomes increasingly angry and is especially venomous at the end.

> I hear you've sailed back safely to Thessaly's shores,
>   a rich man, thanks to the Golden Fleece.
> I congratulate you, not that you make it easy –
>   you should have written to me with news of that.
> Maybe you wanted to stop off at my kingdom (which I   5
>   pledged to you), but didn't have the right winds;
> but, however unfavourable the wind, people do write:
>   I'm Hypsipyle, I deserved to be sent a letter.
> Why did I hear, before getting a letter from you, a rumour
>   that Mars' sacred bulls were yoked,   10
> the dragon's teeth were sown and produced a crop of
>   warriors who didn't need you to slaughter them,
> and the ram's Golden Fleece (which was guarded by a sleepless
>   serpent) was bravely seized by you?
> Oh, if I could say to those who doubt this, 'He wrote me   15
>   this himself,' I'd be really somebody!
> Why complain of my dilatory husband's neglect of his duty?
>   If I'm still yours, then you're very kind to me.
> I'm told that some barbaric witch came with you
>   and shares your bed (which was promised to me).   20
> Lovers are credulous. I hope that people will say that
>   I was rash and wrongfully accused my husband.
> A stranger from Thessaly came here recently. He'd
>   scarcely set foot in my palace when I asked him:
> 'How's my Jason?' He was embarrassed, at a loss,   25

his eyes fixed on the floor in front of him.
At once I jumped up, tore the front of my dress in grief and shouted:
    'Is he alive, or must I now join him in death?'
'He's alive,' he said. Lovers are fearful. I made him swear
    by the gods, and even then hardly believed you lived.   30
I calmed down and began to ask about your exploits;
    he said Mars' bronze-footed bulls had ploughed,
the dragon's teeth had been sown in the earth as seeds
    and suddenly armed warriors grew from them,
earthborn men who died fighting each other   35
    and lived out their lives in a single day;
and the snake had been conquered. I asked again
    if Jason was alive, hoping and fearing in turn.
He told me all about you, eagerly running on, and
    in his naivety revealed something that wounded me.   40
Ah, what about your promise of fidelity, the bonds of marriage
    and the wedding-torch (that should rather light my pyre)?
We didn't have a furtive affair: the marriage-gods were there –
    Juno and Hymen with garlands on his head.
No, it wasn't Juno or Hymen but a grim and bloody Fury   45
    that carried the ill-omened wedding-torch before me.
What did the Argonauts and the Argo have to do with me?
    Why did your helmsman steer the ship here?
The ram's spectacular Golden Fleece wasn't here,
    and Aeetes didn't have his capital on Lemnos.   50
At first I was determined to drive off the armed strangers with
    my female fighters, but an evil fate drew me on.
The women of Lemnos know all too well how to defeat men;
    I should have defended my land with such brave troops.
You got help from my city, I took you into my home and heart,   55
    and you stayed while two summers and winters sped by.
At harvest-time in the third year, pressured into sailing away,
    you said to me in a suitable flood of tears:
'I'm being forced to go, Hypsipyle. Provided fate lets me return,
    I leave as your husband, and I'll always be your husband.   60
But I pray that the child of mine in your womb
    survives and we both become parents.'
After that, I remember, the tears ran down on to your
    lying lips and you couldn't speak any more.
You were the last of the crew to board the sacred Argo,   65
    which flew off, with its sails billowing in the wind.
The speeding keel churned the blue waves;
    you gazed at the land, I at the water.
I rushed off to a tower with an all-round view of the sea.

My face and chest were drenched with tears.   70
I looked out through my tears, and my eyes (obliging
   my loving heart) saw further than usual.
Also bear in mind my faithful prayers and fearful vows,
   which (as you're safe) I must repay, despite everything.
Should I repay my vows, for Medea to benefit by them?   75
   I'm sickened, filled with rage and love.
Should I make offerings at temples for the survival of a man
   who's left me, and sacrifice in thanks for my loss?
Certainly I never felt secure and was always afraid your father
   would choose a bride for you from some Greek city.   80
I feared Greek women – the damage came from a barbarian slut;
   I was wounded by an unexpected enemy.
You're not captivated by her beauty or her qualities: she knows
   spells and gathers dread herbs with an enchanted knife.
She applies herself to bringing down the reluctant moon from its   85
   course and shrouding the sun's chariot in darkness;
she halts winding rivers, stops the flow of the water,
   she makes woods and rocks come alive and move around;
she wanders among tombs, with her hair and robe unbound,
   and gathers specific bones from still warm pyres;   90
she curses people in their absence, pierces wax images of them,
   driving slender needles into their poor hearts,
and does things I'd rather not know. Character and beauty
   should inspire love; it's wrong to use magic potions.
Can you hug *her*, enjoy a quiet night's sleep and not be   95
   afraid when alone in the same bedroom with her?
Clearly she has tamed you as she did Mars' bulls, and she
   charms you with the sorcery used on the savage serpent.
What's more, she's keen to be attached to the exploits of you
   and your men, diminishing her husband's glory.   100
And one of Pelias' supporters imputes your feats to her
   magic (and has followers to believe him),
saying: 'It wasn't Jason, it was Medea from Colchis who
   took down the ram's Golden Fleece from the tree.'
Your mother (ask her advice!) and your father don't approve   105
   of a daughter-in-law who comes from the frozen north.
Medea should look for a husband in her own area – by the Tanais,
   in marshy Scythia or on the remote banks of the Phasis.
Fickle Jason, more changeable than a breeze in spring,
   why does your pledge to me count for nothing?   110
You left as my husband – why haven't you returned as that?
   Let me be your wife now you're back, as I was when you went.
If you're impressed by high birth and royal names, note that I

am famed as the daughter of Thoas, descended from Minos;
    my grandmother was Ariadne, wife of Bacchus, who transformed   115
        her and her crown into one of the brightest constellations.
My wedding-gift to you will be Lemnos, with its fertile soil,
        and slaves (you can have me among them).
And now I've given birth too; congratulate us both!
        I loved being pregnant by *you*, Jason.   120
I was also lucky in having twins, yes two
        babies, with the help of the goddess of childbirth.
If you ask who they're like, they're the image of you,
        just like you, apart from not knowing how to lie.
I very nearly had them carried to you as envoys for me,   125
        but the thought of their savage stepmother stopped me.
Medea frightened me. Medea's worse than a stepmother.
        Medea can turn her hand to any crime.
Would my boys be spared by the woman who could hack up her
        brother and scatter the bits all over the countryside?   130
But they say you prefer *her* to your wife Hypsipyle.
        Oh, you're insane, unbalanced by Colchian witchcraft.
That girl committing adultery with you was despicable:
        we were joined together, you and I, in a faithful marriage.
She betrayed her father, I snatched mine from death;   135
        she abandoned Colchis, I'm still on my Lemnos.
But so what, if a dutiful daughter's going to lose out to some criminal,
        who won herself a husband with a dowry of treachery?
I condemn what the women did here, but I'm not surprised:
        such resentment turns even great cowards into warriors.   140
Tell me, if you and your crew had been driven here by adverse
        winds and you'd entered my harbour (as you should have done),
and I'd gone to meet you with the two babies (no doubt
        making you pray for the earth to open up and swallow you),
how would you have faced me and the boys, you criminal?   145
        What sort of death would your perfidy have deserved?
You would have been safe and sound – I'd have seen to that –
        not because you deserve it, but because I'm gentle.
As for your mistress, I'd have personally splashed her blood all over
        my face and yours (which I no longer see thanks to her magic).   150
I'd have been a Medea to Medea! But if just Jupiter
        on high looks at all favourably on my prayers,
let that successor to my bed be made to feel the agony
        that I do by someone with a code of conduct like hers.
I'm deserted, a wife and mother of two, so let her lose   155
        her husband after she's had two children,
and not keep for long the man she's stolen, and leave him worse off,

and go into exile, searching everywhere for refuge!
Let her be as cruel to her children and her husband
 as she was to her brother and her poor father!   160
Unable to escape by land or sea, let her try the air, and
 wander helpless, hopeless, red with the blood she's shed!
I was cheated out of my marriage, so that's my prayer.
 Live on, man and wife, in your doomed relationship!

This is real tragedy here. After helping Jason, marrying him and becoming pregnant by him, Hypsipyle has been forgotten by him, and supplanted by a rival, an inferior and ominous rival in her eyes. She has had no word from him, and will not hear from him or see him again ever. On top of that there is more misery ahead for her. The women of Lemnos eventually found out that she spared her father and wanted to kill her for her treachery. In one tradition they murdered him and sold her into slavery; in another she fled but was captured by pirates and sold. In either case she ended up as the slave of king Lycurgus in Sparta. In addition to her humiliating loss of status there was more danger for her there. She was ordered to look after the king's child, but at one point was distracted and the child was killed by a snake. She was very nearly put to death for that, until another king intervened, saving her life and winning for her a return to Lemnos with her two sons.

The bulk of this epistle consists of appeals to Jason. It is sad to see a queen reduced to this, and it is especially sad that these appeals never were likely to work, as the queen does not realize how despicable a person Jason is (he later goes on to drop Medea and his two children by her and marries a Greek princess, because that will bring him more power, influence and money). At 1–8 she begins with calm remonstrance, trying to make him feel embarrassed for not coming to Lemnos or writing. She combines that with disarming congratulations and an excuse for his non-appearance (5f.), so as not to be too heavy, but also a gentle reminder that she deserved better treatment, as Hypsipyle (his wife and benefactress), so that he will experience guilt and pity her. However, the fact that he has not even bothered to write makes it clear that he does not care for her at all; and someone as self-centred as Jason will not be touched by remorse or feel sympathy for her. At 9–16 between plaintive references to the absence of a letter she lists his exploits, dwelling on them in celebration and suggesting that she still relishes the news of her brave man's great personal achievements. But poignancy is wasted on him, and he will know how vital Medea was to his success; and Hypsipyle spoils all this flattery at 97f. by openly ascribing it to her. At 17–22 reminders that they are married and (in 19f.) an attempt to shame him and turn him off Medea (as a 'barbaric witch') are toned down by humility in 18 and an easy way out for Jason at 21f. However, apart from the fact that it would not be a good idea to show weakness like this, the polygamist is obviously not at all concerned about their marriage, and would not be embarrassed by his infidelity, and has actually found Medea and her magic very useful to him rather than repellent. As you can discover for yourself, Hypsipyle continues like this for most of the rest of the letter, running on and on with such patent, humiliating and feeble appeals, vainly using the same ploys with the same aims.

Her emotional state adds to the futility, as it leads her to undermine her pleas thoughtlessly. At the start of the epistle she is trying to control herself, but the more she writes (and mulls over the situation) the more animated and angry she becomes. Her continuing love for Jason is clear throughout, but she is incensed about Medea, who intrudes as early as line 19. Strong emotions break out at 41ff. and there is an even more irascible outburst at 75ff. From line 75 on Medea and the queen's hatred and fear of her dominate the letter, and giving vent to her feelings makes Hypsipyle write things that would have alienated Jason (see 97f., 124, 132, 139f. and 149f.). Then in an emotional crescendo Hypsipyle loses control totally at 151ff., where she ends with savage curses (cursing Jason as well as Medea) that represent no sort of appeal to her husband but would completely subvert all her earlier entreaty and scare him off.

There is tragic irony too, in the whole letter (aimed at getting back as terrible a husband as Jason) and in Hypsipyle's great sadness at the departure of such a person (67ff.). It is also grimly ironical when she complains of his treachery and wishes exile on Medea, as she herself will soon suffer exile for betraying the cause of the Lemnian women. And by the end of the letter she has degenerated into something as bad as her hated rival: after calling Medea a barbarian and a murderess, who curses people and dooms them to death, at 149ff. Hypsipyle herself imagines splashing Medea's blood all over her face and Jason's, and she herself curses Medea and dooms her and Jason.

So far we have been concentrating on the emotional impact, but there is also an important intellectual element, as usual in Ovidian poetry, and the lines affect the head as well as the heart. Sophisticated readers who know the story in full and are acquainted with earlier treatment of it will find much more in *Heroides* 6 and will see beyond the obvious pathos to more subtle aspects. There is an admixture of cleverness, even some wit and humour, and much of literary interest as well.

There is ingenuity in the setting for this epistle: Ovid makes Hypsipyle complain about the disregard of her marriage and threaten her treacherous husband and his new woman on the island of Lemnos, where because of conjugal violations her subjects killed their unfaithful spouses and the female captives they took up with instead. Ovid has also been adroit in making Jason here abandon the queen and his two children for someone more helpful to him when he is married to Hypsipyle (which he is not in other accounts) because that makes him act in keeping here with what he will do with his later wife Medea and his two children by her, so that there is a sort of pre-echo of his coming maltreatment of his Colchian bride. As well as neat symmetry there is also contrast, as in *Her.* 6 we see not the standard picture of Medea as the wronged wife enraged with her rival, but Medea as the rival, and Hypsipyle as the wronged wife enraged with her rival. And Ovid has been clever in the curse on Medea that he ascribes to Hypsipyle at 151ff., as much of it comes true later on.

There are also some facetious touches for the detached reader to appreciate. When you read *Heroides* 12 and learn how exactly the story continues you will be able to see more of this kind of thing in this poem, but some of it will be apparent to you now. For example, at 79f. actually Hypsipyle's fears about Jason having a Greek bride *are* justified, as Jason will take a Greek wife (after Medea). In connection with 107f. it really *would* be much better for Medea to look for a husband in her own area (rather than marrying Jason). At 115f. rather quaintly Hypsipyle brags that her granny is a star! In connection with 136–40 she prides herself on still being on Lemnos (but she won't be for long) and condemns the Lemnian women (when she will have more grounds for complaint against them soon). See if you can find more instances of this on your own (consider, for instance, the wit in 151 and the pictures conjured up of the great heroes at 51ff. and of Medea at 95f.). This humour is most often dark and grim, so as not to be too jarring amid all the tragedy.

From a literary point of view, Ovid here will naturally have been looking to an episode in a very famous and influential predecessor and will have expected his readers to have an eye to that too, so that they could spot the differences in the Ovidian account. In the third century BC a Greek called Apollonius of Rhodes wrote an epic on Jason's quest for the Golden Fleece. In that the Lemnos encounter was essentially a brief, light-hearted fling enjoyed by both Hypsipyle and Jason, a matter of sexual attraction and pleasure rather than deep passion. Here is Jason's departure in Apollonius (1.886ff.):

> . . . as Jason was leaving, Hypsipyle took hold of
> his hands and prayed, in tears at losing him:
> 'Go. May the gods bring you and your comrades home
> again unharmed with the Golden Fleece for the king,
> granting your dearest wish. This island and my   890
> father's sceptre will be waiting for you, if after you
> return from Colchis you want to come back here.
> You could easily collect a host of followers from
> other cities. But you won't want to do that,
> I don't foresee that happening myself.   895
> But remember Hypsipyle when you're far away and after
> you get home. And leave me your instructions (which I'll
> gladly carry out) if heaven allows me to become a mother.'
> Jason appreciated her words and said in reply:
> 'Hypsipyle, may the gods make all that turn out well.   900
> But don't get your hopes up about me, because it's
> enough for me to live in my own country, with Pelias'
> permission, if only the gods set me free from my ordeals.
> But if I'm not fated to return to the land of Greece
> from my distant voyage, and you give birth to a boy,   905
> send him when he grows up to Iolcus in Thessaly
> to console my parents for their grief over me (if he
> finds them still alive), and to care for them at their
> own hearth and home well away from king Pelias.'

With that he boarded the ship first. The other heroes   910
followed him on board, sat down at their benches and took
hold of the oars. The helmsman released the mooring-cables,
which were attached to a sea-beaten rock. Then they
struck the water vigorously with their long oars.

Apollonius' queen there (as throughout the episode) is a gentle character: she is upset but resigned, tells Jason to go, wishes him well and accepts that he probably won't return to her. She is also only possibly pregnant by him, not married to him and not passionately in love with him (in fact he has only been with her for a couple of days, not for years). Ovid's Hypsipyle is very different from that in personality and circumstances, as our poet goes for a version that is sad and bitter, and turns the queen at the end into the single most vicious and violent heroine in the *Heroides*. If you compare the above lines with the description of the actual parting in Ovid (57ff.), you will find many significant discrepancies which highlight the pathos in the Latin poem. Also of interest is the fact that we get a new point of view for the episode, as here only in extant literature are we shown things from Hypsipyle's perspective; and nowhere else in what has survived does she learn about Medea or write to Jason.

Hypsipyle is queen of a society of women without men, and the male poet Apollonius represents them as vulnerable and in need of males. All of this recalls the Amazons, mythical female warriors who lived on the borders of the known world. They generally shunned and hated men, using them only for breeding purposes, then killing or mutilating any male babies that they produced, while raising female ones as fighters, and removing their right breasts, so they could better handle a bow and a spear unimpeded (hence supposedly the Greek name A-mazon = 'No-breast'). In literature they are presented as bizarre, inferior and barbaric, because they invert traditional Greek norms for women by having sex as they please, ruling themselves and going off hunting and fighting, rather than being chaste, submissive to men and staying at home and looking after their family. Many heroes fought them, and always beat them, showing the triumph of (male-centred) Greek civilization over barbarism.

One of the most memorable Amazons was another queen without a man – Penthesilea. Quintus Smyrnaeus in book 1 of his *Posthomerica* presents a stirring and moving picture of Penthesilea and her Amazons taking part late on in the Trojan War on the side of Priam. When she arrived at Troy, the Trojans flocked out to see her and were amazed at her beauty, which was both glorious and terrible, and at her entrancing smile. At dawn the next day she rode into battle with her Amazons, leading a great horde of Trojans. Lured on by Doom, she was relentless, driving the Greeks in terror before her, hurling spears and hacking down men with her huge battle-axe. But then Achilles confronted her. He disdainfully reminded her of his great prowess and told her that her final hour had come. Then (at 1.592ff.):

So saying, he charged, brandishing in his powerful hand
the long, murderous spear made for him by Chiron,

and quickly wounded warlike Penthesilea above
her right breast. Her dark blood spurted out.   595
Immediately the strength left her body and she
dropped the great battle-axe from her hand. Black night
clouded her eyes, and she felt agony deep inside her.
But even so she was still breathing and saw her enemy
now about to drag her from her swift horse.   600

As she wondered whether to draw her sword and fight on or yield, Achilles
impaled her and her horse with his spear (at 1.619ff.):

...Achilles' eager spear went right through
Penthesilea and her magnificent horse.   620
She quickly fell to the ground and her death. But there was
nothing unbecoming as she tumbled in the dust, nothing shameful
to bring discredit to her fine body. She lay on her swift horse,
stretched out face-down, transfixed by the long spear, convulsing.

When the Trojans saw that she had been struck down they fled to Troy in terror,
weeping for her. Achilles stood over her and spoke exulting words. Then (1.654ff.):

So saying, Achilles wrenched his ashen spear out of
the swift horse and dread Penthesilea. They both   655
gasped their life away, killed by the same lance.
He pulled from her head the helmet that glittered
like the rays of the sun or Zeus' radiant lightning.
As she sprawled there in the dust and blood, the face
revealed beneath her lovely eyebrows was beautiful,   660
even though she was dead. The Greeks thronged around and
were amazed when they saw her, looking like a blessed god.
She lay in her armour on the ground like Zeus' daughter
Artemis sleeping, when that relentless huntress is tired
from shooting arrows at swift lions on long mountain-ridges.   665
Aphrodite crowned in splendour, mate of mighty Ares,
personally made her a wonder of beauty even in death,
so that the noble Achilles would feel some pain too.
Many of the Greeks prayed they might have a wife
like her to sleep with when they returned home.   670
Achilles was filled with endless grief because he had
killed her and not taken her as his glorious bride
back to Phthia, that land of fine horses (for in stature
and beauty she was flawless, like an immortal).

For more on Amazons see Lefkowitz 15ff. and Blok.

Heroides 7

DIDO TO AENEAS

Placed right after *Heroides* 6, this epistle forms a natural pair with it: in both poems we find a queen who gave hospitality and help to a voyaging hero and had an amatory relationship with him but subsequently left by her lover, who sailed off to success on his quest. But Ovid rings the changes and demonstrates his versatility by producing here a different tone in his treatment of the same basic situation (see further below on all the irreverent levity). Monotony is also avoided by means of divergence in points of detail (e.g. this time the hero is a moral man, who has not yet departed; there is no other woman involved; and the outcome is dissimilar, as this heroine goes on to commit suicide very soon). You should be able to spot further differences for yourself as you read *Heroides* 7.

Virgil had recently depicted the love affair between Dido and Aeneas in the opening books of his famous epic the *Aeneid*, where the Trojan meets her, tells her of his adventures so far and enters into a doomed relationship with her. Ovid here assumes readers' knowledge of that account. At the fall of Troy, when further resistance was futile, Aeneas (son of Venus) escaped from the burning city, accompanied by his wife and his young son (Ascanius), and carrying on his shoulders his aged father (Anchises), who held the statues of the gods of Troy. He had agreed to meet with their servants at a shrine outside Troy, but when he got there he found that in the haste and confusion his wife had disappeared. Distraught, he rushed back into Troy to try to find her, and a mysterious phantom of her appeared to him and informed him that it was the will of heaven that she remain there. When he rejoined his father and son outside Troy, he found many other Trojan survivors gathered there. He sailed off with them as their leader, seeking a new home, and for seven years they roamed the Mediterranean Sea in their search for it. During that time Anchises died, and it was revealed to them that the promised land for them lay in Italy, in Latium, the area around the river Tiber where Rome was eventually built.

Italy proved elusive, but the Trojan fleet was finally nearing Latium when their arch-enemy the goddess Juno caused a massive storm, which drove the ships all the way to north Africa. There they were given a warm welcome by Dido, queen of the rising city of Carthage. She had been very happily married to Sychaeus, but her evil brother Pygmalion had killed him in the hope of acquiring his wealth. Dido and her supporters had fled with the treasure and landed in Africa, where she founded her splendid city, surrounded by enemies. She had sworn to remain faithful to Sychaeus, but fell deeply in love with Aeneas, because (to ensure that the Trojan was safe at Carthage) Venus sent her other son (Cupid) to inspire an irresistible passion for Aeneas in the queen. Then Juno, hoping to capitalize on the situation and keep the hated hero from Latium, engineered the start of an affair. When the Trojans and Carthaginians were out hunting together, she caused a storm, and Aeneas and Dido fled for shelter to the same cave, and began their relationship there. Feeling guilty, the queen called it a marriage, although there was no formal wedding, and Aeneas did not view himself as her husband.

At first they were happy together, but a rejected suitor (the African chieftain Iarbas) complained to Jupiter about their liaison, and Jupiter sent down Mercury to remind the Trojan of his fated mission to found a new settlement in Latium and to order him to leave. Terrified by the god, Aeneas decided that he had to obey the divine command, but he was in agony over Dido. He got his men to prepare the fleet secretly, while he waited for the best moment to approach her. But she found out first, attacked him for treacherously abandoning his wife, angrily rejected his defence and stormed off. But then, as she watched the fleet's preparations, the love-sick queen felt that she had to try to win him over again. It is at this point that Ovid has her write this letter and send it to him (in Virgil she sends her sister Anna, who had encouraged her to begin the affair with the Trojan, to make a final, futile appeal). Aeneas was visited by Mercury again and ordered to leave once more. When he did obediently sail off, Dido committed suicide, mounting a funeral pyre and throwing herself on his sword (which he had given her as a gift). Aeneas did settle in Latium, and eventually from his line came Romulus and Remus, who founded Rome.

> This is like the song of a dying white swan
> > that has collapsed in the moist grass by the river Meander.
> I'm not writing to you in the hope that pleas of mine could
> > move you — a god's against this letter I've started.
> But as I've wasted my kindness, reputation, fidelity and   5
> > chastity for nothing, wasting words doesn't matter.
> Are you determined to go nonetheless and abandon miserable Dido?
> > Will your ship and your pledge to me both be whisked away by the wind?
> Aeneas, are you determined to cast off your mooring-ropes and your wife
> > in search of a kingdom in Italy (you know not where)?   10
> Doesn't new Carthage touch you or its rising ramparts
> > or the sceptre of sovereignty ceded to you?

You shun what you've done, look for things to do, leaving the land
    you've found and ranging the world to find another.
Suppose you find it – who will hand it over to you as yours?   15
    Who will give their territory to strangers to occupy?
No doubt there's another lover waiting for you, another Dido,
    and there's another pledge for you to make, and break.
When are you likely to found a city as splendid as Carthage
    and survey your subjects from your citadel on high?   20
Even if your prayers all come true and don't keep you waiting,
    where will you get a wife to love you like me?
I burn for you, like candles of wax coated with sulphur,
    like incense devoutly placed on a smoking altar.
Aeneas is before my eyes all the time I'm awake;   25
    at night in sleep my thoughts return to Aeneas.
True, he's ungrateful and indifferent to my kindness;
    if I had any sense, I'd want to be rid of him.
But I don't hate Aeneas, though what he plans is wrong;
    I resent his treachery, but resentfully love him more.   30
Venus, spare your daughter-in-law; Cupid, embrace your
    brutal brother and make him a soldier of yours.
I started it (I'm not ashamed), so let me do the loving,
    and let him be around for me to care about.
I'm deluded, that's a delusive fantasy I'm conjuring up;   35
    he doesn't have Venus' temperament.
No, you were born from rocks and mountains and oaks
    growing on lofty crags and from savage wild animals
or a sea like the one you see here churned up by gales again –
    and yet you're ready to run away across these hostile waves.   40
Where to? Through a storm. (I hope that ally can stop you for me.)
    See how the East Wind heaves up the seething water!
Let me owe to the gales the favour I'd rather owe to you;
    the wind and the waves are more just than you.
To be fair to you (*why* am I being fair?), I'm not worth dying for   45
    while you run far away from me across the sea.
You're indulging a very, very costly hatred,
    if death means nothing, provided you're free from me.
Soon the winds will fall, the waves will be flat and level
    and the god Triton will skim the sea on his blue-green horses.   50
I wish that you too were changeable, like the winds!
    And you will be, unless you're harder than oak.
As if you didn't know what the frenzied ocean can do!
    Why trust it, after all your bad experiences at sea?
Even if the sea grows invitingly calm and you cast off,   55
    that immense expanse of water holds many terrors.

Those who've broken their word shouldn't brave the sea:
    that's a place where perjury gets punished,
especially when a lover's been wronged, as Venus, the Cupids' mother,
    was born naked from the waves at Cythera, they say.   60
I'm afraid to harm as you harm, or to destroy my destroyer;
    I'm frightened my enemy may be shipwrecked and drown.
I pray you survive, as that will destroy you better than dying:
    instead of that you'll be well-known for causing my death.
Come on, imagine you're caught in a violent tornado (don't   65
    let this be an omen!) – what will go through your mind?
Your thoughts will turn at once to your perjured, lying tongue
    and Dido forced to die by Trojan treachery.
Before your eyes will stand the spectre of the wife you deceived,
    miserable, bloodstained, her hair unbound in grief.   70
What makes it worth having to say then, 'I deserve it, forgive me!'
    (thinking the falling thunderbolts are hurled at you)?
Wait a little for the sea's savagery and yours to abate:
    a safe voyage will be a great reward for delaying.
You may not care about that, but spare the boy Ascanius!   75
    It's enough for you to be famous for killing *me*.
What have the boy and Troy's gods done to deserve such an end?
    Will the sea engulf the statues you saved from the flames?
But you don't have them, you traitor. You didn't carry your father
    and their images from Troy, as you boast to me.   80
You're all lies, and you didn't start the deceit with me.
    I'm not the first to be hurt by you.
If anyone wonders where handsome Ascanius' mother is –
    she died, alone, abandoned by her brutal husband.
You told me this, which should have warned me. I deserve the pain   85
    as punishment (which won't be as great as my mistake).
I've no doubt in my mind that your gods condemn you:
    you've been tossed at sea and on land for seven winters.
You were cast ashore, and I gave you a welcome and a safe anchorage;
    I'd hardly heard your name when I gave you my throne.   90
But I wish I'd been content to be no more obliging than that
    and the rumour about our love making had been buried.
The damage was done on the day when that dark rainstorm's sudden
    downpour drove us into a sloping cave.
I heard a sound, and thought the nymphs had cried out,   95
    but it was the Furies signalling my doom.
My lost virtue, punish me! Sychaeus' violated. . . .
    to which I'm going, ah, full of shame.
In a marble shrine covered in front with foliage and white wool
    I have a statue of Sychaeus, which I regard as sacred.   100

I heard myself summoned from there by his well-known voice
  four times; he said himself faintly, 'Dido, come!'
I am coming, I'm coming right now (I'm bound to you in marriage),
  but slowly, because of shame at my offence.
Pardon my crime: I wasn't deceived by someone unworthy,   105
  thanks to him that lapse of mine is not something hateful.
He has a divine mother and dutifully carried his aged father,
  so I hoped he'd do the right thing and stay on as my husband.
If I had to do wrong, the wrong I did was for a respectable reason:
  if only he was faithful, I'd have nothing to regret.   110
My destiny follows the same course right up to the end,
  still with me during the final hours of my life.
My husband was cut down at the altar inside our home,
  and my brother enjoys the profits of that terrible crime.
Driven into exile, I left my homeland and my husband's ashes;   115
  I had a fraught journey, pursued by my enemy.
I escaped the sea and my brother, landed on these shores
  and bought the coastal strip I gave you, you traitor.
I founded a city and set in place wide-reaching walls
  that arouse envy in neighbouring regions.   120
There was a swell of war, war to test the female foreigner;
  I only just provided myself with troops and crude city-gates.
I attracted a thousand suitors, who have now merged their forces,
  complaining I married some nobody rather than them.
Why not hand me over in chains to African Iarbas?   125
  I'd hold out my arms and let you commit that crime.
And there's my evil brother, who longs to spatter his hands
  with my blood, as he spattered them with my husband's.
Put down those sacred statues of the gods: your touch profanes them,
  it's wrong for a man with unholy hands to worship them.   130
Since you were destined to worship those gods if they escaped
  the flames, they're sorry they escaped the flames.
You're abandoning me when I may be pregnant too, you criminal,
  with a part of you concealed inside my body.
The poor child will share in its mother's doom,   135
  and you'll be responsible for the death of your unborn son.
Ascanius' brother will die along with his mother, and a
  single calamity will carry off the two of us together.
'But the god commands me to go.' I wish He'd ordered you not
  to come and Trojans had never set foot in Carthage.   140
This must be the god who guided you into wasting many
  years on wild seas, tossed by hostile winds.
You'd hardly expend so much effort to return to Troy,
  if it still was as it was when Hector was alive.

You're headed for the Tiber, not your native Simois, and of
    course even if   145
    you reach the land you long for, you'll be a stranger there.
Italy hides, conceals itself and avoids your ships:
    you'll grow old in your quest and be lucky to find it then.
Stop your wandering and instead accept as your dowry my people
    and the treasure that Pygmalion wanted but I brought here.   150
You'd be better off transferring Troy to Carthage
    and holding royal power and the sacred sceptre here.
If your heart is hungry for war, if Ascanius wants somewhere
    to fight and win the right to a victory-parade,
I'll provide an enemy for him to beat, so he lacks for nothing: 155
    there can be warfare here as well as terms of peace.
I beg you, by your mother, by your brother Cupid's arrows,
    by Troy's sacred gods that are with you in exile
(and I hope that those Trojans who were spared by savage Mars
    in the war live on and you lose no more of them,   160
and Ascanius prospers for all the years allotted to him
    and the body of aged Anchises rests in peace),
spare this house, which hands itself over to your control.
    What do you accuse me of, apart from loving?
I'm not some Greek from Thessaly or mighty Mycenae;   165
    no husband or father of mine stood against you at Troy.
Call me hostess, not wife, if you're ashamed of marriage to me;
    provided I'm yours, I'll put up with being anything.
I know the seas that break on the shores of Africa:
    at fixed times of the year they permit and prevent sailing.   170
When the breeze permits sailing, you'll spread your canvas before the wind;
    for now your ship stays beached behind the light seaweed.
Let me watch for the right time; your departure will be safer,
    and I myself won't let you remain, even if you want to.
Your men demand a rest as well, and your mangled fleet   175
    is half-repaired, necessitating a short delay.
You've been kind to me, and may be generous again, and I'm
    pregnant (I hope), so I ask for a little time
while the sea and my love calm down, and with time and practice
    I learn how to manage to bear my misery bravely.   180
Otherwise I intend to pour out my life:
    you can't be cruel to me for long.
I wish you could see what I look like as I write this!
    I'm writing with your Trojan sword here in my lap,
and tears roll down my cheeks on to the drawn sword,   185
    which will soon be soaked with blood instead of tears.
How well this gift of yours fits with my doom!

It's not costing you much to set up my funeral.
This isn't the first time my heart's been pierced by a weapon:
    it already bears the wound of savage love.   190
Anna my sister, my sister Anna, my guilty accomplice in sin,
    soon you will make the final offerings to my ashes.
SYCHAEUS' DIDO won't be inscribed on my marble tomb,
    when I'm cremated; my epitaph will be merely this:
AENEAS PROVIDED HER REASON FOR DYING AND THE SWORD;   195
    DIDO'S OWN HAND STRUCK THE FATAL BLOW.

A more detailed examination of Virgil's treatment of this tale will make clear
the poignancy of his account (against which Ovid was reacting here). In the *Aeneid*
the epic poet deliberately makes us feel for Dido from the start, so we will become
involved and appreciate properly the tragedy of her death. We are given our first
glimpse of her in book 1, when Aeneas is exploring the coast of Africa to which his
ships have been blown by the storm caused by Juno. His mother Venus appears to
him, disguised as a local huntress, directs him to Carthage for help and tells him the
story so far of its queen. It is a very positive picture of Dido that she presents, one
that suggests sympathy and admiration on the goddess' part, and thereby encourages the same reactions in readers. Virgil's narrative technique increases the force
of a tale that is gripping and moving in itself. He induces us to pity his heroine
from early on, and to respect her more and more as the passage progresses. He also
gives us in her brother Pygmalion a real villain to hate, to engage us further, and
includes various realistic and vivid details, to make the story come alive. He lingers
on Dido's love for her husband, on his murder and the subsequent deception of
the queen and on the appearance of her husband's ghost to her (so all of that has
its full impact on us), and he then picks up the pace, in line with Dido's briskness
and vigour as she sails off with followers to a new home. This is what Venus says to
Aeneas at 1.338ff.:

'You see the kingdom of Carthage, Tyrians and Agenor's city.
But the bordering land is the Libyans', that untameable warrior nation.
Dido reigns as queen. She came from the city of Tyre,   340
fleeing her brother. It's a long story of crime, a long
complicated tale, but I'll tell you the main events in outline.
Her husband was Sychaeus (the man with the most gold in Phoenicia),
and he was loved by that poor woman deeply and passionately.
Dido was a virgin when her father joined her in wedlock to him,   345
and that was her first marriage. But the king of Tyre was her brother
Pygmalion, a monster surpassing all other men in evil.
Madness came between them, dividing them. Blinded by love
of gold, the impious king caught Sychaeus off guard at his altar
and killed him with his sword in secret, ignoring his sister's love.   350

He concealed his crime for a long time, made up many stories
and with empty hope cruelly deluded the distraught loving
wife. But in a dream the ghost of her unburied husband
actually came to her, raising his face, which was strangely pale.
He showed her the savage altar and the wound in his chest made   355
by the sword, revealing all the house's hidden evil.
Then he urged her to hurry away, to leave the land of her fathers;
and to help her on her journey he unearthed an ancient treasure –
a mass of gold and silver known to nobody else.
That roused her to get herself and some followers ready to flee.   360
They gathered, those who felt a savage hatred for greedy
Pygmalion or feared him intensely; they seized some ships which happened
to be ready for sea, loaded the gold and sailed,
taking the tyrant's treasure with them. In command was a woman.
They arrived at this place, where now you will see the mighty   365
walls of new Carthage and its citadel rising high.'

The Trojans are given a warm welcome by Dido thanks to Jupiter, who
instils in her friendly feelings for Aeneas and his men. But Venus is fearful
because of Carthage's association with the Trojans' enemy Juno. To make sure
that Aeneas is safe there, she sends Cupid to fire the queen to a frenzy of passion
for the hero. When Dido puts on a banquet for her guests, Cupid is substituted
for the boy Ascanius, carrying marvellous gifts from Aeneas. At 1.712ff. in a sinister, doom-laden scene the sympathetic poet lingers on the terrible moments
of this disastrous infatuation. There is horror in the childishness and (perverted)
affection of what is in fact a mighty and callous divinity, in the psychological attack on the heroine (playing on her frustrated maternal desires), in the
mysterious vagueness over the actual process of possession, and in the insidious
effacement of the memory of Sychaeus. Horrifying too is the response of the
unwitting Dido, who is fascinated with Cupid and actually takes him on her
lap, again and again.

Most of all ill-fated Dido, doomed to the
imminent plague of love, can't get her fill and catches
fire as she gazes, affected as much by the boy as the gifts.
After hanging from Aeneas' neck, embracing him and sating   715
the great love of the man who thinks he's his father, he goes
for the queen. Her eyes and all her attention are fixed on the boy,
and she fondles him on her lap, several times. Poor
Dido's unaware that a powerful god's possessing her. Remembering
his mother Venus' wishes, he begins to obliterate gradually   720
the memory of Sychaeus and tries to preoccupy with a living love
her long dormant affections, her heart that's unused to passion.

One of the really sad things about this whole Carthaginian episode in the *Aeneid* is the fact that Dido is a pawn, a victim of gods with conflicting interests. Her violent and ultimately fatal love for Aeneas was caused by an external supernatural force, which she was powerless to resist – Cupid, who was dispatched unnecessarily by the over-protective Venus. Next Juno, trying to hinder the Trojan from reaching Latium, con-trived the intimate meeting in the cave – without which the affair might well never have started (otherwise why did Juno set it up?). Then Jupiter got involved (after Iarbas' com-plaint) and in concern over Aeneas' mission sent down Mercury to order him to leave.

In *Aeneid* 4, when Dido discovers, before Aeneas can break the news gently to her, that he is secretly preparing to sail away, she goes raving through the city and then attacks him in an extremely emotional speech. Initially her rage dominates, but she is soon making a futile attempt to get him to stay. The proud queen in her desperation is forced into using various appeals, showing humility, revealing her dependence on him and trying to arouse pity:

'Traitor! Did you actually hope you could keep your terrible   305
crime secret, leave this land of mine without a word?
Can nothing keep you here? Not our love? Not the pledge you
once made to me? Not the cruel death in store for Dido?
And are you working hard to ready your fleet in winter weather,
hurrying to sail across the sea in the midst of northern gales?   310
You're cruel. Tell me, if it wasn't some foreign land and unknown
home that you're bound for, and ancient Troy was still standing,
would you be sailing for Troy over this heaving sea?
Is it *me* you're running from? By these tears and your pledge
(I'm a poor fool who's left herself nothing else to appeal by),   315
by our wedding, by the marriage we entered on, I beg you,
if I've shown you any kindness, or anything about me was
pleasing to you, pity my falling house, and, if
it's not too late for pleas, give up this plan of yours.
Because of you the peoples of Libya and Numidian chieftains   320
hate me, the Carthaginians are hostile; and because of you
I've lost my honour and the good name that I had, my only hope
of immortality. You're leaving me to be killed (by who?),
my guest – I can only call you that, not 'husband' any more.
What am I waiting for? For my brother Pygmalion to destroy my   325
city or for African Iarbas to take me away as his captive?
At least if before you ran off I'd had a child by you,
if some little Aeneas was playing in my palace
with a face to recall yours in spite of everything,
I wouldn't feel completely deceived and deserted.'   330

Deeply upset, Aeneas defends himself on the grounds that they are not married and the gods are forcing him to go to Italy against his will. She rounds on him furiously, accusing him of ingratitude and cruelty, telling him to go off to Italy, but expressing the hope that he will be punished by shipwreck on the way, and threatening to haunt him after her death. The anguished Aeneas returns to his fleet, obedient to heaven's command, and his men eagerly get ready to depart. At this point Virgil's queen is forced by her passionate love to initiate another approach to the hero. She is reduced to humility again, and is this time even more humble (but in vain). Sadly now Aeneas has degenerated further, from a guest to a seeming enemy, and Dido has given up on the idea of him staying on permanently and just wants him to delay his departure, so she can learn how to cope. She appeals to her sister Anna to help her in a speech for which Ovid substitutes his letter:

> 'Go, sister, and make this humble appeal to my arrogant enemy:
> I did not swear with the Greeks at Aulis to exterminate   425
> the Trojan race or send a squadron of ships to Troy,
> and I didn't tear up the ashes of his dead father Anchises from his grave;
> so why does he close his callous ears to my appeals?
> Where's he rushing? As a final gift for his poor lover
> let him wait for a favourable wind and smooth sailing.   430
> I'm not begging any more for the marriage we once had and he betrayed
> or for him to forgo glorious Latium and give up his kingdom there;
> I'm asking for nothing – just time, rest and respite for my passion,
> until my fortune teaches me how to lose and grieve.
> Pity your sister. Tell him I'm begging for this final   435
> favour, which I'll repay with interest when I die.'

Virgil was widely recognized as a master poet, and his *Aeneid* was *the* national poem (about the illustrious Trojan origins of the Roman race), said to rival the *Iliad* itself. Ovid did feel respect for his renowned predecessor; but Virgil did also represent a challenge (a great author to top) and provide a tempting target (the lofty and revered *Aeneid*). There is supreme cheek in our young poet taking on the sublime Virgil and a major and tragic episode in his epic, and being so flippant and subversive while doing so. Ovid intentionally draws attention to his source by means of lots of echoes, as he puts his own stamp on it. He gives it a new form (the letter) and a new narrator (Dido), and he makes numerous variations, twists and additions to Virgilian words and details. All of this tinkering with a sacred text baffles and outrages some readers, while others find it stimulating and amusing. There is pathos in *Heroides* 7, but Ovid was too intelligent to try to compete with Virgil in that area. Instead he caps him in other ways and works in lots of irreverent levity, making for a piquant mixture. So, for example, at *Aeneid* 4.9 Virgil made Dido address Anna as *Anna soror* 'Anna my sister', so Ovid improves on that in 191 by making the queen write to her *Anna soror, soror Anna* 'Anna my sister, my sister Anna', producing a doublet that is wittily apt, as this is the second time that Dido so addresses her. He deflates the divine guidance for Aeneas in Virgil's epic by means of the sarcasm at 141f., and he mocks the *Aeneid*'s idea of Rome being Troy reborn with the notion of Rome's great enemy Carthage as

Troy reborn in 151. He even works in some obscene verbal play in 134, where in the context of pregnancy the wording easily conjures up (as well as a baby) penetration by a penis. But Ovid has most fun with Dido and Aeneas.

He creates his own Dido, building on his predecessor's version. He tops Virgil by giving the new, improved heroine all the arguments that she used on Aeneas at *Aeneid* 4.305ff and 424ff. and extra ones. So at 9ff. and 145ff. she points out to him that he already has a kingdom and a loving wife (so why go off to somewhere unknown, where he won't found as splendid a city as Carthage or get a wife as loving as Dido?); she warns him that perjurers are often punished by storms at sea (57ff.); and at 75f. and 153ff. she claims that she has Ascanius' welfare and happiness at heart. The Ovidian Dido is also an elegiac figure rather than a majestic queen of epic, employing much of the vocabulary and imagery of elegy (for instance, with a metaphor common in love poetry, she pictures the warrior Aeneas as a soldier in Cupid's camp in line 32). She is also a stylish writer, as is highlighted at the start of the letter with some neat turns at 5–6, 8, 9 and especially the couplet at 13–14 (with its repetition of words and sounds, beginning in the Latin with *facta fugis, facienda petis*). Such stylistic elegance for a distraught lover has its droll side, and there is also sly humour in some rather undignified aspects to Ovid's Dido. She shows a comical ignorance in 31 and 36, as she does not know that Venus is largely responsible for her problems and has a callous attitude to her. And, getting carried away, she is inconsistent (contradicting 79f. at 107, 131f. and 158) and seems to exaggerate and tell fibs at 115f. (according to Virgil she was not driven off, but left of her own accord, and she was not pursued by her brother), at 121f. (there was no actual war in the *Aeneid*), in 123 (in the epic she did not have anything like as many as a thousand suitors) and at 175f. (in Virgil at this stage Aeneas' ships were already repaired and his men were keen to leave Carthage rather than stay on and have a rest there).

There is also playfulness in connection with Aeneas, the venerable ancestor of the Roman race (and of the emperor Augustus himself), as Ovid gleefully seizes on his rather questionable action of parting from Dido and aggravates the problem. Virgil tried to exonerate somewhat the proto-Roman and hero of his poem, while bringing out the tragedy of the situation and showing the hard choices necessary and the pain involved in starting a new life for one's people. He made it clear that there was no marriage, that Aeneas still loved the queen deeply, and that he was agonized at leaving her and did so against his will (a devout man intimidated by the gods and mindful of his destiny and his son's future). But he did still leave her, turning away from and causing the death of a woman who was passionately in love with him and had done so much for him and his men; and a hero with a mission should not have allowed himself to enter into an affair in the first place. Ovid provides a much less sympathetic picture of the Trojan. His Dido writes to him at far greater length than she spoke in the *Aeneid*, and this facilitates increase of her criticism of him. As in Virgil, she attacks his ingratitude, treachery and cruelty, but does so more extensively, and she also posits other faults, calling him unjust, a liar and (the dutiful Aeneas!) someone who does not care for his father and the gods. And this time Aeneas does not get to defend himself and the poet does not attempt to excuse him. So there is a much more negative presentation of him here, as Ovid employs Dido to really snipe at and undermine the great hero. In particular our poet makes Aeneas look even worse for quitting Carthage. This Dido is even more pitiful and pleading than Virgil's, underlining her love and kindness at many more points than in the epic; but he still goes. In place of a vague hint that she might possibly commit suicide in Virgil (*Aen.* 4.308, 323) here she openly announces, more than once, that she definitely will kill herself, and dwells on her upcoming suicide at the end; but Aeneas still departs. And whereas Virgil's heroine had wished that she had a child by him, the Ovidian queen represents herself as quite possibly pregnant (at 133ff. and 177f.), so that his departure may well cause the death of their son as well; but without waiting to establish if she is with child, Aeneas sails away.

Virgil didn't finish with Dido and her story in the fourth book of the *Aeneid*. Surprisingly she (or rather her ghost) reappears in book 6, when Aeneas goes down to the Underworld to meet the spirit of his father and receive important instructions from him. As he makes his way through the land of the dead he comes to the Mourning Plains, a region for the souls of those who have died of love. There is a forest there, where they hide away, among them Dido. We really feel for the queen, just a faint phantom now, wandering disconsolately, and suggestively enclosed by gloom and dwarfed by the huge wood. As Aeneas speaks to her, she starts to move off, but halts when he asks her to, and finally has to wrench herself away. This suggests that amidst all her anger, hatred and hurt she still has not totally escaped her profound love for him, although she does now manage to control that passion; and she will not look at the hero, probably in part because she does not trust herself to do that. At least she is reunited with her beloved Sychaeus there, although her wandering and stopping to listen to Aeneas leave one wondering if her love for her old husband is entirely unadulterated and unclouded.

Virgil also wants us to feel sympathy for Aeneas. He shows us how much his hero still loves Dido and how distraught he is over having left her and caused her death. Aeneas is desperate to explain his actions to her and to exonerate himself, but fails. On top of the upset of seeing her in that terrible place, she is bitterly hostile to him and will not talk to him or even look at him. And in a final rejection of him she runs away and rejoins Sychaeus in what has to be a close relationship, whereas the Trojan now has no lover.

At line 450 he catches sight of her among other heroines who were destroyed by love:

> Among them Phoenician Dido wandered in that vast wood,   450
> her wound still fresh. The Trojan hero stopped beside
> her and just recognized that dim figure amid the gloom,
> as a man sees or thinks he has seen the moon
> rising amid the clouds at the start of the month.
> Immediately he spoke words of sweet love to her, in tears: 455
> 'Poor Dido! So it was true, the news I heard, that you were

dead, that you'd put an end to your life with a sword?
Ah no, was I responsible for your *death*? I swear by the stars,
by the powers above, by anything sacred in the world below,
I did not leave your shores of my own free will, my queen.   460
No, it was the stern commands of the gods that drove me,
as they force me now to pass through the gloom, this jagged
wasteland, this abyss of night; and I just couldn't believe
that by going away I would cause you such terrible agony.
Stop! Let me look at you a little longer. Who are you running   465
from? Fate won't let me talk to you ever again.'
With these words Aeneas, in tears, tried
to soothe her burning, glaring rage. She
kept her eyes fixed on the ground, turned away from him,
and when he began to speak her face remained unmoved,   470
like solid, hard flint or a crag on Mount Marpessus.
Finally she wrenched herself away and ran, still hostile, back
into the shadowy wood, where her husband of former days,
Sychaeus, responded to her anguish and returned her love.
Despite that Aeneas, horrified at her unjust fate, gazed   475
after her from afar, weeping and pitying her as she went.

On Dido in subsequent literature and in music and art see Grafton & Most &
Settis 268f.

Heroides 8

HERMIONE TO ORESTES

Hermione was the daughter of Menelaus (king of Sparta in Greece) and Helen (who eloped with the Trojan prince Paris when Hermione was a little girl). While Menelaus was off besieging Troy for ten years with a huge Greek army to get his beloved wife back, Hermione's grandfather Tyndareus betrothed her to her cousin Orestes (son of Agamemnon, commander-in-chief of the Greek forces at Troy and brother of Menelaus). Hermione and Orestes were married, but subsequently, while still at Troy, in ignorance of that fact Menelaus promised her to Pyrrhus (son of Achilles, who was the greatest of the Greek warriors in the Trojan war, until he was killed by the god Apollo). After the fall of Troy Menelaus returned with Helen, and Pyrrhus turned up to claim Hermione, seizing her and carrying her off against her will. In this letter she appeals to Orestes to get her back. Her appeal was successful and he did recover her on the death of Pyrrhus (killed by Orestes himself or by another person or persons).

For clarity other allusions made in the course of *Her.* 8 require brief explanation. Andromache (line 14) was the widow of the Trojan hero Hector, and when Troy was taken her son was murdered and she was enslaved. At 47f. and 117 reference is made to the ancestry of Hermione and Orestes, which stretched back all the way to Jupiter: he had a son called Tantalus, who fathered Pelops, and one of Pelops' sons was Atreus, who was the father of Agamemnon and Menelaus. At 49ff. Hermione touches on an unpleasant bit of family history: when Agamemnon got back from Troy, he was murdered by his wife and her lover Aegisthus, and later Orestes got revenge for his father by killing the two murderers. At 66ff. other relatives of Tantalus are mentioned – Helen's mother Leda, who was raped by Jupiter in the form of a swan; and Hippodamia, the wife of Pelops, who won her in a chariot race and drove off with her.

> Pyrrhus, who's as haughty as his father Achilles, holds me 3
> prisoner here contrary to the laws of gods and men.

I did what I could – refused to be held here willingly –   5
  but I'm a woman, not strong enough to do more than that.
I said: 'What are you doing, Pyrrhus? I *have* a man,
  a lord and master, who will punish you.'
Deafer to that than the sea, he dragged me into his palace,
  as I tore my hair in grief and shouted your name.   10
If a barbarian horde had taken Sparta and carried off
  the women, would I have suffered worse than this as a slave?
When the Greeks won the war and set wealthy Troy on fire,
  they didn't maltreat Andromache as badly as this.
But if you care for me, as a husband should,   15
  boldly claim what's yours by right, Orestes.
If someone opened your stalls and stole your cattle, you'd fight;
  but you'll hold back when your bride's been stolen?
Follow my father's example of claiming back an abducted wife;
  he went to war for her, as a husband should.   20
If he'd done nothing, snoring away in the palace she'd left,
  my mother would still be married to Paris.
Don't muster a thousand ships with swelling sails
  or an army of Greek warriors – come yourself!
Even so you could have done that to get me back: there's nothing wrong 25
  in a husband enduring fierce fighting for a beloved bride.
Then again we have the same grandfather – Atreus, son of Pelops:
  if you weren't my husband, you'd be my cousin.
Husband, please help your wife; cousin, help your cousin!
  Both your titles press you to do your duty.   30
With all the authority of his age and way of life, revered
  Tyndareus gave me to you, as was his right as my grandfather.
My father didn't know that and promised me to Pyrrhus;
  my grandfather acted first, and so takes precedence.
When I was married to you, my wedding harmed nobody;   35
  if I become Pyrrhus' wife, you will be hurt.
And my father Menelaus will pardon this love of ours:
  he himself yielded to winged Cupid's arrows.
As he let himself love, he'll allow his son-in-law to do that too;
  his love for my mother will be a useful precedent.   40
You are to me what he is to her, and Pyrrhus plays
  the part once played by the Trojan stranger Paris.
Let Pyrrhus take endless pride in Achilles' exploits:
  you too have a father with achievements for you to recount.
Agamemnon ruled all the Greeks, including Achilles himself: 45
  he was commander-in-chief; Achilles was just one of the soldiers.
Like Pyrrhus you are in a fifth generation descended from Jupiter,

if you count back through your great-grandfather Pelops and his father.
And you're brave. The killing you did was awful, but you had
    no choice – your father put the weapon in your hands.   50
I wish you'd had a better occasion for showing courage in action,
    but the cause was imposed, not chosen by you.
But you did it all, cutting Aegisthus' throat, so he bloodied
    the palace which your father had bloodied before.
Pyrrhus criticizes you for this, finding fault with what should be   55
    praised, and despite doing that doesn't avoid my eyes.
I burst with anger, both my heart and my face swell,
    my breast is scorched painfully by pent up rage.
After someone has maligned Orestes in front of me, am I
    just a weak woman, without a savage sword in my hand?   60
I can cry at least; my rage comes out in tears;
    tears flow down my chest like a stream.
They're all I have; I have them always, and shed them always;
    my cheeks are wet and unsightly from the constant flow.
There couldn't be a family curse, straying down to my time, that   65
    makes all us female descendants of Tantalus ripe for ravishing, could there?
I won't complain about Jupiter disguising himself as a swan of the river
    and tell how he deceived Leda with his plumage.
Where Corinth's long isthmus keeps two seas apart,
    Hippodamia was taken away on a stranger's chariot.   70
Helen was carried off across the sea by her guest Paris,   73
    making the Greeks go to war to get her back.
I hardly remember it myself, but I do remember. The whole   75
    palace was filled with grief, filled with anxiety and fear.
Her father, sister and twin brothers were in tears, while her
    mother Leda appealed to her own Jupiter and the other gods.
I myself tore my girlishly short hair and kept on shouting:
    'Are you going away without me, mother, without me?'   80
(For my father was away.) To prove I'm a member of that family,
    see, I've been provided as prey for Pyrrhus.
I wish his father hadn't been shot by Apollo:
    he'd condemn the outrage committed by his son.
Achilles didn't like back then and wouldn't like now to see   85
    a man weeping for the wife taken from him.
Ah, has some crime of mine turned the gods against me
    or should I be complaining of some unlucky star harming me?
When I was little I didn't have my mother, and father was at war;
    both were alive, but I was an orphan twice over.   90
Mother, during my childhood you weren't there for me
    to lisp girlish words of love to you.

I never tried to clasp your neck with my tiny arms,
    you never enjoyed having me sit on your lap.
You didn't fuss over my appearance, and when I got married   95
    you didn't get the new bedroom ready for me.
I went to meet you when you came home, and – honestly –
    I didn't know what my mother's face looked like.
I realized you were Helen because you were so beautiful;
    you asked which one was your daughter.   100
Marriage to Orestes is the only bit of good luck that I've had;
    I'll lose him too, if he doesn't stick up for himself.
Pyrrhus holds me captive, though my father returned victorious:
    that's the gift I got out of the destruction of Troy.
I'm miserable, but in the daytime, when the Sun drives his   105
    bright chariot on high, I enjoy some freedom from pain;
at night, shut in the bedroom, wailing and groaning
    bitterly, I lie down on my bed of sorrow
and, weeping instead of sleeping, as much as I can
    I shrink from the man, as if from an enemy.   110
Dazed by pain, and forgetting how things are and where I am,
    I've often touched Pyrrhus' body unwittingly;
when I sense the terrible thing I've done, I recoil from him,
    thinking my hands defiled by that hateful contact.
I often come out with your name instead of his   115
    and treasure my verbal slip as a good omen.
I swear by our luckless family, by our ancestor Jupiter,
    who makes earth, sea and his own sky tremble,
by the bones of your father (my uncle) lying in his tomb,
    which got revenge thanks to your bravery,   120
I'll either die young, killed before my time, or I'll be your wife,
    and we two descendants of Tantalus will be united.

As with *Her.* 7, we are again involved in the aftermath of the Trojan War. But there are obvious differences in the character and circumstances of this heroine, and in the purpose and effect of her letter. The tone diverges too: the extensive frivolity of 7 has gone now. This cannot be a tragic epistle in view of the happy outcome, but it is a very affecting one, thanks to the main thrusts of Hermione's appeal to Orestes. She is touchingly afraid that he will not tackle a savage like Pyrrhus, and so she spends a lot of the letter trying to psych him up, stressing his bravery, maintaining that his ancestry is as distinguished as Pyrrhus' and so on (see further Jacobson 48ff.). But she tries even more to arouse pity for herself. So she points out that she was deprived of her father and especially her mother when she was a child, something that she goes on about twice and at length (at 75ff. and 89ff., in a flashback that gives us a brand-new take on Helen's elopement and a picture of a letter-writer's girlhood that is unique in the *Heroides*). To appreciate properly the pathos in those two passages, note the nature and number of sad details highlighted, the emotive adjectives and nouns, and the repetition of significant words (including negatives). On top of that earlier loss Hermione is now deprived of her beloved Orestes, when marriage to him was the only good thing in her life (101). And this gentle, weak and sorrowful young woman is in the power of the vicious Pyrrhus.

Contemporary readers would have particularly felt for her because of the recent depiction of Pyrrhus in Virgil's *Aeneid*, where during the fall of Troy he plays a brutal role in the attack on Priam's palace and the death of the king himself. A survey of Virgil's lines (spoken by Aeneas as he recalls what he witnessed on that final night of his city) will bring out what a terrifying and cruel monster now holds poor Hermione captive (and what a formidable opponent faces Orestes). At the start of 2.469ff. the sinister Pyrrhus is outside the palace, dancing about with nervous energy and in his eagerness to get inside and start killing, and he is all glittering bronze (almost non-human). By way of reinforcement he is compared to a dangerous, deadly and repulsive snake. As he breaks in he is a figure of violence and fury, unstoppable and pitiless, not given pause by pathetic and helpless females (like Hermione), and once inside he goes mad slaughtering people.

> In front of the entrance-hall itself, right in the gateway, Pyrrhus
> prances, exulting, aglitter with gleaming weapons of bronze,   470
> like a swollen snake that has fed on poisonous herbs and hidden
> away underground during the cold winter, but now has
> shed its skin and is young again and glistening,
> coiling its slippery back into the light, its chest upreared,
> towering up to the sun, darting a three-forked tongue from its mouth.   475
> With him huge Periphas and warlike Automedon
> (Achilles' charioteer), with him all the young warriors from Scyros
> advance on the palace and hurl firebrands on to the roof.
> Pyrrhus himself at their head seizes an axe and tries to
> smash through the stout door and tear the bronze doorposts   480
> from their sockets. Now he has hacked out a panel
> and made a huge, gaping hole in the tough oak.
> The heart of the palace stands revealed, the long halls are exposed;
> the inner rooms of Priam and the kings of old stand revealed;
> they see armed defenders standing just inside the doorway.   485
> The interior is chaos and tumult, groans and anguish;
> deep within, the vaulted building wails with the howls
> of women; their cries rise to strike the golden stars.
> Terrified mothers wander about in the vast palace, clinging
> to doorposts, embracing them and kissing them goodbye.   490
> Pyrrhus drives on with all his father's violence; bars and even
> guards can't withstand him; under a battering-ram's repeated

blows the door totters and falls forward, wrenched from its sockets.
Violence forces an entry. Greek troops burst in, charging,
butchering the guards and filling the entire building,   495
more frenzied than a foaming river that overflows, bursting its
banks and overwhelming the dykes with its flood, and rushes
into the fields in a mass, dragging cattle and their
stalls all over the plains. With my own eyes I saw in the
doorway Pyrrhus in a killing frenzy and the two sons of Atreus,   500
I saw Hecuba, her hundred princesses and Priam over an altar,
polluting with his blood the flames which he had consecrated himself.

That reference to the killing of Priam is elaborated at 2.526ff. The king has gone
to an altar in his palace for sanctuary along with his wife (Hecuba) and his daughters, but there Pyrrhus is responsible for the death of one of his sons right in front
of him (and the women), after running the youth down (and quite possibly playing with him, like a cat with a mouse). When the old man bravely attacks Pyrrhus
verbally and feebly throws a spear at him, instead of being understanding and just
brushing him aside, Pyrrhus is contemptuously curt in his reply (and actually jokes),
before butchering this venerable king cruelly (in his own son's blood, before his
wife and daughters) and sacrilegiously (at an altar, in a grim parody of a sacrifice).

Look – Polites, one of Priam's sons. He had escaped death at
Pyrrhus' hands, but now fled down the long colonnades amid
enemies, amid weapons, and ran through the empty halls,
wounded. Pyrrhus pursued him hotly, on the point of seizing
him, pressing him hard with a spear that was poised to strike.   530
Finally he emerged before the faces and eyes of his parents
and collapsed, pouring out his life in a river of blood.
Although clutched tight in death's grip, Priam didn't
hold back or keep quiet, curbing his rage.
He shouted: 'If there's any righteousness in heaven that cares   535
about such things, may the gods show you fitting gratitude and
give you your due reward for this monstrous crime, this
outrage! You made me witness my own son's murder in
person, you defiled a father's eyes with the sight of death.
You claim Achilles was your father. You liar! He didn't treat his   540
enemy Priam like this. No, he respected my rights as a suppliant
and my trust in him, he gave me back for burial Hector's
bloodless corpse and allowed me to return to my city.'
So saying, the old man hurled his weak, unwarlike spear.
It was immediately repelled by the clanging bronze   545
shield and hung uselessly from the top of its centre.
Pyrrhus said: 'Very well then, you'll go as a messenger to my

father Achilles with news of all this. Remember to tell him
about my deplorable conduct and the degeneracy of his son.
Now die!' While speaking, he dragged Priam to the actual altar,   550
trembling and slipping in pools of his son's blood.
He entwined Priam's hair in his left hand, while with the right
he raised his flashing sword and buried it to the hilt in his side.
This was the end of Priam's destiny, this was the doom
that carried him off, seeing Troy in flames and his   555
citadel in ruins, this man who was once the proud lord
of so many peoples and regions of Asia. He lay on the shore, a mighty
trunk, the head hacked from his shoulders, a nameless corpse.

To supplement the emotional impact of *Heroides* 8, there is some typical Ovidian
cleverness and complexity in kaleidoscopic play with character. Ovid's Hermione
is Hermione, but she also takes on the guise of other heroines. She depicts herself
as a second Helen at 19, 23ff. and 41f. In that role some of what she writes is very
much what one would expect of that personage: a Helen of Troy *would* be against
a large Greek force being sent to fetch her back (23f.) and *would* be critical of the
Greek warrior Pyrrhus and want him to be opposed and thwarted. But there are
also piquant inversions, in a Helen of all people objecting to being abducted and
claiming to be unhappy over sharing a bed with her abductor, and in *her* loving her
husband, counting marriage to him the one good thing in her life and asking him
to get her back.

Hermione also recalls Orestes' sister Electra, who in the tragedy by Euripides
called *Electra* (at 668ff. and 963ff.) had to embolden her cautious and irresolute
brother to get him to kill their father's murderers (first Aegisthus and then their
mother Clytaemnestra). In *Her.* 8, as in Euripides' *Electra*, we find a female relative
shoring up the courage of Orestes when he has done nothing so far, urging him
(successfully) to act against an adulterer and (at 49ff.) condoning the execution of
Aegisthus and Clytaemnestra. Again there are some interesting twists. This Electra,
unlike Euripides' heroine, is passive, inert and totally reliant on Orestes. This is also
a gentler Electra: in contrast to her Euripidean counterpart, she does not hate her
mother for treating her badly, and she does not press Orestes to commit murder
specifically.

In *Heroides* 3 Briseis is involved with Agamemnon and Achilles. Hermione, who
is involved with the son of Agamemnon and the son of Achilles, also resembles
her. Like Briseis, Hermione is a young woman high-handedly taken away from a
Greek hero whom she loves by another Greek hero, and she writes to her man,
on whom she is completely dependent for release, asking him to stir himself and
recover her. Once more Ovid rings the changes. For instance, whereas Briseis is a
foreigner, slave and concubine, Hermione is a Greek, of free birth and a wife, so that
Pyrrhus' abduction of her would have been viewed as more serious and shocking.
And while Briseis was taken from Achilles by Agamemnon, Hermione was taken

from the son of Agamemnon by the son of Achilles, so there is a sort of tit for tat, as history repeats itself with a spin. Try to find some more parallels and variations, and see what you think of the remarks in Fulkerson 87–102 on the connection between *Heroides* 3 and 8.

Not much has survived of ancient literature about Hermione, but we do have one other extensive depiction of her, and it is a very different Hermione in a divergent version of her story that we find there. Euripides in his tragedy entitled *Andromache* tells how Pyrrhus came back from the Trojan war with Hector's sorrowing widow as his captive and impregnated the poor woman. Then in his desire for a legitimate heir he married Hermione, but she was unable to get pregnant. She blamed this unfairly on magic by Andromache, and persecuted her and her son. While Pyrrhus was away at Delphi, Hermione and her father tried to kill the child and Andromache, who had taken refuge at a temple of the goddess Thetis. However, Pyrrhus' grandfather (Peleus) arrived, rescued Andromache and drove off Menelaus. Without her father's support Hermione was afraid to face Pyrrhus and feared that he would kill her for the attempted crime. At that point her cousin Orestes turned up, and she begged him to take her away with him to save her from Pyrrhus' rage. Orestes announced that he had been promised Hermione before Pyrrhus, and took her off to marry her, having already arranged for the murder of Pyrrhus at Delphi.

Hermione's first appearance on stage at 147ff. sets the tone for what follows and establishes her from the start as a most unsympathetic figure. She is harsh and haughty, flaunting her wealth and royal authority, reminding Andromache of her servile status and piling on the humiliation. Her accusations are unreasonable, and in her speech there is an unpleasant mixture of snobbery, contempt, spite, envy and bigotry.

> This sumptuous, splendid crown of gold and the
> richly embroidered robe that I am wearing
> are mine, not some present to honour me
> from the house of Peleus and Achilles: 150
> my father Menelaus from the land of Sparta
> gave them to me together with a large
> dowry, and so I can say what I like.
> But you, a slave-woman, a captive taken in war,   155
> want to get rid of me and take possession of this
> house; you make my husband hate me, because
> my womb is barren and dying due to your potions.
> You Asiatic women are experts in that
> sort of thing; but I'll put a stop to it.   160
> This temple of Thetis, its altar and inmost shrine,
> won't help you at all; you're going to die.
> Suppose some god or mortal did want to save your life –
> you must stop being proud as if still rich,
> and cower humbly, and grovel at my feet,   165

sweep my house and sprinkle with your own
hands river water from my golden pitchers,
realizing where you live now. You have no Hector here,
no Priam, no gold. This is a Greek city.
You slut, you're so perverted that you bring yourself   170
to go to bed with the son of Achilles, who killed your
husband, murdered your man, and to bear him a
child. That's the way all you barbarians are:
fathers sleep with their daughters, sons with their mothers,
sisters with their brothers, very close relatives slaughter   175
each other, and no law prevents any of this.
Don't you introduce that kind of thing here. It's
immoral for a man to have charge of two women at once.
Anybody who wants to lead a decent life
is content to look to a single sexual partner.   180

Ovid has an eye to Euripides' heroine also. As early as line 14 he makes Hermione write of Andromache being maltreated by Greeks, which is an obvious pointer
to the maltreatment of her by Hermione herself and her father in the tragedy; and
by way of reinforcement at 55f. he clearly echoes Pyrrhus' criticism of Orestes for
murdering his mother at *Andromache* 977. As part of his play with character Ovid
presents a young woman who is diametrically opposed to the Euripidean version.
In place of the hard and arrogant figure who relished her royal power Ovid gives us
a gentle, meek and weak person. In *Her.* 8 she is held against her will and longs to
escape the union with Pyrrhus, whereas in the *Andromache* she wants to live on in
the palace as queen and is keen to stay married to Pyrrhus. And Ovid's Hermione
is cruelly oppressed instead of being a cruel oppressor herself.

With his sad lines on Hermione as a little girl Ovid was working within a literary tradition of achieving pathos by means of children that went all the way back
to Homer. In book 6 of the *Iliad* Hector leaves the battle to get the women of Troy
to pray to Athena for help in the fighting, and while in Troy he encounters his
wife Andromache and his baby son Astyanax. The boy will later be killed by Greek
warriors when Troy falls, so there is a melancholy undertone to lines 466ff. There
Hector reaches for the child, but Astyanax shrinks back crying, frightened by his
father's helmet with its horsehair crest nodding grimly from its peak. Hector and
Andromache burst out laughing at that. Then the hero takes off his helmet, dandles
his son in his arms and prays to the gods for the boy to grow up to be a mighty king
of Troy and for people to say that he is a much better man than his father when he
returns from war with bloody armour taken as spoil from the enemy, making his
mother glad.

Ovid made similar use of a father and son in book 8 of his *Metamorphoses*. At
195ff. he depicts the boy Icarus watching his father (the wonderful craftsman Daedalus) making wings for their arms so they can escape by flying away. The innocent Icarus smiles as he playfully tries to catch feathers stirred by the breeze and

softens the wax with his thumb – all of which foreshadows the climax, when the child, despite his father's anxious warnings, gets carried away with the exhilaration of flight and flies too close to the sun, which melts the wax holding together the feathers for his wings. Ovid catches the awful moment as the boy moves his now bare arms up and down, but without wings can get no purchase on the air. He calls out to his father, before plunging to his death in the sea. Daedalus cannot find him and keeps on frantically shouting 'Icarus' until he sees the feathers on the water, and curses his own skill.

Literary epitaphs for children can also be very moving. Callimachus produced one with an eloquent brevity and simplicity (*Greek Anthology* 7.453):

> Philippus buried here his twelve-year-old son,
> > Nicoteles, his great hope.

Martial (11.91) wrote a longer and more harrowing one for a young slave girl:

> Aeolis' daughter Canace lies buried in this tomb;
> > her seventh winter was the last one for this little girl.
> How unjust, how criminal! You, traveller, on the verge of tears,
> > must not complain about the brevity of life in this case.
> Sadder than her death is the manner of her death: a hideous   5
> > infection disfigured her face and settled on her tender mouth,
> and the cruel disease ate away her very kisses,
> > and only a part of her lips were left for the black pyre.
> If the Fates had to come swooping down so swiftly,
> > they should have come some other way.   10
> But death was quick to block the path of her charming voice,
> > so her tongue couldn't soften those pitiless goddesses.

Still more harrowing is Tacitus *Annals* 5.9. In the first century AD a man called Sejanus achieved a position of great influence in the court of the Roman emperor Tiberius, but suddenly fell from power and was killed. Tiberius then attacked Sejanus' allies and family, including a son and daughter. In describing the children's end (strangled by a noose) Tacitus employs pathos as part of his criticism of the callous emperor:

> They were taken off to prison. The boy understood what was going to hap-
> pen, but the girl was so unaware that she kept on asking where they were
> dragging her and what she'd done wrong. She said she wouldn't do it any
> more, and she could be warned off by a spanking. Contemporary authors
> report that, since it was believed to be unheard of for a virgin to be subjected
> to capital punishment, she was raped by her executioner, next to the noose.
> Then they were strangled, and their young bodies were thrown on to the
> Gemonian Steps.

Heroides 9

DEIANIRA TO HERCULES

The last wife of the super-hero Hercules during his time on earth was the Greek heroine Deianira. To win her hand, he had to fight a rival suitor, the river-god Achelous, whom he defeated, breaking off the deity's horns as he wrestled with him. When returning home with his bride, Hercules came to the river Evenus, which was severely swollen by heavy rains. A Centaur (half-man, half-horse) called Nessus offered to carry her over the river on his back while Hercules made his own way. The hero agreed and swam across, but then heard her cry and looked back to see Nessus trying to rape her. He promptly shot the Centaur with an arrow. To get revenge, as he was dying Nessus gave Deianira his tunic soaked in his blood, telling her that the blood had the power to revive waning love. Years later Hercules conquered the Greek town of Oechalia, killing its king (Eurytus) and taking his daughter Iole captive. But he fell in love with her and had her go on ahead of him back to his home. There Deianira became aware of his feelings for Iole, when she arrived, and so she sent him a tunic smeared with Nessus' blood. At this point, confident that his love for her would be renewed in this way, she writes this letter, in which she reprimands him for his infidelity and mocks him for his undignified carryings-on. However, while she is still writing, news reaches her that Nessus' blood is in fact an agonizing poison, which is burning and killing Hercules (who has put on the tunic), and she resolves to commit suicide at the end of the epistle. She did go on to kill herself. Hercules died too, having made a pyre on the top of Mount Oeta and mounted it as it burned. The fire purged his mortal elements, and he mounted to heaven and became a god. The story is told in full at Ovid *Metamorphoses* 9.1ff.

In the course of this poem Deianira makes numerous references that need explaining. Hercules was the illegitimate son of Jupiter and Alcmene, the wife of king Amphitryon (who passed as the father of Hercules). The god joined two nights together to extend his love-making and father a mighty son. His wife Juno hated her rival's child, and when he was still a baby sent two snakes to kill him, but he throttled them in his cradle. He grew up to be a great benefactor of mankind, travelling widely and cleansing the earth of various wild animals, monsters and other enemies of humanity. At the implacable Juno's instigation king Eurystheus (who ruled over Hercules as one of his subjects thanks to a ruse of hers) imposed the twelve Labours on him. These supremely difficult tasks included killing an invulnerable lion at Nemea (he strangled it, skinned it and wore its impenetrable hide ever after); exterminating the Hydra, a monstrous snake with several heads, each of which grew back twofold when severed; bringing back alive to Eurystheus a huge boar that lived on Mount Erymanthus; fetching the man-eating mares of the savage king Diomedes; seizing the cattle of Geryon, a giant with three bodies; and going down to the Underworld to carry off Cerberus, the three-headed dog that guarded Hell. Hercules successfully performed all these assignments. He also supported the sky on his shoulders, while the giant Atlas (who normally held it up) went to get the golden apples of the Hesperides for the hero as another one of his Labours. Hercules put to death Busiris too, a cruel king of Egypt who sacrificed strangers, and Antaeus, an African giant who was invulnerable as long as he was in contact with the earth (so he was hoisted off the ground and throttled). As well as alluding to all that, Deianira complains that her husband demeans these achievements by his many love affairs, and she dwells in particular on his erotic entanglement with the beautiful oriental queen Omphale. Hercules was forced to serve as her slave, and got involved in some undignified cross-dressing in the process. She made him do women's work (spinning) and dress in women's clothes, while she wore his lion-skin and carried his weapons. Towards the end of *Heroides* 9 Deianira refers to her own ill-fated family, including her brother Meleager. When he was born, his mother was told that it was fated for him to die if a particular log was consumed by fire. She hid the log in a chest to protect his life, but when he killed her brothers in an altercation, she burned the log; she then committed suicide in remorse.

> I'm pleased that Oechalia's been added to the list of our achievements;
>   I'm upset that the conqueror's been conquered by his captive.
> A disgraceful rumour has suddenly reached the cities of Greece
>   (and you need to do something to disprove it) –
> that the man who Juno and an endless series of labours   5
>   never broke has been subjugated by Iole.
> Eurystheus would want this to be true, and so would your stepmother
>   Juno (who'd be delighted at this stain on your life's work),
> but not Jupiter, who supposedly found just one night of
>   love-making too short for fathering as great a hero as you.   10
> Venus has harmed you more than Juno did: Juno's persecution spurred
>   you on; Venus humiliates you, her foot on your neck.
> Look at the world, the expanses of land surrounded by the blue
>   Ocean – all pacified and protected by your mighty hand.
> Peace on earth and safety at sea are due to you; you have   15
>   done an immense amount of good in the east and the west.

You've already borne the heavens that will bear you,
    substituting for Atlas until he supported the sky again.
If you crown your former achievements with a stigma,
    all you've done is publicize your contemptible disgrace.   20
Are *you* the one they say gripped and throttled the two snakes
    when in your cradle, already a child worthy of Jupiter?
You began well, but end badly; your last deeds don't match the
    first; the man you are and the boy you were are different.
The hero who a thousand wild animals, hostile Eurystheus   25
    and Juno couldn't defeat is defeated by Love.
But they say I married well because I'm called Hercules' wife
    and my father-in-law thunders on high in his swift chariot.
Mismatched bullocks don't plough well together; so too a woman
    who's inferior to her great husband is overshadowed by him.   30
That seems an honour, but damages those burdened with it;
    if you want a suitable marriage, marry an equal.
My man is always away (more of a guest than a husband)
    in pursuit of terrifying wild animals and monsters.
At home, on my own, I busy myself with chaste prayers, tormented   35
    by the fear that he'll be killed by some savage enemy,
and anguished by thoughts of snakes, boars, ravening lions
    and dogs that will fasten on him with their triple jaws.
Insubstantial images in my dreams and omens sought in the
    secrecy of night and at sacrifices worry me.   40
In my misery I snatch at unreliable whispered rumours;
    my fear is killed off by wavering hope, my hope by fear.
Your mother's away, sorry she ever attracted mighty Jupiter;
    your father Amphitryon and your son Hyllus aren't here either.
I'm the one affected by unjust Juno's lasting anger   45
    and Eurystheus being in control thanks to her trickery.
As if that's not enough for me to endure, you have affairs
    when you're away, ready to impregnate any woman at all.
I'll say nothing about Auge, who you raped in Parthenius' valleys,
    or the child of yours born to the nymph Astydamia;   50
I won't criticize you for king Thespius' fifty daughters,
    not one of whom was left untouched by you.
I *will* mention one mistress (a recent offence) – the Lydian
    queen Omphale, mother of your son Lamus.
The river Meander, which winds constantly through the same regions   55
    and often makes its weary waters twist back on themselves,
saw necklaces hanging from the neck of Hercules
    (which had supported with ease the weight of the sky).
Weren't you ashamed to put gold bracelets around your strong arms
    and to cover your solid muscles with jewels?   60

And those were the arms, of course, that killed the deadly Nemean
    lion, whose skin you wear now over your left shoulder.
You actually put a woman's turban on your shaggy hair!
    Your usual garland of white poplar suits it better.
You don't feel it was degrading to wear   65
    a Lydian girdle like a promiscuous girl?
Didn't you think of your victory over vicious Diomedes,
    the savage who fed his horses on human flesh?
You conquered Busiris, but if he'd seen you dressed like that,
    he'd certainly have been ashamed of having such a conqueror.   70
Antaeus would have ripped the ribbons from your hard neck
    to avoid the mortification of having lost to a she-man.
They say you held a wool-basket among Ionian slave-girls
    and were really scared of your mistress' threats.
Those hands were victorious in countless labours, but you   75
    didn't refuse to touch a smooth basket with them,
and you used your strong thumb to spin your portion of coarse wool,
    giving back the full amount as thread to your notorious mistress?
As you twisted it into strands with those hard fingers,
    your mighty hands shattered the spindle again and again.   80
At your mistress' feet . . .
    you told of your feats (which you should have concealed) –   84
no doubt how as a baby you throttled those immense snakes,   85
    which as they died wrapped their tails around your hands,
and how the boar that had its lair on cypress-clad
    Erymanthus dented the ground with its great weight.
You also mentioned the heads nailed up on Diomedes' palace,
    and his horses, which were fattened on men he killed,   90
and that threefold monster with his great herd of Spanish cattle –
    Geryon, a single person, but with three bodies –
and Cerberus, the dog with three heads branching from one body,
    and with menacing snakes entwined in his fur,
and the Hydra, reproducing when wounded and amply reborn,   95
    growing two snaky heads for every one cut off,
and the giant Antaeus, who you held up, pinned between
    your left arm and your left side, strangling him,
and the Centaurs, mistakenly confident because they had hooves and
    human arms, and routed by you on the ridges of Thessaly.   100
How could you tell of all that while wearing a distinguished purple
    dress? Didn't your clothes make you hold your tongue?
Omphale even adorned herself with your arms –
    famous trophies taken from her captive.
Go on – take on airs, enumerate your brave exploits;   105
    she was the real man, you have no right to that title.

Greatest of heroes, you're inferior to her, in so far as it was
    a greater feat to conquer you than those you conquered.
All your achievements are credited to her; hand over what was
    yours; your girlfriend is the inheritor of your glory.   110
Oh, the disgrace! She covered her soft flank with the
    rough pelt of the shaggy Nemean lion.
You're mistaken without realizing it: that's spoil taken from you,
    not the lion; you beat the animal, and she beat you.
Scarcely strong enough to carry a spindle loaded with wool,   115
    a woman carried your arrows black with the Hydra's venom,
armed herself with the club that fells wild animals and looked
    at herself in a mirror equipped like my husband!
However, I merely heard all that, and could disbelieve the rumours;
    the pain I felt from what came to my ears was bearable.   120
But with my own eyes I saw a foreigner (my rival Iole)
    brought here, and I couldn't conceal my suffering.
You didn't let me turn away; that captive came right through
    the centre of the city, so I had to look at her despite myself.
And she wasn't like a prisoner, with unkempt hair   125
    and a suitably sad face eloquent of her misfortune.
She strutted around, a vision thanks to all that gold,
    dressed just the way you were with Omphale.
Head held high, she presented her face to the crowd as if you'd
    been defeated, her town still stood and her father was alive.   130
Perhaps you'll drive away Deianira (a fellow-Greek), and Iole
    won't be called your mistress but will be your wife.
An infamous marriage will unite a disgraceful pair –
    Hercules of Thebes and the daughter of Eurytus.
Warning myself of this makes my mind reel; I go cold   135
    all over, and my hands lie limp in my lap.
You've loved me and many others, but me as your lawful wife.
    You fought over me twice (don't feel regret at that!):
the river-god Achelous sadly gathered his horns on his wet bank
    and bathed the brow you tore them from in his muddy water;   140
and you shot down the Centaur Nessus in lotus-bearing Evenus,
    and he dyed that river red with his horse-blood.
Enough of that! As I write this, news has reached me that
    my husband is dying from that poisoned tunic of mine.
Ah, what have I done? What has my mad love driven me to?   145
    Deianira, you're a bad wife; why hesitate to die?
Your husband's being mangled amid Mount Oeta's heights –
    will you live on, when you're responsible for such an awful crime?
If I've done anything so far to make people think that I am
    Hercules' wife, I must prove it now by killing myself.   150

Meleager will see how clearly I am a sister of his.
  Deianira, you're a bad wife; why hesitate to die?
Ah, our family's cursed: my uncle seized the high throne of my father,
  who is now alone, destitute and crushed by old age;
my brother Tydeus is an exile in some foreign land,   155
  while Meleager's life depended on a fateful firebrand;
and my mother plunged a sword into her own heart.
  Deianira, you're a bad wife; why hesitate to die?
All I pray, by the very sacred bonds of our marriage, is that
  you don't think your death is due to some plot of mine.   160
When Nessus' lustful heart was struck by your arrow,
  he said: 'This blood has the power to inspire love.'
But it was poison, and I sent you a tunic smeared with it.
  Deianira, you're a bad wife; why hesitate to die?
And now farewell, my old father, my sister Gorge, my   165
  native land, my exiled brother, and today's light
(the last that I'll see); and farewell to you, my husband
  (oh, if only you could fare well!), and to you, Hyllus, my son.

There is the usual variation, in connection with tone (pathos does not predominate this time) and situation (there is no Trojan War link now; and there is another woman in the background here). So too the addressee is the vigorous Hercules, who has already achieved so much, in contrast to the inert Orestes, who still needed to be urged to act. This is also the only one of the *Heroides* to feature a refrain (the repeated line at 146, 152, 158 and 164). And it is the only one in which there is a dramatic development as news suddenly reaches the writer of an event in the outside world (Hercules being killed by the tunic); and this takes the epistle off in a surprising new direction and gives it a novel twofold thrust (initially it is aimed at ending the affair with Iole, but then it turns into reaction to the news about the tunic).

This is one of the *Heroides* whose authenticity has been challenged, and critics have maintained that large parts of *Her.* 9 or even the whole poem were the work not of Ovid but of an imitator. There seems to us no good reason for doubting that Ovid composed the letter (for the arguments against Ovidian authorship and for convincing rebuttal of them see Jacobson 228ff. and Fulkerson 108). However, this controversy does concern issues which are very relevant to the overall interpretation of the piece, and it usefully encourages readers to probe the purpose and weighting of Deianira's words. Scholars have been perplexed by and critical of substantial portions of the epistle, and raise important questions in connection with them. Why is there such a long passage on the *former* affair (now *over*) with Omphale (which has been classified as a long inorganic digression)? Why is there so much about Hercules' Labours and other feats (seen by some as tediously repetitious)? And how effective or otherwise is the refrain (which has been characterized as a makeshift device to render unnecessary a description of Deianira's grief)? Our answers to these questions will emerge in the following paragraphs. But you should consider them for yourself now and make up your own mind about what the point is in each case.

At the time of writing this letter Deianira has already sent to Hercules the tunic, which she assumes will have restored his feelings for her. But he could, of course, love Iole as well as Deianira, and he could have a liaison with the former while being in love with the latter, so this epistle is initially intended as a reinforcement to the tunic, to make him give up his affection for his captive. To achieve that end she utilizes various ploys. She shows him that she loves him (e.g. by identifying with him in the very first line, by going on and on admiringly about his exploits, and at 35ff. by highlighting her fears for his safety). She tries to make him pity her too (for instance, at 2, 29ff., 45ff. and 119ff.). Above all she tries to make him feel ashamed of his philandering and see that he thereby disgraces himself. She does this by claiming that in committing adultery he is not living up to his great feats (repeated reference to them also drives home that point) and by dwelling at 53ff. on her best example of his humiliation due to love (the entanglement with Omphale) and bringing out forcefully, memorably and at length how demeaning that was (and no doubt this incident still rankles and she wants to let off steam about it too). In this way she will be hoping to dissuade him from degenerating and degrading himself further, with Iole (see 3ff., 7f., 12, 19f. and 23ff.). When the news about Hercules' death-throes arrives at 143, she keeps on with her letter, but the purpose of her writing changes. In particular now she is keen to let Hercules know that sending the tunic was an innocent mistake on her part and she tries to steel herself to commit suicide (hence 147f., 149f. and the refrain). Her final farewell at 165ff. intimates that she has succeeded in that attempt.

Obviously this is a sad story, and the two deaths are particularly tragic. To help you appreciate the full force of them, here are detailed accounts of them. The fifth-century BC Greek tragedian Sophocles produced a play based on this incident called the *Trachiniae*. In it Hyllus, the son of Deianira and Heracles (the Greek name for Hercules), is with his father when he puts the tunic on, and he goes on home ahead of the dying Heracles and in all ignorance denounces his mother as a murderess and describes his father's torment. As a result Deianira kills herself at 900ff. First she roams the palace, hiding in shame, and looking at familiar people and things for the last time. Next she rushes into her bedroom, where she reveals how very important her marriage was to her, and then commits suicide briskly and resolutely. The pathos is increased at the end by Hyllus' lamentation, which underscores the tragedy of her death and shows his guilt and misery over mistakenly accusing her and precipitating it.

> When she went into the palace, on her own,   900
> and saw her son in the courtyard preparing a stretcher
> to take back with him when he went to meet his father,
> she hid herself where nobody could see her.
> She fell on the altars, crying out that they would now

be neglected, and the poor woman wept whenever she   905
touched any of the household things that she'd used in the past.
She wandered from room to room in the palace,
and if she saw any of her beloved servants,
she wept as she gazed at them,
crying out miserably at her own fate.   910
Suddenly she stopped, and I saw her   912
rush into the bedroom she shared with Heracles.
I concealed myself and stayed out of sight,
watching her. I saw her take blankets and   915
make up the bed she shared with Heracles.
When she'd finished doing that, she jumped up
on to the bed and sat down in the middle of it.
She broke into floods of hot tears and
said: 'My bridal bed, my bedroom, goodbye   920
now forever: I'll never come back again
and sleep here with my husband.'
That was all she said. Then, with tensed
hands, she unfastened her dress, by pulling
out the gold pin above her breasts, and   925
uncovered all her left side and arm.
I ran as fast as I could and
told her son what she was planning.
I rushed there and we raced back, only to
find that meanwhile she had driven a two-edged   930
sword through her side into her heart.
When he saw this, her poor son screamed. He knew
that his anger had driven her to that, and
he had learned, too late, from the palace servants that
she had acted in innocence, tricked by the Centaur.   935
Then the boy sobbed over her in his misery,
and went on and on wailing and kissing her,
and threw himself down at her side
and lay there, groaning again and again
that he had accused her unjustly and cruelly,   940
in tears because he would now live the rest
of his life deprived of both his father and his mother.

When it comes to Hercules' end, Ovid at *Metamorphoses* 9.159ff. catches well the horror as well as the poignancy. After the tragic irony of an act of piety activating the poison that kills Hercules, there is a full and vivid picture of its awful effect on the brave hero. Not sparing his readers, Ovid appeals to various senses and presents a flurry of precise and telling details that have great cumulative impact.

As soon as the fire was lit, he offered prayers and incense
and poured wine from a bowl on to the marble altar.   160
The virulent poison was warmed and released by the fire;
it seeped away and spread through his entire body.
As long as he could, he stifled his groans with his usual courage.
When the pain became unendurable, he pushed over
the altar and filled wooded Mount Oeta with his shouts.   165
At once he tried to rip the deadly tunic off. Where it was
torn away it tore away skin, and (writing this makes me shudder)
some of it stuck to his body, resisting his attempts to pull it off, while
what did come away exposed lacerated limbs and his massive bones.
The burning poison made his very blood hiss and boil,   170
like a white-hot strip of metal dipped in a trough of cold water.
On and on, the greedy flames sucked up his vital organs,
dark sweat poured out from his whole body,
his scorched sinews crackled and the invisible venom
melted his marrow.   175

There is pathos in *Heroides* 9 too. In addition to those deaths looming in the background, sympathy for Deianira is built up. She feels eclipsed by her husband (29ff.), and his adventuring leaves her isolated and fearful (33ff.). She has been badly treated by him, despite being a loving wife, and his repeated adultery obviously upsets her deeply. And when she tries to remedy the situation with Iole, she makes a terrible mistake, which causes her great grief and leads her to end her life. However, our irreverent poet also reacts against the inherent sadness of the story and serious literary treatments of it. Here again we find a lively admixture of humour, wit and irony, to ensure that the poem does not lapse into mawkishness and engages the head as well as the heart.

Although Deianira is making a serious point about Hercules disgracing himself, she does so with an amusing mockery and tartness that is intended to really get to her husband, and so the dilation on his stay with Omphale and on his achievements also has a droll aspect. She ridicules him at length with her description of his incongruous and grotesque cross-dressing and spinning, working in especially entertaining taunts in 66, 71f. and 74. There is as well much bitter joking in the humiliation of the great conqueror being conquered himself and being subjugated by a woman and love, with witty verbal play in 2, 25f., 107f. and 113f.

All of that is deliberate on the part of Deianira. Her words are also often unintentionally funny and ironical. It is horribly inappropriate for her to attack and poke fun at her husband, given that she is in the process of ending his life in a particularly painful way. A major topic that she pursues is the addressee brought low by a female and by love, when she is herself a female bringing him low because of her love for him. She dwells on him as a conqueror and killer too, unaware that she is herself conquering and killing him. This kind of thing operates in connection with individual lines as well. In 17 she speaks of him reaching the heavens, when she has sent him the tunic that gets him there (deified), sooner than she expects. In 33 she complains with exaggeration that he is always away, while ensuring that he really will be permanently away. At 57ff. she writes at length about feminine attire that humiliated him, having sent him masculine attire that will destroy him. At 74 he is said to have been afraid of his mistress' threats, but he should rather have been afraid of his wife's gift of the tunic. See if you can spot for yourself this kind of irony at 11, 23f., 35f., 37, 47, 99f., 102, 113, 116, 122 and 129f. There are other facetious touches too. At 9f. Deianira ineptly cites the archetypal adulterer Jupiter (to a product of one of his affairs) as one who would disapprove of his passion for Iole. And there is a comic coincidence at 141ff., as she talks glibly of the death of Nessus and his blood and then immediately receives news of its deadly effect on her husband. There are even diverting elements at 145ff. In connection with the refrain, after going on and on about what a bad husband Hercules was, she now has to go on and on about what a bad wife she is; and by spending time saying repeatedly 'why hesitate to die?' she is in fact delaying her death. Also, if one bears in mind the bigger picture, the end of Hercules' mortal existence led to his deification (and to the end of Juno's persecution of him), which was a definite improvement for him, so that Deianira's grief and suicide are ultimately inappropriate.

Heroides 9 fits into a long literary tradition of frivolity regarding Hercules. In ancient literature he was a far more versatile and interesting character than the stereotypical strongman depicted on television and in the cinema, and we find a host of different versions of the hero there (see Galinsky 1972). For example, as well as being big and brawny, he could also be ingenious, or stupid, a civilizer and benefactor of mankind, a man of great appetites (for food, wine and women), a compassionate person, a savage, a jolly good fellow, a role model thanks to his virtue and fortitude, a figure of pathos and a figure of fun. In the latter connection he was often portrayed on stage in comedies and satyr plays (which had a pronounced comic element).

In Aristophanes' *Frogs* the god Dionysus intends going down to the Underworld because he longs to bring back to earth his favourite poet, Euripides, who has recently died. He applies for directions to Hercules, who had already gone down there to bring back Cerberus. No intellectual, this Hercules is baffled by his longing, until Dionysus compares it to the hero's craving for pea soup; then he immediately grasps the seriousness of the situation. When the god asks about the quickest way down to the Underworld, Hercules flippantly suggests that he hang himself, poison himself or jump off a high tower; but then he tells him the route down for a living person, while mischievously stressing its horrors (such as numerous monsters and a lake of liquid excrement in which sinners have to lie). When he does get into the Underworld, Dionysus finds that the hero had made a big impact when he went down. He dined at an inn there (!), where he devoured sixteen loaves of bread, twenty orders of stew, lots of garlic, huge quantities of fish, masses of cheese and the baskets containing it. When the two women who ran the inn asked for payment, he bellowed in rage, drew his sword and chased them, forcing them to hide in the loft. And when he left, he stole the mattresses.

Euripides wrote a drama called *Alcestis*, which performed the function of a satyr play and contained its lighter elements. In it we see again an amusingly undignified Hercules. Queen Alcestis dies, but when the hero turns up at the palace, on his way to perform one of his Labours, her husband conceals her death from him, making him think that the dead person is just some orphan whom they have taken in. He does this because he is a good host and wants his guest to enjoy himself properly. He insists on giving him food and drink, and Hercules indulges his appetites to the full. One of the servants, who misses his mistress deeply, comes out on stage to complain about Hercules' riotous behaviour inside the palace, and then Hercules comes out, tipsy, and annoyed that the slave is miserable and frowning. Like many drunks, he wants others to be happy too and tries to snap the man out of his sullenness. Also like many drunks, he imagines that he has found the secret of life and is keen to pass on his findings. He is genial and hearty, and also rather patronizing, as he solemnly reveals his great 'wisdom' (after giving it a careful build-up at 779–81). In reality his observations are obvious, and his message is simply that one should enjoy oneself while one can (drinking and making love), which does make sense, but is hardly very profound, hardly amounts to impressive philosophy and was in fact trite and commonplace (and so the servant's immediate response to this speech is: 'I know that'). Imagine Hercules slurring his words as he comes out with the following:

> Come over here, so I can impart some wisdom.
> Do you know the nature of our mortal lot?   780
> I think not. How could you? Well, listen to me.
> Death is a debt that all men must pay,
> and there is no mortal who knows for sure
> if he is going to live through the morrow.
> For Fate moves in mysterious ways,   785
> which cannot be taught or grasped by any craft.
> So, now that you've listened and learned all this from me,
> cheer up, have a drink, think of each day that you live
> as yours but everything else as belonging to Fate.
> And give honour to Aphrodite, the loveliest, sweetest of   790
> gods to humans. For she is a kindly goddess.
> Forget everything else and take my advice,
> if you think I'm speaking sense, as I imagine
> you do. So, no more of this excessive grief!
> Rise above this trouble, put a garland on your head   795
> and have a drink with me. I'm absolutely certain that
> the wine will ambush you, assault your sense and
> put an end to this clotted sullenness of yours.
> We are mortals and should think like mortals.
> As for all those solemn types with knitted brows,   800
> in my judgment at least, their life isn't
> really a life at all, it's catastrophe.

As far as we can tell from surviving literature, within this tradition such humour in connection with the death of Hercules (and Deianira) was not found before Ovid, so there is typical novelty here. Ovid was also apparently the first to introduce the god Faunus into the Omphale episode in a clever and entertaining reprise of that incident at *Fasti* 2.305ff. (on which see Murgatroyd 84f., 223f. and 253ff.).

Heroides 10

ARIADNE TO THESEUS

Ariadne was the beautiful young daughter of Minos, who was king of the large Greek island of Crete. A son of his called Androgeos died during a visit to mainland Greece. Minos held the Athenians responsible for his death, and by way of punishment demanded that they sent to Crete each year a tribute of seven young women and seven young men, who were devoured by the monstrous Minotaur. Minos' wife Pasiphae had been afflicted by a deity with an irresistible passion for a bull, which she gratified by getting the bull to mount her (concealed inside a fake wooden cow). The offspring of this mating was the savage Minotaur, which had the body of a man and the head of a bull, and was shut up in an inextricable maze called the Labyrinth.

Theseus (son of the Athenian king Aegeus) ended the tribute by going as one of the seven young men and putting the Minotaur to death. When this handsome hero arrived on Crete, Ariadne fell deeply in love with him. Greatly concerned for his safety, she helped him by giving him a ball of thread to let out behind him as he entered the Labyrinth and to follow back to get out of the maze after conquering the monster. In return he promised to marry her and spend the rest of his life with her. He killed the Minotaur, and to escape Minos' anger quickly sailed off with Ariadne. On the voyage back to Athens they spent the night on an island (Dia), but Theseus callously abandoned her while she was still asleep, and she woke to see his ship disappearing in the distance. Shortly after that she wrote this letter.

Elsewhere we learn that she prayed to Jupiter to punish Theseus, and her prayer was granted. Theseus' father Aegeus had been very worried about his son's chances on Crete and had sent him off on a ship with a black sail, telling him to replace it with a white one if he was successful. Theseus was made to forget to change the sail. When his father saw the ship coming back with a black sail, he assumed that Theseus was dead and committed suicide. So the hero returned to his father's death and to misery and mourning. But there was a happy ending for princess Ariadne. The god Bacchus turned up on Dia in a tiger-drawn chariot with his companions (his female worshippers called Bacchantes and the minor country divinities named Satyrs). He saved her, claimed her as his bride and carried her off to live on Olympus with him. In some versions she was made immortal; in others she or her golden crown (a wedding present) was raised into the sky to become a constellation.

I've found every species of wild animals gentler than you.
  Better to have entrusted myself to any of them rather than you.
I send the letter you're reading, Theseus, from the shore
  where you left me behind when you sailed away,
where I was brutally betrayed by my sleep and by you,   5
  with your insidious crime against me while I slept.
It was the moment when the earth is first sprinkled with crystal
  frost and the birds begin their plaintive song amid the leaves.
Not properly awake, and languid from sleep, I turned on my
  side and reached out to take hold of Theseus –   10
he wasn't there! I moved my hands back and tried again,
  feeling all around the bed – he wasn't there!
I was lying on my own. Fear shook me awake,
  and I leapt up, absolutely terrified.
Immediately I beat my breasts, loudly, and   15
  tore my hair still tangled from sleep.
In the moonlight I looked for something other than shore;
  there was nothing for my eyes to see but shore.
I ran this way and that, haphazardly,
  my girlish feet slowed down by the deep sand.   20
Meanwhile I shouted 'Theseus' all along the shore;
  the concave cliffs echoed your name.
The place itself called out to you as often as I did:
  the place itself wanted to help poor Ariadne.
There was a mountain – a few bushes are visible on its peak,   25
  from which hangs a cliff, eroded by roaring waves.
I climbed up (given strength by the state I was in) and then
  looked out, scanning the deep sea far and wide.
From there – for I found the winds cruel as well as you –
  I saw your sails stretched tight by a southerly gale.   30
After seeing what I thought I didn't deserve to see,
  I was colder than ice and half-dead.
But my grief didn't let me languish for long; it roused me,
  roused me, and I called out 'Theseus' at the top of my voice.
'Where are you rushing off?' I shouted. 'Theseus, you criminal,   35
  come back! Turn the ship round! It's a person short.'
As these cries didn't reach you, I beat my breasts too,

flailing and wailing out words as well.
So you could at least see me, if you didn't hear me,
    I signalled with wide waves of my hands,   40
and I placed my white dress on the end of a long branch,
    to remind those who had clearly forgotten about me.
And now you were snatched from my sight. Then I finally wept;
    before that my tender eyes had been paralyzed by pain.
What was there for my eyes to do except cry for me,   45
    when I couldn't see your sails any more?
Either I wandered around alone with streaming hair,
    like a worshipper of Bacchus spurred on by the god,
or I sat, chilled, on a rock, looking out to sea,
    as stony as the stone on which I sat.   50
I often went back to the bed which we'd shared,
    but wouldn't be seen sharing again,
and touched your imprint (all I could touch in place of you)
    and the bedding which grew warm from your body.
I threw myself on to it, and drenched it with tears, shouting: 55
    'Two people lay down on you – give back two people!
We both came here – why don't we both leave together?
    Treacherous bed, where's my other, and greater, half?'
What am I to do? Where should I go, alone on an uninhabited
    island? I see no sign of ploughing by men or oxen.   60
There's sea on every side of the land, no sailor anywhere,
    and no ship to sail off on an uncertain course.
Suppose I was given companions and a boat and winds –
    where should I make for? My own country won't have me.
Even if I have a successful voyage over peaceful seas,   65
    even if Aeolus controls his winds, I'll be an exile.
I won't visit my homeland, that island of a hundred cities,
    well-known to Jupiter, who spent his childhood there,
since by my actions I betrayed my just father Minos
    and his kingdom of Crete (names so dear to me).   70
When I gave you the thread as a guide to lead you back,
    so you wouldn't die in the maze after beating the Minotaur,
you said to me: 'I swear by the very dangers facing me
    that you'll be mine as long as we're both alive.'
We're alive, and I'm not yours, Theseus – if a woman *is* alive   75
    who's been buried by the deceit of a perjurer.
You criminal, you should have clubbed me as well as my brother:
    killing me would have freed you from your pledge.
Now I'm not just thinking about what will happen to me and all
    the things that can happen to any abandoned woman: 80
I'm picturing death in a thousand forms,

and dying isn't as bad as waiting to die.
At any moment, I suspect, here or over there
  wolves will come to tear my flesh with greedy fangs.
Who knows if this land also nurtures tawny lions?   85
  Perhaps the island has savage tigresses too.
They say the sea casts ashore huge seals! And who's
  to prevent me being stabbed in the side by swords?
So long as I'm not captured and bound in cruel chains,
  and made a slave, with masses of wool to spin —   90
for my father is Minos, my mother is a daughter of Apollo and
  (something that stands out more in my memory) I was betrothed to you.
Whenever I've looked at the sea and the land with its long shoreline,
  to me the land and the water are very threatening.
There was the sky, but there I fear divine apparitions.   95
  I'm abandoned, prey and food for ravening animals.
But if men do live here and plough the fields, I don't trust them:
  maltreatment has made me fearful of foreigners.
If only Androgeos was alive, and Athens hadn't paid for
  its crime by sending its youths to their deaths,   ⸳   100
and your right hand hadn't been raised on high, Theseus,
  to kill the Minotaur with that knotty club,
and I hadn't given you the thread to show you your way back,
  the thread that your hands often.took up again and tugged!
Personally I'm not surprised that the victory was yours   105
  and the beast was brought crashing down to the ground.
Your heart of iron couldn't have been pierced by his horn,
  your chest was safe, even if unprotected:
you had flint there, you had adamant there,
  there you have a Theseus harder than flint.   110
Cruel sleep, why immobilize me? If I had to sleep,
  I should have done so for ever, plunged in endless night.
Winds and breezes, you were cruel as well, far too
  ready to blow, and concerned to make me cry.
The hand was cruel that has killed me and my brother, as was   115
  the 'pledge' (meaningless term) that you gave when I asked for it.
Sleep, wind and that pledge conspired against me,
  a single girl, betrayed by those three agents.
So, I won't see my mother weeping when I'm about to die,
  and there won't be anyone to close my eyes?   120
My sorrowful soul will pass from me into this foreign air,
  and no friend will lay me out and anoint my body?
Will sea-birds perch on my unburied bones and be
  my tombs? My kindness deserved better than that.

You'll go to Athens' harbour and be welcomed home,   125
    you'll stand there proudly, before the gaze of your people,
and you'll tell a fine tale about the man–bull's death
    and about the rocky Labyrinth's confusing maze.
Tell of me too, abandoned on a deserted island.
    I mustn't be quietly removed from your roll of honours.   130
Your father isn't Aegeus, you're not the son of Pittheus'
    daughter Aethra: rock and sea were your parents.
I wish the gods had made you see me from the top of the stern:
    my sad figure would have brought tears to your eyes.
Look at me now – you can't with your eyes, but in your mind –   135
    clinging to a rock that's pounded by the restless waves.
Look at my hair, loosened as though I were mourning the dead,
    and my clothes heavy with tears like rain.
My body is shivering, like a crop of corn swept by northerly gales,
    and the letters traced by my quivering fingers are shaky.   140
I won't base pleas on the help I gave you (as it turned out badly for me);
    don't be grateful at all for what I did.
But don't punish me either! Even if it wasn't true that I
    saved you, you have no reason for causing my death.
In my misery I'm stretching out to you over the broad sea   145
    these hands that are weary from beating my mournful breasts;
I'm sadly showing you what's left of the hair that I've torn in grief,
    and I'm begging you by these tears, caused by what you've done: 150
Theseus, turn your ship round and sail back here!
    If I die before you arrive, you'll take my bones with you.

One can understand perfectly why the abandoned Ariadne is distraught and fears for her life, but in fact nothing bad happens to her. So this is another epistle which is both affecting and amusing, and which is written by a heroine who is ignorant of how things will turn out and so comes out with unintentionally comic remarks. But this time the levity is deceptively delayed, so that for the first 34 lines there is straight pathos, which makes a change from the tonal mix in *Her.* 9; and this time there is no dark humour. The background circumstances and purpose of this letter differ too, and there is a favourable outcome in store for this writer.

Ovid is here again reacting to a literary forerunner. Catullus (approximately 84–54 BC) in his poem 64 had recently produced a memorable version of Ariadne abandoned on the island of Dia, complaining at length and praying for punishment for Theseus. This should have readily sprung to mind for those reading *Her.* 10, and, to make sure that it did, Ovid included many echoes of the lines of Catullus (see e.g. Jacobson 215ff.), so that readers would assess the Ovidian piece in the light of its model. Catullus' depiction of Ariadne waking up on the beach as Theseus sails away

(64.52ff.) is one of the most moving passages in ancient literature and is especially relevant to *Her.* 10.

> For, looking out from the wave-sounding shore of Dia,
> Ariadne with the wild frenzy of love in her heart
> gazes at Theseus sailing away on his swift ship;
> even now she does not believe what is before her eyes,   55
> naturally, as she has only just woken from treacherous sleep
> and sees herself abandoned, miserable, on the lonely shore.
> With no thought for her the youth flees, his oars beating the waves,
> leaving behind his empty promises for the gale to dissipate.
> From afar, from the seaweed line, Minos' daughter, like a marble   60
> statue of a Bacchante, stares at him, ah, stares at him with
> sad eyes and is tossed on great waves of anguished emotions.
> She has lost the delicate headband from her blonde hair
> and the light dress that covered her chest
> and the smooth band that bound her milk-white breasts –   65
> all these have fallen everywhere from her whole body
> and the waves are playing with them at her feet.
> But at that moment she did not care about her floating
> dress and headband, but, ruined, was hanging on you,
> Theseus, with all her mind, all her heart, all her soul.   70
> Ah the poor girl, driven mad with constant grief by Venus,
> who sowed thorny cares in her breast,
> from the time when fierce Theseus, after leaving
> the winding shores of Athens' port,
> reached the Cretan palace of unjust Minos.   75

Catullus begins his narrative at the most dramatic and poignant point of the whole story. At 53f. for pathos he brings out the fact that Ariadne is still madly in love, contrasting her with Theseus, who feels nothing for her and, after using her, is getting away from her as fast as he can. The poet builds up further sympathy for her at 55f., where she can't believe her eyes because she has just woken up, confused and defenceless, and still loves Theseus and thinks he feels the same way, and in 57 with the combination of three sad details in rapid succession. Effectively the spotlight in this whole passage is very much on the heroine, although at 58f. there are two lines on Theseus (this is a contemptuous brevity: he does not deserve more than the briefest mention – just enough to make the situation and his cruelty clear). Line 60 underlines Ariadne's separation from him, and depicts her as having wandered down from higher up on the beach (where they slept) to the edge of the sea, trying to see the ship better and/or get closer to her man. She is then compared to a statue of a female worshipper of Bacchus. Like a statue she is silent and unmoving, with a fixed stare, and impervious to the weather. She also has the disordered clothing and frenzied emotions typical of Bacchantes (and like them she will soon be protected by and devoted to Bacchus, as his wife). At 61f. Catullus repeats for stress the verb 'stares' (this futile action is all she can do now) and adds her mournful eyes (picture them!) and his own exclamation of sympathy ('ah') to encourage the same reaction in his readers. He then includes a metaphor which suggests that Ariadne was in a turmoil, helplessly tossed to and fro by successive waves of powerful emotions. At 63ff. the loss of clothing (flimsy garments loosened for sleep and caught by the gale) makes her seem vulnerable, as Catullus reminds us that she is a beautiful princess with fine clothes, so that we will view her as somebody special and feel for her more. At 68–70 there is psychological insight: she does not care at all about her nakedness and her lovely clothes being spoiled because she is so wrapped up in the lover who is callously abandoning her (note the emphasis in the triple mind, heart and soul). In 71 the poet again shows his own involvement and encourages ours by referring to her as 'the poor girl'. He also brings out the wildness and painfulness of the passion that she felt for the hero from first seeing him in that line and in the metaphor in 72, which represents Venus as digging into the heroine's breast and then thrusting into it sharp, spiky thorns.

In *Heroides* 10 Ovid starts at the same point in the tale and also puts the focus on Ariadne, and it seems initially (at 1–34) that he is producing another sad account. In fact he expands on Catullus there to heighten the emotional impact. At 1–6 he adds the plaintiveness of the princess' protests to Theseus. At 7ff. he catches the moment of waking vividly and in more detail, and makes her speak, so that we can see (and hear) the scene in all its poignancy. At 25ff. he brings out even more the abandonment and isolation, as this Theseus has put even more distance between Ariadne and himself (she has to climb a cliff to see his sails). So it looks as if in his response to Catullus 64 Ovid is not just giving the narrative a new (epistolary) form but also aiming at outdoing the pathos in his source. And he does achieve that at 1–34, to show that he can do it. But he is also mischievously misleading us there with a lengthy tease about his real attitude to this episode. At 35–42 he suddenly undercuts the mournful mood, as (mindful of the happy ending) he brings in a flurry of frivolous points and starts to give his version a different (tragicomic) tone. The levity begins with Ariadne's cries at 35f. directed at the parting ship and pointing out that it was a person short (as if Theseus could hear her all that way off, and as if he didn't realize that he had sailed away without her!). It continues with her actions in the following lines. At 37f. as her words are not loud enough to get to him she supplements them by beating her breasts, but the hero is hardly likely to hear those blows if he could not catch her shouts, and she must have been really pounding away if she wanted the sound of that to reach his ears (and Ovid works in some flippant verbal play in *verbera cum verbis*, which I have rendered with 'flailing and wailing'). At 39f. she engages in vigorous (and patently pointless) semaphore. At 41f. she resorts to a flag (which is equally futile, and looks like a witty twist by Ovid to the white sail that Theseus forgot to raise), and she is still labouring under the preposterous misapprehension that he could somehow have risen from the bed where he slept with her and then simply forgotten her.

In the rest of the poem amid the obvious pathos there are many more facetious flashes. The poet inserts grotesque touches in the picture conjured up in 77 of Theseus clubbing Ariadne to death, her references to the monstrous Minotaur as her brother (77, 135), the idea of seabirds eating her corpse and so becoming her tombs (123f.) and the (surreal) enormously long hands that she stretches out over the sea to Theseus in Athens at 145f. The princess herself indulges in sarcastic wit over Theseus' heart being so hard that it would be proof against the Minotaur's horns (107ff.) and over the honour he won in deserting her (130). More often she says unintentionally amusing things. So in 75 she wonders if she is alive, when she is alive enough to be composing this letter. In 87, with real bathos, she is terrified of being attacked by seals. In 136 she ludicrously depicts herself as penning this epistle while clinging to a sea-beaten rock (and so it's no wonder that she is shivering and producing shaky writing at 139f.) and then portrays herself (so alluringly!) as partially bald in 147. See if you can spot similar silliness at 55–8 and 111–18. In addition, many lines are entertaining when one bears in mind the ending of the episode. So at 59–63 the answer to her questions about what should she do and where should she go is do nothing at all and stay exactly where you are (as Bacchus will be along shortly); when she complains that there is no sailor and no ship there, we recall that there will soon be a god there with a chariot; and when she speculates about possibly being given companions, we know that she *will* be given Bacchus and his companions any minute now. At 79f. she maintains that she is thinking about all the things that can happen to any abandoned woman, but she does not envisage what will happen to her. And at 133 she wishes that the gods had made Theseus look back and see her from his ship, but one of the gods will do much more than that for her in a moment. Look for similar irony and humour based on the actual outcome of the story at 48, 83–6, 95, 96 and 119–24. You might also ask yourself why Ovid subverts Catullus 64. Is it because he is incorrigibly lightweight and frivolous, or are there sound literary reasons for this?

Ovid was obviously taken with Ariadne as a subject and he returned to her in his poetry several times, relating different parts of her story, with different spins. In book 1 of his *Ars Amatoria* (a jocular poem of instruction on how to conduct a successful love affair) he introduces her in a digression, to show that Bacchus is a lover himself (and as such is favourable to love, providing the gift of wine and thus facilitating dinner-parties, which present numerous opportunities for advancing an affair). There the poet plays the same trick on readers about his attitude to the heroine, but not at such length. He begins this account with an air of supreme sympathy and sadness at the plight of the abandoned princess, and with several reminiscences of Catullus 64.52ff. to suggest that this version will be in the manner of his predecessor. Then, going for a gradual and smooth transition to humour this time rather than a sudden switch, he gives a few hints that he might not be so serious after all. At 533f. he talks of Ariadne's tears suiting her (passing such an odd and jarring comment on her attractiveness at this point makes one suspect that he can't be entirely in earnest); and in 535 he notes that the breasts that she was beating in grief were extremely soft (that voluptuous and appreciative comment is subtly disruptive and suggests that he isn't all that sorrowful). Then in 537 as soon as her question (about what will happen to her) is out of her mouth it is answered, as

Bacchus' retinue makes a dramatic entrance and we are reminded at once of what will happen to her (she will be carried off by the god). Now the levity surfaces fully, and gaiety and fun dominate the remainder of the passage, with particularly diverting touches in the antics of drunken Silenus (an old, Satyr-like divinity of the countryside), in Ariadne's melodramatic swoon at 539f. and her inappropriate reaction later to Bacchus (her saviour and future husband) and in his handling of her (the god turns out to be a fast worker and a smooth operator, eloquent and masterful). By way of a change from *Heroides* 10, this time after the deception is over there is just humour (with the addition of lots of farce), and in this narrative the poet concentrates on the advent of Bacchus and his attendants and the happy ending.

The girl from Crete was wandering, distraught, on unknown sands,
    where tiny Dia is pounded by the sea's waves.
Just as she was, straight from sleep, dressed in a loosened
    tunic, barefoot, her blonde hair unbound,   530
she kept on shouting 'Cruel Theseus!' to the deaf waves,
    as an undeserved downpour of tears drenched her tender cheeks.
She kept on shouting and weeping together, but both suited her;
    she was not made less attractive by her tears.
Beating her breasts (which were extremely soft) again, she said: 535
    'That traitor has gone away – what will happen to me?'
As she said 'What will happen to me?' cymbals sounded along
    the whole shore and tambourines struck by frenzied hands.
She fainted from fear, breaking off what she'd just been saying;
    the blood drained from her swooning body.   540
Look – Bacchantes, their hair tossed on to their necks;
    look – lively Satyrs, the retinue that precedes the god;
look – drunken old Silenus only just keeps his seat on a sagging
    ass and skilfully grips and holds on to its mane.
While he pursued the Bacchantes, and they ran away
    and towards him,   545
    while the poor horseman urged on his mount with a stick,
he slipped from the long-eared ass and fell on his head;
    the Satyrs shouted: 'Come on, dad, get up, get up!'
Now in his chariot canopied with grape-clusters the god
    held the golden reins loosely over his team of tigresses.   550
Ariadne went pale, forgot Theseus and lost her voice;
    three times she tried to flee and was restrained by fear.
She trembled, like barren corn-ears stirred by the wind,
    as a light reed shivers in a watery marsh.
To her the god said: 'Here I am – a more faithful lover.   555
    Don't be afraid. You'll be Mrs. Bacchus from Crete.
Have the sky for your gift: there you'll be gazed at as a star;
    you'll often guide ships in doubt, as the Cretan Crown.'

> So saying, in case she was scared of the tigresses, he jumped down
>> from the chariot (the sand gave way to his foot's impress). 560
> Enfolded in his arms (not strong enough to fight), she was
>> carried off – gods can manage all kinds of things.
> Some sing the wedding-song, some shout Bacchic cries,
>> as the god and his bride come together in the sacred bed.

There are two other significant references to this myth in Ovid, where the poet again rings the changes. At *Metamorphoses* 8.169–82 he presents a summary of events from the Minotaur being shut up in the Labyrinth to Bacchus' rescue of Ariadne and her crown being turned into a constellation. There he covers more incidents than he does in any of his other accounts of this episode, and he adroitly packs them all into just 14 lines, with a much reduced role for the princess this time, and a witty compression of her lengthy complaints when deserted into just two words (*multa querenti* in 176). He concludes with a novel focus – on the actual process of her diadem's metamorphosis.

At *Fasti* 3.461ff. Ariadne is used in a different way – to explain the origin of the Cretan Crown constellation, whose rising has just been mentioned by Ovid in this poetic calendar. He takes her story further on here in a sequel which has no parallel and looks like a brand-new addition of his own. In this passage the heroine, now married to Bacchus, scolds herself for being upset over Theseus' ingratitude, as that had a fortunate conclusion for her. But then Bacchus returns from his conquest of India with a beautiful princess whom he finds very attractive and seems to have abandoned his wife for her. Ariadne goes off on her own and walks along the beach, weeping and complaining to herself at great length about her husband's treachery, wishing he would be true to her, asking him why he saved her on Dia and protesting that he used to promise her heaven. At the end (507ff.) it is suddenly revealed that the god had actually been there all along, quietly walking behind her and listening to her whining on about him and addressing him, and he kisses her tears away and now does actually give her a place in heaven, and transforms her crown into a group of nine stars. In addition to the comical picture conjured up, there is humour in Bacchus behaving rather as Theseus had but making things turn out well for Ariadne once more, and in the heroine criticizing herself for her ultimately inappropriate reaction to Theseus' treatment of her but then reacting in exactly the same ultimately inappropriate way all over again in connection with Bacchus' treatment of her (not having learned her lesson). There are also lots of clever and complex connections with the narratives in Catullus 64, *Heroides* 10 and *Ars Amatoria* 1 (on which see Murgatroyd 264ff.).

On later treatments of Ariadne see Grafton & Most & Settis 67f.

Heroides 11

CANACE TO MACAREUS

Now we are taken on to a letter which is consistently serious and sad, and which takes the form of a suicide note (compare *Heroides* 2) rather than a plea for the return of the addressee. This time the love is incestuous (compare *Heroides* 4), and a child has been born as a result of the affair, and taken off to die. And here there is no prospect of marriage and no happy ending in store.

Canace, daughter of Aeolus (the king who controlled the winds), fell in love with her brother Macareus and got pregnant by him. When the baby was born, her father found out about its birth and was furious. He ordered the child to be taken out to a lonely spot and left as prey for the wild animals, and he sent her a sword so she could kill herself. She writes this letter to Macareus as she is about to commit suicide, asking him to bury the remains of her son with her in a common tomb.

In a version of the story which may well have been known to Ovid and his readers Macareus approached his father and won a reprieve for Canace, then ran to tell her that, but arrived too late, and put an end to his life with the same sword that she had used on herself. So there could be added poignancy here, if we are to imagine that while Canace is writing this Macareus is winning a pardon from Aeolus for her and rushing to her with the good news, but not quickly enough.

> But if any of my words are unclear due to illegible smears,
>   it will be my blood that's smeared my letter.
> My right hand holds a pen, my left holds a drawn sword,
>   and an unrolled scroll of paper is placed on my knees.
> There's a picture for you of Canace writing to her brother,
>   one that I think might please my hard father.
> I could wish he was here in person to see my death and to
>   examine the suicide he's responsible for with his own eyes.
> He's cruel, and much more ferocious than his winds,

5

so he'd have looked on my death-wound with dry eyes.   10
Living with the savage gales under his command has to have
     an effect, and his character now matches theirs.
He controls the South Wind, the West, the Thracian
     North and the winged and violent East.
Ah, he controls those winds, but doesn't control his furious temper: 15
     his faults are even more extensive than his realm.
What good to me is my link to heaven via my ancestors
     and being able to count Jupiter among my relatives?
Does that make the sword I hold any less harmful (this
     deadly gift, this weapon unfit for a woman's hand)?   20
Oh, Macareus, how I wish that I'd died
     before we were joined together as one!
Brother, why did you ever love me as more than a brother,
     why was I to you what a sister shouldn't be?
I burned too, warming to you, and feeling some god in my   25
     heart, exactly as I'd often heard Him described.
My face was pale; I'd lost weight and grown thin;
     I was eating very little, forcing it down;
sleep wasn't easy, each night was as long as a year,
     and I kept on groaning, though not in physical pain.   30
I couldn't explain to myself why I was doing all this;
     I didn't know what a lover was, but I was one.
My old nurse first sensed what the trouble was;
     my nurse first said to me: 'Canace, you're in love.'
I blushed and looked down at my lap in embarrassment –   35
     indicative enough of a confession, even though I said nothing.
Then, no longer a virgin, I was pregnant. My womb was secretly
     swelling, weighing me down and making me tired.
My nurse brought all kinds of herbs and all kinds
     of medications and boldly inserted them,   40
to abort (this was my only secret from you)
     the foetus that was growing inside my womb.
Ah, too full of life, the child resisted the techniques
     used against him by his hidden enemy and survived.
Now after nine months a new Moon (the Sun's exquisite   45
     sister) was driving her glittering chariot across the sky:
I didn't know the reason for the sudden pains inside me;
     I was a raw recruit, with no experience of childbirth.
I cried out, couldn't keep quiet. My old accomplice said: 'Don't
     give your guilty secret away!' and covered my mouth.   50
Ah, what could I do? The pain made me groan, but the
     nurse and my fear and shame itself told me not to.
I stopped groaning, tried to take back the words I'd let slip

and forced myself to swallow my tears.
Death was before my eyes, the goddess of childbirth wouldn't
   help me,   55
   and, if I died, my death would also reveal my great guilt;
but you leaned over me (your tunic and hair torn in grief),
   pressed your chest on mine, warming me back to life,
and said to me: 'Sister, live, my dear, dear sister, live;
   don't kill two people by letting one body die!   60
Take strength from hope of something good: you'll marry your brother
   and be his wife as well as the mother of his baby.'
I was dead, believe me; but I revived at your words,
   and gave birth to that child of sin.
Why so glad? Aeolus was seated in the heart of the palace,   65
   and we had to sneak away from him the proof of my sin.
My nurse carefully concealed the infant under corn-ears,
   white olive-branches and slender headbands,
pretended to be performing a rite and spoke words of prayer;
   the people and my father himself made way for the rite.   70
She was near the doorway – the baby cried, revealing himself,
   betraying himself, and my father heard.
Aeolus snatched up the infant, exposing the fictitious rite;
   the palace resounded with his roars of fury.
As the sea ripples when grazed by a light breeze,   75
   as an ash-tree's branch quivers in the warm south wind –
you'd have seen my pale body trembling just like that;
   I set the bed quivering beneath me.
He rushed in, shouting about my disgrace for all to hear,
   and scarcely keeping his hands off my miserable face.   80
I was ashamed, and speechless. All I could do was weep;
   my tongue was paralyzed by chilling fear.
Now he'd ordered his little grandson to be abandoned
   in some lonely spot, as prey for dogs and birds.
The poor boy wailed – you'd have thought he understood –   85
   and begged his grandfather, the only way he could.
How do you think I felt then, brother –
   you can gather that from how you feel yourself –
when I watched my enemy take my own flesh and blood into
   the towering forest, to be eaten by mountain wolves?   90
He left the room. Then finally I could beat my
   breasts and tear my cheeks with my nails.
Meanwhile one of my father's attendants arrived, with a sad
   look on his face, and spoke these shameful words,
handing me a sword: 'Aeolus sends this, and says what   95
   you've done must make you realize what it's for.'

I do realize, and I'll use that savage sword bravely,
    burying my father's present in my chest.
Is this the gift that you give me away with, father?
    Is this the dowry that will make your daughter rich?   100
Marriage-god, you've been foiled; take your wedding-torches
    and run far away from this evil place in horror.
You black Furies, bring me your torches and
    light my funeral pyre with their flames.
My sisters, I hope you have better luck and are happily married;   105
    but remember me after death takes me from you.
The child's a few hours old – what crime did he commit?
    He's scarcely been born – how has he harmed his grandfather?
How could anyone think he could possibly deserve to be killed?
    Oh, the poor boy's being punished for *my* crime.   110
Ah, my son, how I grieve for you – the prey of frenzied wild
    animals, torn apart on the day you were born.
Son, you pitiful proof of a doomed love, this
    was your first day of life and this was your last.
I wasn't allowed to shed over you the tears I owe you   115
    or to offer shorn locks of my hair at your tomb;
I didn't lean over you and take kisses from your cold lips.
    Ravenous wild animals are rending my own flesh and blood.
I'll stab myself and follow the ghost of my baby;
    I won't be called a mother or bereaved for long.   120
Macareus (the husband your poor sister hoped for pointlessly),
    please gather up the scattered remains of your son,
bring them back to his mother and put them with me in my tomb;
    let one urn, however small, hold the ashes of us both.
Live on, remembering me, and shed tears on my wound;   125
    lover, don't recoil from the body of the girl who loved you.
Please carry out the instructions of the sister you cared for
    too much; I will obey the instructions of my father.

    In Ovid's day most people viewed sexual relations between close relatives with
revulsion, and marriage between them was prohibited in law. So accusations of
incest were used to attack political opponents. In the middle of the first century
BC, to raise a laugh and to smear his personal enemy Clodius, Cicero in his speech
Pro Caelio implied an incestuous connection between Clodius and his sister Clodia,
referring to him as 'the woman's husband – I'm sorry, I mean brother – I always
make that slip.' Incest is also part of the negative tradition concerning several of
the emperors, like Caligula and Nero in the first century AD. Agrippina engineered
the succession of her young son Nero, so that she could be the power behind the
throne, but he became estranged from her. According to the historian Tacitus it
was said that she tried to retain power through incest, offering herself to her son

when he was drunk, and exchanging lascivious kisses with him (and when he subsequently murdered her he examined her dead body and praised its beauty). Some years before that Caligula was supposed to commit incest regularly with each of his three sisters in turn. The biographer Suetonius has lots of anecdotes in that connection. He tells us that Caligula's favourite sister was Drusilla, and he ravished her while he was still a minor and was caught in bed with her by their grandmother. Later, when she married, he took her from her husband and openly treated her as his wife. When she died, he declared a period of public mourning, during which laughing, bathing and dining with one's family were punishable by death. Afterwards, whenever he had to swear a public oath, he swore by the divinity of Drusilla. He didn't love the other sisters so much, and often let his boyfriends sleep with them.

Ovid, who was interested in unusual and perverse forms of love, had handled the rather lurid topic of incest in *Heroides* 4 and would return to it in the *Metamorphoses*. As you know, he liked to set himself challenges and demonstrate his versatility. So here, after being outrageously flippant about Phaedra's passion in *Her.* 4, he turns things right around and is serious about the subject. He also builds sympathy for an incestuous lover (a figure most would find repellent). Look at the letter again to see for yourself how he does that, and then move on to the next paragraph, where we offer our analysis of that process.

Ovid uses a range of techniques to make someone who is guilty of incest (and pregnant as a result) not just acceptable to readers but also affecting. For a start there is omission of potentially alienating material: there is nothing on the actual act of sex, no sensuality, no sloppy endearments and, although the heroine does accept that what she has done is wrong, there is no condemnation of it as something repulsive and terrible (rather she and Macareus are very much in love and want to get married). The timing of the letter is significant too: their misdemeanours are in the past, and the princess is now on the point of suicide, after all the upset of the failed abortion (attempted out of fear), the painful and dangerous birth, the discovery of the baby, the death-sentence for her and the loss of the child she has come to love, without even a chance to bury or mourn for him. Placement is also effective: this epistle is even sadder for coming right after *Her.* 10 with its humour and happy ending in the background; and Canace seems still more innocent and touching in contrast to the earlier incestuous female in the collection (the experienced, lustful and harmful Phaedra of *Her.* 4). Aperture plays a part: Canace foregrounds her enforced suicide and the cruelty of her father, creating compassion for herself for twenty lines before she even mentions her relationship to her brother. And from line 73 to the end of the poem (providing an aptly gloomy frame) the emphasis is on Aeolus' murderous rage, which extends to his own daughter and an innocent infant. There is cumulative impact in such a long passage on that, and there is particularly poignant closure at 111ff. The narrator is important too, as the heroine obviously gives her own colouring to her presentation of events and depicts herself in a positive light (much more a victim of her father than an incestuous lover). Many critics have been moved by the Canace on show here, and Jacobson 163 characterizes her as 'loving, gentle, delicate, pitiful, yet with a carriage of dignity, quiet resolve, and resignation.' We would add that she also comes across as naive and vulnerable, and tragically feels guilty over her part in her baby's death (110). That self-portrayal is reinforced by the sympathy shown for the heroine by the nurse and by Macareus, which subtly encourages a similar reaction in readers.

Ovid returned to the topic of incest later and handled it differently yet again, taking a whole new tack. At *Metamorphoses* 10.300ff. we find the tale of Myrrha, a beautiful Arabian princess who fell in love with her own father and had sex with him in his darkened bedroom (without the king knowing who the girl in his bed really was). When he finally found out, she fled to escape his homicidal fury and was subsequently turned into the myrrh-tree. Her story is told by Orpheus, the famous musician of Thrace, who failed to recover his dead wife from the Underworld, and who then turned his back on women, singing a series of songs which celebrated love for boys and showed females in a much less favourable light. The extensive contrasts with the treatment of incest in *Her.* 11 make Ovid's mitigating techniques in the epistle stand out clearly. In the *Metamorphoses* passage we see a deeply critical attitude to incest and to the incestuous girl, put in the mouth of an unsympathetic narrator (unlike Canace). He gives a very negative thrust to his account at the start, and he constantly describes Myrrha's behaviour as evil and invests it with revulsion. Orpheus begins his narrative as follows:

> 'This story is horrific. Daughters and fathers, keep well away from it;   300
> or, if you can't resist my song, give no credence to this
> part of it, don't believe that this happened; or, if you do
> believe that it happened, believe that it was punished too.
> However, if nature allows an outrage like this to be witnessed,
> I congratulate the people of Thrace and this part of the world,   305
> I congratulate this land, on being far away from those regions
> which engendered such evil. Arabia's myrrh surpasses all
> its balsam, cinnamon and costum, its frankincense exuded
> from trees, and its other flowers, but the crime that was
> involved in acquiring this new tree was too great.   310
> Myrrha, Cupid personally denies that his arrows wounded you
> and says that his torch had nothing to do with your offence.
> One of the Furies blasted you with a firebrand from Hell
> and her venomous vipers: it's a sin to hate a parent,
> but your love is a greater sin than hatred.'   315

Orpheus goes on to say that when she realized that she was lusting after her own father, Myrrha tried to talk herself out of it, but used specious arguments against the criminality of incest and did not succeed in suppressing her passion. She veered this way and that over what to do, couldn't sleep and decided to end her shame by hanging herself. Her old nurse, on guard outside the bedroom door, heard her preparations for suicide and rushed in to stop her. When she pressed Myrrha, to find out why she wanted to kill herself, the princess finally confessed to her wicked love for her father. The nurse shuddered in horror and tried to persuade her to give it up. But Myrrha said she would kill herself if she couldn't satisfy her desire, so the nurse decided to help her. While the queen was away at a festival, the nurse informed the king that there was a beautiful young girl who wanted him, and he told her to bring the girl to his bedroom that night. Myrrha was made uneasy by a presentiment of evil, but set off at midnight to commit the crime. At this point Orpheus builds atmosphere, an aptly dark and ill-omened atmosphere:

'She was coming to her crime. The golden moon fled from the sky,
which was totally black; the stars hid behind dark cloud, and of them
the two which first covered their faces were Icarus and Erigone   450
(who'd been raised to the heavens for her devoted love for her father).
Three times Myrrha was checked by an inauspicious stumble; three
times a funereal screech-owl sang its ominous song of death.
But she went on, her shame lessened by the shadows and black night.
Her left hand clung to her nurse, and she moved her right hand in front   455
of her, blindly feeling her way. Now she reaches the bedroom,
now she opens the door, now she's led inside. But her knees
shake and give way, the blood drains from her face, she
goes pale, and her courage fails her as she advances.
The closer she is to the crime, the more she shudders, regretting   460
her rashness, wishing she could go back unrecognized.
As she hesitated, the old woman led her by the hand to the
high bed. As she handed her over, she said: 'Take her,
Cinyras, she's yours,' and brought the doomed couple together.
The father took his own flesh and blood into that bed of horror,   465
encouraging the frightened girl and calming her fears.
And perhaps he called her 'daughter' (in keeping with her youth)
and she called him 'father', so words would compound the crime.
Filled with her father, she left the bedroom, bearing his evil
semen in her hideous womb, the child conceived in sin.   470
They committed the same crime the next night, and on others after that.
Finally Cinyras, eager to know the mistress with whom
he'd copulated so often, brought in a lamp and saw his
daughter and the terrible thing he'd done. Speechless, appalled,
he snatched the gleaming sword from the scabbard hanging nearby.   475
Myrrha ran off, and escaped death thanks to the
night's murky darkness.'

Orpheus then tells how she wandered beyond her father's kingdom, exhausted, afraid of death but sick of life. Finally she prayed to the gods, saying that she repented and saw that she deserved a dreadful punishment, but asking them to change her into another form, in case she contaminated by contact the living if she survived and the dead if she died. A god heard her and changed her into the myrrh-tree. When she went into labour, the goddess of childbirth split the tree-trunk, and so her baby was born – the beautiful Adonis (whose story Orpheus goes on to tell).

Before that passage Ovid had also handled the theme of incest at *Metamorphoses* 9.454ff. (on Byblis' love for her brother). The usual variation is in evidence. Contrast the narratives about Myrrha and Byblis, looking for differences in connection with the narrator and his attitude, the characterization of the heroine and the actual events of the two episodes. If you need help with this or want to go into it in more detail, see Nagle.

There would have been added interest for Ovid's Roman readers in comparing his Aeolus with another version of that character, in Virgil's *Aeneid*, and Ovid carefully directs us to that epic Aeolus by means of a clear verbal echo in line 65 (*media sedet Aeolus aula* 'Aeolus was seated in the heart of his palace' recalls *Aeneid* 1.56 *celsa sedet Aeolus arce* 'Aeolus is seated on a lofty peak'). Typically Ovid goes in for modification (Virgil's king of the winds is a bachelor and submits to a female) and especially deflation (the Virgilian Aeolus is a god; he comes across as a very impressive figure in view of his power over the mighty winds and the momentous storm that he causes; and he is not depicted as cruel and nothing more than a stern father).

In book 1 of the *Aeneid* Juno, the queen of the gods and an implacable enemy of Aeneas and the other survivors of the fall of Troy, catches sight of them sailing close to Italy, where they are destined to settle and prosper. She is incensed at that, and decides to attack the Trojan fleet with a violent storm (even though she cannot stop what is fated, she is malevolent enough to want to cause them major problems and delay them). To achieve this, she approaches Aeolus, the minor god in charge of the winds.

> Turning over these thoughts in her blazing heart, the goddess 50
> came to Aeolia, the land of clouds, a region filled with
> frenzied gales. Here king Aeolus masterfully
> curbs and confines and keeps imprisoned in a huge cavern
> the battling high-winds and bellowing hurricane-blasts.
> As they roar resentfully round the barriers, the mountain reverberates 55
> with mighty rumbles. Aeolus is seated on a lofty peak,
> holding his sceptre, and soothes their passion and restrains their rage.
> If he didn't, they'd certainly seize and rush away with
> land, sea and boundless sky and sweep them through space.
> Almighty Jupiter, fearing this, hid them away 60
> in a gloomy cave and settled soaring, massive mountains
> on top and assigned a king who'd keep to a fixed agreement
> and know how to rein them in and let them run free, as ordered.

Chillingly the proud queen of heaven hates the Trojans so much that she is prepared to lower herself and coax a lesser deity. In the speech to Aeolus that follows she is calculating and employs a variety of approaches. Initial friendliness and flattery are combined with subtle reminders of her status and power. Next she uses strong language to make her request forceful, and rather intimidating too. Then comes the offer of a lovely nymph as a wife, well aimed at a lonely bachelor. In his appropriately shorter speech Aeolus shows some self-importance, but above all awe and deference, and readily accepts Juno's offering. Ominously she has now succeeded in enlisting the help of another god to get her way, and now a terrible tempest is unleashed by Aeolus to fall on the Trojan fleet and drive it all the way to Africa (to Dido's Carthage).

> Juno now used on him these words humbly:
> 'Aeolus, the father of gods and king of men gave you   65
> the power to calm the waves and raise a swell with the wind.
> A race that is my enemy is sailing the Etruscan Sea,
> transporting into Italy Troy and its conquered gods.
> Batter your winds berserk, smother and sink their ships,
> or scatter those aboard and strew the sea with their bodies.   70
> I possess fourteen nymphs with exquisite bodies,
> and out of them all the loveliest one is the beautiful Deiopea.
> I'll unite you in lasting wedlock and formally make her yours.
> To repay the great favour I ask, she'll live with you for all
> the years to come and make you the father of beautiful children.'   75
> Aeolus replied: 'Oh, your majesty, your task is
> to decide what you want; my duty is to perform your commands.
> I owe to you this little realm of mine, this sceptre
> and Jupiter's goodwill. It's thanks to you I can feast with the gods.
> You make me the lord of storm-clouds and hurricane-blasts.'   80
> So saying, he reversed his spear and struck the side of the
> cavernous mountain. Like an army in line, the winds whirled out
> through the exit provided, swirling and sweeping across the land.
> They swoop on the sea. Together the South and East Winds
> and the South-West Wind with squall after squall heave all of it up 85
> from its lowest depths, and roll to the shore enormous waves.
> Now men are screaming and rigging is screeching.
> Clouds abruptly snatch away the daylight and the sky
> from the eyes of the Trojans. Black night settles on the water.
> There's thunder from pole to pole, and the sky keeps flickering with fire. 90
> It all holds out the threat of instant death for the men.

As you are working from a version of the *Heroides* in English rather than from the original Latin, it is important for you to have an idea of this translation's aims and methods and to realize that there are different types of translations. You should also be aware of the potential hazards of relying on translators, who have their own strengths, weaknesses and agendas (you are at their mercy, and this serves you right for not learning Latin!). Examination of a sample passage from *Heroides* 11 should be illuminating.

Look first at this literal translation (keeping very close to Ovid's Latin) of lines 55–66:

> Death was before my eyes, and Lucina denied aid   55
>   – and, if I had died, death too would have been a serious indictment of me –
> when, leaning over me, with torn tunic and hair,
>   you warmed back to life my chest pressed by yours
> and said to me: 'Live, sister, oh my dearest sister,
>   live, and don't destroy two by means of the body of one.   60
> Let good hope give strength; for you are going to be married to your brother.
>   You will be the wife also of the man through whom you are a mother.'
> Dead (believe me), nevertheless I revived at your words,
>   and the crime and burden of my womb was born.
> Why do you congratulate yourself? Aeolus sat in the middle of his palace;   65
>   my crime had to be secretly removed from the eyes of my father.

Obviously that literal translation is at several points clumsy, stilted and obscure (which Ovid's Latin was not), and in this way it actually erects a barrier between the reader and the poem. The version in our book is aimed primarily at Classical Civilization students and is meant to be reliable but also readable and readily intelligible. Consequently it works in some brief explanation of references (like Lucina), but it does not introduce anything that is not present or implicit in the Latin. It does not omit anything significant either. It goes for a couplet for couplet correspondence and tries not to sound too prosaic or flat. Compare our version (reprinted below) with the literal translation above to see how well it meets those aims.

> Death was before my eyes, the goddess of childbirth wouldn't help me,   55
>   and, if I died, my death would also reveal my great guilt;
> but you leaned over me (your tunic and hair torn in grief),
>   pressed your chest on mine, warming me back to life,
> and said to me: 'Sister, live, my dear, dear sister, live;
>   don't kill two people by letting one body die.   60
> Take strength from hope of something good: you'll marry your brother
>   and be his wife as well as the mother of his baby.
> I was dead, believe me; but I revived at your words,
>   and gave birth to that child of sin.
> Why so glad? Aeolus was seated in the heart of the palace,   65
>   and we had to sneak away from him the proof of my sin.

There are also other kinds of non-literal translation. So, for example, the English poet John Dryden (1631–1700) produced a rendering of this poem which in terms of elevation and imaginative use of language far surpasses the one in this book. However, it is not as easy to read or as close to the Latin, as you can see from his lines representing the same passage.

> Death was in sight, Lucina gave no aid;
> And e'en my dying had my guilt betray'd.
> Thou cam'st, and in thy count'nance sate despair;
> Rent were thy garments all, and torn thy hair:
> Yet feigning comfort, which thou couldst not give,
> (Prest in thy arms, and whisp'ring me to live:)
> For both our sakes, (saidst thou) preserve thy life;
> Live, my dear sister, and my dearer wife.
> Rais'd by that name, with my last pangs I strove:
> Such pow'r have words, when spoke by those we love.
> The babe, as if he heard what thou hadst sworn,
> With hasty joy sprung forward to be born.
> What helps it to have weather'd out one storm?
> Fear of our father does another form.
> High in his hall, rock'd in a chair of state,
> The king with his tempestuous council sate.
> Through this large room our only passage lay,
> By which we could the new-born babe convey.

Dryden wanted to produce versions which would be pleasant and entertaining for people of good sense who were not scholars, and which would be eloquent and graceful, indulging in some liberty of expression where necessary, while conveying the sense of the Latin and the spirit of the author. In the above lines he went for what contemporary readers would have viewed as poetry. This involved quite lofty diction and rhyme (hence the insertion of the third and fifth lines above, which are not in Ovid). Hence also the 'noble' sentiment in the gratuitous addition of the verses on the power of words and the baby springing forward to be born. Dryden also tried to minimize any offence to delicate sensibilities by omitting Ovid's remarks about Canace being the mother of her brother's baby and the child being the crime of her womb. Dryden's final four lines represent a lengthy expansion to explain the point of Ovid's reference to Aeolus seated in the palace, so that readers can follow the drift more easily, and he also takes the opportunity to introduce some more sublimity there while he is at it. Compare Dryden with the literal translation to see if you can spot more of this type of thing.

Heroides 12

MEDEA TO JASON

In contrast to *Heroides* 11 this much longer letter is not a meek suicide note, and is not purely tragic (but has much dark humour as well as pathos). The situations are dissimilar too (Medea is far from her family, and is not in an incestuous relationship, but has been jilted by her husband), and so are the natures of the writers (Medea is hard, pro-active and powerful).

For the earlier part of Jason's quest for the Golden Fleece see the introduction to *Heroides* 6. Because she had fallen in love with Jason, Medea agreed to the request to help the Argonauts made by her sister Chalciope (whose sons had been rescued by the Greek heroes and had joined them), and she enabled Jason to perform the tasks set by her father Aeetes and to seize the Fleece, and then she sailed off with him back to Greece, getting married to him on the way. However, when Jason presented the Golden Fleece to Pelias in Thessaly, the king went back on his word and refused to give up his kingdom. Medea then pretended to quarrel with her husband, took refuge with Pelias' daughters and got friendly with them. She offered to use her magic to make Pelias young again if his daughters killed him, but when they did that, she did not rejuvenate him. She and Jason fled and ended up in the wealthy city of Corinth in central Greece. They settled there and had two sons, but after all Medea's help Jason suddenly left her to marry Creusa, daughter of Creon (the king of Corinth). Medea was enraged and began to make threats, so was sentenced to exile by Creon along with her children. She pretended to accept banishment for herself, but begged Jason to see if he could persuade the royal family to let the boys escape exile. She persuaded him to go with them to Creusa with gifts from her – a fine robe and crown, ostensibly to win her over. In fact the robe and crown were impregnated with a napalm-like magic substance, and when she put them on they stuck to her and burned her to death. Creon turned up and in his grief embraced his dead daughter, only to be burned to death too by the same substance. Medea set the palace on fire, and then, to hurt Jason further, she killed their two sons, and denied him access to the bodies, flying off to her refuge in Athens on a chariot drawn by dragons, which her grandfather (the sun-god) had given her.

Heroides 12 is written just as Medea is starting to utter the threats that lead to the decree of banishment from Corinth and before she has finalized her plans for revenge.

> But (I remember) though a princess of Colchis, I found time
> > for you when you asked me to help with my magic.
> The Fates, who spin the thread of a mortal's life,
> > should have ended mine and killed me then.
> I could have died well then. All my life   5
> > since that time has been punishing.
> Oh, why did the Argo ever go in quest of the
> > Golden Fleece, rowed by its young crew?
> Why did we Colchians ever set eyes on that ship
> > and you Greeks drink from our river Phasis?   10
> Why did I find your blond hair and good looks
> > and your charming, lying tongue all too attractive?
> But I did. Otherwise when that unfamiliar ship
> > with its bold heroes had reached our shores,
> thoughtless Jason would have gone against the bulls' flaming   15
> > breath and scorched mouths without magic protection
> and would have sown the dragon's teeth (every one an
> > enemy) only to be cut down by his own crop.
> So much treachery would have died with you, you criminal,
> > and I'd have been spared so much suffering!   20
> I'll take what pleasure there is in attacking the ingratitude of
> > someone who's been helped – the only joy I'll get from you.
> You were told to sail your untried ship to Colchis
> > and landed in our prosperous kingdom.
> I was there what your new bride is here;   25
> > my father was as rich as hers is.
> Hers rules Corinth with its two seas, mine everything as far
> > as snowy Scythia at the far end of the Black Sea.
> Aeetes welcomed you young Greeks hospitably,
> > and you reclined on his embroidered couches.   30
> It was then that I saw you and found out what you were;
> > that was the start of my mental collapse.
> I saw you and died, I burned with a fire new to me,
> > like a pine-torch burning on an altar to mighty gods.
> You were handsome, I couldn't resist what was fated   35
> > for me, and my eyes were ravished by yours.
> You realized, you traitor. Who succeeds in hiding love?
> > It flares up clearly, giving itself away.
> You were told you had to put a yoke on the hard necks of

the fierce bulls, which weren't used to ploughing.   40
 They were Mars' bulls, with cruel horns and muzzles;
  they breathed forth terrifying fire;
they had feet of solid bronze and nostrils sheathed in bronze,
  which was also blackened by the blasts of their breath.
You were also ordered to scatter all over the field with your   45
  doomed hand seeds that would produce a horde of men
meant to attack you with weapons born along with themselves –
  a harvest hostile to the one who sowed it.
Last of all you had to elude by some ruse or other the
  sleepless eyes of the snake guarding the Fleece.   50
When Aeetes had finished, you all got up sadly from the
  purple couches, and the whole company retired.
What help to you then was mighty Creon, his daughter
  Creusa and her dowry – the kingdom of Corinth?
You went off, despondent. I watched you go with tears in my   55
  eyes, and with a faint murmur I wished you well.
I went to bed in my room, badly wounded by love,
  and spent the whole night long crying.
I saw before my eyes the bulls and the evil harvest;
  I also saw the serpent that never sleeps.   60
I felt both love and fear, and the fear increased the love.
  Next morning my dear sister came in
and found me lying face-down, with dishevelled
  hair, and everything wet with my tears.
She asked me to help the Argonauts; I granted Jason her   65
  request, and gave him what she begged.
There's a dark grove of pines and leafy oaks,
  which the sun's rays can scarcely penetrate;
in it there is – or was – a shrine to Diana, with a golden
  statue of her sculpted by foreign hand.   70
Do you recognize the place, or have you forgotten it as well as me?
  We met there, and you spoke first, treacherously:
'Fortune has given you complete control over my wellbeing;
  and my life and death are in your hands.
To be able to kill is enough, if you take pleasure in power itself;   75
  but you will win greater glory by saving me.
I beg you, by my troubles (which you can end), by your noble
  lineage and your divine grandfather (the all-seeing Sun),
by the triple face and secret rites of Diana,
  and by any other gods you Colchians may have,   80
young lady, have pity on me, have pity on my men;
  help me, and make me yours forever.
If by some chance you don't spurn a Greek for a husband

(but how could the gods be so very kind to me?),
I'll die, and my spirit will vanish into thin air,   85
    before I take to my bed any bride but you.
Let Juno the goddess of marriage be my witness
    and Diana whose marble shrine this is.'
Your speech (and this is just a small part of it) and the clasping
    of my hand touched my naive, girlish heart.   90
I also saw tears (they played their part in your deception);
    and I was just a girl, quickly taken in by your words.
You yoked the bronze-footed bulls without being burned,
    and ploughed the hard earth, as ordered,
and sowed in the furrows not seeds but envenomed teeth   95
    which produced warriors with swords and shields.
Even I, who'd given you the magic salve, sat there
    pale at the sight of the sudden armed men,
until (a miracle!) those earthborn brothers drew
    their weapons and fought each other.   100
Suddenly the sleepless sentinel, bristling with rustling
    scales, swept across the ground, coiling and hissing.
Where was your rich dowry and royal bride then
    and the Isthmus of Corinth that separates two seas?
I am now a barbarian in your eyes, after everything,   105
    I now seem to you a pauper, and malignant;
but I was the one who closed its fiery eyes in a magic sleep
    and gave you the Fleece to safely steal away.
I betrayed my father, gave up my throne and my country;
    my reward is being able to live here in exile.   110
A pirate from overseas plundered my virginity; I left
    behind a wonderful sister and a mother I loved.
But I didn't leave you behind, my brother, when I fled
    (this is the only place where my pen falters).
What I dared to do I don't dare to write down;   115
    I should have been hacked apart too, along with you.
With nothing to fear after that, I wasn't afraid to trust
    myself to the sea, though only a woman, and now a criminal.
Where is heaven's power? We deserve to be punished at sea –
    you for being deceitful, I for being gullible.   120
The Clashing Rocks should have crushed and smashed us,
    clamping us together in a bony embrace!
Or ravening Scylla should have drowned us as food for her dogs
    (Scylla should have harmed ungrateful men)!
Charybdis, who sucks in and spews out sea three times a day,   125
    should have drawn us under the waves off Sicily.
But you returned victorious and unscathed to Thessaly's cities

and laid the Golden Fleece before your country's gods.
Need I mention Pelias' daughters, who harmed their father out of
    devotion, their girlish hands hacking his body?   130
Though others criticize me, you must praise me:
    I've been forced to do wrong so often because of you.
You dared – I'm so angry (rightly angry) that the proper words
    fail me – you dared to say: 'Leave my royal home!'
I left your home, as ordered, taking along our two sons   135
    and my love for you (which is always with me).
Suddenly I heard the words of a wedding-song
    and saw brightly gleaming torches,
and a flute played the wedding-march for you two,
    a sound more mournful than a funeral dirge for me.   140
I was terrified. I didn't yet believe such wickedness existed,
    but still my heart was all cold with fear.
A crowd rushed up, shouting the wedding-chant repeatedly:
    the nearer the cry, the worse it was for me.
My slaves turned away, weeping, and hiding their tears: 145
    who'd want to pass on such terrible news?
It was better too for me not to know, whatever it was;
    but my heart was sad, as if I did know.
My youngest boy, either just by chance or because
    he was keen to see, stood at the front door.   150
He said: 'Mother, just come here! Father's leading a
    procession, dressed in gold and driving a chariot.'
Immediately I ripped my clothes and beat my breasts
    and scratched my face in grief.
I felt an urge to plunge into the crowd and tear   155
    the garlands from their neatly combed hair.
I scarcely restrained myself from tearing my hair, shouting
    'He's mine!' and grabbing hold of you.
I hope this delights the father I wronged, the Colchians I abandoned;
    let my brother's ghost accept this offering to him –   160
me deserted and deprived of my throne, country, home
    and husband, who was on his own everything to me.
So, I managed to subjugate serpents and mad bulls,
    but I could not subjugate this single man.
I repulsed fierce flames with my magic expertise,   165
    but I can't escape the fire of love myself.
My very skills and spells and herbs are deserting me;
    my powerful Hecate and her rites are quite useless.
I loathe the daytime, my nights are wakeful and hateful,
    soft sleep abandons me in my misery.   170
I can put to sleep a serpent, but not myself;

everyone profits from my industriousness more than me.
My rival is caressing the body I saved from death;
  she is enjoying the reward for my hard work.
Perhaps too, when you're trying to show off to your stupid   175
  wife and say things my enemy would like to hear,
you come up with new criticisms of my looks and my foreign ways.
  Let her laugh and take pleasure in my faults!
Let her laugh, lying on her purple couch, exalted –
  she will weep, burnt even worse than me.   180
So long as I have a sword and fire and magic potions,
  no enemy of Medea will escape vengeance!
But if by any chance pleas touch your heart of steel,
  hear what I have to say now, curbing my pride.
I'm begging you, as you often begged me;   185
  I'm kneeling at your feet without hesitation.
If you despise me, show some thought for our boys:
  a stepmother will be cruel, a terror to sons of mine.
They really look like you, I'm touched by the resemblance,
  and whenever I see them, my eyes fill with tears.   190
I beg you, by the gods, by my grandfather the Sun,
  by the boys (our mutual pledges) and all I've done for you:
be my husband again (I gave up so much for that, madly),
  be true to your word and repay my help to you.
I'm not asking you to face bulls and warriors or to use   195
  your powers to conquer and quiet a serpent;
I want *you* – I've earned you, you gave yourself to me
  and I became a parent along with you.
Do you ask where's my dowry? I paid it out on the
  field that you had to plough to win the Fleece;   200
and the spectacular, thick Golden Fleece is my dowry
  (if I asked for that back, you'd refuse);
and the survival of you and your crew is my dowry.
  Go on, compare the wealth of Corinth with that, you bastard!
It's thanks to me that you're alive and actually able to be   205
  ungrateful and have a powerful wife and father-in-law.
Soon you'll all be – but why tell you your punishment in
  advance? My rage will give birth to massive menace.
I'll go where rage takes me. I may regret what I do,
  but I also regret looking out for my unfaithful husband.   210
I'll leave that to the god who now has my thoughts in a turmoil.
  My mind is definitely devising something drastic.

Sadly, if understandably, love is not much in evidence in this letter. Medea does
mention her love for Jason, but usually sets it in the past, and only twice and briefly

does she say that she still feels that way about him (at 136 and 166, and in the latter case she wants to escape her passion). Love is overshadowed by other powerful emotions, like injured pride, jealousy, indignation, suspicion and bitterness. So most of the epistle is taken up with complaints and criticisms of Jason, and she does not get around to asking for a reconciliation until late in the letter. She has reached the point where love is nearly dead, hatred and desire for vengeance have nearly taken over and entirely justified anger is getting the better of her (this happens firstly at 175ff., and then more strongly at 207ff., so that the poem closes aptly and ominously with rage and revenge).

Medea's motivation for writing *Heroides* 12 is rather complex. As she herself states at 21–2, she wants to let off steam and get some satisfaction from giving Jason a piece of her mind. It would appear that she also wants to make him feel bad and hurt him, and worry him with her threats. She seems conflicted as well. She says that she still loves him, and she does ask him to get back together with her (at 183–206), but consciously or unconsciously she makes it very probable that he will refuse her request. She undermines it in advance with all the alienating censure and abuse. She surrounds it with threats, at 180–2 and 207–12, and Jason would come away from the letter with that latter passage (at the very end) uppermost in his thoughts. And as well as leaving it late she words her appeal in a way unlikely to win him back: she does not try to convince him that she will give up her resentment (in fact she makes digs during the appeal itself) or that she really loves him or that they will be happy together again, but unflatteringly demands him back as someone she has earned, and for the sake of the children. It looks as if this is his last slim chance for reconciliation and an escape from vengeance, and in her heart of hearts she would really rather he did not take it. He would then realize subsequently that he brought retribution on himself by his ingratitude and could actually have avoided it by accepting the offer in this letter, so that he might feel some personal responsibility.

That is all very sad and grim. Jacobson 109ff. sees only that in the poem, and as a result criticizes it for sameness and simplicity and calls it 'unfortunately dull'. But, as so often with Ovid, there are layers and nuances that make for interest and bite. This is in fact a typically dexterous and ingenious performance by the poet, and in addition to the emotional impact there are also important intellectual aspects. If *Heroides* 6 was a tragicomedy with the stress on the tragic, *Heroides* 12 is a tragicomedy with an emphasis on the comic (the darkly comic). His Medea is serious, but Ovid himself is having fun.

One of the interesting things that Ovid is doing here is giving us a new perspective. In *Heroides* 6 we had Hypsipyle's point of view, and she (naturally enough) gave us an entirely negative picture of Medea as a barbarian slut, a repellent witch, a treacherous, dangerous and murderous woman. What we get now is a much more positive version, as Medea tells her own story with her own colouring. She foregrounds her royalty and kindness, her misery and her regret at helping Jason, putting them at the start of her letter to give them prominence. She plays up all she has done for him and how badly he has treated her by going on at length about all that and returning to it repeatedly. She plays down the questionable and bad things she has done (the betrayal of her father and the murders of Apsyrtus and Pelias), passing over them quickly, and also intimating that her love for Jason was to blame in each case. She presents herself as a naive and vulnerable young girl who was taken in by his seductive words, and who has subsequently been caused great pain by being abandoned by him for a new wife.

This is all rather involving and provocative. Two (male) critics are not convinced by Medea's words here. Isbell 104f. describes her as 'a perfect model of depravity' and claims that she is not rehabilitated in the eyes of the reader and her argument is so flawed that she cannot be pitied. Jacobson 113 and 118–20 calls her a 'dastardly villain' and says that there is little good to be said for her and her personality is contemptible. What do you think? Is there truth in what Medea says here? Do you feel sorry for her at this point in her story to a greater or lesser extent? Is she the only (or the real) criminal in all of this? Use the text of *Heroides* 12 to support your case.

There are further connections between *Heroides* 12 and 6. For a start, there are obvious similarities. Both are letters to Jason written by heroines upset that they have been abandoned by him, along with their children, despite being married to him; and in *Heroides* 12 we find yet another woman who has fallen for his charm, tears and lying assurances. Readers may find these correspondences saddening and/ or amusing (these princesses never learn!). Certainly there is diverting irony in these links: for instance, Hypsipyle thinks herself so superior to the barbarian, but in fact she is much closer to her than she realizes; and Medea is enraged at being supplanted by a royal successor, but (as these parallels bring out) she herself is a royal successor who supplanted and enraged another. There are clever and entertaining twists too: for example, at 6.83ff. Hypsipyle complains that Medea enthralled Jason by means of magic, but at 12.163f. Medea complains that she could not do just that; and at 6.149f. the Greek wishes that she had committed murder, killing her rival, while in 12 we are reminded that the barbarian has already committed murder, and she will before long go on to kill her rival, exactly as she threatens in her letter. There are many other ties between 6 and 12, which you can find and explore for yourself. For some more of them, and for different ways of looking at them, see Lindheim 125ff. and Fulkerson 43ff.

There are funnier aspects, for those who have a nasty sense of humour. There are so many clear hints of what Medea is going to do that we are invited to feel a gleeful anticipation, reflecting on what a crazy fool Jason is to mess with a woman like this and how he is going to get his richly deserved come-uppance very soon. In particular the frequent references to fire, heat and burning are witty, in a way that makes you both cringe and smile, as they foreshadow the incineration of Creusa, Creon and their palace. The black comedy is in evidence from the very beginning of the poem in all the point and play and spin there. Look back at the first twenty verses and note the following. Lines 1–2 lead us to reflect that Medea will find time for Jason again soon, and will use her magic to hurt him rather than help him. At 3f. a murderess wishes that she had been killed herself! In connection with 5, if she didn't die well then, she can at least kill well (efficiently). In 6 she is talking of her life being punishing for her, but there will be more punishment, for Creusa, Creon and Jason. Along with Medea at 7–10, many others will wish that the Argo had never sailed to Colchis. In line 12 she criticizes Jason's charming, lying tongue not long before she charms him with her lies about the robe and crown being gifts to win over Creusa. At 15–18 there is the irony of Medea saving Jason's life only for him to ruin hers. In 18 the killer makes a joke about killing, with grim play on the crop cutting down rather than being cut down. In 19 she accuses another of being treacherous and a criminal! And 20 prompts the thought that many others would have escaped suffering too (at her hands).

The rest of the poem also contains the same kind of bleak humour and wit, often centring around her treachery, deceitfulness and ruthless murders. Examine, for example, Jason's speech at 73–88 for irony in him saying all that to Medea in the light of what he went on to do and what ensued from that (her attitude, actions and mastery of the situation in Corinth). And look at the words put into her mouth at 129–42, prefiguring the daring crimes that she will shortly commit.

There are variant versions of the rest of Medea's story. According to Ovid in his *Metamorphoses*, while taking refuge in Athens with king Aegeus, she married him. But when his illegitimate son Theseus turned up, she tried to poison Theseus unsuccessfully, and had to use her magic to summon up clouds or a mist so that she could escape death (it is not clear exactly how). Ovid leaves her disappearing mysteriously like that and says no more about her subsequent career. Other authors tell us that she went to the east, where Medus (her son by Aegeus or by an oriental king) became the founder of the powerful people called the Medes, and that she returned to Colchis, where her father had been dethroned, and returned him to royal power. At the end of her life she went to the paradise called Elysium and there married and lived with the great Greek hero Achilles.

It is interesting and instructive to consider the ethical aspects of the Medea myth and to ask ourselves if women should view Medea as an empowering role model. She does rise above gender stereotypes, asserting herself and exacting a well-deserved vengeance. But many would view her actual methods of avenging herself and the extent of her revenge as problematical. These are complicated issues.

Is Medea a feminist in *Heroides* 12? You can't get any more provocative than that when talking about the protagonist of this letter. On the one hand, Medea comes off as a woman demanding to be on an equal footing with Jason (at times seeing herself as a hero, e.g. at 181f.), but, on the other hand, she wishes to be restored as the hero's wife (so re-establishing her subordinate status). Some feminist readings unconvincingly see the duplicate nature of Medea's characterization as a means on the part of the heroine to re-attract Jason: Medea portrays herself at one moment as innocent like Jason's current love interest (Creusa), and in the next as a strong, independent woman like Jason's previous wife Hypsipyle (see further Lindheim 125ff. and Fulkerson 49). But Medea insults Creusa whenever she does mention her, so any parallel of naivety is lost (and is slim at best with only two references to Medea's innocence (99ff. and 111), which are placed in the past); and Jason abandoned Hypsipyle, so why would Medea compare herself to a loser? What's more, these readings do not take into account Medea's attacks on Jason – is Medea really trying to win the hero back, when she frequently hurls vitriolic remarks in his direction?

Clearly there is a two-sided depiction of Medea and, to a lesser extent, of Jason in *Heroides* 12, whereby each undergoes a reversal of gender roles. A long-standing tradition of gender-switching can be found in the Greek tragedies of Euripides and Aeschylus to reinforce the importance of the realities of people's roles in society, as Foley 148ff. has noted. But what about Ovid? This poet likes to push the envelope and, occasionally, poke fun at the idiosyncrasies of his characters. Here in Medea's appeal to Jason the reversal of the protagonist's role appears to be on steroids! It may well be that Ovid is ridiculing the tradition itself. In hyperbolic fashion, then, Ovid appears to be exploring the limits to which his character is both masculine and feminine.

The feminine persona of Medea unmistakably comes across in the varied and extreme emotions that she experiences and expresses in her letter. Complaints mixed with grief, fear and threats suggest that this heroine may not be entirely stable (an understatement!) now that Jason has rejected her. She even mentions the fact that upon meeting Jason her mental collapse started (at 32). She begins by complaining about how punishing life has been since she met and fell in love with Jason (5ff.). Medea recalls the inner turmoil she endured imagining Jason's defeat at the hands of her father (57ff.), her naive willingness to help him win the Fleece (89ff.) and her jealousy over Jason's repudiation of her and subsequent marriage to Creusa (133ff.). Fear for her children's future results in Medea's pleas to him to take her back (183ff.), but these pleas are quickly replaced by vindictiveness – she calls Jason a bastard who would be nothing without her (204). Finally, her vindictiveness culminates in a warning that her rage is uncontrollable, and is rather in the hands of the gods (211f.). Throughout, Medea oscillates between sorrow, panic and rage, with the rage taking over by the end of the letter.

Ovid further defines Medea as feminine by her role as 'other'. The poet plays up her aspect as a sorceress and her foreign background, traits that portray the heroine as strange or different, qualities which ultimately cast Medea in a negative light and, as a result, in a feminine one. So, repeated reference is made to Medea's use of magic, and her ability or inability to wield it. The letter opens with her aiding Jason by using her magic (2). She refers to her help as 'magic protection' (16) and a 'magic salve' (97), and tells how she defeated the obstacles placed before Jason with 'magic sleep' used against the serpent at 107 and 'magic expertise' used against the flames at 165. Mention of Diana/Hecate, the goddess of magic (at 69, 79 and 88) and reference (at 167f.) to how ineffective her magic powers are now at keeping Jason with her similarly point to Medea's strangeness and thus her otherness.

With almost equal frequency Ovid draws attention to Medea's otherness by allusions to her foreign background. In the opening line of the letter Medea calls herself a princess of Colchis, pointing to her status as a foreigner head on and suggesting that, even as this second-rate outsider, she still felt obliged to help Jason. She goes on to mention Colchians/Colchis four other times (9, 23, 80 and 159), really driving home the point that she is not Greek, unlike Jason's current squeeze. In comparison to Creusa, Medea charges that she herself is a barbarian in Jason's eyes (105) and imagines how he and his new wife mock her ways as foreign at 177. What sets her further apart is the label 'exile' (110) which Medea applies to herself. True, she is an exile from her homeland – that comes with the territory of betraying her father and killing her brother – but now she is an exile from her home and Jason, so she is 'other' even more than she thought she ever would be.

If Ovid portrays his Medea as feminine by means of her riotous emotions and otherness, then he wittily turns everything on its head when at the same time he also depicts her as masculine with aggressive and heroic qualities. She is a powerful figure – she repeatedly reminds Jason that it was her magic that enabled him to succeed. But Medea is powerful in other ways too. Despite her current regret, she writes how she was responsible for her brother's brutal murder (13ff.), she does not hesitate to mention how she opposed her father (109 and 159) and she warmly (pun intended!) refers to Creusa's upcoming demise at her hands (180).

Nowhere does Medea appear more masculine than when she seemingly presents herself as the hero. Three times the sorceress refers to Jason's tasks (15ff., 39ff. and 93ff.), each time with greater description and growing horror, and with each mention of them Medea points out either Jason's hopelessness or just how she enabled his success. Medea's masculine side comes across even more when she muses on how both she and Jason should have died a heroic death at sea – killed by the Clashing Rocks or Scylla or Charybdis (121ff.). Finally, Medea exclaims at 181f. that no enemy will escape her vengeance while she carries, of all things, a sword, and later at 197 she claims that she earned Jason; the sword, the word 'enemy' and the prize in the form of a person all belong to the very masculine heroic world in which apparently Medea sees herself.

Jason, on the other hand, comes across as a rather feminine character and, as a foil, contributes to our viewing the protagonist Medea in a masculine light. For instance, Jason is passive, even humble, at times. When Jason learns of the tasks, he is saddened (51) and despondent (55), and when he asks Medea for her help, Jason begs her (77ff.) and is described as having tears in his eyes (91). Moreover, any heroic qualities are absent from Jason. For instance, Jason's accomplishment of the tasks set by Aeetes is based on Medea's aid, and, when the tasks are described, the hero's contributions are minimal (e.g. the epic encounter between Jason and the earthborn men at 99f. is reduced to the earthly creatures *only* attacking each other; contrast Apollonius of Rhodes 3.1340ff.). Lastly, rather than giving a description in glowing terms, Medea refers to Jason as a criminal (19), a traitor (37), a treacherous speaker (72), deceptive (91 and 120), ungrateful (206) and unfaithful (210) – all negative terms more suited to the standard characterization of a feminine figure.

Finally, special attention ought to be given to the close of the letter, wherein Ovid manages an amusing coup de grâce regarding his characterization of Medea. The poet has spent a great deal of time craftily portraying the sorceress as a figure whose feminine traits are often overshadowed by masculine behaviour. Actually, up to this point Medea has been significantly masculinized, primarily by her own actions, not to mention the lacklustre description of Jason. But at 204ff. the heroine is shown at her worst/best, and, make no mistake about it, the illusion of a hermaphroditic Medea is shattered by the very feminine creature depicted there. Medea is irrational, mentioning her rage twice and claiming that her thoughts are in a turmoil. In her eyes, Jason is not only a bastard but also ungrateful and unfaithful. Lastly, she is menacing, threatening that what she is preparing is going to be horrific (in her words, massive and drastic). Ovid has built Medea up as heroic, more so than even Jason, so we may have anticipated a close with a masculinized Medea, but the poet quickly dispels this notion, playfully offering up an extremely off-putting, negative and, accordingly, incredibly feminine portrayal of Medea.

Do we have here an instance of feminism gone awry?

What do you think about Medea's killing of her children? We tend to gloss over the fact that Creusa is going to be murdered, and many readers might applaud Medea for the bad-ass she is for giving what for to Creusa, but what about her kids? Ovid doesn't describe the impending murder but rather alludes to it instead, allowing the reader to imagine the upcoming horrific fate of the hero's children. For all that Medea is a pathetic creature, treated poorly by her husband, abandoned after everything that she has given up and done for him, do you sympathize with her knowing that what she is about to do is so awful? Do you suppose that killing one's children was as horrible a crime in ancient times as it is today? And what do you think specifically of a mother being the culprit?

Here are a few things to consider as you develop your own thoughts about the crime. As Patterson 104f. astutely notes, while it is true that infanticide was practiced among the Greeks without penalty, the killing of a child already recognized as a member of the *oikos* (house) was subject to the laws of homicide. Sealey 278 takes great pains to point out that a homicide warranted different punishments depending on whether it was intentional or unintentional. In Classical Athens, the perpetrator of an intentional homicide was subject to death by the state, whereas a person guilty of involuntary murder was exiled, though a pardon could be sought afterwards.

In the western world today, the murder of a child, infant or otherwise, is considered a homicide, and the punishment varies depending on extenuating circumstances. But the mother as murderer adds a different dimension to the discussion. When we hear on the news that a mother has murdered her child, our first reaction tends to be one of stunned disbelief, followed by the question 'How could she do that to her own child?' We are outraged and find the act morally repugnant. The media tend to stay with the story for a few days, perhaps because of the incomprehensibility of the act, and further investigation often uncovers issues of mental illness. This revelation, of course, is followed by judicial procedures and some sort of penalty. In the case of Medea, however, it is worth noting that she is never punished for her children's murder by a court or by the gods. Actually, as the myth goes, she flees to Athens and devises other schemes of self-interest, and when she does die she marries Achilles and remains with him in the Elysian Fields (Apollonius of Rhodes 4.811–15).

It may come as a shock to learn that Medea is not punished, but she is, in fact, no longer a part of the society in which such punishment would take place. In ancient Greece, whether she was a daughter, sister or wife, the place of a woman was in her *oikos* (house). Women did not vote, nor did they have many duties or responsibilities outside of the home (aside from religious activities), especially if they were of the upper crust. So, a look at Medea through this sociological lens would reveal a woman who has long removed herself from her *oikos* and, accordingly, the constraints of society (see Foley 148ff. for more on the female/house vs. male/city in drama). Despite her present remorse, as indicated in the letter at 113ff., Medea willingly abandoned her role as daughter by betraying her father in order to help Jason – she deserted her *oikos* and, as a result, her place in society. So, when she murders her brother, it should come as no surprise.

While it is true that she does become Jason's wife, and so re-establishes herself within the *oikos*, it seems that once you abandon the *oikos* and society's norms, there is no return. Medea laments angrily the fact that Jason has ordered her and their children out of the *oikos* (133ff.), and it is now at this critical state of flux that we see the sorceress plotting. There is no going back to being a daughter, and though she begs to be a wife again to the hero, the insults that Medea spews at Jason (knowingly) undermine her efforts. What's left to her is her role as a mother, but because she is out of the *oikos* (as are her children) she appears not to be bound by her maternal role nor by society's laws which govern mothers. And so, by the end of *Heroides* 12 our last glimpse of Medea as she alludes to the imminent murder of her children is of her in her role as 'other'.

Medea was a very popular subject for ancient poetry, and interesting accounts of different parts of the myth were produced by famous authors like Pindar, Euripides, Apollonius of Rhodes, Seneca and Valerius Flaccus (on these see further Griffiths 14ff. and Clauss & Johnston). Ovid in particular was clearly fascinated by her. In addition to *Heroides* 6 and 12, he wrote a tragedy called *Medea* (of which sadly only two lines survive). He also devoted a whole poem (*Tristia* 3.9) to her murder of her brother. In it he describes how, after eloping with Jason and the Fleece, she slowed down her father's pursuit of them by killing and dismembering Apsyrtus, strewing his limbs far and wide, so they would take a long time to collect, and setting up his pale hands and bloody head on a high rock, so that her father would see them and stop to recover the body. Ovid also told her story from Jason's arrival to her disappearance after the attempt on Theseus' life at *Metamorphoses* 7.1–424, showing us in more detail the naive and vulnerable young girl who got entangled with a smooth operator and because of him and her experiences with him went to the bad herself (although here she already possessed in herself the seeds that led to her degeneration, like passion, pride and problems over self-control).

We will go into *Metamorphoses* 7 in more detail, to give you a fuller picture of Ovid's Medea and of some of the incidents only briefly mentioned or alluded to in the letter. In that long narrative the epic hero Jason is debunked from the start. His exploits on the way out to Colchis are minimized in the opening lines. So too, when it comes to the trials performed by him for Aeetes, his actions are played down, while the vital importance of Medea's aid is played up. Something similar happens when it comes to the seizing of the Fleece (which was hung up in a tree) prior to the return to Iolcus (the port in Thessaly from which Jason set out) at 7.149ff.:

> The remaining task was to drug with magic herbs the sleepless snake,
> a striking sight with its crest and three-forked tongue and   150
> hooked fangs, the dread guardian of the Golden Fleece's tree.
> After she had sprinkled on it a herb's soporific juice
> and recited three times words which bring peaceful slumber,
> which check heaving seas and rapid rivers, sleep came to
> those eyes which had never known it. The heroic son of Aeson   155
> seized the Fleece and, proud of this spoil, and taking with him
> as additional spoil the woman who gave it to him,
> he returned in triumph to the port of Iolcus with his wife.

Here the female is the real achiever, while Jason is undercut. Ovid begins by stressing how formidable the snake is, and then has *Medea* dispatch it (*she* is the one acting, and *her* even more formidable powers predominate). She takes them there and deals with the guardian, while Jason just nips in at the end to profit by all that. In view of that the designation of him in 155 seems decidedly mock-solemn. In the final few lines he starts to assert himself, but again he is undermined: he is absurdly proud of another's achievement; he regards her as a prize (a mere thing, on a par with the Fleece); he apparently does not thank her; and their marriage is minimized and passed over very quickly, suggesting something hurried and perfunctory.

When they are back in Greece, Ovid begins to stress still more the powerful sorceress side of Medea. When Jason begs her to extend the life of his aged father, she uses her magic to perform the miracle of rejuvenation, seeming more and more awesome, and a little frightening too. Then her evil aspects come to the fore, and she is depicted as chillingly manipulative, calculating, sadistic and ruthless, as she murders Pelias (for no stated reason) and employs his daughters (who have done her no harm at all) in the killing. There is real horror here, but also black humour. She pretends that she has broken up with Jason, takes refuge with Pelias' (comically gullible) daughters, wins their hearts with a show of friendship and is careful to mention the rejuvenation of Aeson. As their own father is old, they ask her to do that for him too (in fact begging her to slaughter their father, if they only knew it). She agrees, and then carefully sets up a trial run, killing a ram by cutting its throat, plunging it into a cauldron containing a magic mixture and swiftly and painlessly transforming it into a very young and healthy lamb. This performance is intended to impress and reassure the girls and to get them to countenance the murder of their father. It succeeds, and they beg her again to give him back his youth. Now we see how (deliciously) cunning and callous Medea is. She keeps the daughters in suspense for three days before proceeding with the operation (to make them keener to act). She puts Pelias to sleep, so they will find it easier to stab him. She comes out with a strong speech, urging them to action and playing on their devotion to their father. She allows Pelias at the end to awake from his magic sleep, so that he will see that he is being stabbed to death by his own daughters. And there is a final bit of cruelty, when she plunges Pelias into the cauldron, so that the girls will expect his rejuvenation, in vain.

> And now the king (and with him his guards) lay relaxed
> in a sleep like death, which had been produced by
> incantations and the power of Medea's magical tongue.   330
> His daughters, as ordered, entered the room with her and stood
> around his bed. She said: 'Cowards! Why hesitate now?
> Draw your swords and drain his old veins,
> so I can refill them with young blood!
> Your father's life and age are in your hands.   335
> If you have any love for him, and your hopes for him are real,
> do your duty by your father, use your weapons to free
> him from old age, stab him and make his blood flow!'
> That made those who loved him most the first to harm him,
> thinking it a crime not to commit this crime. But none could   340
> bear to watch herself wounding him. They averted their eyes,
> turned away and struck at him fiercely and blindly.
> Though streaming with blood and half-butchered, he raised
> himself on his elbow and tried to get out of bed. Encircled by
> so many swords, he stretched out his pale arms and said: 345
> 'Daughters, what are you doing? Who gave you weapons to kill
> your father?' Their courage and their hands faltered.
> Medea cut short his words by cutting his throat
> and plunged his mangled body into the hot water.

Again the girls are absurdly naive, not questioning why they rather than Medea should have to kill Pelias, or why they should all have to stab him and inflict many wounds, whereas a single stroke slit the ram's throat. And there is a grimly comic picture of them hacking away at him blindly in 341f. Medea's nasty sense of humour is also in evidence, as she has fun about their father's life in their hands in 335 and teases them about their hopes in 336. We can also see the poet's own wit here, in the verbal play at 339f. and 347f., and in the stupid question that he puts in the mouth of Pelias at 346 (QUESTION: 'Daughters, what are you doing?' ANSWER: 'We're killing you, daddy.').

Mischievous as ever, after leading his readers to expect a full account of the deaths of Creusa and Creon and the boys (foreshadowed at the end of our letter), Ovid passes over them very quickly at 7.394–7. Euripides in his tragedy entitled *Medea* is much more full, in particular over the first two deaths, which are reported to Medea by a messenger. He tells how Jason and his sons went to Creusa with the marvellous robe and crown and he asked her to accept the gifts and persuade her father not to banish the boys. The narrative that follows is carefully ordered. At 1156–66 the tension starts to mount as Creusa puts the presents on. Look for (believable) realistic touches there and irony and foreshadowing of her death. At 1167–77 there is a dramatic progression as the princess feels the effect of the robe and crown. Examine those lines for vivid and small points of detail that bring out the horror. At 1177–82 there is a brief respite, to lower the emotional pitch (why?), and it looks as if Creusa is dead (why does Euripides mislead us like this?). But then she comes to, and we get more and more horrific details at 1183–1203. Analyze the various elements that give those lines real impact. Finally at 1204ff. there is another death, when Creon turns up and is killed because of his love for his daughter and in a grotesque parody of affection. Look for various instances of pathos in that passage.

When she set eyes on the finery, she gave in	
and agreed to everything he had asked, and before	
Jason and his boys had gone far from the palace,	
she took the exquisite robe and put it on,	
and placed the golden crown on her head,	1160
arranging her hair in a bright mirror,	
and smiling at her lifeless reflection.	
Then she got up from her chair and walked across	
the room, taking delicate steps with her white feet,	
thrilled at the presents, looking back again and again	1165
to see how the robe hung at her ankles.	
But then we saw something terrifying.	
She goes pale, staggers back sideways,	
shaking all over, and only just manages to	
collapse on to her chair, nearly falling to the floor.	1170
An old servant, thinking (I suppose) that a frenzy	
from Pan or some other god had come upon her,	
gave a cry of joy, until she saw the white froth	
oozing from her lips, her eyes starting from	
their sockets and her body draining of blood.	1175
Then she changed her cry of joy to a great	
shriek. At once servants rushed off to Creon's rooms	
and to Jason, to report the awful thing that	
had happened to the new bride. The whole	
house rang with lots of running footsteps.	1180
And now a sprinter running the return leg of a course	
of two hundred yards would be reaching the finish-line	
when the unfortunate girl broke her silence and opened	
her eyes, coming to with an appalling groan.	
She was being attacked by twofold agony:	1185
the golden diadem around her head was	
streaming awesome, all-consuming fire,	
and the delicate robe (the gift of your children)	
was eating into the poor girl's delicate flesh.	

She leapt up from the chair and ran off,   1190
on fire, tossing her head this way and that,
trying to shake off the gold crown. But it stayed
firmly stuck to her, and when she tossed her
hair, the fire only blazed up twice as much.
She collapsed on the floor, crushed by catastrophe;   1195
she was unrecognizable, except to her father.
Her eyes looked unnatural, her lovely
face was gone and blood mixed with
fire was trickling from the top of her head,
and the flesh was dripping from her bones   1200
(like leaking resin), invisibly devoured by your poison.
It was a hideous sight. We were all afraid to touch
the corpse, in view of what had happened to her.
Her wretched father, not knowing how she had died,
suddenly entered and threw himself on the body.   1205
He immediately sobbed, put his arms around it
and kissed it, saying: 'My poor girl, some
god must have made you die this degrading death,
taking you from me when I'm old and close to the grave.
Ah, my child, I wish I was dead too.'   1210
When he had finished groaning and wailing,
the old man wanted to get up, but he
stuck to her delicate dress, like ivy clinging
to laurel-branches. Then a grim wrestling began.
He wanted to stand up, but she clung   1215
to him; and when he pulled hard, he kept on
tearing strips of aged flesh from his bones.
Finally his suffering was too much for the poor
man and he breathed his last, snuffed out.
The girl and her old father lie next to each other,   1220
corpses. A catastrophe! Enough to make anyone weep.

Euripides had built up a lot of sympathy for Medea in his play, but these two horrific deaths, described in detail and vividly, raise a moral issue (do we condone murder?) and mean that our sympathy for Medea must be diminished. It is diminished still further when she leaves the stage and slaughters her two children. This time Euripides employs a different technique for putting across death. Conventionally, in Greek tragedy an act of extreme violence could not be shown on stage, but it was an acceptable way of representing it to have somebody on stage reacting to it as it happened off stage. So at 1271ff. the children cry out for help as they are being killed, while the (intimidated) chorus dither over going to their assistance and end up too late to do anything. This is all stark and effective enough: much is left to our imagination; there is the grim silence of Medea throughout; and the boys' cries are soon stopped, so that the murder is over with chilling speed.

The final scene of the play provides a bleak and dispiriting close. Medea appears aloft in a chariot drawn by dragons and, as a final blow, refuses to let Jason have his sons' bodies. Then two of the most famous lovers of myth begin trading insults while their children's corpses are still warm, and the impotent Jason is reduced to ineffectual appeals, as Medea disappears, and we witness one evil overcome by a stronger evil. If you want more on this powerful and thought-provoking tragedy see Grube 147ff. and Allan.

That play and adaptations of it have been put on for thousands of years (see e.g. Hall & Macintosh & Taplin 1ff.). A 1972 version by a Romanian director was set in a café basement (into which the audience were led by candle-bearing actors) and had a chained Medea cursing in Greek and a Jason who spoke only in Latin, to bring out the gulf between the two characters. In 1974 H. Müller's *Medeaspiel* had Medea (tied to a bed on stage) giving birth and then ripping up the child and hurling its limbs and intestines at Jason. Jackie Crossland's 1992 play *Collateral Damage* is a feminist retelling of the story with comic elements that depicts Medea as an innocent victim falsely accused of being a murderess.

Medea has also proved to be an immensely popular subject for many genres of post-Classical literature outside of tragedy, and also for opera, ballet, film and art (see Hall & Macintosh & Taplin 4, 100ff., 144ff., Clauss & Johnston 297ff., Griffiths 103ff. and http://en.wikipedia.org/wiki/Medea). There is a great mass of material which really repays investigation and shows how this fascinating figure has been constantly reinterpreted and redeployed.

In literature Christa Wolf's *Medea: Stimmen* (translated by Cullen) is a new take on the myth with multiple narrators and lots of modern relevance (especially to the collapse of East Germany). This Medea is not a killer and not a witch, but a healer and wise woman. Brown-skinned and woolly-haired, she and some others from Colchis are refugees in Corinth, where she and her children fall victim to intrigue and xenophobia. This is a novel of ideas, which has much to say, about things like male power, state control, the immigrant experience and the pretensions and arrogance of 'civilization'.

For an interesting dance version of the story see *Medea: A Ballet in One Act* performed by the orchestra and ballet troupe of the Tbilisi Z. Paliashvili Opera and Ballet State Theatre (available on DVD from Kultur), especially scenes 14 (Creusa receives the fatal cloak), 15 (Medea's triumph and tragedy) and 16 (Jason's despair).

Two films in particular are worth seeing, in their different ways. *Jason and the Argonauts* (released by Columbia in 1963) is an enjoyable 'Sunday afternoon movie'. It has lots of action (including a climactic fight with skeletal earthborn men), and it is often unintentionally amusing (for instance, the Argonauts seem to wear diapers, and Aeetes has a very silly beard which his mother obviously knitted for him). Not surprisingly, given when and where it was made, this cinematic version demotes and diminishes Medea (so that the typical Hollywood hero is not upstaged by her but performs his great feats with minimal help from her), presenting her as a saccharine and colourless bimbo. Essentially she is a female with a pretty face and prominent chest, while Jason is a handsome and neat male. They are Ken and Barbie, and this is Ken and Barbie's Greatest Adventure. Much more serious, and much more difficult and challenging, is the 1970 film *Medea* (in Italian, with subtitles), directed by Pasolini. This is a free adaptation of Euripides' play, which, like its source, questions civilization and ponders the human psyche. But Pasolini takes all that off in a new direction with a radical updating. He depicts the clash between two cultures – the primitive, instinctual culture of the Colchians (typical of the third world) and the more advanced and rational culture of the Greeks (typical of the modern western world). He shows that the latter culture exploits the former, stealing from it and devaluing what it takes, and that the two cultures cannot co-exist harmoniously, so that catastrophe results when they come into contact. In this deliberately disturbing film Pasolini jolts us into thinking, brings out the strangeness and savagery of the myth and alienates us in line with his own feelings of alienation. He gives back to Medea a major role in the action and really develops her character, especially her dark side (she is sensual, barbaric and cruel, and also strange and enigmatic).

Medea is as fascinating in the visual arts. Her power as a sorceress was a popular theme of sixth- and early fifth-century BC Attic vase paintings, and, interestingly, these vases are the first evidence we have of the death of Pelias. Medea is recognizable on the vases with this theme from her dress, her tall headdress and especially the box of drugs she holds. In the particular scene on the Pelias hydria (type in Pelias hydria in the Google Images search engine and view the first image) the sinister aspect of the rejuvenation (i.e. Pelias' murder) is not foregrounded, as Medea appears to be convincing Pelias himself of the merits of a quick dip in her cauldron filled with some nice refreshing herbs! And so, as in the earliest vase paintings, the interest lies in Medea's power.

One of the most striking vase paintings from the late fifth century BC (a bell crater of about 400 BC) shows Medea in her finest barbarian garb (type in Flight of Medea in the Google Images search engine and view the first image). She is in the magical chariot given to her by her grandfather, the Sun, and her position above the other characters reinforces her distance from everyone, and her status as a woman foreign to Greek culture. Her dress, outer garment and tiara are oriental (her headdress is very Phrygian) in their decoration and they add to her portrait as a non-Greek – she is in fact entirely 'other' in this painting. Elements of the fantastic and supernatural are played up with the wingless dragons that draw her chariot, itself encircled by a huge sun, and the presence of hideous Furies on either side of her (reminding us that the boys' murder will be punished). True to the play by Euripides that has influenced this image, Jason helplessly and pitifully looks on, as his dear sons lie slain on the altar (in the play Medea carries them away in the chariot, and on the vase this change also helps to stress her distance from those who should be closest to her). The pathos of the situation is stressed via the placement of Jason's clothing, which seems to be almost slipping down, and his expression of humiliation and grief due to his former wife is evident. The anguish of the children's tutor and nurse adds to the tragedy of the scene, as these characters clutch at their hair in disbelief and horror. In the vase paintings subsequent to the production of Euripides' tragedy the emphasis shifts to this type of portrayal in which the focus is on Medea as a child murderer – the same association that we still have today with her name.

Equally interesting is a later fourth-century BC volute crater attributed to the Underworld Painter (type in Underworld painter Medea in the Google Images search engine and view the first image). The dense crowding of figures illustrates a clear shift in artistic taste, as the image of Medea on the cusp of stabbing one of her sons (at the bottom left) is not the central image; instead the unsuccessful attempt to remove a poisonous crown from Creusa's head inside her father's palace dominates. This type of vase painting, which shows many scenes of a myth in multiple registers (here Medea's Corinthian escapades), is regularly believed to have been inspired by tragedy and is typical of Southern Italian vases influenced by the theatre. The fullness of the painting seems almost overwhelming in contrast to the power of a single dramatic moment so effectively captured in the bell crater mentioned above. As in the earlier image, Medea is again sporting a very eastern mode of dress, complete with headdress, outer garment draped over her shoulder and tunic with decorated sleeves, all of which signal her foreignness. The horror of Medea's sinister nature is played up in the image of her seizing the boy's hair as he stands on an altar, a place of refuge. To add further to the poignancy of the scene, Jason is prevented from reaching his son as Frenzy bearing torches in his serpent/dragon-drawn chariot waits to carry Medea off. As in the preceding image, the focus remains clearly upon the 'otherness' of Medea, who is altogether different from the rest of the female figures in the painting.

Medea has remained a very popular subject in all artistic media to this day. The 1836–8 painting of Medea by the French artist Eugene Delacroix (type in Medea Eugene Delacroix in the Google Images search engine and view the first image) is a magnificent example of the continuing fascination with the heroine, her unnatural act of child-murder and her iconoclasm. Delacroix's decision to capture her on the point of slaying her sons illustrates this continued interest in her deviation from female norms. The artist's own brief comments on the painting indicate that Medea is being pursued, as does her backward glance and lengthy stride. A quick look at the painting may leave us wondering whether she has clasped her sons tightly to her body to rescue them from their pursuer, but a more careful examination conveys to the viewer Medea's unstable emotional state, effectively communicated in a number of ways. Her physical form has marked masculine aspects. She has broad shoulders, and her musculature is accentuated by the use of chiaroscuro, as the whiteness of her flesh contrasts with the shadows cast. Her angular jaw-line is also accentuated by the shadow-play. The painting has a pervasive darkness, with the sole light entering the cave in the upper left corner, thus lending itself to the overall ominous atmosphere. Furthermore, the three figures are foregrounded against a gloomy and indistinct area, so that the knife which will stab the boys is nearly lost. The lack of movement in the background is in stark contrast to the writhing of the children and their mother's movement as the children try to escape from her violent clutches. Though Medea's breasts are bare, there is no suggestion of sensual femininity or nurturing concern for her sons, and the rigidity of expression on her face illustrates rather her resolve and defiance. Delacroix's choice of colour for clothing in the painting requires little comment. The redness of her cloak is naturally suggestive of impending bloodshed, and the choice of rose for her dress creates a neat contrast between notions of femininity and the character of Medea.

Also stimulating is the striking 1964 metal sculpture entitled *Medea* by Eduardo Paolozzi (type in Eduardo Paolozzi Medea in the Google Images search engine and view the top row of images). There is much that is intriguing and suggestive here. For example, the piece is extraordinary and mysterious; it is nearly seven feet tall (as Medea towers over lesser figures) and made of (hard) welded aluminium; and the square centre looks like (powerful, relentless) machine parts. Do the legs remind you of any particular creature, and how relevant is that creature to Medea and her story?

Heroides 13

LAODAMIA TO PROTESILAUS

By way of a change we now move on to a consistently sad letter from a loving wife (who has no rival to worry about) to a loving husband (who parted from her unwillingly), and instead of complaints, criticisms and threats of death we find here affection, solicitude for the man's wellbeing and horror at the idea of him dying. Like *Her.* 11, this is a mournful epistle by a powerless female, with no happy ending in store, and the writer's suicide in prospect, so the two poems form a purely tragic frame around the tragicomic *Her.* 12, with all its dark humour.

The young heroine Laodamia married Protesilaus, a king in Thessaly (northern Greece). After a brief period together married (in one tradition only one day and night) they were parted when he had to sail off to join the huge army that was gathering at the Greek port of Aulis with the intention of getting Menelaus' wife Helen back from the Trojan prince Paris, with whom she had eloped when he stayed with them as a guest. However, a contrary wind blew, and the fleet of a thousand ships could not sail off to Troy. It is when she gets news of this that Laodamia writes this letter. She is miserable at his absence, deeply concerned about what might happen to him at Troy (with its rivers Xanthus and Simois, its Mount Ida, and the nearby island of Tenedos), and she begs him again and again to be careful there and to come back safe to her.

The contrary wind was caused by the goddess Diana, who had been offended by the commander-in-chief of the Greek forces (Agamemnon, the brother of Menelaus). She only relented and gave the Greeks the wind they needed for their voyage when he sacrificed to her his own daughter Iphigenia, whom he lured to Aulis by pretending that he was going to marry her to the mighty hero Achilles. The grimness of all this was well brought out by the first-century BC poet and philosopher Lucretius at 1.83ff. in an attack on religion, which he viewed as mere superstition:

> Superstition has been the cause of criminal and impious actions –
> for example, at Aulis the appalling defilement of

virgin Diana's altar with the blood of Iphigenia   85
by the foremost heroes, the elite leaders of the Greeks.
The headband was tied around the girl's hair
and hung down evenly over both cheeks.
She became aware of her father standing sadly in front
of the altar and attendants at his side hiding the knife   90
and her people in tears at the sight of her. Immediately
she sank to the ground on her knees, struck dumb with fear.
At such a moment the fact that she was the
king's first daughter couldn't help the poor girl.
Men's hands lifted her up and led her, trembling, to the altar,   95
not so she could be escorted by a loud wedding-song
in the traditional solemn ceremony, but so that at the
time of her marriage she could fall a sinless victim
in a sinful rite, miserable at being sacrificed by her father,
so the fleet could sail off successfully and enjoy good luck.   100
Such was the wickedness that superstition managed to motivate.

So there was a sombre start to the expedition. The sombreness continued. There
was an oracle that the first Greek to touch Trojan soil would die. That person was
Protesilaus. In many accounts (which Ovid clearly had in mind at 65ff.) he was
killed by Hector, Troy's great defender. It is possible that by the time that Laodamia
writes this letter the fleet has already got its wind and sailed away and Protesilaus
has died (the image of him that appears to her at 109f. might be his ghost, showing
the pallor of death and coming out with unspecific complaints). This would suddenly increase the tragedy and sense of futility here. Out of the different versions
of the heroine's own subsequent death Ovid follows the one that involves a wax
statue of her husband that she kept to comfort her (see 155ff. and *Remedia Amoris*
723f.). Her father ordered it to be thrown on to a pyre, so that she would not torment herself any more, and she then jumped into the fire after it, unable to bear her
grief, and was burnt alive.

From loving Laodamia of Thessaly to her Thessalian husband.
    Greetings. I wish I could come with this letter in person.
They say you're still at Aulis, detained by a wind.
    But where was this wind when you hurried off from me?
That's when the waves should have obstructed your ship;   5
    that was the right time for a savage sea.
I'd have given you more kisses and more final instructions –
    there's a lot that I wanted to say to my husband.
You were rushed away from here; the sort of wind that the sailors
    wanted, but I didn't, was there to summon your sails.   10
It was a wind that suited sailors, not a lover.
    You released me from your embrace, Protesilaus,

I didn't finish giving you my final instructions
   and I scarcely managed to say that sad 'goodbye'.
The north wind swooped, snatched and stretched your sails,   15
   and now my Protesilaus was far away.
I took pleasure in gazing at my husband as long as I could,
   and my eyes kept on following yours;
when I couldn't see you, I could see your sails,
   and I stared at your sails for a long time.   20
But when I didn't see you or your speeding sails,
   and there was nothing to gaze at but sea,
the light went along with you, and darkness engulfed me;
   I'm told I paled, my knees gave way and I collapsed.
Your father, my old father and my dejected mother   25
   only just managed to revive me with cold water.
They were kind, did their duty, but did me no favour:
   I resent not being allowed to die in my misery.
I was brought back to consciousness, and to pain too:
   wifely love gnawed at my faithful heart.   30
I can't be bothered to let a maid comb my hair,
   and I've no desire to wear robes of gold.
I'm agitated, driven this way and that, like Bacchantes
   maddened (we believe) by their god's vine-leafed wand.
The local ladies gather here and shout out to me: 35
   'Laodamia, wear your royal finery!'
Yes, of course I'll slip on a costly purple dress,
   while he wages war beneath Troy's walls,
I'll get my hair done while he has a helmet on,
   I'll put on new clothes while he carries hard weapons?   40
Let them say my neglected state is the only way of matching
   your hardships. I'll be in mourning throughout the war.
Deadly Paris, your handsomeness means ruin for your people;
   you were a treacherous guest – be as poor a fighter!
If only you'd found fault with Helen's face   45
   or she hadn't been attracted by yours!
Menelaus, your distress over your stolen wife is excessive:
   ah, your revenge is going to make lots of people weep.
That's a bad omen. Gods, please avert it from us; let my man dedicate
   his weapons to Jupiter in thanks for a safe return!   50
But I'm afraid whenever I think of that appalling war,
   and my tears flow like snow melted by the sun.
Troy, Tenedos, Simois, Xanthus, Ida – just the sound of
   those names is almost enough to make me afraid.
Paris wouldn't have dared to steal her if he couldn't   55
   defend himself: he knew his own might.

He was (they say) a splendid sight, covered in gold,
    wearing clothes that showed the wealth of Troy,
and with a strong force of the ships and men used in fierce war –
    how small a part of his princely power was with him?   60
Helen, daughter of Leda, I suspect that's what won you over,
    and I believe that can harm the Greeks.   62
Avoid Hector, whoever he is, if you love me: remember him,   65
    and keep his name inscribed on your heart.
When you've evaded him, remember to evade others,
    and imagine there are many Hectors there.
Whenever you get ready to fight, make sure you say:
    'Laodamia told me to save my life and hers.'   70
If it's fated for Troy to fall to the warriors of Greece,
    it will fall just the same if you're not wounded at all.
Let Menelaus attack the enemy head on when he fights: 73
    a husband *should* win back his wife from the midst of the enemy.   76
Your case is different: you just fight to survive
    and to return to your lady's devoted arms!
Trojans, please spare one enemy out of so many,
    don't make my life-blood flow from his body.   80
He's not suited to clashing with bare steel and presenting
    a fierce breast to troops ranged against him.
He can make love much more vigorously than he makes war;
    fighting is for others, loving is for him.
Now I confess – my heart moved me to call you back, I wanted to,   85
    but I held my tongue, for fear of saying something ill-omened.
On the point of leaving your ancestral home for Troy,
    you stumbled on the threshold – a bad sign.
When I saw that, I groaned and said to myself:
    'Please let this be a sign that my man will return!'   90
I'm telling you this now so you won't be bold in combat;
    make this fear of mine vanish completely into thin air.
There's also a prophecy marking someone out for an undeserved fate –
    the first Greek to touch Trojan soil.
I pity the woman who'll be the first to mourn her dead husband.   95
    May the gods keep you from wanting to be keen!
Among the thousand ships let yours be the thousandth, the final
    one to cleave the sea that the others have wearied.
And here's another warning: leave your ship last!
    The land you're hurrying to isn't Greece.   100
When you come back to me, use oars and sails together
    and quickly set foot on your own shore.
Whether the sun has set or is high in the sky,
    come to me quickly by day and by night,

but more so at night – nights are lovely for girls   105
   who are lying with someone's arms around their neck.
Alone in bed, I seek sleep with its deceptive dreams,
   enjoying false pleasure in place of the real thing.
But why is the image of you that comes to me
   pale, and why does it complain so much?   110
That jolts me awake, and I pray to the phantoms of the night.
   I make offerings at all the altars in Thessaly.
I burn incense, which I wet with my tears, so
   the flames flare up, as if sprinkled with wine.
When will I hold you, back home again, in my loving   115
   arms, and melt and languish with happiness?
When will you go to bed with me, and tell me
   about your glorious exploits as a soldier?
While you tell me, although I'll enjoy listening,
   I'll kiss you and you'll kiss me repeatedly.   120
Well-told stories are always interrupted like this;
   such pleasant pauses make the tongue more fluent.
But when I think of Troy, I think of the winds and the waves;
   anxious fears crush and kill hope of your return.
I'm also worried because you're all preparing to sail off when   125
   the winds forbid it and the ocean is against it.
Who'd want to return home when the wind forbids it?
   But you're leaving your homeland when the sea prohibits it!
Neptune himself bars the way to the city whose walls he built.
   Where are you rushing? Go back home, all of you!   130
Greeks, where are you rushing? Listen to the winds prohibiting that!
   This didn't just happen, all of a sudden: a god is delaying you.
This massive war is just to get back some filthy slut!
   Turn around, you ships of Greece, while you still can!
What am I doing? Recalling someone is a bad omen. I take it back.   135
   May a gentle breeze waft you over a calm sea!
I envy the women of Troy: even if they'll see the dismal
   deaths of those they love, and have the enemy nearby,
the new bride there will personally put the helmet on her brave
   husband's head and hand him his weapons.   140
While handing him his weapons, she'll kiss him
   (the type of task they'll both enjoy),
and she'll escort him on his way and instruct him to return,
   saying: 'Be sure to bring back these weapons to Jupiter!'
He'll remember his wife's recent instructions and   145
   fight cautiously, with his home in mind.
When he comes back, she will remove his shield, undo his
   helmet and take his weary body in her arms.

But I know nothing for sure; anxious fear makes me
    think that whatever could happen has happened.   150
However, while you're off fighting in a remote region,
    I've got a wax image to remind me of your face.
I speak coaxing words to it and the loving words that are
    rightfully yours, and it accepts my embraces.
Believe me, the image is more than you might think: 155
    give the wax a voice, and it'll be Protesilaus.
I gaze at it, hold it in my arms instead of my real husband
    and complain to it, as if it could reply.
I swear by your return, by you yourself (a god in my eyes),
    by our wedding-torches and the fire in my heart (which is just as hot), 160
I'll go to join you, wherever you summon me,   163
    whether – ai! – my fears come true or you survive.
I'll close this letter with a brief demand: 165
    if you care for me, take care of yourself.

Ovid here employs various techniques of characterization and (we feel) demonstrates much psychological insight in this realistic and touching depiction of a young new bride. In Roman society of his day most females were about fourteen when they first married, and in line with that we see in his Laodamia a girlish naivety and vulnerability and typical raw emotions, raging hormones and deep infatuation.

With regard to characterization, what we find here is the indirect method, whereby the author does not state openly (directly) that someone has a certain quality but leaves readers to infer it from the person's words and/or actions. Laodamia tells us a lot about herself here by speaking (writing) intimately and at length, and she also mentions several revealing acts of hers (e.g. the swoon when the sails disappear from view at 23f., the neglect of her appearance at 31ff., her pursuit of dreams of Protesilaus at 107f. and her behaviour with the wax image at 153ff.). Ovid is also selective in his portrayal of the heroine. Writers frequently give us the big picture, informing us about a character's earlier history, background, environment, accomplishments and so on, but our poet effectively focuses on Laodamia at a particular moment and her feelings then. Contrast is another useful tool in this connection, and Laodamia's gentleness, passion and conjugal devotion stand out even more after Medea's violent rage, hatred and almost total loss of love in *Heroides* 12. First impressions are important too in our estimate of people, and repetition of a point or trait gives it emphasis. So at 1ff. we are made very much aware of the heroine's love ('loving' in 1, picked up by 'lover' in 11; and all the kisses in 7), her delight in her married status (there is relish in her use of 'husband' in 1 and again in 8, and often later on in the poem) and her concern for Protesilaus (evident in all the 'final instructions' she wanted to give him in 7 and also in 13); there we see as well the tunnel vision of a wife (in 3, where 'you' in the Latin is singular, and she thus ignores all the other Greeks) and her inability even now to get over his departure, as she dwells on it, and complains of the speed of it in 4 and once more in 9. Distinctive touches and telling details (i.e. things that really get to you) make a character come alive and have impact – like the extreme behaviour for a young woman in not being at all concerned about how she looks at 31ff. (in a quite odd attempt to get close to her man), her identification with him via the life-blood in 80, her fantasy at 137ff. (where, with projection, the Trojan wife enjoying proximity to her husband is a substitute for Laodamia herself) and her memorable and rather bizarre relationship with the wax statue at 151ff.

As for psychological insight (on which see also Jacobson 202ff.), we have already mentioned several life-like traits of Laodamia as the loving new wife. We can add to that her fixation on her husband, who is now the most important person to her in the world (her parents figure only briefly, at 25–7), and whom she tells to look after himself at Troy over and over again, rather obsessively. But naturally after such a short period married she does not yet really know Protesilaus: she claims at 81ff. that he is not much of a fighter, but in fact he was (she betrays naivety about the wider world too at 55ff., where she imagines that Paris is a great warrior and does not know who Hector is). Ovid also presents a convincing picture of a girl who has recently experienced an erotic awakening, and so shows a certain sensuality (in 83, 105f. and 115ff.) and sexual frustration (at 107f.), as well as missing hugs and kisses (in 120, 154 and 157). She is too young, too much in love and too much in lust to be able to cope with the loss of her man. Hence the sudden lurches to new topics in her letter (rather than a smooth, calm progression) and her frequent lack of logic (look for this especially in 44, 45f., 61, 79 and 137ff.). Hence in particular her great gloom – evident not only in her anxiety and fear but also in the accumulation and repetition (almost without relief) of elements such as tears, misery, pain, mourning, darkness, ferocity, fighting and bad omens.

All of this makes for a dark tone for *Heroides* 13, and so does the overall futility and the presence throughout of grim hints and sombre irony. Again and again there is allusion to the deaths of Protesilaus and Laodamia (see, for instance, 28, 80, 87f. and 93f.) and the heroine comes out with remarks which are sadly inappropriate in view of the way things turn out (see, for example, 38, 67f., 95ff. and 115ff.). In fact Ovid was working within a mini-tradition of dark depictions of Laodamia and Protesilaus in recent Latin elegy.

Earlier Catullus (approximately 84–54 BC) had worked thought-provoking allusion to this pair into a disturbed and moving poem of his (68). His Laodamia there is essentially a very passionate figure, who cannot endure the loss of her beloved husband (and so commits suicide, as is intimated at 83f.). He highlights her great beauty in line 105, and at 107–30 he goes on at length about the ardour of her amatory frenzy. She operates in the poem as an intriguing and depressing parallel to his girlfriend (who is unfaithful to him). In this piece Catullus thanks his friend Allius for providing a house where he could meet with his mistress for assignations that had to be secret because she was married to another man. At 70ff. he depicts his girl (calling her a goddess) as arriving there and then likens her to Laodamia going to Protesilaus' home. The comparison is richly suggestive and casts a shadow over the poet's liaison (see if you can see how, before moving on to our comments after the translation).

> My radiant goddess went there, stepping softly,   70
>   and set down her dazzling foot on the smooth threshold,
>   resting her weight on her shining sandal,
>   just as Laodamia, on fire with love for her husband,
>   once went to the house that Protesilaus had
> begun building in vain, since he hadn't appeased the Lords   75
>   of Heaven with the blood of an animal sacrificed to them.
> (Goddess of retribution, may I never be so attracted to something
>   that is undertaken rashly without the consent of those Lords!)
> How much the starved altar craves a bloody offering
>   Laodamia learned when she lost her man.   80
> She was forced to let go of her new husband's neck
>   before the coming of a couple of winters had satisfied
> her hungry love in long nights, so she could bear
>   to live on when her marriage was cut short.
> The goddesses of fate knew that this was not far off,   85
>   if he went to fight before the walls of Troy.

In the comparison of Catullus' girl to Laodamia there is an implication that like the heroine she is supremely beautiful, superior to ordinary mortals and a special person. The poet underscores Laodamia's passion here (and later in the poem), but his mistress cannot be deeply in love with him in view of her infidelity, so he is being pathetically optimistic over this aspect. Catullus also brings out here how difficult Laodamia found it to cope with losing her man, and he is thereby probably being hopeful again – about his girlfriend finding it hard to deal with permanent deprivation of him. He dwells on the unhappy side of the mythical marriage, so that an ominous gloom is prominent, and attaches to Catullus' own troubled relationship. And, if his girl is equivalent to Laodamia, he would correspond to the tragic and doomed Protesilaus (although he does try at 77f. to dissociate himself from that hero and from the action that led to the separation).

Subsequently Propertius (an older contemporary of Ovid) also employed this myth in connection with his liaison, but he changed the focus and the thrust. In 1.19 he concentrates on Protesilaus, implicitly comparing himself to the hero, and alluding to the version of the story in which after his death at his request he was allowed by the powers of the Underworld to come back to earth and be briefly reunited with his dear wife (when he had to leave her, she pined away or committed suicide and went to join him in the land of the dead). The mythical figure again denotes intense passion, but here Propertius uses Protesilaus as an example to show that love can actually rise above and go beyond death (in contrast to Catullus 68, where Laodamia cannot deal with her husband's demise and so overcome death).

Protesilaus is cited to prove the poet's point that like the hero he will still be totally devoted to his woman (Cynthia) after he has died (although he does have fears about her feelings for him then).

A powerful and challenging poem, 1.19 is addressed to and aimed at Cynthia, and its purpose is to ensure that they have a blissfully happy affair while still alive (25f.). Since (according to him) there is no doubt about his own involvement, he must be attempting to get her to be more committed and loving. Typically Propertius (who has been called the first neurotic of European literature) goes about achieving this in an extreme and morbid fashion. There is a seething mixture of intense emotions here. He doesn't just assure her of his lasting affection and flatter her (13ff.), but tries to make her feel sorry for causing him worry about her and to win pity by holding out the prospect of himself dead and in the Underworld (and still in love). To bring home the reality of death and the afterlife, which he will surmount, there is a build-up of grisly details and macabre language, which produces a forbidding atmosphere. (Incidentally it is interesting to compare and contrast Propertius 4.7, where Cynthia's ghost comes back to *him* after her death and complains of *his* lack of fidelity.)

My Cynthia, I'm not afraid now of the grim ghost-world,
    I don't care about my destined end on the final pyre,
but what I do dread more than the funeral rites themselves
    is the possibility of being deprived of your love when I'm a corpse.
Cupid is firmly fastened on my eyes, so I couldn't let slip   5
    from my mind and lose my love for you when I am dust.
Down there, in the darkworld, the Thessalian hero
    Protesilaus could not forget his delightful wife,
but, yearning to touch his darling with his phantom hands,
    he returned to his ancient home as a spectre.   10
Whatever I am down there, I'll always be called your ghost:
    a powerful love crosses even the shores of death.
Down there, if a crowd of the beauties who the Greeks
    won as spoil from Troy came to me,
I'd find none of them more attractive than my beautiful   15
    Cynthia; and even if you're fated to be kept from me
by a lengthy old age (may Earth be just and grant this!),
    I'll cry tears of joy and love your skeleton.
If only, while still alive, you could feel that for my ashes!
    Then, wherever I was, death would not be bitter for me.   20
Cynthia, how I fear that cruel Cupid may make you spurn
    my grave and drag you away from my dust
and force you against your will to dry your falling tears.
    Even a faithful girl bends before continual threats.
So, while we can, let's be blissfully happy lovers: 25
    however long, no love is long enough.

Ovid would of course have been aware of these elegiac predecessors, and in *Heroides* 13 he makes his own contribution to this mythical cycle. He follows them both in spotlighting the deep love, but returns to Catullus' focus on Laodamia. However, he goes beyond external beauty and gets inside her mind, really developing her as a person (rather than a symbol of passion). He also creates a darker mood than both Catullus and Propertius thanks to the length of his treatment and the accumulation of gloomy material.

Laodamia conforms broadly to the standard figure of the Good Wife in myth, but because her married life is so short, another tragic aspect of her story is the fact that she does not have time to enter fully into that role and is denied various elements of it. Typically such a Good Wife loves her husband with devoted fidelity, and gives him help and support; she produces a child or children, and cares for her offspring, performs various domestic tasks and supervises the slaves; she is also quite capable of making a sacrifice for the good of her family or city. Famous examples include Penelope (who stayed faithful to her spouse during his absence for twenty years), Andromache (who was a loving mother and remained devoted to her husband long after his death), Evadne (who was so distraught at the demise of her man that she threw herself into the flames of his funeral pyre and died) and Alcestis (whose husband, king Admetus, was allowed to escape death if he could find another prepared to die in his place, and she was the only person ready to do this for him).

At Euripides *Alcestis* 158ff. a servant describes how Alcestis readied herself for death when the fatal day arrived. This passage highlights several aspects of married life which Laodamia was sadly unable to enjoy, while also being very moving in itself. At the start the queen puts on a brave face and demonstrates great self-control and altruism as she herself prepares her body for her funeral. Then her piety and loving concern for her children are in evidence, as she prays to numerous gods for them (rather than for herself), deeply concerned about their future wellbeing even at this point in her life. Once she enters her bedroom and is out of the public gaze, realistically she does give way to her emotions, showing the importance to her of her husband and her marriage, but not whining or complaining. She finds it hard to leave the bedroom and face people again (quite possibly trying to hide from death), but when she does manage that, we see how close she is to her two children and to the servants, and how they love and respect each other.

> When she realized that the appointed day
> had come, she washed her fair skin with water
> from the river, took out clothing and finery   160
> from a cedar chest and dressed herself becomingly.
> She stood in front of Hestia's altar and prayed:
> 'Mistress, as I am going beneath the earth,
> I'll kneel before you and pray this final time:
> look after my orphaned children; give the boy   165
> a loving wife and the girl a noble husband;

don't let my children die before their time like their
mother, but let them prosper and enjoy a long
and pleasant life in their own fatherland.'
She went to all the altars in Admetus' palace,   170
put garlands on them and prayed, plucking
foliage from the myrtle branches that she carried.
She didn't cry, didn't sigh, and her lovely face
didn't go pale at the thought of the coming catastrophe.
After that she rushed into her bedroom and up to her bed,   175
and it was only then that she wept, saying:
'Oh my marriage-bed, in which I lost my virginity
to the man for whose sake I am dying, goodbye.
I don't hate you. But you're responsible for a
unique sacrifice – because I won't betray you and my   180
husband, I'm dying. Some other woman will acquire you;
she'll be luckier perhaps, but not more virtuous.'
She fell on to the bed, kissing it and soaking
all of it with a flood of streaming tears.
When she'd finally had enough of weeping,   185
she tore herself from it and walked away, drooping.
Again and again, as she was leaving the room, she turned
round and flung herself back on to the bed once more.
The children kept on crying, holding on to their
mother's dress. She took them into her arms and   190
kissed them goodbye in turn, as she was about to die.
And all the servants in the palace kept on crying,
out of pity for their mistress. She held out her right
hand to each one, speaking to even the lowest
of them, and they all spoke to her in reply.   195

Heroides 14
HYPERMESTRA TO LYNCEUS

There was a war over the kingship of Egypt between two Greek brothers – Danaus (who had fifty daughters) and Aegyptus (who had fifty sons). The writer of this letter, Hypermestra (one of the Danaids = daughters of Danaus), says that Aegyptus and his sons seized the kingdom and drove Danaus and his girls into exile. They fled to Argos in Greece. Aegyptus and his boys subsequently pursued them there, and he forced his brother to marry the young women to their cousins (according to one account to stop them wedding other men who might help them get revenge, according to another so Aegyptus could have them in his power and kill them). The marriages took place in the palace of Pelasgus (a current or former king of Argos). Danaus secretly gave his offspring swords and told them to kill the new grooms on their wedding-night when they fell asleep. All the Danaids did this except for Hypermestra, who bravely and nobly spared her man (Lynceus), because she regarded killing him as a crime and not the way a wife should treat her husband. Out of fear of her brutal father she nearly put Lynceus to death, but, after veering to and fro over what to do (see 53ff.), she woke him up instead and told him to flee. He awoke to see her with a sword in her hand, and she didn't have time to explain it then, but got him to slip away under cover of darkness. The next morning Danaus was enraged when he discovered that Lynceus had escaped death and imprisoned her in chains. At this point, certain that she will be executed, she writes this letter, asking Lynceus to come to her aid or at least to give her a proper funeral and a tomb with an inscription recording her good deed. There was a happy ending, although there are different versions of what actually happened later. In one tradition Danaus relented and reunited his daughter with Lynceus; in another Lynceus returned and killed Danaus and/or his other girls; while in another Hypermestra was put on trial in Argos but was acquitted, and her sisters and father were condemned instead. It was also said that Hypermestra and Lynceus stayed married and she bore him a son, who founded a royal dynasty in Argos.

In the course of her epistle Hypermestra links her own story to that of her ancestress Io, claiming that she too must be a victim of Juno. Io (the daughter of a river-god) was a beautiful young nymph loved by Jupiter. Juno changed her into a heifer by way of punishment. Io wandered far and wide in distress over her altered appearance, and also maddened by a gad-fly sent to sting her by Juno. Finally, the god of the river Nile restored Io's original form. She subsequently became a major goddess (the Egyptian Isis).

There are obvious differences between this letter and the last with regard to background-situation, purpose of the epistle and tone (especially in view of the outcome there is not deep tragedy here). In addition, as Ovid is now nearing the end of the single *Heroides*, he brings in some major changes to enliven and add variety. So this is the only one of the poems that is not amatory (Hypermestra is not yet in love with her husband), and it is also the only one in which one heroine tells another heroine's story at length. At the same time there are many correspondences which pair this letter with *Heroides* 11 (on which see Fulkerson 79–82).

From Hypermestra to the sole survivor out of so many brothers
    (the rest now lie dead, murdered by their evil brides).
I'm held prisoner in the palace, confined, loaded down with chains;
    I'm being punished for my devotion to my husband.
Since I shrank from plunging a sword into your throat, I'm charged   5
    with a crime; if I'd dared to commit one, I'd be praised.
Being charged is better than gratifying my father like that;
    I don't regret not having blood on my hands.
My father can burn me with the blazing marriage-torches that
    I didn't violate, he can aim them at my face,   10
or cut my throat with the sword he unscrupulously gave me,
    murdering me in the way I wouldn't murder my husband.
But he won't make me say 'I'm sorry' as I die. A wife
    who regrets her devotion to her man isn't devoted.
He and my savage sisters should feel sorry, for their crime,   15
    as people normally do after doing something bad.
When I remember that night defiled by blood, I get scared;
    my hand suddenly trembles, making it hard to write.
You might imagine me capable of killing my husband, but I
    shrink from even writing about the killing done by others.   20
However, I'll try. Dusk had just fallen on the earth; it was
    the final part of the day, the first part of night.
We sisters were led into mighty Pelasgus' palace, where
    Aegyptus in person welcomed his sons' (armed) brides.
Everywhere gilded torches gleamed; in this unholy wedding   25
    incense was sprinkled on reluctant altar-fires;
the crowd invoked the marriage-god, but He fled their invocations;
    Juno herself departed from here (her favourite city).

Look – the grooms, fuddled with wine, escorted by noisy friends,
    and with fresh garlands on their perfumed hair,   30
joyfully rush into the bedrooms (their tombs) and lie down
    on the beds that can function as funeral-biers.
Now they lay there asleep, overcome by wine and food,
    and there was deep sleep throughout unsuspecting Argos.
I thought I heard around me the groans of dying men,   35
    and I *did* hear them; what I feared was a reality.
I went pale, my mind froze, my body grew cold
    and I lay there on my new bridal bed, chilled.
Like slender corn-ears quivering in a gentle west wind,
    like poplar leaves shaken by a chilly breeze –   40
that's how I trembled, or even more than that. You yourself
    lay helpless, in the grip of the sleep the wine brought on.
The thought of my violent father's orders drove away my fear;
    I got up and grasped the weapon in my trembling hand.
I won't lie: my hand just managed to raise the sharp sword   45
    three times, and each time it sank back down again.
I moved to your throat – let me tell you the truth –
    I moved my father's weapon to your throat.
But fear and devotion to you prevented that cruel crime;
    my pure right hand shrank from acting as commanded.   50
In my anguish I tore my purple dress and tore my hair,
    and then I said to myself quietly:
'You've got a vicious father; carry out your parent's
    orders; let Lynceus here join his brothers.
I'm a female, a girl, gentle by nature and because of my youth;   55
    my soft hands aren't suited to fierce weapons.
No, come on, while he lies there, be as brave as your
    sisters, who have probably all killed their husbands.
If this hand of mine was capable of committing a murder,
    it would be covered in blood from killing me.   60
They deserved to be murdered like this for seizing their uncle's kingdom
    and making us helpless wanderers with our helpless old father.
Suppose they *did* deserve to be murdered – what have I done wrong,
    to be punished by not being allowed to be a devoted wife?
I'm a girl. What do I want with a sword, with weapons of war?   65
    Wool and the distaff are more fitting for my fingers.'
As I complained to myself like this, the words made me weep,
    and the tears fell from my eyes on to your body.
You tried to throw your sleepy arms around me in an
    embrace, and nearly cut your hand on the sword.   70
By now I was afraid of dawn arriving and my father
    and his servants. I woke you up, saying:

'Come on, Lynceus, up! You're the sole survivor out of all your brothers.
 If you don't hurry, it'll be night everlasting for you.'
You get up in a panic. All the torpor of sleep disappears.   75
 You see a soldier's sword in my fearful hand.
When you ask me why, I say: 'Escape, while night lets you!'
 While dark night lets you, you get away; I stay.
In the morning Danaus counts the sons-in-law lying murdered.
 There's one missing (you), making the crime incomplete.   80
He can't bear the loss of the death of a single relative
 and complains that not enough blood was shed.
I'm seized by the hair, dragged from my father's feet
 (my reward for my devotion to you) and imprisoned.
Obviously Juno's anger continues, on from the time   85
 when Io became a heifer and then became a goddess.
But it was punishment enough for that tender girl to moo,
 no longer beautiful and able to attract Jupiter.
A new-made cow, she stood on the banks of her father's river
 and saw in his water horns she'd never had before.   90
She tried to complain, but mooed instead, terrified by
 her appearance, terrified by her voice.
Poor Io, why so frantic, amazed at your reflection?
 Why count the feet created for your new form?
Mighty Jupiter's famous mistress, rightly feared by Juno,   95
 you satisfy your great hunger with leaves and grass,
and drink at a stream, stunned to see what you look like in it,
 and afraid you might wound yourself with your horns.
Recently you were so well-off as to seem worthy even of
 Jupiter, but now you lie naked on the bare ground.   100
You speed across sea, land and rivers whose gods are related to you:
 the sea, the rivers and the land let you through.
Why run away, Io, roaming over long stretches of ocean?
 To escape your face? You won't succeed.
Where are you rushing? You flee your horns and follow behind   105
 them, leading yourself on and going along with yourself.
The Nile at its seven-mouthed estuary removed the form of
 the maddened heifer and restored the features of Juno's rival.
Why talk of things long ago told me by grey-haired old people?
 Look, I've cause for complaint in my own life: 110
my father and my uncle are at war; we are driven from our
 kingdom and home; we're exiled to the ends of the earth.
Out of so many brothers only a single one survives.   115
 I weep for those who were killed and for the killers.
As many sisters as brothers-in-law are lost to me:
 let both those groups receive my tears.

See, because you survive, an agonizing punishment's in store for me.
> God help the guilty, when I face charges for a good deed   120
and die in misery, leaving just one brother alive
> out of that depleted group of a hundred relatives!
But, Lynceus, if you care at all for your devoted cousin,
> and deserve the gift of life that I gave you,
come and help me, or leave me to die and secretly   125
> lay my dead body on a funeral pyre,
shed many faithful tears over my remains and lay them to rest;
> and let a short epitaph be engraved on my tomb:
EXILED HYPERMESTRA, WHOSE DEVOTION WAS UNFAIRLY PUNISHED,
> FOR SAVING HER COUSIN FROM DEATH ENDURED IT HERSELF.   130
I would write more, but the heavy chains are dragging my
> hand down, and fear itself is draining my strength.

So far Ovid has poked fun at some of his heroines and has been sympathetic to others. Now he shows great respect for one of them. His Hypermestra is a touching character for whom we feel pity, but above all she is an admirable figure who possesses many sterling qualities.

She is highly moral. Of particular importance to her is *pietas* (which in her case means a dutiful fidelity to her obligations to her new husband), and so the words *pius* and *pietas* (translated as 'devoted' and 'devotion') recur throughout her letter. So too she demonstrates integrity in dealing with an ethical quandary: a female was also expected to have a sense of duty towards her father, but she reaches the (humane) conclusion that his orders are wrong, as murder is a crime. She is also very honest: she admits to Lynceus that she came close to killing him (while carefully explaining why she came to have a sword in her hand when he awoke); and she does not try to win him over by pretending that she spared his life because she loves him (given the circumstances, it is not surprising that she does not feel love for him, and if she had felt it so soon, she would surely have mentioned it; compare Jacobson 125f.). In addition to her morality, she also gives clear signs of independence. She thinks for herself and is mentally strong, reaching her own decision about Lynceus and acting on it (in contrast to her weak and passive sisters). And when she does act (at 73–8), she is efficient: she copes well under pressure, and is brisk and commanding, telling the man what to do, and not wasting precious time then in explanation of the sword in her hand but just making sure that he gets away safely. Of course, she is also extremely brave, in standing up to her vicious parent when she knows that she will be severely punished by such a person, and in facing the prospect of death at 125ff. In her present predicament a quiet dignity is in evidence: she does not whine or give way to paroxysms of grief or abjectly beg Lynceus to rescue her. In fact she uses an indirect and subtle approach to him, with various ploys aimed at him throughout the epistle, in line with her intelligence. For example, she stresses her devotion (so he will reciprocate) and his unique survival (so he will feel particularly grateful), and she tries to win his sympathy by mentioning her past fears, present maltreatment and awful prospects; and she tells the story of Io to represent herself as under a grim family curse (persecuted by vindictive Juno), linking herself with her ancestress, whose plight she brings out to gain pity for her own similar sufferings as a latter-day Io (to whom Juno may yet do something equally drastic), and touching on the nymph's eventual salvation thanks to a male as an adroit hint to Lynceus. Finally, just in case Hypermestra might appear a bit austere or hard or calculating, Ovid puts across constantly (especially at 17ff., 55f., 65ff. and 116ff.) what a gentle, sensitive and feeling young woman she is (and those qualities are accentuated by the contrast with her callous and brutal father).

'Authentic realism' is a term applied to a particular way of looking at literature about women which really involves the reader. With it the text is read as a means of gaining insight into their lives (especially seeing how patriarchy limits their possibilities) and as a vehicle for change in women's view of themselves. If the women represented in the literary piece are in accord with the female reader's idea of what women are like, then they are deemed to be authentic and realistic (rather than male stereotypes of the feminine). In addition, since female characters affect the self-image of the reader of the same sex (who identifies with them), in the view of the authentic realistic critic they should be positive figures for emulation (strong, vigorous, resourceful etc.) rather than the silent and passive types that male writers often portray. On this reading strategy see further Mills & Pearce & Spaull & Millard 51ff. In line with this approach examine *Heroides* 14 for the accuracy of its representation of the female experience (e.g. in connection with parental authority and moral dilemmas) and analyze Ovid's Hypermestra as a role model (a resisting and ultimately triumphant victim of a male oppressor etc.).

Ovid's older contemporary Horace uses Hypermestra's story in a different way and takes a light-hearted approach to it. His *Odes* 3.11 is concerned with Lyde, a sexually inexperienced young woman who is obstinately rejecting the poet's advances. He appeals to the lyre and the inventor of that musical instrument (the god Mercury) for a poem that will seduce her. In so doing he lists the powers of the lyre, which include (in the hands of the supreme musician Orpheus, as he sang in the Underworld to get back his dead wife Eurydice) soothing Cerberus, hell's ferocious guard-dog, and charming the legendary sinners enduring terrible punishments down there. There is witty exaggeration in the arch implication that Lyde is as hard to affect and win over as them. Among the sinners mentioned by him are the Danaids who for murdering their husbands were condemned to spend eternity down there in futile attempts to fill with water a container that had holes in its base. Horace playfully pretends that just by chance he has lit on the perfect story for Lyde to hear, and at 25ff. he presents that myth with a message in a condensed, selective version that suits his purposes. He begins with the Danaids, who show Lyde how she should *not* behave and how sexual crimes are subject to severe penalties. There is a mock-solemn equation here of Lyde's refusal with their murderous conduct and an over-the-top suggestion that she is as cruel as them and will undergo similar retribution. Having gained impact by putting that grim picture of crime and punishment first, Horace next dwells at length on Hypermestra, making her an

appealing figure as he employs her to intimate how Lyde *should* behave (i.e. be kind
to her man and concerned about his wellbeing). Examine Horace's characterization
of Hypermestra here and his presentation of her tale, bearing in mind that all this
is done for Lyde's benefit.

Lyde must be told about the crime and notorious	25
punishment of those girls (the vat empty of	
water, which leaks away through its base) and the	
doom which, though delayed,	
awaits crimes even down in the Underworld.	
Those wicked women (what could be worse than what they	30
did?), those wicked women brought themselves to murder their	
bridegrooms with pitiless swords.	
One out of the many was worthy of the marriage-torch	
and was magnificently deceitful to her	
treacherous father, a girl who won	35
everlasting renown.	
She said to her young husband: 'Get up, get up,	
or you'll be put to sleep for a long time by those	
you don't fear. Escape your father-in-law	
and my criminal sisters,	40
who, like lionesses pouncing on calves, are all	
(ah no!) savaging their men. I am gentler	
than them. I won't stab you or lock	
you up in this room.	
Let my father load me down with cruel chains,	45
because I spared my poor husband out of pity,	
or banish me on a boat to the furthest	
regions of Numidia.	
Go where your feet and the sea-breezes take you,	
while night and Venus are on your side, go, and good	50
luck to you! Carve on my tomb a mournful epitaph	
in memory of me.'	

   Earlier in the first century BC the poet and philosopher Lucretius had a different take on the Danaids. In his *On the Nature of the Universe* he tried to free his
readers from the stifling influence of religion (which according to him was mere
superstition). In line with that he offered a rational explanation of the myths of
such punishments in Hades, claiming that the torments did not actually exist but
were allegories of what goes on in life on earth. At 3.1003ff. he maintained that the
daughters of Danaus symbolize people who are never satisfied:

   Next, to be forever feeding an ungrateful mind
   and never fill it and satisfy it with good things

(as when the seasons of the year come round,   1005
bringing us their fruits and various charms,
we are never filled with the fruits of life) –
this, I think, is the meaning of the tale of the girls
in their prime pouring water into a jar full of holes,
which cannot be filled by any method at all.   1010

What we have seen so far in Ovid and others about Hypermestra's sisters is very negative and not very informative. Aeschylus will now redress the balance for us and give us fresh insight. In the fifth century BC he produced a tragedy called the *Suppliants* which depicts the Danaids sympathetically at an early stage in the story, before the murders. Here they have fled from Aegyptus and his sons to Greece and have arrived at Argos, where they are given asylum, but Danaus suddenly catches sight of the ships of their brutal cousins pursuing them and intent on taking them in marriage. When he tells them of this, the girls (who form the chorus in the play) give voice to their terror and their yearning for escape and are so distraught that they contemplate suicide. To add to the impact of the powerful emotions, there is a macabre beauty in the lofty language, striking sound and spectacle (picture this being performed in the theatre by fifty masked members of the chorus in exotic costumes, singing the lines and dancing with expressive gestures to the sound of a pipe).

Ah, land of hills, which we rightly revere, what will
happen to us? Where can we run to here in hope
of somewhere some pitch-dark hiding-place?
If only I could become black smoke, soar
towards the sky-god's clouds,   780
completely invisible, imperceptible,
and dissipate like dust!
We cannot escape catastrophe any more.
My heart is dark and trembling.   785
I'm destroyed, crushed by fear of what father saw.
I'd sooner meet my fate in a knotted
noose than let a man I loathe touch
my flesh. I'd rather die   790
first and become one of Hades' subjects.
Where can I find an airy throne, up there
where the rain-clouds turn into snow,
or a bare, lonely, beetling crag, above
goat-reach, a haunt of vultures,   795
a place past human perception,
which will witness me plummeting
down, down to escape a corrosive
marriage contrary to my wishes.

After that the dogs and birds of the area can prey   800
on my corpse and devour it – I don't care.
For the dead are free from
adversity's misery.
Let death come and claim
me before the marriage-bed does.   805
What path can I cut now
to escape, to evade marriage?

We have already mentioned the Ovidian Hypermestra's motivation for recounting what happened to Io and commented on how this reveals her intelligence. Over and above that Ovid makes his character do this so that he can present a deftly streamlined version of the myth of Io (with stress on her suffering and subsequent rescue, i.e. aspects relevant to Hypermestra's purposes), and also so that he can add variety to the collection by introducing into it narrative embedding (telling one story inside another). This inset facilitates some characteristically ingenious and elaborate effects. There are numerous parallels to appreciate: both Io and her descendant were tender girls and victims of Juno, who fell from positions of eminence, were maltreated and felt fear. The lines on Io contain foreshadowing too, of eventual salvation for Hypermestra as well. There are also enlivening contrasts: in addition to differences in circumstances, time and setting, the embedded tale constitutes a brief interlude which for a change switches right away from Hypermestra's situation and moves up on to the divine plane; and, although the heroine is entirely serious there as in the rest of her letter, Ovid ensures that thanks to the way in which she puts across events and Io's reactions to them the uninvolved reader may glimpse some unintentionally comic touches (at 91f., 94, 98 and 103–6). There is also more complex play, as one mythological female tells another mythological female's story in the midst of telling her own. At 87 Hypermestra, who is being punished severely, with worse in store, says that Io's metamorphosis into a heifer was punishment enough. At 91 our complaining heroine depicts her ancestress as unable to complain. At 101ff. a girl who did not flee describes one who did flee and tells her that fleeing is futile, and a static figure (a powerless mortal) portrays a wide-wandering figure, who became a powerful immortal.

Heroides 15

SAPPHO TO PHAON

Ovidian authorship of *Heroides* 15 is hotly disputed. We are among those who believe that the poem was composed by Ovid (for arguments see Jacobson 277f., Palmer 420ff. and Thorsen 96ff.; note also that the woman's attempt here to win over her man is consistently and comically inept in a way that is typically Ovidian, rather like Phaedra in *Heroides* 4). Even if the letter was not in fact by Ovid, it is well worth studying.

In contrast to *Her.* 14 this is an amatory epistle again, and it is disrespectful and very funny. But the biggest change lies in the fact that this is the only one of the *Heroides* in which the writer is not a mythological character but a real-life historical personage, and the only one in which homosexual love figures.

Sappho was a famous lyric poetess (i.e. someone who produced poetry which was sung to a musical accompaniment provided by the stringed instrument called the lyre). She was born, apparently from an aristocratic family, in about 630 BC on the Greek island of Lesbos (off the coast of Turkey). She had a daughter, and so was presumably married, but on Lesbos she headed and possibly instructed a literary and musical circle of young women, to whom she refers in her verse with affection and love. Some critics have doubted that she was a lesbian, but Ovid clearly saw her as one (see 15ff. and 201 below on her female partners). This poem centres around what all scholars agree is an invented story about her love for Phaon, who is never mentioned in the lines by her that have survived. According to the tale he was a young ferryman who worked the route between Lesbos and the mainland, and one day he conveyed in his boat Aphrodite (the goddess of love) disguised as an old woman, and did not charge her. In return she made him the most handsome of men. He had an affair with Sappho, but left her, moving on to the island of Sicily, off the toe of Italy. She subsequently threw herself into the sea from a cliff on the Greek island of Leucas, hoping to be healed of her love for him, as was supposed to happen for unhappy lovers who survived the leap, but she did not survive it. Ovid has her write this epistle as a final appeal to Phaon before she goes off to Leucas.

At 89f. she refers to Endymion, a beautiful young shepherd loved by the goddess of the moon, who put him to sleep permanently, so that she could always visit him for sex. See the glossary for the other mythological allusions below.

> Tell me, when you looked at these words eagerly penned by me,
>> did you immediately recognize the handwriting as mine
> or wouldn't you know that this short letter comes from
>> Sappho, if you hadn't read the writer's name?
> And perhaps you ask why I'm producing elegiac   5
>> couplets when I'm more suited to lyric poetry.
> I must mourn my love – elegy is the genre of mourning;
>> lyric verse isn't appropriate for my tears.
> I burn with passion, like a fertile field blazing up when its crop
>> is on fire and wild east-winds drive on the flames.   10
> Phaon, you're far away in Sicily, near Typhos' Etna;
>> I'm possessed by a heat as great as Etna's fires.
> I can't come up with poetry to be accompanied by the lyre's
>> orderly strings; that's the product of a mind without worry.
> The girls of Pyrrha and Methymna have no charms   15
>> for me, nor do those anywhere else on Lesbos;
> I despise Anactoria, I despise fair Cydro;
>> I don't find Atthis attractive any more
> or the hundreds of others here who I have loved without reproach:
>> the love that many girls had is yours alone, you traitor.   20
> You have beauty and are the right age for love's fun
>> and games – o beauty that ambushed my eyes!
> Pick up a lyre and quiver – you'll be Apollo (an epiphany);
>> grow horns on your head – you'll become Bacchus.
> Apollo was Daphne's lover, and Bacchus was Ariadne's,   25
>> yet neither girl could write lyric verse.
> But I am inspired by the Muses to write exquisite poetry,
>> and my name is now celebrated throughout the world.
> My countryman Alcaeus doesn't win more praise,
>> even though his lyric verse is loftier than mine.   30
> If unkind nature has denied me good looks, offset that
>> lack by taking my talent into account.
> I may be small, but I have a reputation that fills every
>> land on earth; I'm as big as my reputation.
> I'm not fair-skinned, but Perseus found Cepheus' Andromeda   35
>> attractive, and she was dark (from darkest Ethiopia);
> and white doves often have mates of a different colour,
>> and black turtle-doves are loved by green parrots.

If nobody can be your girl unless you think her beauty
   worthy of yours, nobody will be your girl.   40
When I read you my poems, you thought me good-looking enough then;
   you always swore my words made me supremely attractive.
I'd sing them, I remember (lovers remember everything),
   and while I sang them, you'd give me stolen kisses.
You praised my kisses too, and I pleased you in every way,   45
   but especially when we made love.
Then you particularly liked my sensuality and my
   constant liveliness in bed and my sexy talk
and, after we'd reached a climax together, the deep,
   deep languor of our exhausted bodies.   50
Now new prey – the girls of Sicily come to you.
   What's Lesbos to me? I want to be a Sicilian.
O send that runaway back to me from your island,
   you young women and you older women of Sicily!
Don't let his seductive, lying tongue deceive you: 55
   what he says to you he said before to me.
Divine Venus, enshrined on Sicily's Mount Eryx,
   I'm yours, so protect your poetess.
Is misfortune still dogging me, continuing as it began,
   inexorably set on its cruel course?   60
I was six years old when I shed tears on the ashes
   of my father, cremated before his time.
My stupid brother was ensnared, burned with love for a prostitute,
   lost his money and thoroughly disgraced himself.
Now he's poor, and sails the blue seas, rowing hard,   65
   trying to recoup his shameful loss in shameful ways.
Because I gave him lots of good, loyal advice, he hates me –
   that's what I get for my frankness and devotion!
And, as if there wasn't enough to wear me out endlessly,
   I've got my little daughter to worry about too.   70
And finally there's you – yet another cause for complaint.
   There's no smooth sailing on the sea of love for me.
Look, my hair's all over the place, hanging on my neck in a mess,
   and I don't wear any rings with sparkling stones;
my dress is shabby, I don't have a gold hairpin in   75
   and my hair isn't perfumed by the gifts of Arabia.
I'm miserable. Who should I dress up for alluringly?
   You're the only reason for dressing up, and you're not here.
My tender heart is susceptible to Cupid's swift arrows;
   there's always a reason for me to be always in love –   80
whether the fates prescribed this as a rule for me at my birth
   and didn't spin an austere thread of life for me,

or writing poetry affects my personality, and Thalia (the Muse
    who instructs me) makes my character tender.
Is it surprising if I've been swept away by someone of the age   85
    when the downy beard begins and men can be captivated?
Dawn, I feared you'd carry him off, as you carried off Cephalus,
    and you would, but Cephalus holds your affections.
If the Moon, who sees everything, saw Phaon,
    she'd command him to sleep for all time.   90
Venus would have taken him to heaven in her ivory chariot,
    but she sees that her Mars could also find him attractive.
Not yet a youth, no longer a boy (and so of service to me),
    the pride and great glory of your generation,
come here, handsome, sail back to my arms! I'm not   95
    asking you to love but to let yourself be loved.
As I write, the tears well up in my eyes and spill over:
    see how many blots there are in this part of my letter.
If you were so set on leaving, you might have done so with more
    decorum, and just said: 'Goodbye, you girl of Lesbos.'   100
You didn't take with you my tears or kisses, you didn't let me be
    frightened of the heartache ahead by alerting me to it.
I have nothing of yours except the wrong you did me,
    and you have no token to remind you of your lover.
I didn't give you parting instructions, but I wouldn't have   105
    given any, except that you shouldn't forget me.
I swear to you by our love (may it never be far from us!)
    and by the nine Muses, who are my divinities,
that when somebody said to me: 'Your sweetheart's running away,'
    I couldn't weep or speak for a long time.   110
There were no tears in my eyes, no words on my lips;
    my mind was numb with the cold chill of fear.
When my grief found its bearings, I felt no shame at beating
    my breast, tearing my hair and shrieking
like a devoted mother who has lost her son and is carrying   115
    his lifeless body to a heaped up funeral pyre.
My sorrow makes my brother Charaxus swell with joy,
    and he parades before my eyes again and again;
so it seems there's something disgraceful behind my grief, he says:
    'Why's she upset? Her daughter certainly hasn't died.'   120
Modesty and love don't go together. Everyone was watching.
    I tore my dress in grief, exposing my breasts.
Phaon, you're my darling. My dreams bring you back to me,
    dreams more radiant than the beautiful daylight.
I meet you in them, although in reality you're far away;   125
    but the pleasure that sleep gives me doesn't last long enough.

Often I dream that I rest my head on your arms,
    often that I put my arms around your neck.
I recognize the kisses, tongue entwined around tongue,
    which you used to give me and get back from me.   130
Sometimes I whisper sweet nothings, speaking words that
    are almost real, with lips attentive to my feelings.
I'm ashamed to describe the rest, but we do it all,
    and I enjoy it, and can't help but be wet.
But when the sun reveals itself and the world,   135
    I complain that sleep has deserted me so soon.
I go to the caves and the wood that witnessed my rapturous
    love-making – as if caves and a wood could help me!
I rush there, my hair unbound, out of my mind,
    like a woman touched by maddening Enyo.   140
I look at the caves (with their arches of rough volcanic rock),
    which seemed to me as lovely as Mygdonian marble.
I find the forest which often provided a bed for us
    and hid us under the shade of all its leaves,
but I don't find the lord of the forest, and my lord;   145
    it's just a paltry piece of ground: *he* made it attractive.
I have recognized the well-known blades of grass,
    bent over and pressed down by our weight;
I have lain down and touched the spot where you reclined;
    the turf I once treasured has drunk my tears.   150
So too the trees have shed their foliage in mourning,
    it seems, and no birds sing their sad, sweet songs,
except the nightingale – anguished Procne lamenting Itys,
    the son she killed for unholy revenge on her husband.
The bird sings of Itys, Sappho of love deserted, and that's all   155
    there is to hear; otherwise it's as silent as midnight.
There's a sacred spring, which glitters, more transparent than
    any glass (many people think a deity lives there);
above it a water-lotus spreads its branches wide (a grove
    all by itself); the ground is green with soft turf.   160
When I lay down there, in tears and exhausted,
    a water-nymph stood before my eyes.
She stood there and said: 'You're burning with unrequited
    passion; so go to the region of Ambracia.
There Apollo in his temple on high looks down on all the   165
    outspread sea which people call Actian and also Leucadian.
Deucalion, inflamed with love for Pyrrha, threw himself down
    from there and hit the water without suffering harm;
in it his fire went out at once, love turned tail and fled,
    and his heart became impervious to passion.   170

That's the rule there. Go to the high cliff on Leucas
   immediately, and leap from it without fear.'
Her words of advice faded away, and so did she. I got up,
   terrified. I couldn't contain my tears.
Nymph, I'll go, off to the cliff you mentioned. May love's   175
   frenzy conquer my fear and drive it far away!
Whatever happens will be better than this. Breeze, blow beneath
   my body and support it (it's not heavy);
tender Cupid, put your wings under me as I fall, so I don't
   die and people don't blame the Leucadian Sea for that.   180
In thanks I'll dedicate to Apollo my lyre (the instrument
   we both play), with two verses inscribed beneath it:
APOLLO, THE POETESS SAPPHO GRATEFULLY DEDICATES TO YOU
   THIS LYRE, AN APT GIFT FROM HER AND FOR YOU.
But why send your miserable lover to the Actian coast,   185
   when you could come back home again?
You can be better for my health than the Leucadian Sea; if you're
   kind to me, with your looks you'll be Phoebus in my eyes.
Oh, you're fiercer than any cliff or wave, but can you
   bear to be called my killer, if I die?   190
Ah, how much better for my breast to be pressed to yours
   than to be hurled headlong from a cliff.
Phaon, this is the breast that you used to praise,
   that so often seemed talented to you.
I wish I was eloquent now. Grief hinders my art,   195
   and my troubles have checked all my talent.
My old poetic power won't come at my call, and my
   lyre and plectrum are idle, silenced by grief.
My group of girls from Lesbos, married and yet to marry,
   girls from Lesbos named in my lyric verse,   200
girls from the isle of Lesbos loved by me, notoriously,
   don't come to listen to my lyre any more.
Phaon has destroyed all the poetry you once enjoyed
   (ah, I very nearly said just now 'my Phaon');
make him return, and your poetess will return: 205
   my talent's strength or weakness depends on *him*.
Are my pleas achieving anything? Is his uncouth heart moved,
   or not? Are my words futile, swept away by the wind?
I wish it would bring you sailing back to me instead, you cold man.
   That's what you should do, if you had any sense.   210
If you're coming back, and are making garlands for your ship
   in celebration, why tear my heart apart by delaying?
Sail! Sea-born Venus makes the sea safe for a lover.
   The wind will speed you on your way. Just sail!

Cupid himself will sit at the stern and steer your ship;   215
    he'll spread and furl the sails with his soft hands.
If you want to run far away from Sappho of Lesbos
    (though you won't find a good reason for running away),
at least tell me that in a cruel letter, so in my misery
    I can seek my fate in the Leucadian Sea.   220

Sappho was the most renowned poetess of Greece and Rome. She was highly regarded in antiquity, included in the canon of the nine major Greek lyric poets and referred to as a tenth Muse (traditionally there were nine Muses, patron goddesses of verse and song, who were themselves supremely skilled musicians). To judge from what has survived, her writing was predominantly personal and erotic, and was passionate and moving, so that it has a great emotional impact; but it also has the intellectual appeal of melodiousness, subtlety and elegance. She influenced a wide variety of subsequent authors, including Baudelaire, Byron, Catullus, Durrell, H.D., Horace, Pound, Rilke, Swinburne and Verlaine. Because of constraints of space we have to restrict ourselves to some of the most famous pieces by her (mainly fragmentary) to fill out the picture, but for more on Sappho and her poetry and on the reception of both see Johnson, Reynolds and Greene.

In the first fragment her depth of feeling embraces her daughter, in exchange for whom she would (presumably) not take one of the richest kingdoms of the day or some other place (like Lesbos) famed for its beauty. She includes a short simile which implies a lot about Cleis (apart from the relevant properties of flowers in general; note that gold had divine associations, and golden flowers grew in the fabulous paradise called the Isles of the Blessed).

I have a beautiful daughter – my darling
Cleis, who looks like golden flowers; for
her I would not . . . all Lydia or lovely

Another fragment also contains an effective image (for violent mental disturbance caused by love), in which distracting ornamentation is absent, and every word does duty (the wind would be particularly powerful on high, and the choice of oaks for the trees implies a mighty struggle).

And Eros convulsed my
mind like a wind falling on oaks up a mountain.

Sappho also composed marriage-songs for performance at weddings on Lesbos. A simile in one of them likened the bride to a sweet-apple and was melodious and apposite (apples were love-tokens and were connected with the goddess of love and with weddings). There are obvious correspondences between the girl and the reddening sweet-apple in itself. Sappho also draws attention to the apple's lofty position, implying that the bride was special and superior. After that Sappho may be lightly teasing her, raising the possibility that men had just forgotten about her, but then quickly correcting that and stressing the third line; the natural inference is that the bride had remained a virgin.

> just as the sweet-apple reddens on the branch at the top,
> on top of the topmost one; the apple-pickers forgot –
> not forgot completely, but could not manage to reach it.

The next fragment tries to comfort the young woman Atthis in her separation from a female companion who has gone to Lydia for some reason.

> . . . .
> . . . . often turning her thoughts this way
> . . . . she . . . . you
> as an unmistakable
> goddess and enjoyed *your* singing most.   5
> Now she stands out amid the Lydi-
> an women like the rosy-
> fingered moon (after the sun has set)
> surpassing all the stars; light is spread
> over the salty sea and   10
> also over the flowerful fields;
> the dew is sprinkled beautifully,
> roses bloom and soft chervil-
> plants and flowery honeyclover.
> Often roaming, recalling gentle   15
> Atthis with longing she doubt-
> less eats out her sensitive heart.

Here Sappho produces remarks to console Atthis and also poetry to distract and charm her. As well as portraying a picturesque nocturnal scene in lines 6–14, Sappho implies that the absent friend is a pre-eminent beauty among a host of lesser beauties, with her radiance denoted by 'rosy-fingered' (white roses are most pertinent here, so the adjective will refer to pale moon-beams). Sappho will have chosen the moon for her image because for people on Lesbos it rises in Turkey (where the companion is); and perhaps the moon, which could be seen by Atthis, was meant to act as a substitute for her friend, who could not, with 9–11 suggesting the moonlight coming from Turkey to Lesbos and so forming a link between the females. At 10–14 the wide spread of the moon's light stresses the companion's radiance still further, and the effect of the dew (supposedly produced by the moon) may be intended to intimate that she had a similarly invigorating effect on people.

In the next piece (a complete poem for a change) again the poetess is in love with a female and is being rejected by her. So Sappho prays to the love goddess

Aphrodite, asking her to do now what she has done before – come, find out the cause of the trouble and undertake to change the female's mind. There is a solemnity that is apt for a formal prayer, but there is also intimacy here.

> Elaborately-enthroned, deathless Aphrodite,
> wile-weaving child of Zeus, I beg you,
> don't overwhelm my heart with pangs and
> anguish, Mistress,
> but come here, if you ever in the   5
> past heard and paid heed to my voice from
> afar and came, leaving your father's
> palace and yoking
> your golden chariot; and lovely,
> swift sparrows bore you over the black   10
> earth, their massed wings whirling, down from heav-
> en through the mid-air,
> and they arrived quickly; Blessed One,
> with a smile on your deathless face, you
> asked what troubled me this time, what made   15
> me call you this time
> and what I wished you to do, with
> all my mad heart. 'Who must I persuade this
> time . . . to your love? Who's not being
> fair to you, Sappho?   20
> For if she shuns you, she'll soon pursue;
> if she spurns gifts, she'll give them to you;
> if she does not love, she'll soon love too,
> against her wishes.'
> Come to me now too, set me free from   25
> chronic anxieties, bring about
> what my heart wants brought about, and fight
> on my side yourself.

Critics have praised the graphic description of the chariot drawn by the goddess' sacred birds at 9ff. and the lively depiction of the affectionate and informal Aphrodite at 13ff. But this poem is more remarkable as a human document. Cast as a private prayer (on which we eavesdrop), it shows a person at a loss trying to hearten herself (by turning to a superior power and recollecting that things came out well in the past) and, despite emotional turmoil, not being over-familiar or pushy, but deferential and restrained. So she does not over-emphasize her pain, although she makes it clear early on. And she operates more by implicit than explicit appeals: we deduce that she wants the goddess once again to come quickly, smile comfortingly, chaff her reassuringly and above all solemnly promise to remedy the situation rapidly and completely.

Finally there is a very famous fragment addressed to a beloved female, in which Sappho lists the symptoms of deep love that she experiences whenever she looks at the addressee.

> To me he seems to be the equal
> of the gods, the man who sits oppo-
> site you and listens, close by, to you
> speaking sweetly and
> loveably laughing; and that real-   5
> ly jolts the heart in my breast. For when-
> ever I glance at you, I simply
> can't speak any more,
> but my tongue is . . . and silent,
> fine fire has instantly raced under   10
> my skin, my eyes simply can't see, I've
> whirring in my ears,
> and cold sweat covers me, tremors seize
> all of me, and I am paler than
> grass, and I seem to myself not far   15
> away from dying.
> But it is all bearable since . . .

The pathos and the passion come across strongly there. The agonized state at 7ff. stands out more thanks to the contrast with 1–5. For example, the opening (ordinary) scene is followed by Sappho's extraordinary reactions; she pairs the male and female but isolates herself; and the addressee is speaking, while Sappho can't speak. The focus on speech and laughter at 4f. is suggestive (lovers are often particularly fascinated by just one or two qualities). More powerfully, at 7ff. Sappho describes a whole host of extreme effects, gaining impact by adding point after point. The expression there is direct and sparing of adjectives and imagery. And so we find even more striking the phrases 'fine fire' and 'paler than grass' (i.e. grass parched by the sun: a sallow (Greek) skin's pallor is similarly yellowish). At 7ff. Sappho also presents her disordered state in a very orderly fashion. For instance, the first three symptoms and the last three are groups which each form an increasing triad (a set of three in which more space is devoted to the second symptom than the first, and then more space is given to the third than the second); and those groups frame the central group of three (in which each symptom is treated at exactly the same length). The fact that Sappho demonstrated such control when she composed these lines highlights further her lack of control when she looked at the addressee.

Ovid presents a very different Sappho in *Heroides* 15 and subverts this rightly revered poetess. How do you react to that subversion and what do you make of it? Formulate your thoughts on this before reading on.

Some critics find fault with Ovid as a male all too readily taking over a tale that denies a female her natural (lesbian) sexuality and usurping her poetic voice. So

Harvey (in Greene 84ff.) talks of 'sexual mastery and theft' and the 'ventriloquistic appropriation' of Sappho's voice, which Ovid subordinates to his own. Compare also Lindheim 155ff., who views Ovid as using Sappho as a mouthpiece to take away the potential for a woman's multiplicity evident in her fragments and 'controlling both her poetic expression and her expression of women's desire(s)'. And it is true that there is something of a Roman tradition of male writers making negative comments about female homoeroticism.

Another line of approach to *Heroides* 15 would see Ovid as being light-hearted and mischievous (rather than having a serious agenda), finding a tempting target in the highly esteemed Sappho and having irreverent fun with her, just as he did with the male authors Homer (in *Her.* 1) and Virgil (in *Her.* 7), and just as he jokes at his own expense in *Amores* 3.7 (a whole elegy devoted to his embarrassing impotence when in bed with a beautiful girl). We incline rather to this point of view, while allowing that there is also validity in the feminist position outlined above. We feel that Ovid is relishing the whole quaintly comical situation of this famous lesbian totally rejecting females, in love with a man and having sex with a man, and of the venerable Greek poetess talking dirty (45ff.), having wet dreams (133f.) and losing her dignity by openly admitting that and by begging, flattering etc. (in Latin!). Our playful poet also seems to us to be mocking his illustrious predecessor (but gently mocking her: he shows respect for her at *Tristia* 3.7.20), especially by representing this extremely intelligent woman as decidedly silly and by making this great writer produce a thoroughly incompetent piece of writing.

Ovid's Sappho has been surprisingly naive in the past, when Phaon was around: when he claimed that her poems made her supremely attractive (41–4), he will have been merely flattering her so that she would have sex with him (as she virtually admits at 55f.; and he was obviously not that captivated by her verse, as he interrupted her performance of it with kisses; and he did jilt her subsequently). This Sappho is also foolish now. For a start she simply does not take into account the fact that Phaon is just a ferryman, and so is uneducated. We can reasonably assume that he would be unable to read or write, so that her question about him recognizing her handwriting at 1f. and her request for a letter from him in 219 are fatuous. And it is hardly likely that he would know the difference between lyric and elegiac poetry and so wonder why she was producing the latter (5f.). In addition, it is absurdly misguided of her to be so critical of an errant lover. For comments about his lying tongue (55), his lack of decorum (99f.), his inhuman ferocity (189), his uncouth heart (207), his coldness (209) and his lack of sense (210; which is particularly rich in *her* mouth) are scarcely going to win him back. She also clumsily undermines her own position. She dwells on her brother's failings (at 63ff. and 117ff.), which would make Phaon unlikely to want to have any connection with such a family. And she really highlights her own shortcomings. As well as being naturally unattractive (33ff.), she is at present frumpy in her misery (73ff.), has made an embarrassing spectacle of herself on Lesbos bewailing his departure (113ff., 121f.) and is the kind of obsessive female that few men would want to be involved with, having erotic dreams about him (123ff.), revisiting the place where they had intercourse and lying down where he lay (137ff.). All of this would, of course, get him rushing back to her!

Ovid's Sappho also says laughably silly things. She calls this letter (of 220 lines) 'short' in 3. At 53f. she appeals to the women of Sicily to send back to her the divinely handsome Phaon (as if they would!). She refers to herself (a married woman with a child) as a 'girl' in 100. She addresses a breeze at 177f., and supposes that it could hold up her body as she plunges from the Leucadian cliff; and she thinks that the god of love will help her escape from love at 179f. See if you can spot what is similarly silly in her remarks at 191f., 205, 213 and 218. On top of all that, here the great poetess' poeticisms are frequently inept (and Ovid seems to play on that wittily at 195ff., where he has her complain of the loss of her talent through grief). She cannot even manage an effective simile at 9f.: the blazing field to which she compares herself there would soon burn out, unlike her fiery passion. So too her analogies at 37f. are cloddish: birds are not a good parallel for humans, and she actually likens Phaon to a parrot there, a green parrot at that. And she botches the flattery in her mythological allusions at 87ff.: there is bathos in line 88 (which does not in fact amount to a compliment); there is an obvious lack of logic in 89; and 92 conjures up an image of the stern, virile god of war as a homosexual lover captivated by a pretty boy when Venus is around! Look for the same kind of flaws in the simile at 115f. (how apt, and how flattering to Sappho, is that?), the picture at 151–6 (how realistic, and convincing, is it?) and the flight of fancy at 215f. (visualize the scene!). Actually, if you re-examine the whole poem, you will find many more examples of all the above categories of humour. This is a constantly improbable and amusing epistle.

As well as loving Phaon, Sappho was said to have had affairs with the lyric poets Alcaeus (who was at least her contemporary) and Anacreon (who was born about fifty years after her!). There were lots of such stories about Greek poets in antiquity. They are in general unreliable, and many of them are quaint and comic. Supposedly when Euripides fell asleep on Mount Helicon, a bee constructed a honeycomb in his mouth, signifying the sweet song that issued from it (and suggesting that he slept with his mouth open and was a pretty heavy sleeper). The god Pan was heard singing one of Pindar's poems, and the goddess Demeter appeared to Pindar in a dream asking him to write a hymn about her. During a performance of Aeschylus' tragedy called *The Eumenides* the actors playing the Furies (dread deities of vengeance from the Underworld) looked so terrifying that children fainted and pregnant women had miscarriages. Aeschylus himself came to a sad end, when a (rather short-sighted) eagle flying above him with a tortoise in its talons mistook his bald head for a rock and dropped the tortoise on to it to smash its shell. There were also sad ends for Philemon (who laughed himself to death), for the tragedian Sophocles (who choked when he ran out of breath while reciting from a play of his entitled *Antigone*) and for Alcman (who died of lice).

There were improbable tales about Roman poets too, many of them attached to Virgil. As a learned man, who had written about magic and the Underworld in his verse, he was believed in the Middle Ages to have been a wizard. Many of the magic stories are connected with Naples, a city in which Virgil had stayed and in which he was buried. He was said to have founded the city, and to have balanced it on an egg (for some reason best known to himself). He also made for it a butcher's block which kept meat fresh indefinitely, and he created a bronze fly which made ordinary flies stay away from Naples. He kept the local volcano Vesuvius in check by means of a bronze statue of an archer threatening it with an arrow on his drawn bow aimed at it, until a passing moron fiddled with the statue and fired off the arrow. Virgil's bones were placed in a castle overlooking Naples and surrounded by the sea; if they were exposed to the air, the water became violently disturbed, clouds gathered and a storm raged. His magic powers extended beyond Naples. At Rome he constructed a beautiful palace containing statues which represented all the different lands in the Roman empire; each image had a bell in its hand, and when any of the lands was about to revolt from Rome, its statue rang its bell, and a bronze warrior on the roof of the palace brandished his lance at the place in question. Also, while on the fabulous Mountain of Sorrows, Virgil was shown by a spirit a book of magic under a corpse's head; when Virgil opened the book, 80,000 demons instantly appeared and put themselves at his disposal; whereupon the poet, bizarrely, used them to pave a long street. And after Virgil died and his soul arrived at the gates of Hell, the devils there would not let him in, because they were so frightened of his powers as a sorcerer.

Heroides 16

PARIS TO HELEN

This is the first of the double *Heroides*, three pairs of letters in which a hero writes to a heroine and receives a response from her. By means of this literary form Ovid here gives a lively new twist to one of the most frequently treated stories in Classical literature, providing an intimate insight into the thoughts and feelings of two very famous lovers as they are on the point of bringing about one of the longest and deadliest wars in ancient myth. Some of the details mentioned in *Heroides* 16 may be unfamiliar to you, so do quickly scan the following paragraph, to ensure that you comprehend fully and get the most out of this epistle.

When Hecuba, the wife of Priam (king of Troy, in the region of Phrygia) was pregnant with Paris, she dreamed that she gave birth to a huge, flaming torch. A prophet said that this meant that Troy (also known as Ilium) would burn with the fire of Paris (i.e. he would be responsible for its fiery destruction). So when the baby was born, he was left out in the open on nearby Mount Ida to die. But a herdsman found him and brought him up as his own son. When Paris was still young, he drove off some cattle-robbers, and so was given the extra name of Alexander (meaning in Greek 'one who wards off men'). Subsequently his true identity was revealed, and he was welcomed back into the royal family. Paris was later asked to judge which of the goddesses Juno, Minerva (Pallas) and Venus was the loveliest. They all tried to bribe him, and he accepted Venus' offer of the most beautiful woman in the world. This was Helen, the daughter of the Greek heroine Leda and Jupiter, who had taken the form of a swan and copulated with her. Helen was born in the little country town of Therapnae, and when she was still a girl she was so attractive that the hero Theseus abducted her, although he did return her when her brothers came and demanded her back. Now she was the wife of Menelaus, king of Sparta. Paris built a fleet and prepared to sail off to Greece to get her. His sister Cassandra (who was a prophetess, although nobody believed her prophecies, which were always true) predicted that he would bring a conflagration back with him (i.e. his return with Helen would end in the fiery destruction of Troy). When Paris landed, Menelaus gave him a hospitable welcome. During the course of his visit Menelaus went off to view his territory on the island of Crete. It is at this point that Paris writes the present letter and sends it to Helen in an attempt to seduce her. Helen, of course, did elope with Paris, and a huge Greek army besieged Troy to get her back. Many men died in the war, including Paris' brother (the formidable warrior Hector) and Paris. An archer himself, Paris was killed by an arrow which was shot by the Greek hero Philoctetes and guided home by Minerva (this was the heavenly arrow that Cassandra had prophesied would hit Paris). After that Troy fell, was plundered and set on fire.

This is a highly entertaining poem. The whole idea of Paris sending a letter to Helen at this point is rather comical in itself. The great length of the epistle shows how determined and desperate he is to win over Helen, whom he obviously sees as a very tough nut to crack. It is diverting to watch the renowned great lover writhing and striving to get the affair going, especially as running on and on is quite unnecessary. The goddess Venus has personally promised Helen to him, as he often remarks himself. The heroine has already given him encouraging indications of her interest in him, laughing rather than being outraged at his groans when she kisses her husband (229f.), and letting Paris see her breasts (249ff.); but he is apparently too unperceptive or too backward to get the hints. And we know that *of course* he will get the girl (this is one of the most famous love affairs ever) and that their elopement (and the subsequent war) are fated and in accordance with a divine plan. So the longer Paris goes on the funnier it is.

On top of that he doesn't even make a very good job of trying to win her over. In fact Paris is an amusingly undignified and unimpressive hero: driven by love and lust, he is selfish and rash; he is also foolishly unreflecting, or is deliberately putting a positive spin on gloomy prophecies and wilfully closing his eyes to very probable danger ahead as a result of a liaison with Helen. He has four main ploys: he protests his love; he flatters her (via her beauty and fame); he attempts to impress her (with his wealth, his high birth, his father's kingdom, his contact with divinities etc.); and he stresses that Venus has promised her to him (the implication being that Helen has no choice but to accept him, as she can't cross such a powerful goddess). Such arguments seem sound enough in themselves; but they are employed over and over again, as this eager young puppy repeats himself at length and is in danger of overdoing it and boring or even irritating the addressee.

In addition, his remarks are often fatuous and inept. So, for instance, at 36ff. he makes the implausible claim that he was in love with Helen before he even saw her; at 43ff. he actually passes on an ominous dream about himself as a destructive torch, referring it improbably to his burning love for her; at 93ff. he is bumptious and obvious when he talks of all the females who have desired him; at 107ff. he goes on at tedious length about ship-building; and at 187ff. he runs the risk of offending the Greek heroine by criticizing her homeland and birthplace and contrasting it unfavourably with Troy. As you read the poem, look for more examples of silly and misguided comments. Really it is just as well for him that Helen fancies him (as we learn in *Heroides* 17).

There is also a darker tinge to the humour, in the extensive irony, obvious not to Paris but to us, because we know the outcome of this affair. So he goes to such lengths here to bring about ultimately the destruction of himself, his city and many of his family and fellow-citizens. He speaks glibly of the fire of love and of arrows and the wound of love, when Troy will soon be on fire and he will be wounded by Philoctetes' arrow. He describes with relish his judgment and the building of ships to take him to Sparta, all of which leads eventually to disaster. He maintains that fate is smiling on him and a relationship with Helen is fated, but the deadly consequences of that are also destined. And he boasts about Trojan culture, riches and resources, as he takes the first step to putting an end to all of that. See if you can spot more instances of such tragicomic irony in the lines below (e.g. in 84, 91f., 129 and 169).

> From the son of Priam to Leda's daughter – good day!
>> A good day for *me* depends entirely on you.
> Should I speak out or is that unnecessary? Do you already know that
>> I'm inflamed with love, is that more obvious than I'd like?
> I'd prefer it to go unobserved, until the time comes   5
>> when we can take our pleasure without fear,
> but I'm not good at hiding it – who could conceal a love
>> which constantly betrays itself by burning so brightly?
> But if you're waiting for me to say it as well as show it by my actions,
>> I'm on fire – there, that tells you my feelings.   10
> Please pardon my confession, and don't read what follows with a
>> hard expression but with one befitting your beauty.
> I'm already obliged to you: your acceptance of this letter makes
>> me hope that I too may win similar acceptance.
> May that hope come true, may Venus' promise to me of you be   15
>> made good (she was the one who urged this voyage on me)!
> Just so you know, when you're unfaithful with me: I sailed here on
>> divine instructions, aided in my enterprise by a mighty deity.
> I'm asking for a great prize certainly, but one owed to me:
>> Cupid's mother herself pledged you to me in marriage.   20
> Guided by her I made the dangerous voyage from the Trojan coast
>> far across the sea in a ship built by Phereclus.
> She provided helpful breezes and favourable winds: she was born
>> from the sea, and so of course has power over the sea.
> May she stay kind, calm my agitation, as she calmed   25
>> the waves, and bring my desires safely to harbour!
> I didn't fall in love here, I was already on fire when I came,
>> and that was the reason for such a lengthy voyage.
> I didn't get lost, no savage storm brought me here:
>> I deliberately steered for Sparta with my fleet.   30
> And don't imagine that I'm sailing with merchandise to trade:

I already have wealth — may the gods preserve it!
I'm not here as a tourist, to see the cities of Greece:
   the towns in my own kingdom are more sumptuous.
I come for you, betrothed to me by golden Venus.   35
   I wanted you before I knew you.
I had a mental picture of your face before I actually saw it;
   the wound in my heart began with the rumour that told me of you.
Yet, as the bow is so powerful, it's no wonder that I'm in love
   after being hit by an arrow of Cupid's shot from afar.   40
Such is the will of fate. And so you don't try to subvert that,
   listen to a true and trustworthy tale.
By now my mother's belly was swollen with a fully grown foetus,
   but I was still held in her womb, slow to be born.
In her sleep she had a vision and dreamed that her pregnant   45
   womb gave birth to a huge flaming torch.
She got up, terrified, and told old Priam about the dark
   night's dreadful dream, which he referred to his prophets.
One prophet predicted that Troy would burn with the fire of Paris —
   that was the flame in my heart, which now exists.   50
Although people thought I was low-born, my good looks and mental
   vigour showed that my noble lineage had been obscured.
In the midst of wooded Ida's valleys there's a remote
   spot, enveloped by pine-trees and holm-oaks,
where the grass isn't grazed by the gaping mouths of slow-moving   55
   cows or placid sheep or rock-loving goats.
I was leaning against a tree, looking out from there
   at Troy's walls and lofty buildings and the sea —
suddenly the ground seemed to me to tremble beneath the tread of feet —
   I'll tell the truth, though you'll hardly believe it's true —   60
Mercury, the grandson of great Atlas and Pleione,
   swiftly flew down and halted before my eyes
(I hope I'm permitted to speak of what I was permitted to see)
   and there was a golden staff in the god's hand.
At the same time three goddesses — Venus, Pallas and   65
   Juno — set their tender feet on the grass.
I was stunned, a cold shudder made my hair stand on end,
   when the winged messenger said to me: 'Don't be afraid.
You're a judge of beauty. Put an end to the goddesses' quarrel about
   who deserves to beat the other two as the most beautiful.'   70
So I wouldn't refuse, he commanded me in the name of Jupiter
   and immediately soared up through the sky to the stars.
I recovered my wits, suddenly became daring and wasn't
   afraid to gaze at each goddess observantly.
All of them deserved the prize, and as their judge   75

I expressed my regret that they couldn't all win.
However, already then one of them was more attractive,
    so you could tell she was the one who inspires love.
They wanted to win so much that they offered lavish gifts
    in their eagerness to manipulate my verdict.   80
Juno went on about dominion, Pallas about prowess in war;
    I didn't know whether I wanted to be powerful or brave.
Venus laughed sweetly and said: 'Paris, don't be influenced by these
    presents, both of which involve lots of anxiety and fear.
I'll give you someone to love: pretty Leda's still   85
    prettier daughter will come into your arms.'
After she said that, I approved her gift and her beauty
    equally, and she returned to heaven victorious.
Meanwhile – I suppose because fate now decided to smile on me –
    thanks to reliable indications I was recognized as a prince.   90
The royal family was delighted to recover a long-lost son,
    and Troy added that day to its festivals.
Just as I desire you, so girls have desired me;
    you alone can have what many want.
It's not just the daughters of kings and chieftains who have courted me: 95
    nymphs too have cared for me and loved me.
Who was there to surpass Oenone's marvellous beauty? After you
    nobody in the world is more worthy of being Priam's daughter-in-law.
But I despised all of those females once I was
    given the hope of marrying you, Helen.   100
I saw visions of you when awake, I dreamed of you at night,
    when the eyes are inactive, overcome by peaceful sleep.
Loved when not yet seen, what effect will you have on me in person?
    I burned, although the cause of the fire was here, far away.
I couldn't deny myself what I hoped for any longer,   105
    I had to sail off to get the girl I wanted.
Our Phrygian axes hacked down Trojan pine-woods,
    and all the trees that could be used for sea-going ships;
the lofty forests on Gargara's heights were plundered,
    and Ida's mountain range supplied countless timbers.   110
Oak planks were bent to form the hulls for swift ships,
    and a ribbed framework was attached to the curving keels.
We fitted on to the masts their cross-beams and attendant sails,
    and added painted images of the gods to the rounded sterns.
On my boat is depicted the goddess who guarantees your   115
    marriage to me, accompanied by a little Cupid.
After the finishing touch, when the ships were completed,
    I wanted to sail off over the Aegean Sea at once.
But my father and mother kept me from my heart's desire, delaying

the journey I planned with devoted appeals to me;   120
and my sister Cassandra, just as she was, with streaming hair,
   when my fleet was now about to set sail, shouted out:
'Where are you rushing? You'll bring a huge fire back with you!
   You don't know what a blaze you're seeking out over this sea!'
The prophetess told the truth. I've found the flames she spoke of,   125
   and love burns fiercely in this tender heart of mine.
I left the harbour, made use of favourable winds
   and landed in your country, royal bride of Sparta.
Your husband welcomed me hospitably – this too
   happened in accordance with the will and plan of the gods.   130
He showed me everything that was notable and
   worth showing in the whole of Sparta.
But I longed to see your acclaimed beauty,
   and there was nothing else to beguile my eyes.
When I saw it, I was stunned, thunderstruck, and I felt   135
   my inmost heart swell with extraordinary desire.
Venus had a face like yours, as far as I can recall,
   when she came to be judged by me.
If you had come to that contest with her,
   victory for Venus would have been doubtful.   140
Rumour has really spread your name far and wide,
   and every land knows of your beauty.
No other lovely woman anywhere in Phrygia or from
   the furthest east has fame equal to yours.
But trust me on this: your glory doesn't live up to the real you,   145
   and your reputation all but maligns your attractions.
I find here more than it promised, and your glory
   is surpassed by the beauty that caused it.
So the great Theseus had good grounds for his lust, for viewing you
   as worthy spoil, after getting to know all your charms,   150
while you exercised in the gleaming gymnasium, a naked female
   amid naked men, according to Spartan custom.
I commend the abduction; I'm amazed that he ever returned you.
   He should have held on resolutely to such fine booty.
This head of mine would have been severed from my bloody neck   155
   before you were dragged off from *my* bedroom.
Would my hands ever have consented to let *you* go? While I still
   lived, would I have allowed *you* to leave my arms?
If you *had* to be returned, I'd have got something from you first,
   I wouldn't have been completely inactive sexually.   160
I would have taken either your virginity or what could have
   been stolen without the loss of your virginity.
Just give yourself to me, and you'll come to know my constancy;

only the pyre's flames will put an end to the flames in my heart.
I preferred you to the kingdoms which mightiest Juno,   165
    Jupiter's wife and sister, once promised me.
So long as I could put my arms around your neck, I despised
    the prowess in war that Pallas bestowed on me.
I've no regrets, I'll never think I made a foolish choice;
    my mind's made up – I continue to want you.   170
I've worked so hard pursuing you, but you're worth it.
    Just don't let my hope prove to be in vain, please.
I'm not some peasant wanting to marry a noble lady;
    you won't be disgraced by being my wife, believe me.
If you look, you'll find our line contains Jupiter and a Pleiad,   175
    to say nothing of my ancestors after them.
My father rules the realm of Asia, the richest region on earth,
    a territory almost too vast to be toured.
You'll see innumerable cities and buildings of gold
    and temples which you'd describe as fit for their gods.   180
You'll gaze on Ilium and its walls, fortified by lofty towers,
    and made to build themselves by the music of Apollo's lyre.
Why tell you about the throng, the multitude of men?
    There are almost too many people for that land to sustain.
Trojan matrons will hurry to meet you in a dense line,   185
    there'll be more of our young women than the palace can hold.
Oh, how often you'll say: 'How poor my Greece is!' Any house
    at all in Troy, you'll find, contains the wealth of a city.
But it wouldn't be right for me to despise your Sparta;
    the land in which *you* were born is rich in my eyes.   190
But Sparta is a frugal place, not suited to beauty
    such as yours: you deserve sumptuous clothing.
Adornments without end should be lavished on loveliness like
    yours, it should luxuriate in new-fangled finery.
When you see the clothing of the men here from Troy,   195
    what do you think our young women wear?
Just give in to me, and don't disdain a Trojan
    for your husband, you country girl from Therapnae.
Ganymede, who is now with the gods and mixes nectar with water
    for their drinks, was a Trojan, and a member of my family.   200
Tithonus was a Trojan, but he was carried off as her husband by
    a goddess – Dawn, who finally ends night's journey.
Anchises was a Trojan too, and Venus, the mother of the winged
    Cupids, enjoyed intercourse with him on Ida's ridges.

The comedy continues in the rest of this letter. Paris' silliness and ineptitude are
again evident. For example, it is probably not a good idea to remind Helen that

she has a beloved daughter (255), who she would be leaving behind if she went off with him, or to talk of her bringing glory on her brothers (273), when eloping with him would bring disgrace on them, or to suggest that she might be unfaithful to him too, in Troy (295f.). And at 283f. he comes up with a ludicrously feeble pretext for going to bed with her – so he can communicate his thoughts to her at greater length face to face. Most of the main types of irony noted above are also still present at 205ff., but it takes new forms too. Paris is now at several points flippant while on the way to bringing about misery and disaster for Troy and his own death. He of all people calls others simple-minded, stupid and ignorant. And at the end of the epistle he solemnly assures Helen that there will be no expedition to recover her, and foresees no problems if there actually is one after all. You will find lots more irony as you read the lines below (e.g. at 263f., 324, 339f. and 351).

There are other novelties as well, to inject more variety and interest. Although making Paris burble on has its entertaining side, this poem is nearly 400 lines long, and Ovid must have been aware that he might eventually bore some of his readers. So at this juncture he starts to give Paris some additional ploys. The hero now tries hard to win pity, by describing his envy of Menelaus and his torment as a frustrated lover. He also becomes flatteringly and alluringly roguish, and promises Helen great sex. He depicts a very warm welcome in Troy, if she goes off with him. He attacks her husband too. So at 207ff. he goes into detail about all the black sheep in Menelaus' family: his father killed his own brother's children and served them up to him as a meal, making the Sun recoil in horror from the feast; his grandfather killed his own father-in-law in a chariot race, bribing his charioteer Myrtilus to remove the linchpins from his chariot so that it crashed, and then threw Myrtilus to his death in the sea, which was named after him; and Menelaus' great-grandfather Tantalus was a sinner who was punished in hell by being rooted to the spot in a pool of water (which receded when he tried to drink it) beneath a branch of fruit, which was whisked away whenever he tried to eat it. Paris employs humour as well, mocking Menelaus' idiocy in going off to Crete and leaving him and Helen together. There is also wit at 205f., where he depicts Helen (rather than himself) as a judge, at 251f. and 274 (in connection with Jupiter's coupling with her mother Leda) and at 303–6, with play on the amatory sense of 'care'.

Ovid introduces other new elements too. He brings in narrative at 221ff., in the form of a lengthy and lively account of dinner-parties in the palace, with lots of intimate details and voluptuous touches. At 249ff., when Helen reveals her breasts to Paris at a banquet, there is foreshadowing with clever twists of the famous episode at the fall of Troy when Menelaus was about to kill Helen but dropped his sword when he caught sight of her naked breasts. At 323ff. Paris now tries to get Helen to elope with him, not just make love in secret. And at 353ff. the poem ends with open (and comical) allusion to the Trojan War.

If you compare our looks and age, I don't think   205
    you'll judge Menelaus to be preferable to me.
At least I won't give you a father-in-law who makes the bright Sun

recoil and turns His horses back from a terrifying feast.
My grandfather isn't spattered with his father-in-law's blood
    and didn't stigmatize the Myrtoan Sea with a crime.   210
There's no ancestor of mine in a pool in hell, grasping at
    fruit and trying to drink in the midst of water.
But what does this matter, if a member of that family
    has you, making Jupiter his father-in-law?
Oh, it's criminal. He doesn't deserve you, but he has you all night   215
    long, taking his pleasure, with his arms around you.
I get to see you only when the tables are finally laid,
    and even then there are many things that hurt me.
I wish on my enemies dinner-parties just like the ones
    I often undergo, when the wine has been served.   220
I wish I wasn't your guest when before my eyes
    that peasant puts his arms around your neck.
Why not tell all? I burst with envy when he lays
    his cloak over you and fondles your body.
But when you openly gave each other tender kisses, I picked up   225
    my wine-cup and put it in front of my eyes.
When he holds you close, I look down and lose my
    appetite, and the food swells and sticks in my throat.
I've often groaned, and noticed you not holding back
    a laugh when I groaned, you naughty girl.   230
I've often wanted to quench love's flame with wine, but
    it grew, and drunkenness was fire on top of fire.
So that I miss seeing much, I recline with my head turned away,
    but you immediately make me look at you again.
I don't know what to do. It pains me to see those things,   235
    but it pains me more not to look at your face.
As best I can, as much as I'm allowed, I try hard to hide my
    madness; however, the love I conceal reveals itself.
I'm not lying; you're aware of my wound, you're aware of it!
    And I hope you are the only one who knows.   240
Ah, how often have I turned my face aside as the tears came,
    so he wouldn't ask why I was crying!
Ah, how often have I described some love affair, when drunk,
    referring to my own wound with every single word,
giving away things about myself under an invented name!   245
    I was the real lover, in case you don't know.
Yes, and so I could be more saucy in what I said,
    I pretended to be intoxicated more than once.
I remember, your dress was loose and revealed your breasts,
    giving my eyes the chance to see them naked,   250
breasts whiter than pure snow or milk or the swan that Jupiter

turned into when he made love to your mother.
I was stunned at the sight, and the spiral handle of the wine-cup
    that I happened to be holding slipped from my fingers.
If you gave your daughter Hermione kisses, I joyfully   255
    snatched them from her tender lips at once.
Now I sang songs about old love affairs, lying on my back,
    now through nods I made signs that I should have kept secret.
I recently dared to make an ingratiating approach to
    your principal maids, Clymene and Aethra,   260
but all they said was that they were afraid,
    and they left me in the middle of my pleas and appeals.
I wish the gods would make you the prize in a major contest
    and the victor could have you for his bed,
as Hippomenes claimed Atalanta as his reward in the foot-race,   265
    as Pelops took Hippodamia to his arms,
as fierce Hercules in his pursuit of the hand of
    Deianira broke off the horns of Achelous.
To win you, I'd have been bold and brave and done great things,
    and you'd have known that I laboured hard for you.   270
As it is, my lovely, all I can do now is appeal to you
    and grovel at your feet, if you'd let me.
Oh, you bring glory here on your two brothers; oh, you beauty;
    oh, worthy bedmate for Jupiter, if you weren't his daughter!
Either I'll return to Troy's harbour with you as my bride   275
    or I'll be buried here in Sparta, an exile.
My chest has not been slightly grazed by the tip of
    Cupid's arrow: my wound goes deep – to the bone.
My truthful sister prophesied this, I remember –
    that I'd be shot by a heavenly arrow.   280
Helen, don't despise a love allotted by fate –
    if you don't, may the gods listen kindly to your prayers!
I've lots of ideas, but so we can speak at greater length face to face,
    receive me in your bed during the silent night.
Surely you're not ashamed and afraid to violate your vows   285
    and to flout a formal marriage's requirement of fidelity?
Ah, Helen, you're too simple-minded, not to say unsophisticated:
    do you think that loveliness like yours can avoid misbehaving?
You must make yourself less lovely or stop being hard-hearted;
    beauty and chastity are enemies.   290
Jupiter and golden Venus delight in such secret love-making;
    he, of course, fathered you through such secret love-making.
If heredity determines character, fidelity in a daughter
    of Jupiter and Leda is scarcely possible.
Do be faithful, however, when you're in my Troy;   295

please confine your adultery to me alone.
Let's have sex now (our wedding-day will legitimize it,
   if only Venus didn't make an empty promise to me).
Menelaus himself urges you on by his action, if not his words –
   absenting himself to allow his guest to make love secretly.   300
What a wonderfully astute husband – he couldn't find a more
   suitable time for viewing his kingdom in Crete!
In his instructions on the point of leaving he delegated to you
   care of his affairs and your Trojan guest.
I solemnly swear, you're ignoring your absent husband's instructions: 305
   you don't care for your guest at all.
Helen, do you entertain the hope that this man with no brain
   is capable of properly recognizing your beauty's riches?
You're wrong – he doesn't know. If he really valued what
   he has, he wouldn't entrust it to a stranger.   310
Even though you're not aroused by my words and my ardour,
   I'm forced to take advantage of his complaisance –
otherwise I'd be stupid, even more so than him,
   if I let such a risk-free time go by unused.
He's all but brought a lover to you with his own hands;   315
   make use of this simple-minded king's instructions.
The night's so long, and you lie in bed all alone;
   I myself also lie in bed all alone.
Let's get together, you and me, me and you, in bed.
   Our rapture will make that night more radiant than noon.   320
Then I'll commit myself on oath to Greek marriage-rites,
   swearing to you by whatever gods you like.
Then, with an appeal in person, I'll get you to set off to my realm,
   if my confidence in myself is not misplaced.
If you're ashamed and afraid to be seen as willingly accompanying me,   325
   I'll bear all the blame for this offence on my own.
I'll do what Theseus and your brothers did (there isn't a
   precedent closer to you than that to get to you).
Theseus carried you off, they carried off Leucippus' two daughters;
   I'll be classed with them as the fourth example of an abductor.   330
My Trojan fleet is here, equipped with tackle and crews;
   their oars and the wind will soon speed us on our way.
You'll pass through towns ruled by Troy, a mighty queen,
   and the people will think a new goddess is with them.
Wherever you walk, they'll burn cinnamon in your honour,   335
   and sacrificed animals will collapse on the bloody ground.
My father and brothers, my mother and sisters, the Trojan
   women and all of Ilium will bring you gifts.
Ah, I'm hardly telling you even a part of what lies ahead.

You'll find there's a lot more for you than is mentioned here.   340
    If you are abducted, don't be afraid that fierce fighting will follow us
        and that great Greece will mobilize her forces.
Of all the women snatched so far has any been recovered by combat?
        Believe me, there's nothing to fear in connection with kidnap.
Thracians took princess Orithyia captive (for Boreas, they said),   345
        and yet war wasn't made on the country of Thrace.
Jason carried off Medea from Colchis on the first ship,
        but his land of Thessaly wasn't harmed by a Colchian army.
Theseus, who abducted you, also abducted Ariadne,
        but her father Minos didn't call his men to arms.   350
In such matters the terror is usually greater than the actual danger;
        fearing everything that can possibly be feared is shameful.
However, if you want, imagine that a major war does start up –
        I am also mighty, *my* weapons also wound.
Asia has as many resources as your land has;   355
        it's rich in men, rich and abounding in horses.
And Menelaus, the son of Atreus, will not be more courageous
        than Paris or be rated as a better fighter.
When still almost a boy, I recovered our cattle and killed the enemies
        who stole them – that's why I'm also called Alexander.   360
When still almost a boy, I beat young men in various sports,
        and among them were Ilioneus and Deiphobus.
Don't imagine that I'm only to be feared in close combat:
        my arrows strike where I intend them to.
You can't ascribe to Menelaus such exploits in his early youth,   365
        you can't attribute prowess like mine to him, can you?
You can claim he has all kinds of qualities, but not Hector for a brother,
        who, you'll find, on his own is equivalent to an immense army.
You're unaware of my capabilities, of how strong I am;
        you don't know the man you're going to marry.   370
So either there won't be a violent invasion to get you back
        or the Greek soldiers will surrender before my warlike spirit.
And yet I'd be proud to take up arms for such a fine
        bride. When the prize is great, men fight.
Also, if the whole world battles over you,   375
        you'll be famous for all time to come.
Just leave here, hopeful and fearless, as the gods are on our side.
        I promised you pleasure. Demand it with total confidence.

Roman readers familiar with a famous episode in book 3 of Homer's *Iliad* would have particularly appreciated the absurdity of Paris' boasts at 353ff. At the start of that book the Greek and Trojan armies advance to do battle, and Paris steps out to challenge the best of the Greeks to fight with him. Menelaus immediately comes forward to confront him, and Paris' heart fails him and he promptly slips back into the Trojan ranks. Hector attacks him as a pretty boy who disgraces the Trojans with his cowardice, unwilling to stand up to the better man, whose wife he stole. Paris accepts the justice of Hector's taunts and agrees to fight Menelaus (with the winner to keep Helen, and the war then to end). There is a formal truce, and the two enemies arm themselves and stride out, glaring grimly.

> They took up their positions not far from each other on the
> duelling-ground, angrily brandishing their spears. 345
> First Paris hurled his long-shadowing lance
> and it struck the circular shield of Menelaus.
> But it did not break through: its bronze head was bent
> back by the stout shield. Next Menelaus, son of Atreus,
> attacked with his spear, praying to father Zeus: 350
> 'Lord Zeus, let me get revenge on godlike Paris,
> who wronged me first. Crush him at my hands,
> so future generations will shudder at the thought
> of wronging a host who shows them friendship.'
> With that he poised and hurled his long-shadowing lance, 355
> and it struck the circular shield of Paris.
> The mighty lance pierced the glittering shield,
> forced its way through his ornate breastplate
> and sliced right on through the side of his war-shirt.
> But he twisted aside and escaped dark death. 360
> Menelaus drew his silver-studded sword, reared up
> and brought it down on the ridge of Paris' helmet, but the
> blade splintered on it and fell from his hand in pieces.
> Lifting his eyes to the broad sky, Menelaus groaned:
> 'Father Zeus, no other god is more deadly than you. 365
> I really thought that I'd got revenge for Paris' crime,
> but now my sword has shattered in my hand,
> and I threw my spear for nothing – I missed him.'
> He lunged at Paris, seized his helmet's horsehair crest, swung
> him round and pulled him towards the well-greaved Greeks. 370
> Paris was choked by the pressure on his soft throat of the
> embroidered helmet-strap, which he'd tied tightly under his chin,
> and Menelaus would have dragged him off and won great glory
> but for the sharpness of the goddess Aphrodite, who saw
> what was happening and snapped the leather strap. 375
> The helmet came away empty in his massive hand.
> He whirled it around and threw it among the well-greaved
> Greeks, where his loyal comrades looked after it.
> He leapt at Paris again, keen to kill him with his

bronze-tipped spear, but Aphrodite snatched Paris away,   380
concealing him in a thick mist (a very easy feat for a goddess),
and set him down in his fragrant, perfumed bedroom.

After that Aphrodite sends Helen to Paris, and they make love, while Menelaus prowls through the ranks, looking for his enemy in vain. Homer says that if the Trojans had seen him there, they wouldn't have hidden him from Menelaus, as they all hated Paris like black death.

Heroides 17

HELEN TO PARIS

The double *Heroides* are more complex than the single ones because they inter-
lock, and the second in each pair responds to the first and adds to it – clarifying,
correcting, providing a different perspective, bringing out new aspects etc. Within
these doublets there are correspondences, to bring the two poems neatly together,
and also differences, making for enlivening variety. By way of a change from 16
this epistle is much shorter; this time the writer is calm, sensible and realistic; she is
trying to cool down rather than fire up the addressee; and she argues against going
off together to Troy rather than for it. In common with 16 the irony continues
(although it is much less extensive), and again there is a sad undercurrent (as Helen
here takes the next step, facilitating the affair, which will be followed by elopement
and war), and this is also a very amusing letter.

This poem increases the entertainment value of *Heroides* 16 by making it
clear that Helen wasn't such a tough nut to crack after all and Paris didn't need
to go on and on and try so hard with her: confirming the hints of her interest
in him that she has already given (see 16.229f. and 249ff.), and taking them
much further, she here reveals that she is already very attracted by his good
looks, is in love with him and is willing to have a secret affair, and that she
actually got Menelaus out of their way by urging him to go to Crete. There are
comic rebounds too, as when Paris' mention of Oenone and his suggestion that
Helen might be unfaithful to him at Troy backfire. Also diverting is her adroit
fencing, as she responds tartly to his digs (e.g. about her being unsophisticated
and coming from backward Greece) and questions and tops his boasts (for
example, about his bravery and high birth). In addition, because this epistle is
written at an early stage, before the love affair starts, and because she is trying
to lessen Paris' ardour, we are given a quaint and piquant picture of Helen of
Troy, one of the most notorious adulteresses in the world, as a virtuous wife,
leading a perfectly respectable life, entirely free from scandal, erotically naive

and inexperienced in adultery, and criticizing others for deserting a partner and for being fickle, unfaithful and shameless.

However, she is in fact on the point of entering into a liaison. As you read the poem below, ask yourself what exactly she is trying to achieve in it, how she goes about securing her aims and why the letter is so long.

> Now that your letter to me has defiled my eyes,
>   I feel there's little glory to be won from not replying.
> You came here and dared to violate the sacred laws of hospitality
>   and to incite a lawfully wedded wife to infidelity!
> Of course, the land of Sparta received you in its harbour   5
>   after your voyage across the windy waves
> and our palace didn't keep its doors closed to you,
>   even though you came from a different race,
> so you could wrong us to repay such great kindness!
>   Were you a guest or an enemy, entering with such intentions?   10
> No doubt, even though this complaint of mine is so justified,
>   you judge it to be unsophisticated and call it that.
> Let me be unsophisticated by all means, provided I don't forget about
>   decency, and provided my way of life is free from scandal.
> Although I don't feign a severe expression on my face,   15
>   and I don't sit here frowning harshly and stern,
> my respectability is well known, I've led a blameless life so far
>   and nobody enjoys the prestige of having an affair with me.
> So I wonder all the more what gives you such confidence in your project
>   and what's made you hope that you'd get into my bed.   20
> Because I was abducted once (since Theseus used force)
>   do you think I deserve to be abducted a second time too?
> If I'd been seduced, I would have been in the wrong;
>   since I was abducted, what could I do except say 'no'?
> He took me off for his pleasure, but didn't get what he wanted;   25
>   I came back untouched, except by fear.
> I struggled, and that animal only snatched a few kisses
>   from me; he got nothing more than that off me.
> You're so wicked you wouldn't have been content with that –
>   heaven help me! He wasn't like you.   30
> He returned me still a virgin, his restraint reduced his culpability,
>   and it's clear that the young man repented what he'd done.
> Did Theseus repent only for Paris to follow in his footsteps,
>   so my name would always be on men's lips?
> But I'm not angry – who gets annoyed with a lover? –   35
>   if only you're not pretending when you say you love me.
> For I doubt that too – not because I'm not fully aware
>   of my beauty and don't have confidence in it,

but because credulity is usually ruinous for girls,
  and they say that men's words aren't to be trusted.   40
You claim others misbehave and few married women are faithful.
  Who's to stop my name being among the few?
My mother seemed to you a suitable precedent, and makes
  you think you could persuade me by citing her,
but you're wrong about her infidelity: she was deceived, by a   45
  misleading appearance – her lover was disguised as a bird.
I can't plead ignorance of anything, if I were to misbehave;
  there'll be no mistake on my part to mask the criminal act.
She was mistaken, not immoral, and her lover's divinity made up for it.
  They won't call *me* fortunate for having Jupiter as my boyfriend.   50
But you boast of your birth, your ancestors and their royal titles.
  My family is noble itself and illustrious enough.
To say nothing of my father-in-law's descent from Jupiter and all the
  distinction of Tyndareus and Pelops (son of Tantalus),
Jupiter is my father, thanks to Leda, who was taken in by his   55
  disguise as a swan and trustingly caressed the bird in her lap.
Now go and tell all and sundry about the Trojan race's
  origins and Priam and his father Laomedon!
I respect them; but your great glory Jupiter (you'll find)
  is five generations removed from you, one from me.   60
Although I believe your land's dominion is mighty,
  I don't think that Sparta's is inferior to it.
And even if this place is not as rich and has fewer
  men, yours is indisputably a barbarian land.
It's true, your letter is rich in promises of gifts so splendid   65
  that goddesses themselves could be won over by them;
but if I was now willing to overstep the bounds of decency,
  you yourself would be a better reason for committing adultery.
Either I'll maintain my spotless reputation forever,
  or I'll go for you rather than your presents.   70
I don't spurn them, but the most welcome gifts are always
  the ones made precious by the identity of the giver.
It means much more that you love me, that you work hard
  to win me, that you sailed so far in hope of me.
However much I try to conceal it, I also notice your   75
  shameless behaviour these days at dinner:
now you gaze at me with bold, lecherous eyes,
  mounting an offensive which my eyes can scarcely stand,
now you sigh, and now you pick up the goblet right
  after me and drink from the part where I drank.   80
Ah, I've noticed over and over again covert signs being
  made by your fingers and your all but vocal eyebrows.

I've often feared that my husband would see them
    and blushed at the signals you didn't keep secret enough.
I've often said in a low voice or under my breath: 85
    'He has no shame,' and I wasn't mistaken over that.
I also read on the round table's surface under my name
    I LOVE (the letters were drawn out with spilled wine).
But I told you I couldn't believe that by rolling my eyes –
    oh dear, I've already learned you can speak like this! 90
If I'd been inclined to misbehave, I would have been moved by
    such endearments, my heart could have been won by them.
Also you're extraordinarily handsome, I confess, and a
    girl might want to go to bed with you.
Rather than abandoning decency as an adulteress, I'd even 95
    prefer some unmarried woman to be happy with you.
Just learn from examples that one can do without a pretty partner;
    to abstain from blessings and delights is a virtue.
How many young men, do you think, want what you want,
    but are sensible? Or is Paris the only one with eyes? 100
You're not more perceptive than them, you're more bold and rash;
    you're not brighter, but you are too assured.
I wish you'd sailed here on your swift ship when
    I was a virgin courted by a thousand suitors.
If I'd seen you, I'd have ranked you first out of the thousand. 105
    My husband himself will pardon this judgment of mine.
You're slow, too late. The pleasures you hope for have already been
    taken over and appropriated. Another man has what you're after.
But, while I might want to become your wife in Troy,
    at the same time Menelaus doesn't have me against my will. 110
Please stop tearing at my tender heart with your words;
    don't hurt me – you do say you love me.
Let me keep the lot that fortune has assigned to me;
    don't be keen to shame me by plundering my honour.
But you say Venus agreed to that, and in lofty Ida's 115
    valleys three goddesses showed themselves to you naked,
and when one granted dominion and the other military prowess,
    the third one said: 'You'll be Helen's husband.'
I for my part can scarcely believe that heavenly beings
    submitted their beauty to your judgment. 120
Even if that is true, certainly the other part is made up –
    when you say I was given as a reward for your decision.
I don't have such confidence in my body as to think that
    on the authority of a goddess I was the finest gift.
I'm content for my beauty to be commended in the eyes of men; 125
    praise by Venus exposes me to divine envy.

No, actually I *don't* dispute such praise by her, I even incline to it:
    why deny the compliment I desire in my heart of hearts?
Don't be angry because I've been very reluctant to believe you:
    people usually take time to credit something as momentous as this.   130
So I'm delighted firstly that Venus found me so attractive
    and secondly that I seemed the greatest prize to you,
and after you'd only heard of Helen's charms you didn't
    prefer the honours offered by Pallas and Juno.
In your eyes, then, I am valour, I am glorious dominion!   135
    I'd be as hard as iron if I didn't love a heart like yours.
Believe me, I'm not as hard as iron; but I resist loving
    someone who I think can hardly become my man.
Why try to furrow the watery shore with a curved plough
    in hope of a crop ruled out by the very nature of the place?   140
I haven't had a furtive affair; I've never deftly deceived
    my faithful husband (the gods are my witnesses);
and now, as I entrust my words to a secret letter,
    this is for me a new function for writing.
I envy those with experience. I'm ignorant of the world   145
    and suspect that adultery's path is difficult.
My very fear is causing me problems; I'm already in a
    turmoil, and think that all eyes are on my face –
with good reason: I've heard hostile muttering by the people,
    and Aethra has reported certain comments to me.   150
Conceal your love, unless you prefer to terminate it.
    But why terminate it? You're capable of concealing it.
On with the game, but discreetly! We have greater but not
    total freedom as a result of Menelaus' absence.
Certainly he's set out for a distant place, obliged to go by business;   155
    he had sound, solid grounds for suddenly sailing off –
or so it seemed to me. When he was wavering over leaving,
    I said: 'Go, but come back as soon as you can.'
He was delighted at the omen. He kissed me and said:
    'Take care of the house, my affairs and our Trojan guest.'   160
I only just held back a laugh. While I struggled to suppress it,
    all I could say to him was: 'I will.'
He has sailed off to Crete with favourable winds,
    but don't think that means you can do anything you want.
My man is absent, but mounts guard over me in his absence –   165
    or don't you know that kings have a long reach?
My beauty is a problem too: the more you men persist
    in praising me, the more grounds he has for fear.
I enjoy my reputation for loveliness, but it's a nuisance just now;
    it would have been better if I didn't deserve my fame.   170

And don't be surprised that he's gone off and left you here with me:
    he had trust in my character and way of life.
My looks cause fear, my way of life arouses confidence; he is
    reassured by my virtue, made afraid by my beauty.
You say we mustn't waste this freely offered opportunity and   175
    must make use of my simple-minded husband's complaisance.
That both appeals and appals; I haven't made my mind up
    properly yet; I'm wavering, I'm doubtful.
My husband is away, and you are sleeping on your own;
    you're taken by my beauty, as I am in turn by yours;   180
and the nights are long, and we already make love by letter;
    and you're charming (oh dear me, yes!), and we're under the same roof.
God strike me dead if all that doesn't encourage adultery;
    however, there's some fear that holds me back.
I wish you could compel me to do what you can't persuade me to do!   185
    My lack of sophistication should have been disposed of by force.
Sometimes wrong is profitable for the very people who are wronged.
    At all events I could have been compelled to be happy in that way.
Let's rather fight against the love we're starting to feel, while it's still new!
    It doesn't take much water to quench a fire that's just been lit.   190
The love of strangers is unreliable; it strays, like them,
    and, when you hope it's completely dependable, it's gone.
Hypsipyle is witness to that, and so is Ariadne, both
    cheated when marriage to the man didn't materialize.
You are unfaithful too. They say you deserted your   195
    Oenone after loving her for many years.
You don't deny it yourself. In case you don't know it,
    I've investigated very carefully everything to do with you.
Also, even if you wanted to be a loyal and steadfast lover,
    you can't: your Trojans are already unfurling their sails;   200
while you talk to me, making preparations for the night of love you
    hope for, you'll already have a wind to take you home.
Half-way through the voyage you'll relinquish your brand-new delight
    in me; your love will be gone, off with the winds.
Should I go with you, as you urge, see your celebrated Troy   205
    and marry you, the grandson of great Laomedon?
Rumour spreads the word quickly, and I'm not so disdainful
    of it as to let it tell the whole world of my disgrace.
Whatever will Sparta and all Greece, whatever will the
    peoples of Asia and your Troy find to say about me?   210
Whatever will Priam and his wife, whatever will all your
    brothers and your Trojan sisters-in-law think of me?
How will you be able to hope I'll be faithful, how won't
    you be troubled by the example you yourself have set?

Whenever a stranger enters the harbour at Ilium,   215
    he'll make you feel anxious and afraid.
How often will you say to me yourself angrily 'adulteress',
    forgetting that you're reproaching yourself as well as me!
You'll criticize the offence but also be the person who inspired it.
    May the earth cover my face in my grave before that happens!   220
But, you say, I'll enjoy Troy's wealth and sumptuous luxury,
    and I'll get even more presents than those you promise;
I'll definitely be given expensive purple fabrics
    and I'll be rich, with a great heap of gold.
Forgive me for saying it: your gifts aren't worth that much;   225
    somehow this Sparta of mine keeps me from leaving.
If I go to Troy and I'm maltreated, who will help me?
    I won't find my brothers there or my father to aid me.
Lying Jason promised Medea everything,
    but drove her from his home none the less.   230
She didn't have her parents Aeetes and Idyia or her sister
    Chalciope to go back to when she was spurned.
I don't fear anything like that, but Medea didn't either.
    Anticipation often misleads us into high hopes.
You'll find that for every ship now tossed on the ocean   235
    the sea was calm as it left its harbour.
I'm also terrified by the bloody torch which your mother
    dreamed she bore before the day of your birth;
and I'm afraid of the warnings of the prophets who (they say)
    predicted that Ilium would burn with Greek fire.   240
Although Venus is friendly to you because she was victorious
    and beat the other two thanks to your decision,
I fear the pair of goddesses who, if your bragging is
    true, didn't win as a result of your verdict.
I have no doubt an expedition will be mounted if I go with you.   245
    Ah, our love will pick its way through the midst of swords.
Do you think that the Thessalians declared savage war on the
    Centaurs for the seizure of Hippodamia of Atrax,
but Menelaus, my two brothers and Tyndareus will be slow
    to take action if we give them such good grounds for anger?   250
Despite your brave boasts and talk of courageous exploits
    your beauty is at variance with your claims.
Paris, your body is better suited to loving than fighting.
    Leave war to strong men; you be a lover, always!
Tell your acclaimed Hector to campaign instead of you;   255
    bed, not the battlefield, is the place for your services.
I'd avail myself of them, if I had any sense and was a
    little bolder; any sensible girl will avail herself of them –

or perhaps I will be sensible, abandon decency
    and finally surrender, conquered at last.   260
You want us to discuss your proposition in secret, face to face:
    I know what you're after, what you're calling a 'discussion'.
But you're moving too fast; your crop hasn't ripened yet.
    Delaying might help you get what you want.
Enough. I've confided my secret feelings to this letter, and my fingers   265
    are tired from this furtive writing, so let me end now.
Let's continue our conversation through my allies Aethra
    and Clymene, my two attendants and advisers.

Helen is not only more shrewd than Paris but also makes a much better job of achieving her aims in her letter, using some excellent psychology. She begins by pretending to be outraged by his proposals and depicting herself as a respectable married woman and faithful wife, to get him worried and wrong-footed from the start, so that he will value her and be grateful for what she *is* prepared to do with him. She does want to enter into a relationship with him, but there is a danger of detection, so it must be a secret affair and he must be discreet. She tries to damp down the ardour evident in his epistle, so he won't do anything impetuous and open, and give the game away. Hence her various references to the risks and Menelaus' long reach and her criticism of Paris for being too obvious at dinner. Hence too her unaccommodating responses to his approach – countering his claims, showing she has not been taken in by his ploys and assurances, coming out with objections and expressing doubts (about his love and fidelity and the Judgment and Venus' use of her as a bribe etc.). She is trying to calm him down; but she doesn't want to put him off totally. So among the many negative comments she also works in encouragement for him (at 35, 67ff., 91ff., 103ff., 132ff., 153f., 157f., 177ff., 198, 246, 253f., 257ff.). All of that and various abrupt changes of mood and direction take him on something of a rollercoaster ride, to keep him off-balance.

She is willing for an affair, on her terms, but she definitely does not want to go away with Paris. She speaks out strongly against elopement at 205ff., producing various arguments and showing it as something that frightens her (the woman he loves) and will be bad for her and him and his city. So that this refusal will not turn him off completely, she has saved it until late on, after lots of cheering hints for him, and she follows it up immediately with a very positive passage (257ff.) which intimates at length and at the very end (for impact on Paris) that she will enter into a liaison with him. This leaves the ball in his court. Presumably she is now waiting for him to convince her through her maids that in response to this epistle he will content himself with just a love affair and will be circumspect.

Paris ran on and on in his passionate letter, so quite a long reply would seem necessary to lessen his fervour. It also seems reasonable to deduce another reason for the length of *Heroides* 17: Helen is attracted physically to Paris and is in love with him, so she may well be trying to exert some control over her own feelings here, reminding herself repeatedly of the risks and the need to be secretive and convincing herself that eloping is a very bad idea. Tragically after the relationship began she did go off with him after all, causing the war she foresees here and all the other deaths (including that of her beloved Paris).

There is a further layer to this poem, making for intellectual entertainment and deflating epic personages, in the close connection with Latin love elegy (even more developed here than in *Heroides* 4). The basic situation is one commonly found in Tibullus, Propertius and Ovid's *Amores*: Paris is equivalent to the elegist, who loves a *puella*, a sexy and beautiful girl (= Helen), appeals to her, writes elegiac poetry to her and enters into a furtive affair with her, eluding her *vir*, the man currently in possession of her, who guards her and is largely on the periphery, an enemy to be outwitted (the role filled by Menelaus). More than that, Paris and Helen actually conform to Ovid's advice on how to conduct a love affair in the *Ars Amatoria*. So, as the poet recommends at *A.A.* 1.437ff. and 597ff., Paris approaches his girl by means of a letter filled with pleas and promises, and at a dinner party feigns drunkenness so that he can speak freely. He also utilizes the opportunities in that situation mentioned by Ovid at 1.569ff.:

> Here you can make lots of veiled remarks with hidden
> > meaning, so she can realize they are aimed at her,   570
> and you can write compliments on the table in thin smears
> > of spilt wine, so she can read that she's your girl,
> and you can gaze into her eyes with patently passionate eyes
> > (a silent look often speaks volumes).
> Make sure you're the first to grab the goblet touched by   575
> > her lips, and drink from the part where she drank.

So too Helen ensures that Paris believes she loves him (in accordance with *A.A.* 3.673), and employs the tactics of delaying and blowing hot and cold which Ovid urges on his female readers at 3.473ff.:

> Write back after a brief delay: delay always
> > spurs on lovers, so long as it's short.
> However, when propositioned, don't promise you'll give in,   475
> > but don't harshly refuse what the young man wants either.
> Make him simultaneously fear and hope; and in each reply
> > increase his hope and decrease his fear.

There are also some twists to standard elegiac elements. Unlike the elegist this lover is of noble birth, offers lavish presents, is inside the girls' house (instead of being locked out) and will be wounded and die literally (in battle) rather than metaphorically (in love). Unusually for the *puella*, Helen is of high birth and at present chaste and concerned with decency; she does not lie and is not mercenary, rating love as more important than gifts, and not scorning Paris' poetry; and she will be faithful to him. In fact, uniquely for elegy, their relationship will be happy, long-lasting and solid, actually or in effect a marriage, terminated only by Paris' death.

Heroides 17 is also interesting from a narrative point of view. By presenting Helen's thoughts and arguments at this point Ovid gives new life to a very old tale. He produces novel spins and often highlights the pathos of what did happen subsequently by conjuring up a whole series of alternative scenarios based on Helen's protestations, suggestions and fears − she maintains her respectability and stays faithful to her husband; Paris and Helen fight against their love and terminate it; Menelaus finds out what is going on (which would promptly put an end to relations); Paris leaves without her and forgets her; they have a furtive affair only and do not elope; she goes with Paris to Troy, but he is unfaithful to her or suspects her of infidelity (which might well finish the liaison). We are also given here an incomplete narrative, which is intriguing. We know that she will depart with Paris despite her strong opposition to that notion here, but we are left to speculate why. Was it fate and/or the gods? Did she get carried away with passion when she started having sex with him? Did he seduce or pressurize her into leaving? Or was there some other cause?

What are we to make of Helen as she appears in antiquity? Was she the perfect match for Paris? Or, as Oenone says at *Heroides* 5.71, a slut? Can we see her as a modern woman − free to make her own choices and living an erotic life? Is she a femme fatale, resplendent in her ageless beauty that is renowned far and wide? A woman of great elegance and innocence, and a victim of the gods' scheming? Or is she the wilfull and willing harlot who abandons husband and daughter in order to carry on a salacious affair? Or did only a phantom of Helen go to Troy? She is frequently said to be the source of tremendous heartache and destruction for Trojans and Greeks in ancient literature. Yet we also see that she is, perhaps surprisingly, not always cast in a negative light. She is in fact a complex figure, with conflicting portraits, as a glance at several ancient authors' views of her will show.

The Homeric epics encapsulate the very essence of Helen's story and the outcome of her elopement (or in some versions abduction). In an important scene in the *Iliad* Helen identifies the Greek heroes before Troy, pointing them out directly to Priam early in the poem (3.178ff.), and although she is not the direct focus of the epic, she embodies what the men are fighting for − *kleos* (glory) and *geras* (a prize of honour) − two key concepts in heroic culture. But does this Helen, who is found weaving, and who covers her face, weeps and is filled with self-reproach (6.342ff.) and also regret, really seem like she has been a willing participant in the conflict? Even Priam himself tells her that he blames the gods, not her, for the war (3.162ff.), and she states at 3.428ff. that she wishes that Paris had been defeated by her husband Menelaus in their recent duel. In addition to this depiction, several of her key and recurring traits are brought to the fore. Helen's *arete* (excellence), the beauty for which she remains famous, is described as being like that of the immortals, and it is the aspect which is emphasized repeatedly, both by other Homeric characters and by the epithets attached to her by the poet, such as 'of the white arms' and 'shining among women'.

In the *Odyssey* Helen is again a woman of power and beauty, and she performs the important role of hostess in a scene of domestic bliss where, back with Menelaus, she tells Odysseus' son Telemachus the story of her recognizing his father at Troy (4.219ff.). But not once does she ever accept responsibility for the effects of her beauty, and not even long-suffering Penelope blames her (23.220ff.). Two other significant elements are also brought out – Helen knows about drugs and their ability to alleviate men's suffering, and she appears to have prophetic powers, in that she is able to foretell Odysseus' successful return home to Ithaca. She is after all the daughter of Zeus and Leda, and so exceptional qualities are not entirely surprising.

She receives mixed notices in Greek lyric poetry. Round about 600 BC the poetess Sappho was very positive about Helen, depicting her as a great beauty under the sway of love. At about the same time the male poet Alcaeus blamed her for causing bitter grief for Priam and his sons and the destruction of Troy. A little later Stesichorus in his *Palinode* painted an entirely different picture of her, or at least of her culpability. He tells us that Helen never went to Troy, but rather a phantom of her was sent there by the gods, and she herself was whisked away to Egypt, a suitably mysterious place for such a famous woman.

In fifth-century Greek tragedy she figures especially in the dramas of Euripides (*Andromache, Hecuba, Electra, Iphigeneia in Tauris* and *Iphigeneia at Aulis*). References to her by characters in his plays are always hostile, and she is portrayed as clever and treacherous. In Aeschylus' *Agamemnon* at 688ff. the chorus claim that her name is very apt, connecting it with *helein* (= 'destroy'), and criticize her as a destroyer of ships, men and cities. The charge is repeated at 1455ff., and the only person who defends her (at 1464ff.) is her half-sister Clytaemnestra, the adulteress who murders her own husband.

The view of Helen in the *Aeneid*, with its pro-Trojan bias, differs from the earlier Homeric one. In book 2 the Trojan hero Aeneas is up on the roof of Priam's palace, where he has just witnessed helplessly the death of the king, as Troy is captured and burns. Suddenly he catches sight of her seeking refuge in a shrine, and he is so bitter over the suffering she has caused that shockingly this devout hero is on the point of violating sanctuary and killing an unarmed woman, until his mother Venus intervenes. He tells the story in enraged and highly condemnatory lines at 567ff.:

> And now I was the only one left, when I caught sight of
> Helen, silently lurking in Vesta's secluded shrine, keeping close
> to the doorway: the fire provided a bright light for me, as I
> wandered all over the roof and ran my eyes over everything. 570
> Fearing Trojan hostility because of their city's overthrow
> and Greek punishment and the anger of the husband she'd
> deserted, that hateful Fury, that scourge of Troy and her
> own country too, had hidden and was sitting at the altar.
> Rage blazed up in my heart, I burned to get revenge for the fall 575
> of my fatherland and to inflict a criminal punishment.
> 'Will she really get off unscathed, to set eyes on Sparta and

return to her Greek homeland as a queen in triumph?
She'll look on her husband, her father's palace and her children,
attended by a throng of Trojan women as her slaves,   580
after Priam has died by the sword and Troy has gone up in flames
and our shores have sweated with blood over and over again?
No! Even if there isn't anything glorious or notable
in punishing a woman, such a victory is praiseworthy;
I'll be praised nonetheless for exterminating an evil and inflicting   585
well-deserved punishment, and I'll take pleasure in sating my rage
. . . and getting satisfaction for my dead countrymen.'

Later, when down in the Underworld, Aeneas encounters the ghost of the Trojan prince Deiphobus, who became Helen's husband after Paris was killed, and who
was betrayed by her on Troy's final night. He was asleep, and she stole his sword and
then called Menelaus in, hoping that this act of treachery would make up for her
adultery. The ghost retains the cruel disfigurement of the living man facilitated by
Helen (6.494ff.):

Here too he saw Priam's son Deiphobus: his whole body
was butchery; his face had been brutally hacked,   495
his face and both his hands; the ears had been ripped from his
ravaged temples; and his nose had been sliced off – a vicious wound.

This brief survey of a few ancient portraits of Helen leads into the big question
of her guilt. Is she innocent or guilty? Depending on the era to which the narrative
belongs, we find differing views on moral responsibility and the concept of guilt
(see Maguire 109ff.). Whether Helen is a willing participant in her departure from
Sparta (Aeschylus *Agamemnon* 57f.) or a victim of the gods (Homer *Iliad* 3.164) or
Paris (*Iliad* 3.39, 6.281f.), some authors mention a benefit to the abduction in so
far as the Greek world became unified (e.g. Euripides *Andromache* 167f.). And she
is such a beautiful prize that her husband Menelaus is willing to forget the past and
not do away with her as he had intended (*Andromache* 250ff.). The duality of praise
and blame is played out in Helen's entire history. From a contemporary point of
view what we can see is that as a woman Helen is subject to the desires and designs
of men in the male-dominated Greek world. She is the object for which they vie,
and she has little or no say in what happens to her. And it is mainly male authors
who determine the presentation of her in literature.

For more on Helen see especially Grafton & Most & Settis 422ff. and Blondell.

Heroides 18

LEANDER TO HERO

Two young lovers, Leander and his girlfriend Hero, lived in towns on either side of the strait (narrow strip of sea) called the Hellespont (now known as the Dardanelles, in north-east Turkey). He lived on the western side in Abydos, and she lived in Sestos, just under a mile away across the channel. They had to keep their love secret (at 13f. below we are told that he feared detection by his parents, who would presumably have objected to the relationship for some reason). So Leander used to swim across to her at night, guided not by the stars in the sky but by the lamp she lit in her tower. (In 1810 the English poet Byron swam the strait, proving that the crossing was practicable, despite a strong current.) At the time of this letter stormy weather has made the trip too dangerous for a week, and Leander here writes to Hero to assure her of his love and explain why he hasn't visited her. Subsequently (after her reply in *Heroides* 19) he couldn't wait any longer, and tried to swim across the still wild sea, but drowned. His body was washed up on the shore before Hero, and when she recognized it, she committed suicide.

These two lovers are very different characters from Paris and Helen. There is also variety in their circumstances (they are physically separated, both are unmarried, and Leander is still subject to his parents) and in the purpose of this letter (and Hero's epistle). This time pathos is very much to the fore instead of humour, and there are also many more mythological allusions.

Those allusions have subtle and sombre point, and so need to be explained. At 41ff., where there is reference to Boreas (the North Wind) enamoured of and carrying off the Athenian princess Orithyia, we can see a poignant contrast between the mortal Leander and that wind god, who was unstoppable and had a lasting union with his girl. At 49f. Leander wishes that he had the wings invented by the master craftsman Daedalus, which enabled him to fly off with his little boy Icarus, and he mentions the end of that child, who recklessly flew too close to the sun, which melted the wax holding the feathers together, so that he plunged to his doom in the sea below. There is foreshadowing there of the young Leander's own death at sea due to his recklessness. Lines 61ff. concern the moon-goddess' passion for handsome Endymion, by whom she had fifty daughters, and so (unlike Leander now) she had access to her darling and was lucky in love. Ovid may also want us to think of the famous eternal sleep on Mount Latmos of Endymion (at his own request or brought about by the Moon so that she could always visit him), which ensured that he was immortal, in contrast to Leander, although the latter will soon endure an endless sleep (of death) himself. There is also grim prefiguring at 81f.: the heroine Alcyone's beloved husband Ceyx was drowned (in a shipwreck), his body was washed up before her and in deep despair she tried to kill herself, by leaping into the ocean (but she was turned into a bird, the halcyon, and lived on, unlike Hero). With a doubly ominous touch 117 and 139ff. bring up the origin of the name of the Hellespont, which means literally 'Helle's Sea'. The boy Phrixus and the girl Helle were rescued (from being sacrificed) by a flying ram with a golden fleece, and flew east from Greece on it, but as they made their way over the strait Helle fell off the ram and drowned. The young heroine Hero will also die in that area; Leander will not survive, as the hero Phrixus did, but will end his life in the waves there, like Helle. There are mournful associations in the myths attached to the stars mentioned at 151–4: Andromeda was chained to a cliff and waited in terror to be devoured by a sea-monster (before being rescued by the hero Perseus); Ariadne was abandoned and distraught on an island (until Bacchus appeared and claimed her as his wife, turning her crown into a constellation); and Callisto was impregnated by Jupiter and persecuted by Juno, being changed into a bear and very nearly being shot by her own son (but Jupiter saved her from that by placing her in the sky as the Great Bear). Like those females Hero will also suffer. But they all happily escaped their sufferings and had a continued (and glorious) existence in heaven. So too Perseus, Bacchus and Jupiter were powerful and prospered and lived on, in contradistinction to Leander. Finally, at 181f. Leander actually compares himself to a dead person in the Underworld, when he describes the punishment there of the mythical sinner Tantalus, who was for all time rooted to the spot in a pool of water, which always receded when he tried to drink it, and under a branch of fruit, which was always whisked away when he tried to seize it and eat (hence our verb 'tantalize').

There are also many other elements that help make this a dismal poem. Look for them as you read the translation below.

> Leander hereby sends Hero the greetings that he would rather
>   give her in person, if the sea became calm.
> If the gods are friendly to me, if they support me in my love,
>   you'll be disappointed that you're only reading these words of mine.
> But they're not friendly: they stop me getting what I long for   5
>   and don't let me quickly swim across the water I know so well.
> You see yourself the sky blacker than pitch and the strait churned up
>   by the winds, scarcely approachable even for hollow ships.

Only one sailor (a daring man) has set sail from the harbour –
    the one who delivers my letter to you.   10
I would have boarded his ship, but for the fact that when he
    undid its mooring-cables, all of Abydos was watching.
I couldn't have kept things from my parents as before,
    and the love we want hidden would have been revealed.
I promptly wrote this letter, and said: 'Go, you lucky thing!   15
    She will soon reach out her lovely hand to you.
Perhaps she'll even put her lips to you and touch you with them,
    as she tries to break your fastening with her snow-white teeth.'
I spoke those words to myself in a low murmur,
    and let my right hand say the rest on paper.   20
I'd much rather have my hand swim than write
    and diligently take me across those familiar waters.
It's certainly more suited to thrashing through a tranquil sea;
    and yet it is also suited to conveying my feelings.
It's now the seventh night (a period longer than a year to me)   25
    that the sea's been seething and heaving with raucous waves.
If I've had a soothing sleep during those nights,
    may the strait long continue to rage insanely!
Sitting on a rock, I sadly gaze at your shore, transported
    in thought to a place where I can't go physically.   30
What's more, my eyes see or think they see
    a light wide-awake at the top of your tower.
I've taken off my clothes and put them down on the dry sand three times;
    I've tried to complete that arduous journey three times.
The furious sea obstructed my strenuous attempts,   35
    engulfing my head with hostile waves as I swam.
But you, Boreas, wildest of the violent winds,
    why are you intent on making war on me?
It's me you're raging against, not the ocean, let me tell you.
    You couldn't be crueller if you knew nothing of love yourself.   40
For all your coldness, you savage, surely you don't deny that
    you once burned with passion for Orithyia of Athens?
If someone had decided to block your access by air to that delightful girl
    when you were about to carry her off, how would you have taken it?
Please spare me, be gentler, produce a helpful breeze – if you do,   45
    may your king Aeolus have no harsh commands for you!
A pointless request: Boreas roars against my prayer himself,
    and doesn't calm the water churned up by him anywhere.
I wish Daedalus would give me his daring wings now, even though
    the shore where his Icarus fell to his death is nearby.   50
I'll endure whatever happens, provided I can raise into the air this
    body of mine, which has often floated on dangerous waves.

Meantime, while the winds and the strait completely thwart me,
    I turn over in my mind the start of my secret affair.
Night was just beginning (this is a happy memory for me)   55
    when I left my father's house on my journey of love.
Immediately, laying aside my fear along with my clothes,
    I struck out through the yielding water with supple arms.
For most of my swim the Moon provided a flickering light for me,
    like an attendant helping me on my way.   60
Looking up at her, I said: 'Radiant goddess, be kind to me,
    think of your Endymion on Mount Latmos.
In view of your love for him you can't be a prude at heart.
    Please take notice of my secret affair.
Though a goddess, you glided down from heaven in pursuit of that mortal; 65
    let me speak the truth: the one I'm making for is a goddess herself.
To say nothing of her character, which is worthy of a divinity,
    beauty like hers only falls to the lot of genuine goddesses.
Nobody has a lovelier face than hers, except for Venus and you;
    don't rely on what I say – see for yourself!   70
When your silvery rays gleam in a cloudless sky,
    your blazing light surpasses all the stars by far:
that's how much more beautiful she is than all other beauties.
    If you doubt this, Moon, your bright eyes are blind.'
After saying this, or at any rate something close to this,   75
    on I went through water that gave way to me voluntarily.
The waves were radiant with the reflected image of the moon,
    producing the brightness of day in the silent night.
There was no sound anywhere, nothing came to my ears
    apart from the ripple of the water parted by my body.   80
Only the halcyons, remembering beloved Ceyx,
    seemed to me to make some sweet lament.
Now both my arms from the shoulder down were tired out, but with a
    stout effort I raised myself up high on to the crest of a wave.
I saw your light from afar and said: 'There's the girl who gets 85
    me on fire, the light of my life is on that shore.'
Suddenly strength returned to my weary arms
    and the sea seemed gentler to me than it had been.
The love burning in my eager heart makes me
    unable to feel the cold of the chilly water.   90
The closer I approach and the nearer the shore becomes
    and the less that remains to be done, the more I enjoy going on.
And when I can be seen as well as see you, being watched by you
    immediately gives me heart and makes me strong.
Now I also try hard to please my girlfriend with my swimming   95
    and strike out with a flourish for your benefit as you look on.

Your nurse only just managed to stop you wading out into the sea
    (I saw this too, and my eyes didn't deceive me).
But, although she clung to you as you went forward, she didn't keep
    you from stepping into the shallows and getting your feet wet.   100
You hug me in welcome and give me happy kisses – great gods,
    it was well worth crossing the strait for those kisses!
You take the cloak from your shoulders and give it to me,
    and dry my hair dripping with sea–water.
We know what we did after that, and so do the night, and our accomplice 105
    the tower, and the lamp that shows me the way through the waves.
The delights of that night are beyond counting,
    as many as the strands of seaweed in the Hellespont.
The time granted to us for our secret love-making was short,
    so we were all the more careful to make sure it wasn't wasted.   110
And now Dawn, Tithonus' wife, was about to chase away the night,
    and the morning star had risen, leading the way for her –
in a rush we showered a welter of hasty kisses on each other
    and complained that night only allowed us to linger briefly.
I stayed on and on doing that, until the nurse's painful warning   115
    made me leave your tower and go to the chilly shore.
We parted in tears, and I returned to Helle's Sea,
    continually looking back at my girlfriend, as long as I could.
Trust me, this is true: I seem to myself to be swimming when I
    leave Abydos, but shipwrecked when I return here.   120
Also, if you'll believe me, it seems the way to you is downhill,
    while the return from you is uphill, and the water resists me.
I go back to my fatherland against my will (who could believe it?),
    and I definitely remain in my city now against my will.
Ah, why are we united in soul but separated by the ocean,   125
    two people of one mind, but not of one country?
Let your Sestos take me or my Abydos take you;
    I'm as attracted to your land as you are to mine.
Why am I in a turmoil whenever the strait is in a turmoil?
    Why can something as insubstantial as a wind hinder me?   130
By now the curving dolphins know about our love
    and I think that the fish know me.
By now I've crossed so often you can see the track I've worn in the sea,
    like a road that lots of wheels run over.
Before I complained that this was my only way to you;   135
    but now I complain that the winds deny me this way too.
The Hellespont is foaming white with massive breakers,
    and ships that stay in their harbours are scarcely safe.
I imagine the sea was as wild as this when it first got
    the name it bears from Helle being drowned in it.   140

This place is infamous enough as a result of the loss of Helle;
    even if it spares me, its crime is there in its name.
I envy Phrixus, for being carried safely across this savage
    strait by the woolly ram with its golden fleece.
But I don't want an animal or a ship to help me,   145
    so long as I get the kind of sea I can swim through.
I don't lack anything; if it just becomes feasible to breast the waves,
    I'll be ship, sailor and passenger all in one.
I'm not guided by Helice or by Arctos (like the Phoenicians):
    my love isn't interested in the stars commonly used by helmsmen.   150
Let others fix their eyes on Andromeda and the bright Crown
    and the Arcadian Bear that glitters in the frozen pole.
I don't want those who were loved by Perseus, Bacchus and
    Jupiter to point me on my dangerous way:
there's another light, for me much more trustworthy than them;   155
    with its guidance your lover doesn't go astray in the dark.
Provided I saw that, I could carry on to Colchis, to the
    furthest part of the Black Sea, where the Argo sailed,
and I could swim further than the youthful Palaemon,
    than Glaucus, who ate that herb and suddenly turned into a god.   160
My arms are often weary and weak from the continual strokes
    and I can hardly drag them through that huge expanse of water.
When I say to them: 'I'll soon give you a splendid reward
    for your hard work – my girlfriend's neck to clasp',
immediately they're strong, straining towards their prize,   165
    like a swift horse let out of an Olympic starting-gate.
So I keep my eyes on you, my darling, guiding myself by the girl
    who I love, who is more worthy of a place in heaven.
You're certainly worthy of that; but stay on earth for a while yet,
    or tell me how I too can find a way up to the gods!   170
You are here, yet you have little contact with your miserable lover;
    the sea's in a frenzy, and so am I.
What's the use to me of not being separated from you by a broad ocean?
    Such a narrow strait is no less an obstacle to me, is it?
I wonder whether I'd prefer being remote, the whole world away
    from you,   175
    so my girlfriend and my hope of her were far from me.
Now the nearer you are to me, the nearer is the fire of love, burning me,
    and the hope is always with me, but not the girl I hope for.
The one I love is almost close enough to be touched by my hand,
    but, ah, that 'almost' often moves me to tears.   180
I'm like Tantalus, wanting to seize the fleeing fruit,
    and pursuing with hopeful lips the receding water.
So then, will I never hug you except with the leave of the waves,

and will I always be miserable when there's a storm?
Although there's nothing less reliable than the wind and the waves,   185
   will my hopes always depend on the winds and the sea?
Yet it's still summer. It will be worse for me later, at the rising
   of the Pleiades, Bootes and Capra, when the ocean is enraged.
Either I'm less reckless than I think, or my love will throw caution
   aside and send me out into the strait even then;   190
so you don't think I'm promising this because that time is off in the future,
   I'll soon give you a guarantee of this commitment.
If the sea's still rough for a few nights more,
   I'll try to cross even though the waves don't want me to;
either I'll survive and my daring will meet with success   195
   or death will put an end to my anxious love.
But I'll pray that I'm washed up on your shore
   and that your harbour holds my shipwrecked body.
For then you'll cry and see fit to touch my corpse
   and say: 'I was the cause of this man's end!'   200
I'm sure that you're upset by this omen of my death
   and find this part of my letter hateful.
I'll speak no more of that. Don't complain. But please add
   your prayers to mine that the sea puts an end to its anger.
I need a brief period of calm, until I get over there to you;   205
   when I've reached your shore, let the storm go on and on!
There's a dockyard there that's just right for my ship,
   there's no stretch of water where it's laid up better.
Let Boreas confine me *there*, where it's a pleasure to linger!
   Then I'll be slow to swim, then I'll be wary,   210
and I won't curse the unresponsive waves at all or complain that
   the strait is savage when I'm on the point of swimming.
I want to be held by your tender arms and also by the winds,
   prevented from leaving for both those reasons.
When this storm lets me, I'll use my arms as oars –   215
   just keep your lamp constantly where I can see it.
Meanwhile let this letter spend the night with you in place of me.
   I'm praying that I'll follow it after a very short delay.

As you will have seen, in addition to the allusions which were explained above there is much more that makes for mournfulness here, and there is impact in the concentration of so many dismal details (over a full 218 lines). There is great pathos in the situation itself. Two young lovers are cruelly parted from one another, and will soon meet early deaths as a result. Tragically, but for his fear of detection by his parents, Leander could have sailed safely over to Hero with the sailor who carried this letter (11–14), and not been drowned later on, trying to make his own way to her. So too in this epistle we see clearly that Leander is deeply in love, very frustrated and absolutely miserable, and the fact that he is in such a condition after only one week's separation from Hero shows the profundity of his passion. Touchingly he is here desperate to reassure his girlfriend that he loves her, longs to see her again and is only kept away by the extreme danger involved in negotiating the strait. But in his emotional state and because of youthful impetuosity he thoughtlessly comes out with remarks which would upset his darling and make things harder for her, as when he dwells on their blissful first tryst (101ff.) and the pain of their separation then (111ff.) and depicts himself as dead (196ff.). At the same time by recalling that initial encounter Leander would torment himself, and make himself more likely to try to repeat that crossing, especially when he pictures himself coping well with it before and inspired to great feats of swimming by the thought of his girl (85ff., 155ff.).

On top of all that extensive foreboding is created by the frequent mentions of the stormy weather and wild sea which will kill the young man, and by his claim that Hero is a goddess at 66ff. (which might well offend heaven and invite punishment), and by his words of ill omen at 196ff., where he refers to himself as drowned. There is also foreshadowing of his demise at 35f., 83, 161f. and 193f. A depressing futility is in evidence at several points – in the prayer to Boreas to be gentle and produce a helpful breeze at 45f., in the wish for Daedalus' wings at 49f. and in his hopes for a calm Hellespont and a prolonged stay with his girlfriend at 205ff. There is also lots of bleak irony. At 114 and 135f. Hero and Leander complain about things, but they will soon have much more to complain about. In 124 he says that he is remaining in his city against his will, when he should be happy to stay there, until the storm is over. He depicts himself as swimming all the way to Colchis and being a better swimmer than two sea-gods (157ff.), but he won't even get as far as Sestos and will prove to be far inferior to them in the water before long. And in 206 and 209 he imagines himself reaching Hero's shore and lingering there, when he will soon be doing that as a corpse. Look for more irony (for instance, in 183 and 187f.).

Ovid ensures that the pathos is not overdone and achieves a nuanced complexity by working in just a few, slight touches of unconscious humour in Leander's words, thanks to a realistic and affecting naivety and boyish excitability and exaggeration, so that we can smile now and then amid all the sadness. So his appeal to Boreas at 37ff. is quite comically inept, as he is so rude that he is most unlikely to win over the god. He produces an amusingly pedantic correction of himself in 75 ('after saying this, or at any rate something close to this'). He promptly contradicts his claim in 79 that the sea he swam through was totally silent by mentioning noises at 80–2; and he does the same thing again later, maintaining at 162 that he has to get through a huge expanse of water to reach Hero, and then refuting that in 173, 174 and 179. He also asks a silly question in 130 ('why can something as insubstantial as a wind hinder me?'). See if you can find any other instances of such gentle humour (for example, at 131f. and 133f.).

For other versions of this story, including a possible earlier Greek poem known to Ovid, see Kenney 10ff. The late Greek poet Musaeus handled the love of this pair in a rather different way. In the (typically ornate and elaborate) extract quoted below (*Hero and Leander* 86ff.) he describes their first sight of each other. Which poet is more convincing and more moving in presenting Leander's passion? Which one gives a better insight into the youth's thoughts and feelings, and how does he achieve that greater penetration?

> Leander, when you saw that glorious girl you really suffered.
> You didn't want to be goaded and secretly exhausted by love,
> but you couldn't live without the beautiful Hero, now that
> you'd been unexpectedly overcome by Eros' fiery arrows.
> At the bright gaze of her eyes Love's torch flared up, 90
> and the onset of that invincible fire made your heart seethe.
> (For the far-famed beauty of a flawless woman
> is for men something sharper than a winged arrow;
> its route is the eye; beauty glides out of the eye's
> glances and makes its way into the hearts of men.) 95
> Then he was seized by awe, shamelessness, trembling, shame:
> his heart trembled, he was ashamed at succumbing, he felt
> awe at her exceptional beauty, and passion drove out shame.
> Passion made him boldly embrace shamelessness,
> and he quietly went up and stood before the girl. 100
> Looking out of the side of his eyes, he darted out insidious glances,
> nodding without speaking, and trying to allure the girl.
> She understood that the artful Leander desired her
> and was elated at his handsomeness; she herself quietly
> turned her lovely gaze on him again and again, 105
> sending him a message with slight nods of her head,
> and then turning away again. And his heart glowed inside him,
> because she understood his desire and didn't reject it.

At *Metamorphoses* 4.55–166 Ovid tells the story of Pyramus and Thisbe, another pair of parted and doomed young lovers. There is pathos in that passage too, but much more (dark) humour (for example, the lovers talk to a wall, and when they meet together outdoors at night there is a grim comedy of errors and a gruesome simile). Compare and contrast that account with Ovid's tale of Hero and Leander.

Heroides 19

HERO TO LEANDER

The second poem in this pair responds to the first, giving us Hero's (very similar) reaction to the enforced absence of Leander, and taking the tragedy a step further on. Contrasts with *Heroides* 18 make for the usual enlivening variety: for example, 19 is nothing like as densely packed with allusions, contains much less irony and has no unconscious humour to lighten the tone a bit. But the correspondences are much more numerous, and they are very effective. Both letters are filled with pathos and foreboding, so the gloom is reinforced here. There are many other connections which bring out how close and well-suited to each other these two young people are, shortly before their separation becomes permanent. Like Leander, Hero is deeply in love, frustrated and miserable. She also links herself to him: her first and last couplets pick up his first and last couplets; in line 5 she states that she burns with an equal fire; and in 22 she says that she uses almost the same words as he does to berate the sea. In addition, she too finds a week's delay long, speaks about their love-making warmly but with a delicate restraint, fantasizes about him being blissfully trapped in Sestos with her by bad weather and complains to a god and appeals to him in the name of his own love to calm the sea. As you read the translation below, see if you can find any more parallels and echoes, which draw the letters and the lovers together. Also decide what Hero is likely to achieve here.

> Leander, so that I can enjoy in actuality
>   the greetings you sent me in your letter, come!
> For me all delay that puts off our pleasure is long.
>   Pardon my confession: I'm not a patient lover.
> We burn with an equal fire, but my resolve isn't equal to yours;   5
>   I suspect that men have a greater strength of purpose.
> A tender girl's will is weak, like her body –
>   if you delay a little longer, I'll die.

You men expend a lot of time in various pursuits:
    sometimes you hunt, sometimes you farm your delightful land;   10
or the forum or god's gift of oiled wrestling holds your attention,
    or you ride an obedient horse, guiding it with the bridle;
you haul in now a bird with a net, now a fish with a hook;
    you're served wine which makes the evening glide away.
I'm denied all that; there's nothing left for me to do but love,   15
    and that would be so even if my passion wasn't this fierce.
I do what's left for me to do, and love you, my one and only heart's
    delight, even more than you could possibly love me in return.
Either I whisper about you to my grey-haired nurse,
    wondering what stops you from coming to me,   20
or I look out at the sea churned up by the hateful wind
    and berate the water, using almost the same words as you,
or, when the obnoxious waves become a little less savage,
    I complain that you certainly could come, but don't want to,
and while I complain, tears flow from my loving eyes,   25
    which my old confidante dries with her shaking fingers.
Often I look to see whether your footprints are on the shore,
    as if the sand would preserve marks made on it,
and so I can inquire about you and write to you, I ask if
    anyone has come from Abydos or is going to Abydos.   30
Why mention how often I kiss the clothes which you take off
    when you're about to swim back across the Hellespont?
So too, when the light has gone and the friendlier time of night
    has driven off the day and brought out the bright stars,
I immediately place at the top of my tower the wide-awake lamp   35
    as a signal and marker for your customary crossing,
and we while away the lengthy wait with the women's work of spinning,
    drawing out the twisted threads as the spindle twirls.
Do you ask what I say meanwhile during that long, long time?
    Nothing but the name of Leander is on my lips.   40
'Nurse, do you think my darling has already left home,
    or is he too scared, because all his family's awake?
Do you think he's already pulling his clothes off over his shoulders,
    and already greasing his body with rich olive oil?'
She usually inclines her head, not because she cares about our kisses: 45
    it's sleep creeping up on the old woman and making her nod off.
After a very short delay I say: 'He's already at sea for sure,
    stroking out with his supple arms and parting the water.'
When I've spun a few strands and the spindle has touched the floor,
    I ask whether you could be half-way across the strait.   50
Now I look out, now I pray in a timid voice that
    a helpful breeze will make your journey easy.

My ears strain to make out indistinct noises, and I believe
    that every one of them is the sound of you arriving.
After I have spent most of the night being frustrated   55
    like this, sleep steals over my weary eyes.
(Perhaps you go to bed with me against your will, you traitor,
    and come although you don't personally want to come.)
For I dream that now I see you already swimming nearby
    and now I feel the weight of your wet arms around my shoulders,   60
now I put the clothes I usually provide on your dripping body,
    now I warm your chest pressed to mine,
and I'm too embarrassed to describe the many other things,
    which I enjoy doing but must decorously pass over in silence.
Ah no, this is a momentary and unreal pleasure, as it's   65
    always your way to leave me when sleep does.
Oh, if only our passionate encounters could finally be more stable
    and our loving delights could actually be real!
Why have I passed so many nights alone and cold? Why are you
    so often absent, slow to come to me, lingering?   70
I admit, a swimmer couldn't cope with the sea as it is now,
    but last night the wind was gentler.
Why was that ignored? Why did you fear what wasn't going to happen?
    Why was such a good chance to cross not seized by you but wasted?
Even if a similar opportunity to come was given to you right away,   75
    that one was surely better, as it was earlier.
You'll object that the ocean's peaceful appearance changed quickly,
    but, when you hurry, you often arrive in less time than that.
If you'd been caught by the storm *here*, you'd have nothing to complain of,
    I think, and while you held me close, no squall would hurt you.   80
Then I'd surely be delighted to hear the roaring winds,
    and I'd pray for the water never to be calm.
But what has happened to make you more afraid of the waves
    and frightened now of the strait you scorned before?
I remember when the sea was no less fierce and   85
    threatening, or not much less, but you came,
when I shouted to you: 'Be bold, but not so bold as to make me
    miserable and in tears because you've been too brave.'
Where does this new fear come from, where has that daring gone?
    Where's that mighty swimmer who despised the water?   90
But be cautious like this rather than rash as you used to be before,
    and cross the sea in safety when it's calm,
provided you keep on loving me back, as you say you do in your letter,
    provided that fire doesn't turn into cold ashes.
I don't dread the winds that impede my desire as much as   95
    I fear that your love may be like a wind and wander off,

that I'm not worth it all, and I cause you too much danger,
    and I don't seem enough of a reward for your labours.
Sometimes I'm afraid my birthplace may be a problem, and as a girl
    from Thrace I may be called unworthy of a husband from Abydos.   100
However, I can bear everything with more patience than I could bear it
    if you're idling because you're captivated by some rival or other,
and another girl's arms are placed around your neck,
    and a new love is putting an end to our love.
Ah, I'd rather die than be wounded by such a crime of yours   105
    and pass away before you're unfaithful to me.
I don't say this because you've given me some indication that I'll
    be hurt or I've been alarmed by some new rumour,
but because I'm afraid of everything (has any lover not worried?).
    And being absent makes the heart more fearful.   110
How lucky they are, those girls who are with their lover, and so know
    if he's really unfaithful and don't fear non-existent infidelity!
Baseless suspicions upset me as much as an affair I'm ignorant of would do;
    in either case being deluded is equally painful.
Oh, I wish that you'd come, or that it's the wind or your father –   115
    certainly no woman – that keeps you there.
But if I do learn of some female, I'll die of grief, believe me;
    have an affair right now, if you want to kill me.
But you won't have an affair, and my fears of that are groundless:
    it's the malevolent storm that opposes your arrival.   120
Ah, how huge the waves are that pound the shore,
    how dark the clouds are that block and hide the daylight!
Perhaps Helle's devoted mother has come to this strait,
    and this downpour is her tears for her drowned daughter –
or is Helle's stepmother, now changed into a marine goddess,   125
    attacking the sea called by the hated name of her stepdaughter?
This place, as it now appears, is not kind to tender girls:
    Helle died in these waters, and they cause me pain.
But you shouldn't have let any romance be hindered by the winds,
    Neptune, if you remembered your own loves –   130
that is if the stories are true about your misbehaviour with
    Tyro and that highly celebrated beauty Amymone
and radiant Alcyone and Hecataeon's daughter Calyce
    and Medusa, before she had snakes entwined in her hair,
and blonde Laodice and Celaeno, who was admitted into the heavens,   135
    and others whose names I remember reading.
Neptune, the poets tell that these for sure and more
    slept with you, their soft flanks next to yours.
So, when you've experienced the power of love so often,
    why close off our usual route with a tornado?   140

Have mercy, fierce god, and conduct your battle out on the ocean!
  This stretch of water separating two lands is narrow.
As a great deity it is fitting for you to toss great
  ships or even to savage entire fleets;
it's disgraceful for the god of the sea to terrify a swimming youth; 145
  you win less glory from that than from rippling any pond.
He's definitely of noble birth and from an illustrious family,
  but he's not descended from the suspect Ulysses.
Be kind, and save us both. It's Leander who swims, but
  his body and my hopes depend on the same waves. 150
Look, my lamp has sputtered (it's by me as I write),
  it sputtered and gave us a good omen.
See, my nurse drips wine on to the auspicious flame and says:
  'Tomorrow there'll be three of us,' and drinks some herself.
Oh Leander, you've been welcomed deep inside my heart, right into it: 155
  overcome the sea, glide over it and make us three.
Return to your camp, you deserter from our amorous alliance:
  why do I sleep alone in the middle of the bed?
There's nothing to fear! Venus herself will support your venture:
  she was born of the sea, and will smooth your path across the sea. 160
I often have a good mind to go through the midst of the waves myself,
  but this strait tends to be safer for men.
For, when Phrixus and his sister both rode this way, why did
  the female alone give her name to these desolate waters?
Perhaps you're afraid that you won't have enough time to get back again 165
  or you won't be up to the hard work of swimming both ways.
Well then, let's come together in the middle of the sea from our different
  shores, let's meet and kiss on the crest of a wave,
and then let's each go back to our own city once more –
  this won't be much, but it'll be more than nothing. 170
If only one of them would end – either this shame which makes us love
  in secret or this love that's afraid of what people will say!
As it is, passion and concern about public opinion (an ill-matched pair)
  are at war, and I don't know whether to go for propriety or pleasure.
Jason of Pagasae entered Colchis just once, and took 175
  Medea on board his swift ship and carried her off;
the Trojan adulterer arrived at Sparta just once,
  and returned with Helen as his spoil immediately.
But as often as you make for the girl you love, you leave her,
  swimming off when it's dangerous for ships to travel. 180
You have conquered the swollen sea, young man, but please,
  please be sure to fear the strait while despising it.
Boats built with laborious skill are sunk by the ocean:
  do you think your arms are more powerful than oars?

What you want – to swim – is what sailors dread, Leander,   185
    as this is normally their fate if they are shipwrecked.
Poor me! I want to fail to persuade you in urging caution,
    and I pray that you're strong enough to withstand my warnings –
provided you make it to me, and put around my shoulders those
    weary arms that have often struck out through the waves.   190
But whenever I turn to the dark blue waves, my heart
    is chilled and paralyzed by some strange fear.
And I'm equally disturbed by a dream I had last night,
    even though I've averted its bad omen by sacrificing.
For towards dawn, as the lamp was already drowsing,   195
    at the time when we tend to see true visions,
my fingers went slack with sleep and dropped the threads,
    and I laid my head down on a pillow to support it.
At that point I dreamt that I saw unmistakably
    a dolphin swimming through the windswept waves,   200
then the sea threw the poor creature up on to the thirsty sand,
    and the waves and life left it at the same time.
Whatever this means, I'm afraid; don't laugh at my dream,
    and don't entrust yourself to the water unless it's calm.
If you don't spare yourself, spare the girl you love: 205
    I'll never be safe and sound, if you're not safe and sound!
However, the sea is less violent, so I hope it will soon be at peace;
    strike out through it when it's tranquil with all your heart.
Meanwhile, since the strait can't be crossed by a swimmer,
    let this letter sent to you ease the hateful delay.   210

In *Heroides* 18 Leander teetered on the brink of crossing to Hero, but just managed to hold back. In *Her.* 19 she admits at 5f. that she does not have such strength of purpose, and she demonstrates her lack of self-control by asking him to come to her in the very first couplet, and immediately following that up with the persuasive 3–8 (and much more subsequently). We are left to infer that this epistle reached him and pushed him over the edge, making him decide to swim. This means that her final words in line 210 are deeply ironical, and his image of her as the cause of his death in 18.200 comes all too true.

Hero does refer to the danger, and she does tell Leander not to attempt the trip, but not as frequently and not as fully as she should. She does this at greatest length at 183ff., but after all she has written before this it is too little and too late, and she undermines her own words even as she urges him not to come, at 187f. (where she openly admits that she does not want to persuade him to stay where he is), 194 and 207. She also engages in the same kind of subversion of such admonition at 72ff., 93ff. and 129ff. More significantly she includes a great deal that would positively encourage him to swim, and in fact make him very keen to do so. She actually tells him to cross at various points of the poem. She frequently parades her love, and also her loneliness and frustration and misery without him, painting a pathetic picture of herself. Twice she intimates that heaven supports the journey (151ff., 159f.) and holds out the enticing prospect of sex with her (63f. and 158). And she questions his motives for not arriving several times, and suggests that it is because he is a coward and unfaithful, which would make him very eager to get to her and prove himself. If you look through *Her.* 19 again, you will find other such inducements as well.

Hero is conflicted. She is fully aware of the risk, but she is young and passionate, and she loves and misses Leander so much that she writes a rash letter, and in fact thereby destroys her chance of being reunited with him, bringing about the death of the man she loves so much (and her own demise). This epistle may be a conscious and deliberate attempt to get him to brave the sea. But it could also be that she is so naive and impetuous and unreflecting that she drives him to make the crossing without really meaning to do that. Ovid has left this open, to intrigue us, and it is hard to say which of the two possibilities is more tragic.

There is a further aspect to the tragedy (which also means that we cannot be too critical of the heroine). It is easy enough to deduce that she was spurred on to write as she did by his letter (intended to reassure her of his feelings for her), with all its protestations of passion, the lengthy recollection of their blissful first tryst (18.55ff.), the sketch of them happily together in the future (18.205ff.) and the repeated depiction of him making his way to her across the Hellespont. So there is a grim rebound of his well-meaning words, and a sad reciprocity, as these two lovers feed off each other and impel each other to disaster.

There are still more factors contributing to the mournfulness. There are affect-ing (and imaginative) touches throughout, like Hero looking for Leander's foot-prints on the shore (27f.), kissing the clothes he left behind (31f.), speculating about his progress to her (41ff.), fearing that she isn't worthy of him (97ff.) and engaging in the futile fantasy of them meeting in the middle of the strait (167ff.). In addition, numerous contrasts with Leander bring out how the situation is now and has been all along even worse for Hero, so that there is extra pain for her. He cannot sleep, but she has very upsetting dreams. Then there is her enforced passivity: (apart from the joint letter-writing) he could swim in the past and can now try to swim, but all she could do before and can do at present is wait for him. She is condemned to a state of worrying uncertainty too: when he could cross, he knew full well that he was on his way to her, but she didn't; and now he is aware that it is the bad weather alone that holds him back, but she can't be sure of that, and, while he is certain of her love for him, the vulnerable heroine is prey to fears about his commitment to her and his fidelity. There is also a gloomy impact in the climax at 181ff., with all the references there to fear, shipwreck and death, and the clear foreshadowing of Leander's end, especially in the sinister vision of the dolphin, which cancels out the dream of the young man's arrival at 59ff. and the favourable omen of the sputter-ing lamp at 151ff. Note also that hardly anyone else figures in these two poems, so that the focus is squarely on the doomed pair, without any real distractions or relief, which makes for an intensity and a fixation on them in keeping with their own intensity and fixation on themselves.

Ovid only hints at the drowning of Leander and Hero's suicide. Musaeus describes them at 324ff.:

> He was carried along, battered by the overwhelming assault of the
> waves massed all around him; his feet kicked out less vigorously;   325
> his strong hands never rested, but they made no headway.
> A great flood of water poured itself into his throat, and he swallowed
> a mouthful of the irresistible sea, which did him no good.
> A cruel blast of wind extinguished the treacherous lamp
> and with it the life and love of long-suffering Leander.   330
> Dawn arrived and Hero didn't see her bridegroom.
> She looked out everywhere over the sea's broad back
> and condemned and cursed the barbaric wind.
> As the dead Leander had still not arrived, she already had
> a presentiment of his death. She stood there gazing out   335
> vigilantly, seething with abject anxiety, and hoping
> to catch sight of her husband swimming off course,
> now that the lamp was out. At the base of her tower
> she saw her husband's corpse being lacerated on the rocks.
> She tore the finely-embroidered robe from her chest   340
> and hurled herself headlong from the high tower.
> Hero ended her life beside her dead husband,
> and they made each other happy in the finality of death.

In Chapman's continuation of Marlowe's *Hero and Leander* sestiad VI lines 260ff. there is an addition which makes for a more upbeat ending, as the lovers are given an extended existence, changed into goldfinches. Which conclusion is most effective?

> Thus cried she, for her mixèd soul could tell   260
> Her love was dead. And when the Morning fell
> Prostrate upon the weeping earth for woe,
> Blushes that bled out of her cheeks did show
> Leander brought by Neptune, bruised and torn
> With cities' ruins he to rocks had worn,
> To filthy usuring rocks, that would have blood,
> Though they could get of him no other good.
> She saw him, and the sight was much much more
> Than might have served to kill her: should her store
> Of giant sorrows speak? Burst, die, bleed,   270
> And leave poor plaints to us that shall succeed.
> She fell on her love's bosom, hugged it fast,
> And with Leander's name she breathed her last.
> Neptune for pity in his arms did take them,
> Flung them into the air, and did awake them

Like two sweet birds, surnamed th' Acanthides,
Which we call thistle-warps, that near no seas
Dare ever come, but still in couples fly,
And feed on thistle-tops, to testify
The hardness of their first life in their last: 280
The first in thorns of love, and sorrows past;
And so most beautiful their colours show,
As none (so little) like them: her sad brow
A sable velvet feather covers quite,
Even like the forehead-cloths that in the night,
Or when they sorrow, ladies use to wear;
Their wings, blue, red, and yellow mixed appear;
Colours that, as we construe colours, paint
Their states to life; the yellow shows their saint,
The devil Venus, left them; blue, their truth;   290
The red and black, ensigns of death and ruth.
And this true honour from their love-deaths sprung,
They were the first that ever poet sung.

Heroides 20

ACONTIUS TO CYDIPPE

After all the doom and gloom of the letters by Leander and Hero we are now taken on to two entertaining and witty epistles, which have a happy ending, with the lovers united, married and living on. In this way light-hearted pairs (16 and 17; 20 and 21) frame the tragic duo (18 and 19), and there is a happy ending for the whole collection too.

A young man from Cea called Acontius, while attending a religious festival on the Greek island of Delos, caught sight of and immediately fell in love with Cydippe, a beautiful young woman from Naxos, who was also at the festival, along with her mother. While Cydippe was in Diana's temple, Acontius rolled up to her an apple on which he had inscribed the words: 'I swear by Diana to marry Acontius'. She picked up the apple, read out the words (the ancients normally read aloud) and thereby unwittingly bound herself to him on oath. She returned to Naxos and to the marriage arranged for her by her father, but as the day of the wedding approached, she fell seriously ill (due to a fever sent by Diana, as Cydippe was about to break her word). The ceremony was called off, after which she recovered. At the time of Acontius' letter the wedding has been rearranged another two times and she has fallen ill each time, and she is now still on her sickbed, with her fiancé in attendance. Her father has sent to the oracle of Apollo at Delphi for advice on how she might get well again. Acontius has come to Naxos to find out how she is, and he gets to her this letter (trying to win her heart, on top of the oath) before the response from Delphi is received. That will inform her father about Cydippe's oath and urge him to fulfil it, and as a result of that he will marry his daughter to Acontius.

In his epistle Acontius tells Cydippe that Diana is responsible for her sickness, and he presses her to keep her oath because the goddess reacts violently when she sees an offence against her divinity. At 101ff. he cites three examples by way of proof. When the king of Calydon didn't sacrifice to Diana, she sent an enormous boar which ravaged the fields there (the king's son Meleager organized a hunt which disposed of the boar, but in a quarrel over who got its hide he killed his mother's brothers, and in revenge for that she brought about his death). Actaeon, while out hunting, inadvertently saw Diana bathing naked, so she turned him into a stag, and his own hunting-hounds attacked him and killed him. The heroine Niobe boasted that she had more children than Latona (the mother of Diana and Apollo), so the divine pair slaughtered her children, and she was changed into a rock, although her eyes continued to weep for her loss.

As you read the translation below, ask yourself what kind of a person Acontius comes across as in his letter, and how successful his approach to Cydippe is likely to be.

Don't be afraid! You won't read out in this letter another oath for
    your lover. It's enough that you promised yourself to me once.
Look through it to the very end. May you get well again, if you do!
    It pains me that you feel pain in any part of your body.
Why are you blushing before you've seen it? (I suspect that,   5
    as in Diana's temple, your pretty cheeks have gone red.)
I'm asking for marriage, the fidelity you pledged, nothing reprehensible:
    I love you, girl, as your destined husband, not as an adulterer.
Recall, if you will, the words brought to your chaste hands
    by the fruit I plucked from the tree and threw to you: 10
you'll find that with them you give an undertaking
    which I pray that *you* remember rather than the goddess.
I still long for the same thing, but I long for it more keenly now;
    the fire in me has grown and got stronger due to the delay;
my love was never slight, and it has now increased because of   15
    the length of time that's passed and the hope that you gave me.
You gave me hope, and my passionate heart trusted you.
    You can't deny this happened: the goddess is my witness.
She was there, actually present, and noted what you said,
    nodded her head and seemed to have heard your words.   20
I'll allow you to say you were taken in by a trick of mine,
    so long as you mention that love motivated my trick.
The sole aim of my trick was to be joined to you in marriage.
    You're complaining about something that could make you warm to me.
I'm not so crafty by nature or by practice: 25
    believe me, girl, you're the one who makes me clever.
I drew up the words, but it was ingenious Love who bound you to me
    with them (if I have in fact achieved anything).
It was with words dictated by him that I betrothed us,
    and I acquired my legal cunning from Love the lawyer.   30
Describe what I did as a trick and call me deceitful,
    if it is in fact deceit to want to have the person you love.

Look, I'm writing once again, sending an appeal to you:
    this is another 'trick' for you to complain about.
If I wrong you by loving, I confess I'll wrong you forever,   35
    and even though you're wary of being pursued, I'll always pursue you.
Others have used the sword to carry off girls they found attractive:
    will a carefully composed bit of writing by me be seen as a crime?
I wish the gods would enable me to bind you still tighter,
    so you'd find no escape at all from keeping your pledge.   40
A thousand ruses remain – I'm only sweating at the base of the slope;
    my passion will leave nothing untried.
Though it's doubtful if you can be won, I'll certainly try to win you;
    the outcome rests with the gods, but you *will* be won.
Even if you escape some, you won't evade all of the nets   45
    (more than you think) which Love has stretched out for you.
If artifice achieves nothing, I'll resort to weapons:
    you'll be seized and carried off in arms that yearn for you.
I'm not the type of person given to criticizing Paris for what he did
    or anyone who acted as a man so he could be some girl's man.   50
I too – but I say no more. Though death is the punishment for
    such abduction, not having you will be worse than that.
Otherwise, if you weren't so attractive, you'd be pursued with restraint;
    it's your beauty that forces me to be reckless.
You are responsible for this, you and your eyes, which are brighter than   55
    the fiery stars, and which were the cause of my burning love;
your blonde hair and ivory neck are responsible for this,
    and also those hands, which I long to feel clasping my neck,
and your lovely face, demure but refined, and those feet –
    I can scarcely believe that Thetis has such pretty ones.   60
I'd be happier if I could praise the rest of your charms,
    but I don't doubt the whole masterpiece is equally splendid.
It's not surprising if I was compelled by such beauty
    to want to have a pledge spoken by you.
In short, I'll allow that you're a girl caught by a trap of mine,   65
    provided that you're forced to confess that you have been caught.
I'll endure the dislike, so long as I'm duly recompensed after enduring it.
    Why does such a great crime lack its due reward?
Hesione was captured by Telamon, Briseis by Achilles, and each, of course,
    accepted the conqueror as her man and went off with him.   70
I'll let you make accusations and be angry as much as you like,
    provided you let me have the right to enjoy you while you're angry.
I'm the cause of it, and I'll lessen the anger that I've caused,
    if only I get some slight opportunity to placate you.
Let me stand before your face, weeping,   75
    let me add sad words to the sad tears

and stretch out submissive hands to you in an appeal,
    as slaves generally do when they fear a savage flogging.
You're not aware of your authority. Summon me! Why am I charged in my
    absence? Order me to come right now, just like a mistress.   80
You can imperiously tear my hair yourself
    and bruise my face with your fingers.
I'll endure all that; my only fear will be that
    you might possibly hurt your hands on my body.
But don't use shackles or chains to confine me: the bonds   85
    of my steadfast love will keep me in your possession.
When you've thoroughly sated your anger, as much as you want,
    you'll say to yourself: 'How enduring his love is!'
You'll say to yourself when you see me bearing it all:
    'Let such a good slave be my slave!'   90
Now I'm miserable – prosecuted in my absence; and although my case
    is excellent, it's lost, because I have no defence counsel.
Also, however unfair on you what I wrote on the apple was,
    you surely can't complain about anyone else's conduct.
You broke your word to Diana as well as me, and she didn't deserve that;   95
    if you refuse to keep your promise for me, keep it for the goddess.
She was there and saw when you were duped and blushed;
    she heard your words, stored them away and remembers them.
May nothing bad come of mentioning this! She's supremely violent when
    she sees an offence against her divinity (which I hope she won't).   100
I'll cite as a witness to that the Calydonian boar, a savage creature,
    but not as savage as his mother was found to be to Meleager.
Actaeon's a witness too (in days gone by the dogs with which he'd
    previously killed wild animals imagined that he was a wild animal),
and so is the arrogant mother Niobe, who still stands on the soil of   105
    Mygdonia, motionless and weeping, her body turned to stone.
Ah, Cydippe, I'm afraid to tell you the truth, in case you think
    my warning is something made up in my own interests,
but I must tell it: believe me, this is the reason why
    you often lie ill on the very eve of your wedding.   110
The goddess herself is looking out for you, is at pains to save you from
    breaking your oath: she wants you to keep your word and be well.
So it is that whenever you try to prove yourself to be a perjurer,
    she prevents that crime by you every time.
Don't provoke the cruel bow of that proud virgin;   115
    she can still soften, if you'd let her.
Please don't allow your tender limbs to be wasted by fever;
    preserve that beauty of yours for me to enjoy.
Preserve that face, which was born to set me on fire,
    and the gentle blush under the surface of your snowy cheeks.   120

My usual state when you're unwell is something I wish on my
    enemies and anybody who opposes you becoming mine.
I'm equally tormented whether you're getting married or you're ill,
    and I can't say which of the two I'd like less.
There are times when I'm distressed because I'm a cause of pain for you   125
    and I think that you're being hurt because of my cunning.
I pray that my girl's perjury may fall on my head;
    let me be punished, let her be safe!
However, so I can find out how you are, I often
    prowl about anxiously near your doorway.   130
I follow your servants (the maid and the boy) on the sly,
    asking them what good sleep and food have done you.
I'm miserable because I'm not giving you your medicine,
    stroking your hands and sitting beside your bed.
I'm also miserable because I'm far away from you and perhaps   135
    the other man (the last person I'd want) is there with you.
He strokes those hands of yours and sits beside your sickbed,
    hateful to the gods and to me as well as the gods,
and, while he takes your pulse with his fingers, he uses that
    as a pretext to hold your white arm frequently,   140
and fondles your breasts and perhaps kisses you.
    His services don't deserve as great a reward as that!
Man, who gave you permission to reap my crop before me?
    Who enabled you to trespass on another person's land?
Those breasts are mine! The kisses you're taking are mine!   145
    It's disgraceful. Hands off a body promised to me!
Hands off, you criminal! The girl you're touching is going to be mine.
    From now on if you do that, you'll be committing adultery.
Choose somebody not attached, not claimed by another man;
    in case you don't know it, this property has an owner.   150
Don't take my word for it – let the terms of the agreement be recited;
    so you can't say they're fictitious, make her read them out herself.
You, I'm talking to you: get out of this bedroom – it's another man's.
    What are you doing here? Get out! This bed is taken.
Although you too have a verbal agreement like mine,   155
    you'll find that doesn't make your case as strong as mine.
She pledged herself to me, her father pledged her to you; he's her nearest
    kin, but she's surely more closely related to herself than he is.
Her father only promised her, she vowed herself to her lover on oath;
    he invoked men as witnesses, she invoked a goddess.   160
His fear is of being called a liar, hers of being called that and a perjurer;
    you must know which of these two is the greater fear.
To put it briefly, so you can compare the respective dangers, look at

what's happened: she is in bed sick, he is in good health.
Also, we're in competition with different states of mind: 165
    you're hoping for less than I am, and I have more to dread.
You risk nothing in your courtship, refusal for me is worse than death,
    and I already love one who you will perhaps come to love.
If you'd cared for justice and what's right, you'd have felt bound
    to give way before my passion of your own accord.   170
As it is, Cydippe, that savage persists in fighting for his unfair
    cause, so what does my letter come down to?
He's the one behind you being sick and viewed with suspicion by Diana;
    if you were sensible, you'd tell him not to come to your house.
It's *his* doing that your life is so cruelly in danger –   175
    he's behind that, so let him die instead of you!
If you reject him and refuse to love a man damned by Diana,
    then you'll immediately be saved, and I will be, for sure.
Put an end to your fear, girl! Lasting good health will be yours,
    if you just honour the shrine that witnessed your promise.   180
What pleases the gods of heaven is not sacrificing oxen but being
    true to one's word, which should be done even without witnesses.
To get well, some women endure surgery and cautery,
    others do themselves good by taking horribly bitter medicine.
There's no need for all that: just avoid perjury,   185
    keep your promise and keep yourself and me alive.
Ignorance will provide an excuse for your former misconduct:
    you'd forgotten the agreement you read out loud.
Now you've been reminded by this letter and by the trouble
    you habitually have whenever you try to break your word.   190
Presumably, even if you escape that, when you give birth you'll pray
    to her to help by laying her radiant hands on you, won't you?
She'll hear you, and recall the pledge she heard, and ask
    who is your husband and the father of the child.
You'll promise a votive offering – she knows your promises are false;   195
    you'll swear an oath – she knows you can break your word to gods.
I am not the issue here. I care more and I'm really bothered
    about somebody else. It's *you* I'm worried about.
Recently, when you were in a critical state, why did your frightened parents
    weep for you, in ignorance of your misconduct thanks to you?   200
And why should they be ignorant? You could tell your mother everything.
    There's no need for blushes over what you did, Cydippe.
Make sure you describe in order how I first became aware of you
    while she herself was performing a rite to the archer goddess Diana,
how (if you happened to notice this) right after I saw you   205
    I stood stock-still, with my eyes fixed on your body,

in utter amazement at you, and my cloak slipped from my
    shoulders and fell off (a sure sign of love's madness),
and later from somewhere or other the apple came rolling up
    with insidious words cleverly inscribed on it,   210
and because you read them out in holy Diana's presence you bound
    yourself to abide by your promise before a divine witness.
But so that she'll understand the gist of what was written,
    repeat now the words you once read out.
She'll say: 'Please marry the man who the kindly gods join you to;   215
    you swore he'd be my son-in-law – let him be that!
Whoever he is, Diana approved of him, so you should approve of him.'
    That'll be your mother, if she turns out to be a real mother.
However, do see that she asks who I am and what sort of a man I am:
    she'll find that the goddess had the interests of you both at heart.   220
There's an island in the Aegean Sea called Cea, which was
    once much frequented by the Corycian nymphs.
That's the land of my birth; and I'm indisputably descended from
    impressive ancestors (if your family values aristocratic names);
I have wealth too and a blameless character; and even   225
    without all that, I'm bound to you by Love.
Even if you hadn't sworn, you'd want a husband like that; once you swore,
    you should have accepted me, even if I wasn't like that.
Diana of the hunting spear ordered me to write this to you in a dream;
    Love ordered me to write this to you when I was awake;   230
out of those gods his arrows have already wounded me,
    and you must take care that hers don't wound you.
My survival is linked to yours – have pity on me and on yourself;
    why hesitate to help out two people at one and the same time?
If you do help, then on the day when trumpets signal the rite of   235
    dedication and Delos is stained by blood shed in sacrifice,
a golden replica of the successful apple will be set up,
    with the reason for the offering recorded in two short verses:
BY MEANS OF THIS IMAGE OF THE APPLE ACONTIUS DECLARES
    THAT WHAT WAS WRITTEN ON IT HAS COME TRUE.   240
You're weak, and I don't want you to be tired out by too long a letter,
    so I'll close with the usual ending: fare well!

Some readers will disapprove of Acontius' conduct, because he has tricked an
unsuspecting young woman into binding herself to him with an oath, and has
thus been responsible for her falling dangerously ill on three occasions, and with
this letter is trying to manipulate her. Several scholars have felt like this and have
been critical of Acontius, accusing him of being in this epistle coldly calculating,
ruthless and obsessed. This may be right. What do you think? Do you see anything

militating against this point of view? Think about this before moving on to the next paragraph.

In our opinion that serious and solemn approach takes no account of the pervasive wit, humour and cheekiness in *Heroides* 20. It also makes this into a pedestrian poem, a full 242 dull lines, by Ovid. And such an interpretation does not cohere well with *Her.* 21, where Cydippe, after Acontius' obnoxious qualities have supposedly been brought out at length here, intimates that she loves him and gladly accepts him as her husband. You may well disapprove of the ruse with the apple, but it was love that made him do that (something which often makes humans behave badly). As for manipulation, he doesn't *need* to win her heart (he has got her as his wife by means of the oath), but he *wants* to – obviously because he loves her. We think that those scholars are being too severe and too negative about what Ovid presents as simply the eager attempts of an infatuated young man to bring round his beloved. In our opinion Ovid is (rightly or wrongly) having fun yet again, and Acontius' performance was meant to entertain his Roman readers, something which it could easily have done in such a society, especially in view of the happy ending to come.

This is a letter of courtship, so, as well as explaining that she is legally his and risks punishment if she doesn't marry him (as part of the pressure on her), he comes out with a series of ploys to secure her affection. Something which is very important given what he has done to her, he tries hard to convince her of his love and concern for her (as early as 3f. and 8, and frequently after that). He also compliments her on her beauty, offers her subservience, shows a flattering jealousy in connection with her fiancé, tries to impress her with his credentials and so on. And, divertingly, he can be quite deft while doing this: for example, when he attacks his rival at 143ff. and predicts how her mother will react to him at 215ff., his words are aimed at Cydippe. Such overtures would stand a good chance of working. But what are we to make of all the levity, wit and cheek?

He begins the epistle with a joke about her oath (1f.), actually claims that she gave him hope at 16f. (when she swore involuntarily), generously allows her to say that she was taken in by a trick of his in 21, maintains that he is not crafty in 25, is flippant about revered legal matters at 28ff., and so on and so forth. Most outrageous of all is his strained and sophistic exoneration of himself, ascribing the blame for Cydippe's illness to Diana, Love, the young woman herself and his rival. As the above-mentioned ploys and the ruse with the apple show, Acontius is no fool, so he cannot expect to convince her with this (especially as he admits his culpability at 21ff. and 125f.), but must be engaging in banter and attempting to impress her with his mental agility. We believe that with all the humour and impudence he is trying to lighten things up (so she won't be too serious about the whole situation), put himself across as an amusing and roguish type (someone fun to be with) and dazzle her with his cleverness and stylish way with words (on which see further below).

This is all very amusing for us, but he is sailing close to the wind as far as concerns the addressee (when he doesn't really know her), and there is a definite danger that she might find such frivolity and ingenuity inappropriate and offensive. She could easily be put off as well by his remarks at 47ff., 61f. and 143–50, by his naughty attempts to get her to swear again (152, 213f.) and by the threats of divine punishment (even though they are veiled and attributed to worry for her wellbeing). We know that he will get to marry her, but we are left wondering if he will actually win her heart with this letter, or alienate her affections on a temporary or even permanent basis. So on this interpretation *Her.* 20 coheres effectively with *Her.* 21, since (as well as being similarly light-hearted) it makes us keen to read her reply, so we can see how she will react and find out if he has caused a setback for himself on the emotional front.

Acontius' expression is frequently elegant, especially when he is making witty points. It is not always easy to appreciate this kind of thing when you are working with a translation (which serves you right for not taking Latin!). Sometimes the neatness does come across in the English (for instance the verbal play in 50 and the parallel arrangement and effective repetition of words at 195f., 229f. and 231f.). But often it is impossible to do justice in our language to the dexterity. For example, 35f., 43f. and 227f. are much shorter and snappier in the Latin. In 168 (*idque ego iam, quod tu forsan amabis, amo*) the word order in the Latin is pointed. This breaks down as *idque quod tu forsan amabis* ('and one who you will perhaps come to love') *ego iam amo* ('I already love'). The punch comes at the end with *amo* ('I love'), of Acontius' existing passion, deliberately delayed, and placed beside *amabis* ('you will come to love'), of the rival possibly coming to love Cydippe after they marry. The two verbs are put right next to each other (this device is called juxtaposition) to bring out the contrast in the feelings of the two men. There is also alliteration, repetition of the letters a and m, which lends forcefulness to Acontius' *amo* ('I love'). There is juxtaposition and vigorous alliteration at 95f. as well, where Acontius says to Cydippe *si non vis* ('if you refuse') *mihi* ('for me') *promissum reddere* ('to keep your promise'), *redde deae* ('keep [it] for the goddess'). There we find in addition an ABBA arrangement of words (named chiasmus) in *mihi* ('for me') *reddere* ('to keep') *redde* ('keep') *deae* ('for the goddess').

Such attention to style and sound is an important feature of Ovid's poetry in general, and often goes hand in hand with humour. So he makes a female character claim that Roman women are promiscuous and come out with the epigram *casta est quam nemo rogavit* = 'she [alone] is chaste whom nobody has propositioned' (memorably translated by Guy Lee as 'chaste means never asked'). There is also droll compression in Ovid's advice to short girls on how to present themselves to their best advantage: *si brevis es* ('if you're short'), *sedeas* ('sit down'), *ne* ('so you don't') *stans* ('when standing up') *videare sedere* ('appear to be sitting down'). Sometimes he takes all this to flippant extremes, as when he describes the Minotaur (the monster that was partly a human and partly a bull) as *semibovemque virum semivirumque bovem* ('the half-bull man and the half-man bull'). Many enjoy such flourishes, but this sort of thing led an ancient critic called Quintilian to accuse the poet of being too fond of his own ingenuity, and some modern scholars have agreed with that assessment. What do you think?

It may strike you as odd that Acontius wrote the oath on a piece of fruit. However, we do find inscribed apples elsewhere. Most famously, at the wedding of Peleus and Thetis the goddess Strife rolled among the divinities present a golden apple which bore the words FOR THE FAIREST, and which was claimed by Juno, Minerva and Venus. This led to Paris judging the naked charms of the three of them, and awarding the prize of the apple to Venus, who promised him as a bribe the most beautiful woman in the world (Helen), and so set in train the Trojan War. In fact, for Acontius' message an apple was a variously appropriate receptacle. This fruit was connected with marriage in the ancient world: for example, Strabo notes that Persian brides on their wedding-day are allowed to eat only apples and camel-marrow (yuk!). Throwing an apple to someone was a sign of affection. So Plato's epigram (*Greek Anthology* 5.80) to a girl runs as follows:

> I'm an apple. Someone who loves you throws me at you. Give in
>   to him, Xanthippe. You and I are both decaying.

Apples were also commonly love-gifts. For instance, Virgil at *Eclogue* 3.70f. has the shepherd Menalcas sing:

> I've sent my boy all I could – ten golden apples picked from
> a tree in the wood; tomorrow I'll send him another ten.

The fruit also symbolized the female breast. Paulus Silentiarius (*Greek Anthology* 5.291) writes:

> If you gave me these apples as tokens of your breasts, you charming
>   girl, then I bless you for this great favour.

In addition, apples were associated with the deities of love. So Sappho (fragment 25) presides over a rite in a grove sacred to Aphrodite (Venus) and summons the goddess to join her there in some sensuous lines:

> Come here to me from Crete to this holy
> temple, where your lovely grove of
> apple-trees stands, and altars smouldering with frankincense;
> in there cool water babbles through the
> apple boughs, the whole place is shadowed
> by roses, and a trance comes down from
> glancing foliage.

Heroides 21
CYDIPPE TO ACONTIUS

Ovid now presents Cydippe's perspective on the trick with the apple and the idea of marriage to Acontius, and he gives us her reaction to his letter of courtship. Our poet here takes a major step forward in the story and clearly foreshadows the happy ending, as near the conclusion of *Heroides* 21 he makes Cydippe agree to marry the young man and intimate that she loves him. It turns out that like *Her.* 20 this is also a manipulative, clever and light-hearted poem. There are further links in her reassuring allusion to the rival at her bedside, Acontius' claim of Diana's responsibility for the sickness being confirmed here by an oracle of Apollo and the fact that his suggestion that the young woman should tell her mother everything has been taken up by her and carried out. By way of variety, for much of the epistle she attacks his ruse with the oath (which he defended), refrains from saying that she will marry him (whereas he frequently pressed for that) and conceals her affection for him (in contrast to his parading of his love for her).

Cydippe refers to the tale that Delos was originally a floating island, until Latona gave birth there to the healing god Apollo (and his sister Diana) and he rooted it to the sea-bed. She also mentions the tree on Delos which Latona supposedly clutched during her birth pangs and the altar there which Apollo was said to have constructed from the horns of wild goats killed by the huntress Diana. At 177ff. she picks up Acontius' allusions to Actaeon (who saw Diana bathing naked), the king of Calydon (who did not sacrifice to the goddess) and Niobe (who scorned Latona because she had fewer children), and at 209f. she connects Acontius' name with the Greek word *acontion* (meaning 'javelin'). Other mythological references are explained in the glossary.

As you read her letter, ask yourself exactly what Cydippe is up to in it.

> I was very afraid, and read your letter in complete silence,
>   so my tongue wouldn't swear unwittingly by some god.

I think you would have tried to trap me again, if you didn't know
    that one promise from me was enough, as you say yourself.
I wasn't going to read it, but if I'd behaved harshly towards you,   5
    perhaps that savage goddess' anger would have increased.
Do what I will, although I devoutly offer Diana incense,
    despite all that she supports you, more than is fair,
and avenges you with unforgetting anger (as you want me to believe);
    she hardly did as much for her own dear Hippolytus.   10
As a virgin goddess, she should rather have supported a young virgin,
    but I fear she doesn't want me to live much longer.
For I'm chronically ill, for no apparent reason, I'm exhausted,
    and nothing that the doctor does to help me works.
How thin do you think I am now, hardly able to write this reply to you,   15
    and how pale my body, that I can hardly raise on my elbow?
On top of all that I'm now afraid that someone other than the nurse
    who is my accomplice might realize that we're exchanging letters.
She sits before my bedroom door, and when people ask how I am in there,
    she says: 'She's asleep,' so I can write in safety.   20
Sleep is a very good pretext for my protracted seclusion, but later on,
    when it stops being credible because it has gone on so long,
and she now sees people coming who it's hard not to let in,
    she alerts me with the agreed signal by clearing her throat.
I leave my words unfinished, just as they are, and rush to hide   25
    the letter I've started down the front of my dress, trembling.
Afterwards I take it out again and weary my fingers with it:
    my handwriting shows you the labour you cause me.
God strike me dead if you were worth that, to tell the truth!
    But I'm kinder than is right or you deserve.   30
So it's thanks to you that it's so often doubtful that I'll survive,
    and I have been and still am punished for your ploy?
Is this the reward for my beauty, made proud by your
    praise? Being attractive to you means pain for me?
If I'd seemed ugly to you (as I'd prefer), you'd have found fault   35
    with my body, and it wouldn't be in need of medical aid;
I was praised, and now I groan; you two men are now killing me
    with your rivalry, and I am hurt by my own loveliness.
You don't yield to him, and he doesn't consider himself second to you,
    so you hinder his desires, and he hinders yours.   40
I myself am tossed about like a ship which the north wind steadily
    drives out to sea, and the tide and the waves bring back again,
and when the day that my dear parents long for is upon me,
    at the same time a blazing fever consumes my body –
ah, on the very eve of my marriage the cruel queen of   45
    the Underworld knocks at my door prematurely.

By now I'm ashamed and afraid that, although I know I'm not guilty,
 people will think the gods are deservedly displeased with me.
One man claims that my illness is coincidental, another maintains
 that my fiancé has not won heaven's approval;   50
and, just so you don't imagine that gossip has nothing to say against you too,
 others think that you've used spells to make me sick.
My trouble is obvious, its cause is not. You two have rejected peace
 and are fighting fiercely, and I'm the one who gets hit.
Come on, tell me now (none of your usual deceit): as your love is 55
 so harmful, what will you do to someone you hate?
If you hurt the one you love, you'll be wise to love your enemy;
 to save my life, you terrible man, please plan on killing me.
Either you no longer care for the girl you hoped to have
 and are cruelly letting her waste away and die undeservedly, 60
or, if you're begging savage Diana on my behalf but achieving nothing,
 you can't boast to me of having influence with her.
Choose your story: you don't want to placate the goddess –
 you've forgotten me; you can't – she's forgotten you.
I wish I'd never got to know Delos in the Aegean Sea   65
 or not done so at that particular time!
That was when my ship was launched on an ocean of troubles,
 and it was an ill-omened hour for starting my voyage.
I stumbled inauspiciously when I stepped forward and left my home,
 and when I set foot on the swift, painted ship.   70
Yet twice a contrary wind blew on our sails and turned us back –
 ah, I'm mad, that's not the truth – it was a favourable breeze.
It was a favourable breeze that carried me back on my journey
 and hindered a trip that didn't hold much happiness for me.
If only it had kept on blowing against my canvas!   75
 But it's foolish to complain about a wind being fickle.
I was excited by Delos' fame, in a hurry to visit the place,
 and I felt that the boat I was sailing on was sluggish.
How often did I curse the oars for being slow and complain
 that they weren't letting out enough sail to catch the wind! 80
And now I'd passed Myconos, now Tenos and Andros,
 and gleaming Delos was before my eyes.
When I saw it far off, I said: 'Why are you eluding me, island?
 Surely you're not floating around on the great sea, as you used to?'
I set foot on its soil when the daylight had almost gone and the Sun 85
 was now about to unharness his chariot's radiant horses.
After he brought them back for his usual rising,
 my mother told the maid to do my hair.
She herself put jewelled rings on my fingers and a gold crown on my head,

she herself put my clothes on me over my shoulders.   90
Immediately we set out and greet the gods to whom Delos is
    sacred and offer them wine and yellow incense;
and while my mother stains the altar with blood shed in sacrifice
    and places severed entrails on its smoking fire,
my attentive nurse leads me inside the lofty temples as well,   95
    and we roam at random throughout the holy places.
Now I stroll in the colonnades, now I marvel at the gifts
    of kings and at the statues standing everywhere.
I marvel also at the altar constructed of countless horns
    and the tree which Latona strained against as she gave birth   100
and the other sights on Delos (I don't remember and don't
    feel like mentioning everything that I saw there).
Perhaps while I was inspecting all that I was inspected by you,
    Acontius, and I seemed to be an easy prey in my naivety.
I returned to Diana's shrine, set high up on its steps –   105
    no place should have been safer than that.
In front of my feet is thrown an apple with the following verse –
    ah, I nearly swore the oath to you now all over again.
My nurse picked it up and said in amazement: 'Read this!'
    I read out your trap, mighty poet.   110
At the mention of the word 'marry' I was upset and embarrassed
    and felt the blush spread all over my cheeks.
I kept my eyes on my lap, as if they were fixed there,
    those eyes that you made help you gain your objective.
Why are you pleased, you criminal? What glory have you won?   115
    What renown do you have, as a man who tricked a girl?
I didn't square up to you, armed with an axe and shield,
    like Penthesilea in the land of Troy;
I was no Hippolyte, with an Amazonian sword-belt
    of engraved gold, that you took home as spoil.   120
Why exult if your words deceived me and I was
    an incautious girl caught out by your cunning?
An apple caught out Cydippe, as one caught out Atalanta;
    no doubt you'll now present yourself as a second Hippomenes!
But if Love (the boy who you say possesses some torches or other)   125
    did have you under his control, it would have been better to do what
good men usually do, and not ruin your hopes of success by being dishonest:
    you should have won me over with appeals, not caught me out.
When you went after me, why didn't you think you should openly state
    the qualities which would have made me go after you yourself?   130
Why did you want to compel me rather than persuade me,
    if I could have been won by listening to a proposal?

What use to you now is the set form of the oath or the fact that
    my tongue invoked as a witness the goddess who was present?
It's the mind that swears. But I swore nothing with mine.   135
    It alone can add a guarantee to what someone says.
It's a decision, a conscious intention of the brain, that swears;
    the only valid obligations are those incurred deliberately.
If I made an undertaking to wed you willingly,
    claim the rights of the promised marriage which are due to you;   140
but if I gave you only speech without intellect behind it,
    what you have is useless – words without a force of their own.
I did not swear an oath – I read out words that formed an oath;
    that wasn't the way for you to be chosen as my husband.
Deceive other girls like this – with an apple followed up by a letter!   145
    If this is legally valid, extract immense wealth from the rich,
get kings to swear to hand over their kingdoms to you
    and take for yourself whatever you fancy in the whole world.
Believe me, this makes you much mightier than Diana herself,
    if what you write possesses such dynamic divine power.   150
However, after saying all this, after firmly denying myself to you,
    after completing effectively my case concerning my promise,
I admit I fear nonetheless the anger of savage Diana
    and suspect that she is the cause of my sickness.
For why else, whenever there are preparations for the marriage ceremony, 155
    does the bride-to-be become ill and collapse on each occasion?
Three times now the wedding-god has come to the altars put up
    for me and fled, running from my marriage-bed.
He's slow to keep on replenishing the lamps (which revive reluctantly)
    and to wave his torches (whose flames flare up reluctantly).   160
Again and again the perfume drips from his garlanded hair,
    and he trails behind him his cloak, bright from lots of saffron dye;
but when he reaches our doorway and sees tears and fear
    of death and much that is alien to his worship,
with his own hand he pulls the garlands from his brow and flings them down 165
    and wipes away the viscous scent from his glistening hair;
he's ashamed to stir himself joyfully among the mournful crowd,
    and his cheeks become as red as his cloak.
But, ah, my poor body burns up with fever,
    and the bedclothes feel heavier than they should,   170
and I see my parents leaning over me in tears, and the
    wedding-torch will soon be replaced by the torch for my pyre.
Goddess glorying in the embroidered quiver, I'm in pain, spare me;
    take on your brother's role: help me now and save my life.
It's demeaning for you that he eradicates the causes of death,   175
    but you on the other hand have the credit for killing me.

Surely it can't be that when you wanted to bathe in a shady pool,
    I unwittingly looked at the place where you were washing,
or that out of all the gods' altars I neglected yours,
    or that my mother showed contempt for your mother? 180
I've done nothing wrong, except for reading out a false oath
    and showing my literacy with a ruinous line of verse.
You too, Acontius, if your love for me is no lie, must offer incense
    on my behalf; let the hands that harmed me help me.
You're indignant that the girl pledged to you isn't yours yet, 185
    so why carry on in such a way as to prevent her becoming yours?
While I'm still alive you have everything to hope for; why is the savage
    goddess taking away life from me and your hope of me from you?
And don't imagine that the man I'm betrothed to lays his
    hands on me and caresses my feverish body. 190
He does sit beside me, uninvited, as much as he's allowed to,
    but he doesn't forget that mine is a virgin's bed.
Also he already seems to sense something about me:
    he often sheds tears for no apparent reason,
he's not as bold with his endearments, kisses me only 195
    rarely, and calls me his in a voice that is timid.
I'm not surprised he's sensed something, as I betray myself by
    obvious signs: when he comes, I turn away on to my right side,
and I don't speak, and I close my eyes, pretending to sleep,
    and I push his hand off when he tries to touch me. 200
He groans and sighs, without saying anything, and finds that
    through no fault of his he has made me resentful.
Oh dear, you're elated, delighted by this attitude of mine.
    Oh dear, I've confessed my feelings to you.
But if I felt any anger, you would deserve it with 205
    more justification, for spreading the net to catch me.
You write for permission to visit me on my sickbed. You're apart
    from me, but you're causing me harm from where you are.
I wondered why you're called Acontius: it's because
    you have the sharp point that wounds from a distance. 210
At any rate I haven't recovered yet from just such a wound, hit from
    afar by what you wrote on the apple, as if by a javelin.
But why would you come here? You'd see a body in a really
    pitiful state, a notable trophy won by your ingenuity.
I've wasted away and collapsed; my complexion is bloodless, 215
    like the colour of your apple, as I recall it,
and my face is white, without an added red glow beneath the skin.
    Freshly cut marble usually looks like this;
this is the colour of a silver goblet at a banquet,
    pale from the chill touch of ice-water. 220

If you were to see me now, you'll claim you've never seen me before,
    and say: 'I didn't use my skills to try to win that girl.'
To avoid being married to me, you'll let me off my
    promise and want the goddess to forget it.
Perhaps you'll make me swear again, but the exact opposite,   225
    and send me words to read out a second time.
However, I wish you would sit beside me (as you requested yourself),
    looking at the feverish body of your fiancée.
Even supposing your heart was harder than iron, Acontius,
    you yourself would beg Diana to release me from my oath.   230
But, for your information, Apollo's oracle at Delphi
    is being asked how I can recover my health.
A vague rumour whispers now that he too is complaining, on the
    evidence of his sister, about the failure to keep some pledge.
This is what the god, his prophet and the solemnly intoned oracle say –   235
    ah, there's full divine support for what you desire!
Why are they on your side? – unless perhaps you've devised some
    new writing to ensnare the mighty gods when read out.
Since you've got control of the gods, I obey their will of my own accord;
    I'm beaten, and I gladly yield to your desires.   240
I've confessed to mother the agreement my tongue was tricked into making,
    keeping my eyes on the ground, deeply embarrassed.
The rest is your responsibility. Even as it is, I've done more than a girl
    should in not being afraid to communicate with you by letter.
I'm weak, and I've already tired myself out enough with writing;   245
    my sickly hand refuses to do its duty any longer.
Since I want to be joined to you in marriage soon, nothing
    remains except for my letter to add: fare well!

By the time we reach the end of this poem we can deduce that Cydippe was certainly angered by Acontius' trick but is just about over that now (see especially 205) and his letter, with its compliments, show of love and concern, flattering jealousy etc., has got to her and has won her heart. It also appears that his ingenuity and roguish humour and cheek have not in fact backfired. She was not put off by and may well have been impressed by his clever and stylish expression, as she responds with lots of that of her own (for example at 55–64). And it looks as if his levity has succeeded in loosening her up, since she indulges in wit herself (playing on the derivation of his name at 209f.) and makes a joke out of his ruse with the apple (at 237–9) and teases him.

As part of this tease, amusingly, for much of her epistle Cydippe conceals her real feelings for Acontius and says nothing about her willingness to marry him (and she holds all that back with extensive retardation by going into unnecessarily full detail at 17ff., 77ff., 85ff. and 155ff.). As well as not owning up about things Cydippe also positively misleads Acontius (and us) with what she does say. So it would be very worrying for him to find her dwelling so much on all the suffering he has caused her, and being critical and contemptuous about his trick, and wishing that she had never gone to Delos at all. So too she calls him a terrible man (58) and a criminal (115), accuses him of cruelty in 60, is cuttingly sarcastic in 110 and 117ff., and talks of him having ruined his hopes of her in 127. (At the same time, so he won't give up and not read the letter to the end, she works in a few brief and unclear hints that she may possibly have some time for him after all at 33f., 40, 43, 128 and 130.) Entertainingly Cydippe is getting her own back by deceiving Acontius as he deceived her, and manipulating him in return, making him despondent before suddenly adding much to cheer him at 187ff., where she reveals that actually he has everything to hope for with her, and reassures him about his rival, and implies that she does have real affection for him. But even now she plays with him: she doesn't actually go so far as to state openly that she loves him, she takes her time before saying she agrees to marry him (gladly) and she leaves it up to him to set up the wedding, thereby maintaining her dignity and making sure that he values her acceptance of him.

Ovid ends the *Heroides* collection with one of his most appealing heroines. Cydippe often describes herself as a girl (*puella* and *virgo*), and several of her (touching) characteristics evident in *Her.* 21 fit with that. Still under the influence of her mother and nurse, she is timid, modest and naive (as she says herself in 104), and she reveals a girlish excitement over the trip to Delos and the sightseeing there. She is also tender and vulnerable – hence she is won over by Acontius' letter with its assurances of love etc. But she is no push-over, and she actually exerts control in her epistle. She shows spirit getting her own back on the young man. She is also an intelligent young woman. For instance, in addition to the stylistic neatness, she caps his arguments about responsibility and his legalisms with much more logical and just argumentation of her own at 135ff., and she gives a deft twist to his protestation of affection at 183f. Cydippe has a real sense of humour too. On top of the extended mischievous tease of Acontius and the witty play on his name at 209f. and the joke at 237–9 about the gods being ensnared by his writing, there is the wryly mocking exaggeration of the valid powers of the ruse with the oath at 146ff. Look back through the poem for further traits of Cydippe.

The story of Acontius and Cydippe had been told a couple hundred years earlier by a Greek poet called Callimachus in his *Aetia*, a long and learned composition on the origins of various things (cults, cities etc.). Parts of that account have survived (for all the fragments see Trypanis & Gelzer & Whitman 50ff.). *Heroides* 20 and 21 were written with the Greek poem in mind. There are clear similarities: for example, as you will see shortly, *Her.* 20.25ff. echoes *Aetia* fragment 67.1ff., and *Her.* 20.97 looks to *Aetia* fragment 75.26f. But typically Ovid also showed independence and told the tale in his own way. As you read the two fragments translated below, look to see how Ovid made variations on his model, what he added and what he reduced.

In fragment 67 there is reference in 5 to Acontius' home town of Iulis on Cea and at 12ff. to girls on Cydippe's island of Naxos.

> Love himself taught Acontius the trick, when the boy
>> burned with love for the beautiful virgin
> Cydippe (for he wasn't cunning), so he could acquire
>> for all his life the name of lawful husband.
> For he came from Iulis and she came from Naxos to the   5
>> sacrifice of oxen to you, lord Apollo, on Delos.
> Both beautiful stars of the islands, he was from Euxantius'
>> family, and she was a descendant of Prometheus.
> When she was still a little girl, many mothers asked for Cydippe
>> as a bride for their son, offering a dowry of horned oxen.   10
> For no other girl had a face more like dawn than
>> she did out of those who came to the dripping
> rock of hairy old Silenus or set their delicate feet
>> to the dance about sleeping Ariadne.

Unfortunately we have lost Callimachus' lines on Acontius falling in love and trapping Cydippe. The next fragment (75) depicts her back home on Naxos just before her arranged marriage. As one of the various minor differences in detail we see at 1ff. that in the Greek poet her first illness was epilepsy. At 20f. the text is unsure, but it seems that her father (called Ceyx) went to Delphi, and Apollo spoke to him in a dream, as he spent the night in the god's temple, and told him about the oath by Artemis (= Diana). Here is the start of fragment 75:

> In the afternoon an unsightly pallor seized her, as she was afflicted
>> by the disease which we exorcise on to the wild goats
>> and mistakenly call the holy disease. It was so severe then that it
> made her waste away and took her right up to death's door.   15
>> The wedding-bed was spread a second time, and the girl was sick
> a second time, with a quartan fever for seven months.
>> They thought of marriage a third time, and a third time
> again a deadly chill settled on Cydippe.
>> Her father didn't wait any more for a fourth time   20
> to Apollo. The god said this to him during the night:
>> 'A solemn oath by Artemis is preventing marriage for your child.
> For my sister wasn't off causing trouble for Lygdamis then,
>> and she wasn't plaiting rushes in her shrine at Amyclae or washing
> herself clean in the river Parthenios after the hunt,   25
>> but she was at home on Delos when your daughter swore
> that she would wed Acontius, and no other.
>> Ceyx, if you're willing to take me as your advisor
> . . . . you'll make your daughter's oath come true.

For I say that in marrying Acontius to her you won't be uniting lead   30
with silver but a gold-silver alloy with gleaming gold.

    You, the bride's father, have Codrus for an ancestor, while the bridegroom
from Cea descends from the priests of Zeus Aristaeus

    the Icmian, those whose task it is on the mountain crests to lessen
the heat of the fierce Dog-Star when it rises   35

    and to pray to Zeus for the wind that blows lots of
quails into the bird-catchers' linen nets.'

    So spoke the god. The father went back to Naxos and questioned
the girl herself, who revealed the whole story truthfully.

    And she was well again . . . . It remained for you, Acontius,   40
. . . . to go to Naxos to fetch your wife.

    The oath by Artemis was kept, and the girls of Cydippe's own age
sang her wedding-song immediately and without delay.

    Acontius, I don't think that in return for that night
when you took her virginity you would have accepted   45

    then the speed of Iphicles, who skimmed over the ears
of corn, or the possessions of Midas of Celaenae,

    and all men who have experience of the harsh
god of love would corroborate my judgment.

    Cean Acontius, from that marriage a great name was   50
destined to arise – the Acontiadae, your clan,

    who still inhabit Iulis in large numbers and in great
honour. I learned of this love of yours from ancient

    Xenomedes, who once set down your whole island
in a mythological account, beginning with   55

    how it was inhabited by the Corycian nymphs,
who were driven from Parnassus by a huge lion.

We have to be cautious, as we do not have all of Callimachus' narrative, but on
the basis of what we do have it would appear that Ovid (in addition to introducing
the epistolary form with its exchange between the couple) dropped a lot of the
rather dry erudition, added much humour and really developed the characters of
the young people and brought out their thoughts and feelings, giving Cydippe in
particular a new prominence and a voice of her own. For more on the relationship
to Callimachus consider Barchiesi 119ff.

GLOSSARY OF CHARACTERS IN THE *HEROIDES*

Achelous a river-god defeated by Hercules for the hand of Deianira.

Achilles the greatest of the Greek fighters at Troy and the man who killed Hector.

Acontius the lover of Cydippe.

Actaeon a hunter who inadvertently saw Diana naked and was turned by her into a stag and was then killed by his own dogs.

Adonis a very handsome young hero loved by Venus.

Aeetes father of Medea, king of Colchis and possessor of the Golden Fleece.

Aegeus father of Theseus.

Aegina a nymph, ancestress of Achilles.

Aegisthus lover of Orestes' mother (Clytaemnestra), killed by Orestes.

Aegyptus brother of Danaus and father of fifty sons, whom he married to Danaus' daughters.

Aeneas trojan hero (son of Venus) who had an affair with Dido.

Aeolus the king who controlled the winds, father of Canace and Macareus.

Aethra daughter of king Pittheus, and mother of Theseus; also (in *Her.* 16 and 17) the name of one of Helen's maids.

Agamemnon commander in chief of the Greek forces at Troy and father of Orestes.

Ajax a great Greek warrior at Troy, cousin of Achilles.

Alcaeus a lyric poet on Lesbos contemporary with Sappho.

Alcyone one of Neptune's conquests.

Alexander another name for Paris.

Allecto one of the Furies (dread goddesses of the Underworld).

Amphitryon husband of Alcmena who passed as Hercules' father.

Amymone a heroine who slept with Neptune.

Anactoria a woman of Lesbos loved by Sappho.

Anchises father of Aeneas by Venus.

Androgeos   son of Minos, killed in Athens.

Andromache   wife of the Trojan hero Hector, enslaved after the fall of Troy.

Andromeda   an Ethiopian princess rescued from a monster and married by Perseus.

Anna   Dido's sister.

Antaeus   an African giant killed by Hercules.

Antenor   a wise old man of Troy.

Antilochus   a Greek warrior killed in the fighting at Troy.

Antinous   a leading suitor for the hand of Penelope.

Apollo   a god of music and healing, who built the walls of Troy and shot Achilles.

Argonauts   the Greek heroes who sailed with Jason on the ship called the Argo on the quest for the Golden Fleece.

Ariadne   daughter of Minos (king of Crete) and sister of Phaedra; she helped Theseus kill the Minotaur, and was later abandoned by him, and then married by Bacchus.

Ascanius   son of Aeneas.

Astydamia   a nymph impregnated by Hercules.

Atalanta   a beautiful heroine and great huntress loved by Meleager and Hippomenes; she would only marry a man who beat her in a race, and Hippomenes won her by throwing golden apples, which she stopped to pick up.

Atlas   a giant who carried the sky on his shoulders; grandfather of Mercury.

Atreus   father of Agamemnon, and grandfather of Orestes and Hermione.

Atthis   a woman of Lesbos loved by Sappho.

Auge   a heroine raped by Hercules.

Bacchantes   female worshippers of Bacchus.

Bacchus   god of wine.

Boreas   the North Wind, lover of the Athenian princess Orithyia.

Briseis   Achilles' slave girl, taken away from him by Agamemnon.

Busiris   a king of Egypt who sacrificed strangers.

Calyce   one of Neptune's conquests.

Canace   a daughter of Aeolus who loved her own brother (Macareus).

Cassandra   prophetic daughter of Priam.

Celaeno   one of Neptune's conquests.

Centaurs   violent mythical creatures (half-man half-horse) defeated by Theseus and also by Hercules.

Cephalus   a hero loved and carried off by the goddess Dawn.

Cepheus   father of Andromeda.

Cerberus   the three-headed watchdog of the Underworld.

Ceres   a goddess of agriculture and mystic rites.

Ceyx   Alcyone's husband, who was drowned in a shipwreck.

Chalciope   Medea's sister.

Charaxus   brother of Sappho.

Charybdis   a monster (opposite Scylla) that sucked down the sea three times a day, creating an inescapable whirlpool.

Clymene   one of Helen's maids.

Creon   king of Corinth and father of Creusa.

Creusa   the daughter of Creon whom Jason married, leaving Medea.

Cupid   the god of love (son of Venus); sometimes there are several Cupids.

Cybele   a mother-goddess worshipped in the Trojan area by frenzied devotees.

Cydippe   a beautiful young woman loved by Acontius.

Cydro   a woman of Lesbos loved by Sappho.

Daedalus   Icarus' father, a craftsman who invented wings for men.

Danaus   brother of Aegyptus and father of fifty daughters who were married to Aegyptus' fifty sons.

Daphne   a nymph loved by Apollo.

Deianira   wife of Hercules.

Deiphobus   a son of Priam.

Demophoon   a son of Theseus who was given shelter by Phyllis and took her virginity, but then left her.

Deucalion   a hero who loved Pyrrha.

Diana   a goddess of hunting and the wilds, identified with Hecate.

Dido   queen of Carthage, who had an affair with Aeneas.

Diomedes   a savage king of Thrace with man-eating horses.

Dolon   a Trojan spy killed by Ulysses and Diomedes.

Endymion   a handsome young hero loved by the Moon.

Enyo   a goddess who drove her worshippers into an ecstatic frenzy.

Europa   a heroine abducted by Jupiter in the form of a bull.

Eurymachus   a leading suitor for the hand of Penelope.

Eurystheus   a king who ruled over Hercules and imposed the Labours on him.

Eurytus   father of Iole.

Fates   goddesses of fate who spin the threads on which the lives of mortals depend.

Fauns   minor gods of the countryside.

Faunus   a minor rustic god.

Fury   a sinister goddess of the Underworld.

Ganymede   a handsome Trojan prince abducted by Jupiter and made his cup-bearer.

Geryon   a giant with three bodies.

Glaucus   a sea-god.

Gorge   sister of Deianira.

Hecataeon   father of Calyce.

Hecate   a goddess of magic and the Underworld.

Hector   a son of Priam and the Trojans' best fighter.

Hecuba   wife of Priam and mother of Paris.

Helen   the wife of Menelaus who eloped with Paris.

Helle   a young heroine who fell from the golden ram into the sea.

Hercules   the super-hero who performed the twelve Labours.

Hermione   Helen's daughter.

Hero   a beautiful heroine loved by Leander.

Hesione   a heroine taken captive by the hero Telamon.

Hippodamia   ancestor of Hermione and a princess whose father was beaten in a chariot race by Pelops, who thus won her as his wife; also (in *Her* 17) the name of a heroine whom the Centaurs tried to carry off at her wedding, and who was defended by her husband's Thessalian subjects.

Hippolyte   an Amazon queen whose sword-belt Hercules had to seize and bring back as one of his Labours.

Hippolytus   a son of Theseus, loved by his stepmother Phaedra, and dear to the goddess Diana, whom he worshipped with great reverence.

Hippomenes   a Greek hero who beat the heroine Atalanta in a foot-race by throwing golden apples, which she stopped to pick up, and thus won her as his wife.

Hydra   a many-headed snake killed by Hercules.

Hyllus   son of Hercules and Deianira.

Hymen   god of marriage.

Hypermestra   the daughter of Danaus who refused to kill her husband.

Hypsipyle   queen of Lemnos, married and abandoned by Jason.

Iarbas   an African chieftain and suitor for the hand of Dido.

Icarius   Penelope's father.

Icarus   Daedalus' son who flew too close to the sun.

Idyia   Medea's mother.

Ilioneus   a Trojan hero.

Io   a river-nymph who was loved by Jupiter.

Iole   a princess whom Hercules fell in love with after taking her captive.

Irus   a beggar who sided with Penelope's suitors.

Itys   son of Procne, killed by her to get revenge on her husband.

Jason   the Greek hero who went on the quest for the Golden Fleece, and who married Hypsipyle, Medea and Creusa.

Juno   wife and sister of Jupiter, the queen of the gods and goddess of marriage.

Jupiter   king of the gods, husband and brother of Juno.

Laertes   father of Ulysses.

Lamus   son of Hercules and Omphale.

Laodamia   the young wife of Protesilaus.

Laodice   one of Neptune's conquests.

Laomedon   Priam's father.

Latona   the mother of Diana and Apollo.

Leander   the young man who loved Hero and swam to her of a night.

Leda   mother of Helen, raped by Jupiter in the form of a swan.

Leucippus   the father of two heroines who were carried off by Helen's brothers Castor and Pollux.

Lynceus   the son of Aegyptus whose life was spared by Hypermestra.

Macareus   a son of Aeolus, who loved his own sister (Canace).

Mars   the god of war and lover of Venus.

Medea   daughter of Aeetes and a witch, who helped Jason get the Golden Fleece.

Medon   a herald who associated with Penelope's suitors.

Medusa a beautiful heroine loved by Neptune before her hair was turned to snakes.

Melanthius Ulysses' goatherd who sided with Penelope's suitors.

Meleager a Greek hero (brother of Deianira) cursed by his mother for killing her brothers (after they objected when he awarded Atalanta the hide of the huge Calydonian boar killed in a hunt, as she had inflicted the first wound on it) and killed by her.

Menelaus brother of Agamemnon and husband of Helen and father of Hermione.

Mercury the divine messenger of the gods.

Minerva goddess of wisdom and crafts who favoured the Greeks at Troy.

Minos a king of Crete, father of Phaedra and Ariadne.

Minotaur a monster (half-man and half-bull) born of Pasiphae's mating with a bull; it lived in the Labyrinth and was killed by Theseus.

Muses the goddesses who inspire poets.

Neptune the god of the sea, who built the walls of Troy.

Nereus a sea-god, father of Thetis and grandfather of Achilles.

Nessus a Centaur killed by Hercules.

Nestor the aged king of Pylos who fought at Troy.

Niobe a queen who boasted that she had more children than Diana's mother, with the result that they were all killed by Diana and Apollo, and Niobe was turned into a rock.

Nymph goddess of the countryside.

Oenone a water-nymph loved by Paris before he eloped with Helen.

Omphale an oriental queen served and loved by Hercules.

Orestes son of Agamemnon, and husband and cousin of Hermione.

Orithyia an Athenian princess loved by the god Boreas.

Palaemon a sea-god.

Pallas another name for Minerva.

Pans minor gods of the countryside.

Paris the Trojan prince who eloped with Helen, causing the Trojan War.

Patroclus a Greek warrior killed at Troy and a close friend of Achilles.

Pelasgus a king of Argos.

Pelias the king of Thessaly who sent Jason on the quest for the Golden Fleece.

Pelops grandfather of Menelaus and great-grandfather of Orestes and Hermione; he beat Hippodamia's father in a chariot race and thus won her as his bride.

Penelope wife of Ulysses.

Penthesilea an Amazon queen who fought at Troy on the Trojan side.

Perseus a hero who rescued Andromeda from a sea-monster and married her.

Phaedra wife of Theseus and sister of Ariadne, who loved her stepson Hippolytus.

Phaon a ferryman on the island of Lesbos loved by Sappho.

Phereclus builder of Paris' ship.

Phoebus another name for Apollo.

Phoenix one of the Greeks at Troy who went on the embassy to Achilles.

Phrixus Helle's brother who rode on the golden ram.

Phyllis   a princess of Thrace who gave her love to Demophoon but was left by him.

Pirithous   a king of northern Greece who was a great friend of Theseus.

Pisander   one of Penelope's suitors.

Pittheus   the king of Troezen, father of Aethra and grandfather of Theseus.

Pleiad   a divine daughter of Atlas.

Pleione   a sea-nymph.

Pluto   god of the Underworld.

Polybus   one of Penelope's suitors.

Polydamas   a Trojan hero and friend of Hector.

Priam   king of Troy and father of Paris and Hector.

Procne   wife of the Thracian king Tereus, who raped her sister; in revenge Procne killed her son Itys, cooked him and served him up to Tereus; she was then changed into a nightingale.

Procrustes   a murderer killed by Theseus.

Protesilaus   husband of Laodamia, and the first man killed in the Trojan War.

Pygmalion   Dido's evil brother.

Pyrrha   a heroine loved by Deucalion.

Pyrrhus   son of Achilles.

Rhesus   a Trojan ally killed by Ulysses and Diomedes.

Sappho   a Greek lyric poetess who loved Phaon.

Satyrs   minor gods of the countryside.

Sciron   robber killed by Theseus.

Scylla   a six-headed monster, with dogs growing from her lower body, who lived in a cave near the sea (opposite Charybdis) and attacked passing ships.

Sinis   a murderer killed by Theseus.

Sychaeus   Dido's husband who was killed before Aeneas met Dido.

Tantalus   son of Jupiter and father of Pelops and an ancestor of Hermione and Orestes, he was punished in the Underworld with perpetual hunger and thirst.

Telamon   a hero who took captive the heroine Hesione.

Thalia   one of the Muses.

Theseus   an Athenian hero (father of Demophoon and Hippolytus), who abducted Helen when she was young, and who killed the Minotaur and then abandoned Ariadne after she had helped him.

Thespius   a Greek king whose fifty daughters were impregnated by Hercules.

Thetis   a goddess of the sea, famous for her silvery feet.

Thoas   father of Hypsipyle.

Tisiphone   one of the Furies (dread goddesses of the Underworld).

Tithonus   a handsome Trojan abducted by the goddess Dawn and who became her husband.

Tlepolemus   a Greek fighter killed at Troy.

Triton   a sea-god.

Tydeus   a brother of Deianira.

Tyndareus   Hermione's grandfather and husband of Leda.

Typhos   a monster which was defeated by Jupiter and imprisoned under Mount Etna.

Tyro   a heroine seduced by Neptune.

Ulysses   (Greek name: Odysseus) Penelope's husband who fought at Troy and who was hated by Neptune.

Venus   the goddess of love.

SELECT BIBLIOGRAPHY

We list below only those works which are cited in the text and which we have found particularly helpful in the writing of this book.

Allan, W. *Euripides: Medea* (London, 2002)
Armstrong, R. *Ovid and His Love Poetry* (London, 2005)
———— *Cretan Women* (Oxford, 2006)
Atwood, M. *The Penelopiad* (Toronto, 2006)
Barchiesi, A. *Speaking Volumes* (London, 2001)
Barsby, J. *Ovid* (Oxford, 1991)
Benstock, S., Ferriss, S. & Woods, S. *A Handbook of Literary Feminisms* (New York and Oxford, 2002)
Binns, J.W. (ed.) *Ovid* (London, 1973)
Blok, J.H. *The Early Amazons* (Leiden, 1995)
Blondell, R. *Helen of Troy: Beauty Myth Devastation* (Oxford, 2013)
Bolton, M.C. 'Elegy Upside Down: The Inversion of Elegiac and Epic Elements in *Heroides III*', in Deroux, C. (ed.) *Studies in Latin Literature and Roman History VIII* (Brussells, 1997), 218–230
Boyd, B.W. (ed.) *Brill's Companion to Ovid* (Leiden, 2002)
Boyle, A.J. & Woodard, R.D. *Ovid Fasti* (London, 2000)
Bradley, M.Z. *The Firebrand* (New York, 2003)
Brindel, J.R. *Phaedra: A Novel of Ancient Athens* (New York, 1985)
Claassen, J.-M. *Ovid Revisited* (London, 2008)
Clauss, J.J. & Johnston, S.I. (eds.) *Medea* (Princeton, 1997)
Cornillon, S.K. (ed.) *Images of Women in Fiction Feminist Perspectives* (Bowling Green, OH, 1972)
Crossland, J. *Collateral Damage* (Vancouver, 1992)
Cullen, J. *Medea: A Modern Retelling* (New York, 1996)
Dunbabin, K.M.D. *Mosaics of the Greek and Roman World* (Cambridge, 2001)
Felson-Rubin, N. *Regarding Penelope* (Princeton, 1994)
Fetterley, J. *The Resisting Reader* (Bloomington and London, 1978)

Fiorenza, G. 'Penelope's Web: Francesco Primaticcio's Epic Revision at Fontainebleau', *Renaissance Quarterly* 59.3 (2006), 795–827

Foley, H.P. (ed.) *Reflections of Women in Antiquity* (New York, 1981)

Franklin, S.B. *Daughter of Troy* (New York, 2002)

Fratantuono, L. *Madness Transformed* (Lanham, 2011)

Fulkerson, L. *The Ovidian Heroine as Author* (Cambridge, 2005)

Galinsky, G.K. *The Herakles Theme* (Oxford, 1972)

———— *Ovid's Metamorphoses: An Introduction to the Basic Aspects* (Berkeley and Los Angeles, 1975)

Ginsburg, J. *Representing Agrippina* (Oxford, 2006)

Grafton, A., Most, G.W. & Settis, S. *The Classical Tradition* (Cambridge, MA, 2010)

Graziosi, B. & Greenwood, E. (eds.) *Homer in the Twentieth Century* (Oxford, 2007)

Green, P. *Ovid: The Erotic Poems* (Harmondsworth, 1982)

———— *The Poems of Exile* (Berkeley and Los Angeles, 2005)

Greene, E. (ed.) *Re-Reading Sappho* (Berkeley and Los Angeles, 1996)

Griffiths, E. *Medea* (London and New York, 2006)

Grube, G.M. *The Drama of Euripides* (London, 1962)

Hagen, R-M. & Hagen, R. *What Great Paintings Say* Vol. 2 (Köln, 2003)

Hall, E. *The Return of Ulysses* (Baltimore and London, 2008)

Hall, E., Macintosh, F. & Taplin, O. (edd.) *Medea in Performance 1500–2000* (Oxford, 2000)

Hardie, P. *The Cambridge Companion to Ovid* (Cambridge, 2002)

Hartt, F. & Wilkins, D. *A History of Italian Renaissance Art: Painting, Sculpture and Architecture* (New York, 2010)

Hughes, T. *Jean Racine Phèdre* (London, 1988; New York, 1999)

Isbell, H. *Ovid Heroides* (London, 1990)

Jacobson, H. *Ovid's Heroides* (Princeton, 1974)

James, E. & Jondorf, G. *Racine Phèdre* (Cambridge, 1994)

Johnson, M. *Sappho* (London, 2007)

Joyce, J. *Ulysses* (Paris, 1922; there is a modern Penguin edition)

Kane, S. *Sarah Kane: Complete Plays* (London, 2001)

Kelly, M. 'Ovid's Portrait of Briseis in *Heroides* 3', *Antichthon* 33 (1999), 77–80

Kenney, E.J. *Ovid Heroides XVI-XXI* (Cambridge, 1996)

Knox, P.E. *Ovid Heroides Select Epistles* (Cambridge, 1995)

———— (ed.) *A Companion to Ovid* (Chichester, 2009)

Larson, J. *Greek Nymphs Myth, Cult, Lore* (Oxford, 2001)

Lee, A.G. *Ovid's Amores* (London, 1968)

Lefkowitz, M.R. *Women in Greek Myth* (London, 1986)

Lindheim, S.L. *Mail and Female* (Madison, 2003)

Liveley, G. *Ovid: Love Songs* (London, 2005)

Mack, S. *Ovid* (New Haven and London, 1988)

Maguire, L.E. *Helen of Troy: From Homer to Hollywood* (Chichester, 2009)

Mayer, R. *Seneca: Phaedra* (London, 2002)

Michalopoulos, A.N. *Ovid Heroides 16 and 17* (Cambridge, 2006)

Miller, M. *The Song of Achilles* (London and New York, 2011)

Mills, S. *Euripides: Hippolytus* (London, 2002)

Mills, S., Pearce, L., Spaull, S. & Millard, E. *Feminist Readings / Feminists Reading* (Charlottesville, VA, 1989)

Montiglio, S. *From Villain to Hero: Odysseus in Ancient Thought* (Ann Arbor, MI, 2011)

Mozley, J.H. *The Art of Love, and Other Poems* (Cambridge, MA, 1939)

Murgatroyd, P. *Mythical and Legendary Narrative in Ovid's Fasti* (Leiden, 2005)

Nagle, B.R. 'Byblis and Myrrha: Two Incest Narratives in the Metamorphoses', *Classical Journal* 78 (1983), 301–315

Palmer, A. P. *Ovidi Nasonis Heroides* (second ed., Oxford, 1898; repr. Exeter, 2005)

Patterson, C. 'Not Worth the Rearing: The Causes of Infant Exposure in Ancient Greece', *Transactions of the American Philological Association* 115 (1985), 103–123

Raeburn, D. *Ovid Metamorphoses* (London, 2004)

Reynolds, M. (ed.) *The Sappho Companion* (New York, 2000)

Roller, D.W. & Roller, K. 'Penelope's Thick Hand (Odyssey 21.6)', *Classical Journal* 90.1 (1994), 9–19

Rosenthal, A. *Angelica Kauffman: Art and Sensibility* (New Haven, 2006)

Roworth, W.W. *Angelica Kauffman: A Continental Artist in Georgian England* (Brighton and London, 1992)

Sealey, R. 'The Athenian Courts for Homicide', *Classical Philology* 78.4 (1983), 275–296

Showerman, G. (revised by Goold, G.P.) *Ovid Heroides Amores* (Cambridge, MA and London, 1977)

Spentzou, E. *Readers and Writers in Ovid's Heroides* (Oxford, 2003)

Spoth, F. *Ovids Heroides als Elegien* (Munich, 1992)

Stanford, W.B. *The Ulysses Theme* (Oxford, 1954)

Terry, P. (ed.) *Ovid Metamorphosed* (London, 2001)

Thornton, A. *People and Themes in Homer's Odyssey* (Dunedin, 1970)

Thorsen, T.S. *Ovid's Early Poetry* (Cambridge, 2014)

Trypanis, C.A., Gelzer, T. & Whitman, C. *Callimachus Aetia, Iambi, Hecale and Other Fragments, Musaeus Hero and Leander* (Cambridge, MA and London, 1975)

Turner, P. *Ovid: The Technique of Love Remedies for Love* (London, 1968)

Verducci, F. *Ovid's Toyshop of the Heart: Epistulae Heroidum* (Princeton, 1985)

White, P. *Renaissance Postscripts* (Columbus, OH, 2009)

Williams, G.D. *Banished Voices* (Cambridge, 1994)

Wyke, M. *The Roman Mistress* (Oxford, 2002)

Zimmerman, B. 'Seeing, Reading, Knowing: The Lesbian Appropriation of Literature', in Hartman, J.E. & Messer-Davidow, E. (edd.) *(En)Gendering Knowledge Feminists in Academe* (Knoxville, 1991), 85–99

Ziolkowski, T. *Ovid and the Moderns* (Ithaca and London, 2005)

INDEX

Abydos 212, 216, 224
Achelous 99, 103
Achilles 7, 9, 32, 33, 35, 75, 89, 91, 95, 140, 232; *Heroides* 3 32–42
Acontius 3; *Heroides* 20 230–9; *Heroides* 21 240–9
Actaeon 231, 240
Adonis 46, 128
Aeetes 66–7, 132, 134, 149, 206
Aegeus 111, 140
Aegina 34
Aegisthus 89, 95
Aegyptus 164
Aeneas 40, 42, 211; *Heroides* 7 76–88
Aeneid (Virgil) 1, 40, 76, 82–7, 93, 128, 210–11
Aeolus 121, 123, 128–9
Aeschylus 141; *Agamemnon* 40, 211; *Eumenides* 184; *Suppliants* 171
Aeson 66
Aetia (Callimachus) 247–9
Africa 77, 81, 129
Agamemnon 32, 33–6, 37, 38, 56, 57, 89, 95–6, 153
Agamemnon (Aeschylus) 40, 211
Agenor 82
Agrippina 124
Aissa 55
Ajax 33
Alcaeus 184
Alcestis 109, 162
Alcestis (Euripides) 109, 162–3
Alcman 184

Alcmene 99
Alcyone 213
Alexander 186, 197
Allan, W. 149
Allius 159
Amazons 46, 74, 75
Ambracia 177
Amores (Ovid) 3, 4, 6, 48, 120, 208
Amphitryon 99
Amyclae 248
Amymone 224
Anacreon 184
Anactoria 174
Anchises 76, 191
Androgeos 111
Andromache 40, 41, 42, 59, 89
Andromache (Euripides) 40, 96–7, 211
Andromeda 40, 174, 213
Andros 242
Anna 85
Annals (Tacitus) 98
Antigone (Sophocles) 184
Antilochus 8
Antinous 10
Apamea 18
Aphrodite 38, 52, 62, 64, 66, 75, 173, 181, 199, 239
Apollo 9, 60, 114, 174, 177, 178, 230, 231, 240
Apollonius of Rhodes 73–4, 142, 144
apples 239, 243, 246
Apsyrtus 67, 139
Arctos 217

Ares 75
Argo 66, 133, 140, 217
Argonauts 66
Argos 164
Ariadne 22, 43, 45, 111, 205; *Heroides* 10
  111–20
Aricia 54
Aristaeus 249
Aristophanes 108
Armstrong, R. 3, 88
Ars Amatoria (Ovid) 3, 4, 6, 48, 120, 208
Artemis 52, 75
Ascanius 41, 42, 79, 83
Astynanax 41–2, 97
Atalanta 46
Athena 11, 13, 32, 97
Athens 24, 52, 111, 114–15, 140, 143
Atlas 100
Atreus 89, 197, 198
Atthis 174, 180
Atwood, M. 17
Auge 101
Augustus 1, 86
Aulis 85
'authentic realism' 169

Bacchantes 45, 112, 119
Bacchus 22, 112, 113, 119, 120, 174,
  213, 217
Barchiesi, A. 249
Barsby, J. 6
Baudelaire, C. 179
Bellerophon 40
Betto, Bernardino di 18
Black Sea 133, 217
Blok, J.H. 75
Blondell, R. 211
Bootes 218
Boreas 212, 214, 219
Boyd, B.W. 3
Boyle, A.J. 3
Brindel, J.R. 54–5
Briseis 60, 232; *Heroides* 3 32–42
Brussels 18
Busiris 100, 102
Byron, G.G. 179, 212

Caligula 124–5
Callimachus 98, 247–9, 249
Callisto 63, 213
Calyce 224
Calydon 230, 240
Calypso 12, 16
Canace, *Heroides* 11 121–31

Capra 218
Carthage 77, 80, 81, 82, 86–7, 129
Cassandra 40, 61, 186–7, 191
Catholic church 16
Catullus 115–17, 118, 120, 159–60,
  162, 179
Celaeno 224
Centaur 99, 103, 106
Cephalus 46, 176
Cepheus 174
Cerberus 100, 102, 108, 169
Ceres 23
Ceyx 213, 215, 248
Chalciope 132, 206
Chaonia 42
Chaon of Troy 42
Charaxus 176
Charybdis 135, 142
Chaucer, G. 4
Chiusi Vase 17
Cicero 124
Cinyras 127
Circe 18
Claassen, J.-M. 3
Clashing Rocks 135, 142
Clauss, J.J. 144, 149
Cleis 179
Clodia 124
Clodius 124
Clymene 207
Clytaemnestra 40, 95, 211
Codrus 249
Coen, E. 16
Coen, J. 16
Colchis 66, 69, 70, 133, 140, 141, 144, 197,
  217, 219, 225
Collateral Damage (Crossland) 149
Corinth 91, 132–4, 137
Creon 132, 134, 139, 146–8
Cretan Crown constellation 112, 120
Crete 43, 45, 47, 55, 111, 113, 119, 191,
  196, 204, 239
Creusa 132, 134, 139–40, 142, 143,
  146–8, 151
Crossland 149
Cupid 23, 47, 49, 77, 79, 81, 83, 126, 175,
  178–9, 189, 190
Cybele 45
Cydippe 3; *Heroides* 20 230–9; *Heroides* 21
  240–9
Cydro 174
Cynthia 161
Cyprus 30
Cythera 79

Daedalus 97–8, 212, 214, 219
Danaids 164, 169–71
Danaus 164, 167
Daphne 63, 174
Dardanelles 212
Dawn 46, 176, 191
Deianira, *Heroides* 9 99–110
Deiphobus 59, 197, 211
Delacroix, E. 151–2
Delos 240, 242–3, 247, 248
Delphi 96, 230, 248
Demeter 184
Demophoon, *Heroides* 2 22–31
Dia 111, 112, 115
Diana 45, 46, 47, 50, 52, 134–5, 141, 153,
    154, 230, 236, 237, 240
Dido 129; *Heroides* 7 76–88
Diomedes 13, 100, 102
Dionysus 108
Dolon 7, 9, 11
Donne, J. 4
Doom 62, 74
Drusilla 125
Dryads 45
Dryden, J. 4, 131
Dublin 16
Dulichium 10
Dunbabin, R-M. 18
Durrell, H.D. 179

Eclogues (Virgil) 239
Egypt 164
Electra (Euripides) 95
Eleusis 45
Elysian Fields 143
Endymion 62, 213, 215
Epistulae ex Ponto (Ovid) 3
Eros 179
Ethiopia 174
Eumenides (Aeschylus) 184
Euripides 5, 54, 141, 144, 151; *Alcestis* 109,
    162–3; *Andromache* 40, 96–7, 211;
    Electra 95; *Hecuba* 40; *Hippolytus* 43,
    48, 52; *Medea* 146–9; *The Trojan
    Women* 40
Eurydice 169
Eurymachus 10
Eurystheus 100
Eurytus 99, 103

Fasti (Ovid) 3, 63, 120
Faunus 60
Felson-Rubin, N. 11
Fetterley, J. 50

Fiorenza, G. 19, 20
Foley, H. P. 141, 144
Francis I, King of France 19
Fratantuono, L. 3
Frogs (Aristophanes) 108
Fulkerson, L. 5, 104, 139, 140
Furies 22, 68, 124, 184

Galinsky, G.K. 3
Gallus 1
Ganymede 191
Gelzer, T. 247
Geryon 100, 102
Glaucus 217
golden apple 239
Golden Fleece 66–7, 132, 136, 137,
    144–5
Gorge 104
Grafton, A. 16, 51, 88, 120, 211
Graziosi, B. 17
Great Bear 213
Greene, E. 179, 183
Green, P. 3
Greenwood, E. 17
Griffiths, E. 144, 149
Grube, G.M. 149

Hades 170
Haemus 25
Hagen, R. 18, 19, 20
Hagen, R-M. 18, 19, 20
Hall, E. 149
Hardie, P. 3
Hartt, F. 18
Hebrus 23, 25
Hecate 141
Hector 7, 8, 32, 35, 36, 40–2, 58, 64, 80, 89,
    154, 156, 187, 198
Hecuba 40, 56, 57, 94, 186
Hecuba (Euripides) 40
Helen 3, 7, 14, 15, 20, 56, 57, 61, 89, 91–3,
    95, 153, 156, 212, 225; *Heroides* 16
    186–99; *Heroides* 17 200–11
Helenus 40, 41–2
Helice 217
Hellespont 212, 213, 216, 219
Hercules, *Heroides* 9 99–110
Hermes/Mercury 15
Hermione 41; *Heroides* 8 89–98
Hero 3; *Heroides* 18 212–20; *Heroides* 19
    221–9
Hero and Leander (Marlowe) 228–9
Hero and Leander (Musaeus) 220, 228
Hesione 232

Hesperides 100
Hippodamia 40, 89, 91, 206
Hippolytus, *Heroides* 4 43–55
Hippolytus (Euripides) 43, 48, 52
Hippomenes 243
Homer 5, 183; *Iliad* 13, 32, 37–40, 63–4, 97, 197–9, 209, 211; *Odyssey* 10, 12–13, 15–16, 19, 28–9, 39, 210
Horace 1, 15, 169–70, 179
Hughes, T. 54
Hydra 100, 102
Hylas 63
Hyllus 104
Hymen 68
Hypermestra, *Heroides* 14 164–72
Hypsipyle 138–40; *Heroides* 6 66–75

Ibis (Ovid) 3
Icarius 10
Icarus 97–8, 212, 214
Idyia 206
Iliad (Homer) 13, 32, 37–40, 63–4, 97, 197–9, 209, 211
Ilioneus 197
Ilium 186, 192, 196, 206
incest 124–31
infanticide 143
Io 63, 172
Iolcus 66, 145
Iole 99
Iphigenia 153
Irus 10
Isbell, H. 139
Isles of the Blessed 179
Italy 173
Ithaca 12

Jacobson, H. 4, 6, 88, 92, 104, 115, 126, 139, 159, 173
James, E. 51, 54
Jason 197, 206, 225; *Heroides* 6 66–75; *Heroides* 12 132–52
Jason and the Argonauts (Chaffey) 149–50
Johnson, M. 179
Johnston, S.I. 144, 149
Jondorf, G. 51, 54
Joyce, J. 16
Juno 23, 44, 56, 57, 68, 77, 82, 84, 99–100, 101, 108, 128–9, 135, 165, 169, 172, 186, 189, 191, 204, 213, 239
Jupiter 32, 34, 44, 47, 89, 99, 101, 108, 111, 113, 165, 186, 189, 191, 202, 213, 217
Juturna 63

Kane, S. 55
Kauffman, A. 19–21
Kelly, M. 37
Kenney, E.J. 6, 219
Knox, P.E. 3

Labyrinth 111, 115
Laertes 10, 33
Lamus 101
Land of the Dead 15
Laodamia, *Heroides* 13 153–63
Laodice 224
Laomedon 202
Lara 63
Larson, 63
Latium 77
Latona 231, 240, 243
Leander 3; *Heroides* 18 212–20; *Heroides* 19 221–9
Leda 89, 156, 186, 191
Lee, G. 238
Lefkowitz, M.R. 75
Lemnos 66, 67, 68, 70, 71
Lesbos 173, 183
Leucas 173–4, 178
Leucippus 196
Lindheim, S.H. 5, 11, 139, 140, 183
Liveley, G. 3, 6
Lucretius 153–4, 170–1
Lyde 169–70
Lydia 180
Lygdamis 248
Lynceus, *Heroides* 14 164–72

Macareus, *Heroides* 11 121–31
Macintosh, F 149
Mack, S. 3, 6, 36
Maguire, L.E. 211
Mail and Female (Lindheim) 5
Marlowe, C. 4, 228–9
Mars 35, 66, 68, 81, 134
Martial 98
Mayer, R. 51, 54
Meander 101
Medea 20, 66–73, 158, 197, 206; in art 150–2; dance version of story 149; in film 149–50; *Heroides* 12 132–52; popularity in literature 149
Medea: A Ballet in One Act (Tbilisi Z. Paliashvili Opera and Ballet State Theatre) 149
Medea (Euripides) 146–9
Medea (Ovid) 3

Medea (Paolozzi) 152
Medea (Pasolini) 150
Medeaspiel (Müller) 149
Medea: Stimmen (Wolf) 149
Medicamina Faciei Femineae (Ovid) 3
Medon 10
Medus 140
Medusa 224
Melanthius 10
Meleager 35, 46, 100, 104, 231
Menelaus 8, 11, 56, 59, 64, 89, 90, 153,
    186–7, 191, 196, 197–9, 203–4, 206,
    209, 211
Mercury 77, 169
Metamorphoses (Ovid) 3, 38, 40, 50, 97, 99,
    106, 120, 125, 126, 140, 144, 220
Methymna 174
Midas 249
Millard, E. 169
Mills, S. 51, 169
Minerva 20, 32, 56, 57, 186, 239
Minos 43, 47, 70, 111, 114, 116, 197
Minotaur 22, 24, 43, 111, 118
Montiglio 18
Moon 122, 176, 213, 215
Most, G.W. 16, 51, 88, 120, 211
Mountain of Sorrows 185
Mount Erymanthus 100
Mount Etna 174–5
Mount Helicon 184
Mount Ida 186, 191
Mount Latmos 213, 215
Mount Oeta 99, 103
Mozley, J.H. 3
Müller, H. 149
Murgatroyd, P. 3, 63
Musaeus 219–20, 228
Mycenae 81
Myconos 242
Mynes 39
Myrrha 126–8

Naples 185
Nausicaa 28–9
Naxos 230, 248, 249
Neptune 23, 36, 43, 53
Nereus 34
Nero 124–5
Nessus 99, 103, 104
Nestor 8, 9, 11
Nicoteles 98
Nile River 165
Nine Roads 30
Niobe 231, 233, 240

O Brother, Where Art Thou? (Coen &
    Coen) 16
Odes (Horace) 1
Odysseus *see* Ulysses
Odyssey (Homer) 10, 12–13, 15–16, 19,
    28–9, 39, 210
Oechalia 99, 100
Oenone 190, 200, 205, 209; *Heroides* 5
    56–65
Olympus 112
Omphale 100, 101, 102, 107, 110
On the Nature of the Universe (Lucretius)
    170–1
Orestes 41, 89; *Heroides* 8 89–98
Orithyia 197, 212, 214
Orpheus 127–8, 169
Ovid: *Amores* 3, 6, 15, 208; *Ars Amatoria* 3, 4,
    6, 48, 120, 208; *Epistulae ex Ponto* 3;
    Fasti 3, 63, 120; *Heroides* 3–6; *Ibis* 3;
    life 1–3; *Medea* 3; *Medicamina Faciei
    Femineae* 3; *Metamorphoses* 3, 38, 40,
    50, 97, 99, 106, 120, 125, 126, 140,
    144, 220; *Remedia Amoris* 3, 6, 30,
    38, 154; *Tristia* 3, 183
Ovidian Heroine as Author, The (Fulkerson) 5
Ovid's Heroides (Jacobson) 4
Ovid's Toyshop of the Heart (Verducci) 4

Palaemon 217
Pallas 186–7, 189, 191, 204
Palmer, A. 173
Pan 15, 184
Pans 48
Paolozzi, E. 152
Paris 3, 15, 89, 159, 212, 232, 239; *Heroides* 5
    56–65; *Heroides* 16 186–99; *Heroides* 17
    200–11
Parnassus 249
Pasiphae 43, 111
Pasolini, P. 150
Patroclus 7, 8, 32, 33, 36, 38
Patterson, C. 143
Pearce, L. 169
Pelasgus 164
Peleus 239
Pelias 66, 132, 136, 139, 145–6, 150
Pelops 89, 91, 202
Penelope: in art 17–21; *Heroides* 1 7–21;
    popularity in literature 16–17
*Penelope Invoking Minerva's Aid for the Safe
    Return of Telemachus* (Kauffman)
    19–20
Penelopiad, The (Atwood) 17
Penthesilea 74–5

Pergamum 42
Perseus 174, 213, 217
Peter, Saint 16
Phaeacians 28
Phaedra 173; *Heroides* 4 43–55
Phaedra: A Novel of Ancient Athens (Brindel)
    54–5
Phaedra (Seneca) 52, 55
Phaedra's Love (Kane) 55
Phaedra (Sophocles) 88
Phaon, *Heroides* 15 173–85
Philemon 184
Philippus 98
Philoctetes 187, 188
Philonoe 40
Phoebus 178
Phoenix 33
Phrixus 213
Phthia 75
Phyllis, *Heroides* 2 22–31
Pindar 144, 184
Pintoricchio, F. 19, 20
Pirithous 43, 46, 50
Pisander 10
Pittheus 46
Plato 239
Pleiades 218
Polybus 10
Polydamas 59
Polyxena 41
Posthomerica (Quintus Smyrnaeus) 39–40,
    61–3, 74–5
Pound, E. 179
Priam 7, 9, 32, 33, 40, 41, 56, 65, 93–5, 186,
    189, 190, 202, 205
Primaticcio, F. 19
Pro Caelio (Cicero) 124
Procrustes 24
Propertius 1, 160–2, 208
Protesilaus, *Heroides* 13 153–63
Pygmalion 81, 82–3
Pylos 8, 9, 10
Pyrrha 174, 177
Pyrrhus 40, 41, 89, 90, 92–7

Quintilian 238
Quintus Smyrnaeus 39–40, 61–3, 74–5

Racine, J. 54
Raeburn, D. 3
Readers and Writers in Ovid's Heroides
    (Spentzou) 5
Remedia Amoris (Ovid) 3, 6, 30, 38, 154
Remus 77

Resisting Reader, The (Fetterley) 50
Reynolds, M. 179
Rhesus 7, 9, 11
Rhodope 25
Rilke, R.M. 179
Roller, D.W. 17
Roller, K. 18
Rome 86, 185
Romulus 77
Rosenthal, A. 20
Roworth, W.W. 19

Salmacis 63
Same 10
Sappho 3, 239; *Heroides* 15 173–85
Satires (Horace) 15
Satyrs 48, 60, 112, 119
Sciron 24
Scylla 135, 142
Scythia 69, 133
Sejanus 98
Seneca 52, 54, 55, 144
Sestos 212, 219
Settis, S. 16, 51, 88, 120, 211
Shakespeare, W. 4
Sicily 135, 173, 174–5, 184
Silenus 119
Simois 41
Sinis 24
Sirens 18
Sophocles: *Antigone* 184; *Phaedra* 88;
    Trachiniae 104
Sparta 6, 8, 9, 56, 89, 186, 188, 191,
    201–2, 225
Spaull, S. 169
Spentzou, E. 5
Spoth, F. 4
Stanford, W.B. 17
'Stockholm Syndrome' 37
Styx 53
Suetonius 125
Suppliants (Aeschylus) 171
Swinburne, A.C. 179
Sychaeus 82, 83

Tacitus 98, 124
Tanais 69
Tantalus 89, 202, 213
Taplin, O. 149
Tbilisi Z. Paliashvili Opera and Ballet State
    Theatre 149
Telamon 232
Telemachus 7–8, 10, 11, 16, 20
Tennyson, A. 4

Tenos 242
Thalia 176
Therapnae 186
Theseus 22, 43, 50, 53, 55, 59, 186, 191;
    Heroides 10 111–20
Thessaly 66, 67, 81, 132, 135, 145, 153
Thetis 32, 239
Thoas 70
Thornton, A. 11
Thorsen, T.S. 173
Thrace 22, 24
Tiberius 98
Tibullus 1, 208
Tiresias 15–16
Tlepolemus 8
Toledo Museum of Art 19
Tomis 3–4
Trachiniae (Sophocles) 104
Tristia (Ovid) 3, 183
Troezen 46
Trojan Women, The (Euripides) 40
Troy 6, 8, 9, 15, 28, 32, 36, 38, 40, 41, 56,
    75, 79, 81, 86, 154, 159, 186–7, 191,
    206, 209
Trypanis, C.A. 247
Turkey 173
Turner, P. 3
Tydeus 104
Tyndareus 15, 89, 202, 206
Tyrians 82

Ugone, J. 16
Ulysses 28–9, 33, 63, 225; *Heroides* 1
    7–21
Ulysses and Penelope (Primaticcio) 19
Ulysses (Joyce) 16–17
Underworld 53, 100, 108, 169,
    213, 242
Underworld Painter 151

Valerius Flaccus 144
Venus 23, 41, 43, 46, 52, 56, 57, 76, 77,
    78–9, 82, 84, 86, 178, 186, 189, 196,
    229, 239
Verducci, F. 4
Vesuvius 185
Virgil 5, 183–5; *Aeneid* 1, 40, 76, 82–7, 93,
    128, 210–11; *Eclogues* 239

Whitman, C. 247
Wilkins, D. 18
Williams, G.D. 3
Wolf, C. 149
Woodard, R.D. 3
Wyke, 26

Xanthus 57

Zacynthus 10
Zeus 14, 32, 75, 181, 198
Zeus Aristaeus the Icmian 249